THE
OKANAGAN WINE TOUR GUIDE

JOHN SCHREINER
and
LUKE WHITTALL

TOUCHWOOD

Edited by Grace Yaginuma
Cover and interior design by Sydney Barnes
Maps by Eric Leinberger
Photos by John Schreiner unless otherwise stated on p. 511

LIBRARY AND ARCHIVES CANADA CATALOGUING IN PUBLICATION
Title: The Okanagan wine tour guide / John Schreiner and Luke Whittall.
Other titles: John Schreiner's Okanagan wine tour guide
Names: Schreiner, John, author. | Whittall, Luke, author.
Description: Previously published under title: John Schreiner's Okanagan wine tour guide. Vancouver: Whitecap Books, 2014.
Identifiers: Canadiana (print) 20190230541 | Canadiana (ebook) 20190233893 | ISBN 9781771513241 (softcover) | ISBN 9781771513258 (HTML)
Subjects: LCSH: Wineries–British Columbia–Okanagan Valley (Region)–Guidebooks. | LCSH: Wine and wine making–British Columbia–Okanagan Valley (Region) | LCSH: Vintners–British Columbia–Okanagan Valley (Region) | LCSH: Okanagan Valley (B.C. : Region)–Tours.
Classification: LCC TP559.C2 S35 2020 | DDC 663/.20097115–dc23

TouchWood Editions gratefully acknowledges that the land on which we live and work is within the traditional territories of the Lekwungen (Esquimalt and Songhees), Malahat, Pacheedaht, Scia'new, T'Sou-ke and W̱SÁNEĆ (Pauquachin, Tsartlip, Tsawout, and Tseycum) peoples.

We acknowledge the financial support of the Government of Canada through the Canada Book Fund, and the Province of British Columbia through the Book Publishing Tax Credit.

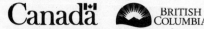 

This book was produced using FSC®-certified, acid-free papers, processed chlorine free, and printed with soya-based inks.

Printed in Canada at Friesens

24 23 22 21 20   1 2 3 4 5

This book is dedicated to the late Harry McWatters, who founded both Sumac Ridge Estate Winery and TIME Winery during a 51-year career in British Columbia wine. He was a towering figure who did much to shape the successful industry.

TASTING ROOM

CONTENTS

WHY WE WROTE THIS BOOK

The answer is easy: we enjoy being around wine people, who are among the most colourful and creative people we know. We like what they produce, and we have come to know many producers intimately. The text usually includes their birthplaces, their ages, and their professional backgrounds. This is seldom available elsewhere. It is our view that this puts the wineries and their wines in a context that enriches your wine-touring experience.

The first edition of *John Schreiner's Okanagan Wine Tour* was published in 2006 by Whitecap Books; it profiled 100 wineries. I updated that book four times, every time the list of wineries grew. The last Whitecap edition, the fifth, was published in 2014 and profiled 196 wineries.

It's been a full six years since the last edition, and the industry has continued to grow at a terrific rate. This book, now published by TouchWood Editions, has been renamed *The Okanagan Wine Tour Guide* to reflect the fact that I've taken on a writing partner, Luke Whittall. And you'll find that this book has 40 more wineries than the last edition. Coverage has been extended to include both Lillooet and the Arrow Lakes. There have never been more wine-touring opportunities in the British Columbia interior.

In most of the tasting rooms, everyone has fun. Visitors to Rust Wine Co. are greeted at the door with a glass of wine. At Ruby Blues Winery, the effervescent Prudence Mahrer waives the tasting fee for anyone who is smiling. And if they are not smiling when they walk into the wine shop, they certainly are by the time they leave. At Van Westen Vineyards, the wines taste even better because of the informal warmth that Rob Van Westen brings to a tasting room that consists of a couple of barrels in a sturdy old apple-packing house. There are also grand tasting rooms at, for example, Burrowing Owl, Hester Creek, Phantom Creek, and

Mission Hill, where wine tastings become memorable occasions.

The Okanagan and Similkameen Valleys are among the world's most scenic wine regions, although this is not always appreciated. Summerland-born Tony Holler, a pharmaceutical entrepreneur who became one of the owners of Poplar Grove Winery, recounts being on a business trip in California in 2004 that included a day in the Napa Valley. He was awestruck by the vineyards and winery architecture until his wife, Barbara, interjected, saying, "Tony, wake up—the Okanagan Valley is far more beautiful than this valley, and it's got a big lake." Deciding she was right, he bought his first vineyard property a few months later on the Naramata Bench and then built a home beside the lake.

Besides wine and scenery, the valleys are fascinating studies in geology, in ecology, and in First Nations culture. We would refer students of geology to a book published in 2011 by the Okanagan Geology Committee, called *Okanagan Geology South: Geologic Highlights of the South Okanagan British Columbia*. The Desert Centre near Osoyoos provides guided walks through Canada's only pocket desert. The self-guided tour at the Burrowing Owl Estate Winery includes information on the fragile environment of the South Okanagan as well as on successful work to restore the burrowing owl population. The excellent Nk'Mip Desert Cultural Centre next to the Nk'Mip Cellars winery interprets the history and culture of the First Nations. The tranquil gardens at the Pacific Agri-Food Research Centre in Summerland offer the perfect spot to relax between winery visits. The Kettle Valley Rail Trail ascends from Penticton and leads along the upper border of the Naramata Bench, providing stunning vineyard panoramas. The Golden Mile Trail on the hills above Tinhorn Creek winery offers breathtaking views of the South Okanagan.

This is the rich tapestry in which the wineries operate. We have never tired of exploring it. Neither will you.

GEOGRAPHY FOR WINE TOURISTS

The following is a quick guide to the wine country's geography, starting with the Similkameen and then arranged from the south to the north. The list of wineries included in each region makes it easier to plan wine tours. This arrangement assumes entering wine country at the south end by way of the Crowsnest Highway (No. 3). Reverse the order if entering wine country from the north, by way of the Trans-Canada and Highway 97. Whether you arrive by air in Kelowna or by car via the Coquihalla, you can turn either north or south in the Okanagan Valley depending on where your favourite wineries are located.

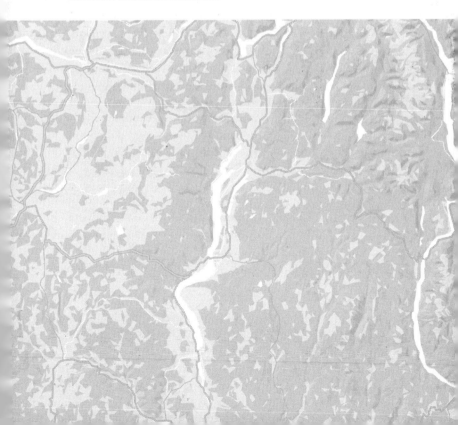

SIMILKAMEEN VALLEY

The Similkameen, where producers are represented by the Similkameen Independent Winegrowers, is a narrow valley, with steep, brooding mountains on both sides and a passive river (except during spring floods) winding along the valley bottom. There is very little rain or snow, and the persistent wind, one of the valley's most important features, cleanses the vines of pests and diseases and facilitates organic viticulture. With about 285 hectares (700 acres) of vineyard, the Similkameen as an appellation is dwarfed by the Okanagan, which is 20 times the size. Under irrigation, all but the late-ripening vinifera grapes grow here in a climate marked by 181 frost-free days, more than 2,000 hours of sunshine, blistering summer heat, and occasional sharply cold winter days.

The valley's vineyards and wineries are all between Keremeos (population 1,500) and Richter Pass—the low mountain pass near the American border through which Highway 3 undulates on its way to Osoyoos. Grapes have grown here at least since the 1960s on well-drained sand and gravel soils. There is benchland on the east side of the valley, above the highway, where apple orchards have been gradually replaced with vineyards. Numerous other farms in the valley grow tree fruit, vegetables, and grains. About half of the farms are organic, perhaps the highest concentration of organic farms in British Columbia.

WINERIES

Clos du Soleil 110
Corcelettes Estate Winery 116
Crowsnest Vineyards 124
Eau Vivre Winery 142
Forbidden Fruit Winery 162
Hugging Tree Winery 208
Liber Farm & Winery 254
Little Farm Winery 262
Orofino Winery 324
Robin Ridge Winery 380
Rustic Roots Winery 390
Scout Vineyard (no tasting room) 408
Seven Stones Winery 416
Vanessa Vineyard 482

OSOYOOS LAKE BENCH

The southernmost vineyards in the Okanagan grow on the Osoyoos Lake Bench. This is one of the narrowest points of the Okanagan Valley—Osoyoos, in fact, is derived from a First Nations word meaning "narrows of the lake"—and one of the hottest. Osoyoos (population 5,100), the Spanish-themed lakeside town against the United States border, averages summertime temperatures that are 3°C to 5°C (5°F-9°F) higher than in Penticton.

This is predominantly red-wine country. The most extensive vineyards are those that Vincor International planted in 1998 and 1999 on the eastern and northeastern side of Osoyoos Lake, on sandy slopes rising about 60 metres above the valley floor. These have been named Bull Pine, Sunrock, Bear Cub, McIntyre, and Whitetail. Leading varieties are Merlot, Cabernet Sauvignon, Syrah, Pinot Noir, and Canada's earliest successful Zinfandel block. Whites are also planted, notably Chardonnay, Sauvignon Blanc, and Viognier. The bench on the western flank of the valley perches slightly higher and has a more complex mix of sand, clay, and gravel. Reds also dominate plantings here. The Osoyoos Larose vineyard high on the western slope grows only Bordeaux reds—chiefly Merlot, Cabernet Sauvignon, and Cabernet Franc.

WINERIES

Adega on 45th Estate
    Winery 30
Blue Sky Estate Winery 74
Bordertown Vineyards &
    Estate Winery 78
Gold Hill Winery 180
Lakeside Cellars 240

Lariana Cellars 246
LaStella Winery 248
Moon Curser Vineyards 296
Nk'Mip Cellars 310
Osoyoos Larose 330
Sonora Desert Winery 430
Young & Wyse Collection 506

THE GOLDEN MILE

In 2015, after extensive soil and climate research, prime vineyards on the west side of the Okanagan south of Oliver received British Columbia's first sub-appellation, the Golden Mile. For the purposes of wine touring, the entire western side of the valley, including vineyards not in the sub-appellation, is referred to as the Golden Mile. It is believed the name once was applied to the 19th-century gold and silver mines, the remains of which can still be found in the hillsides.

The sub-appellation's well-drained gravel, clay, and sandy soils contain complex minerality from Mount Kobau, the stubby extinct volcano above the valley. The vines benefit from morning and midday sun but cool off in late afternoon when the sun drops behind the mountains. The cooler growing conditions of the Golden Mile produce wines, both red and white, with good acidity and bright fruit flavours.

You should hike the hills if you are reasonably fit and wearing good shoes. The 10-kilometre Golden Mile hiking trail extends along the flank of the mountains above the vineyards. One access point is at the north end, near the kiosk dedicated to Fairview, the long-vanished mining town. Another access point is at the uphill end of Tinhorn Creek's vineyard; trail maps are available in Tinhorn's wine shop. The trail provides spectacular views over the Okanagan Valley.

WINERIES

Cassini Cellars 90

Castoro de Oro Estate
    Winery 92

C.C. Jentsch Cellars 94

CheckMate Artisanal
    Winery 102

Culmina Family Estate
    Winery 126

Fairview Cellars 156

Gehringer Brothers Estate
    Winery 176

Hester Creek Estate
    Winery 198

Intersection Estate
    Winery 214

Kismet Estate Winery 228

Maverick Estate Winery 276

Road 13 Vineyards 378

Rust Wine Co. 388

Tinhorn Creek Vineyards 472

vinAmité Cellars 488

Winemaker's CUT 502

BLACK SAGE ROAD

This is the road to drive if you want to see acres and acres of vines, rising up to the low mountains on the east side of the valley. Black Sage Road also shows up on maps as 71st Street. It curls around the eastern side of Oliver (population 4,900), finally petering out at Arterra's Osoyoos Lake Bench vineyards. The views over the valley and also of vineyards crowding the road make this one of the Okanagan's most scenic drives.

Winemakers have discovered that these sandy vineyards, in sun from early morning until the end of the day, grow powerful red wines as well as full-flavoured whites. There are few places in British Columbia where vines grow in leaner soil. Most vineyards are on fine and very deep sand that was deposited a long time ago, when this was the beach of a vast inland lake. In its natural state, the arid earth hosts wiry grasses, tumbleweed, and Northern Pacific rattlesnakes. Irrigation is essential. "It's a really unique little area," Richard Cleave, a retired vineyard manager, says of Black Sage Road. "We get very little rainfall, especially during the summer months, when we get less than three inches on average. We have to use very, very few chemicals. We get very few bugs, so we use very few insecticides. It's just a unique area to grow grapes."

In the growing season, the large swing between hot days and cool nights produces grapes yielding wines with ripe fruit but bright acidity, an ideal combination. While only a handful of wineries are located on or near the road, many premium wineries in other regions use Black Sage grapes, among them Sumac Ridge, Tinhorn Creek, and Mission Hill.

NORTH OLIVER

There are wineries along Tucelnuit Drive, the northern extension of Black Sage Road, and along Highway 97. The Okanagan River and the northern suburbs of Oliver divide the two. The Jackson-Triggs winery, with acres of tanks, is by far the largest wine-processing facility in the Okanagan. It also has the elegant tasting room and wine shop for Jackson-Triggs and Inniskillin Okanagan.

The other wineries here are small and family owned, with informal, friendly tasting rooms. Unlike the year-round hours at Jackson-Triggs, the family wineries are usually open from April to October. Since production volumes are small, it is best to visit early in the season before the wines are sold out.

The Covert winery, while also small, is on a historic family farm on the flank of McIntyre Bluff. The Coverts host popular festivals every summer.

WINERIES

Covert Farms Family Estate 118

Granite Bluff Estate Winery 182

Hidden Chapel Winery 200

Inniskillin Okanagan 212

Jackson-Triggs Okanagan/ Sunrock Vineyards 218

La Casa Bianca Winery 232

Pipe' Dreams Winery 344

Ramification Cellars 362

Red Horses Vineyard 368

Ricco Bambino/Crooked Crown Vineyard 372

River Stone Estate Winery 376

OKANAGAN FALLS

This compact vineyard region, with twisting back roads well worth exploring, includes landscapes of legendary beauty. A view of the vineyards at the Blue Mountain winery, where rows of vines undulate with perfect precision toward a hazy blue horizon, is widely reproduced in industry literature, websites, and even screen savers. A hike to the top of Peach Cliff or a drive to the See Ya Later winery's heritage tasting room affords incomparable views of the region. A back road worth exploring leads east on McLean Creek Road, swinging around to emerge on Eastside Road, not far from Blasted Church Vineyards.

The Okanagan Falls soil types vary so dramatically that some vineyards grow fine Burgundy grapes, and others succeed with Alsace whites and still others with Bordeaux varieties. This is a wine tourist's paradise, with every style of wine available, from sparkling to Icewine. See Ya Later Ranch's Hawthorne Mountain Vineyard boasts the highest-elevation vineyard (536 metres) in the South Okanagan, with an unusual northeastern exposure. As a result, this comparatively cool vineyard produces some of the finest Gewürztraminer and Pinot Gris in the valley.

WINERIES

BC Wine Studio 46
Blue Mountain Vineyard
    and Cellars 72
Bonamici Cellars 76
Liquidity Wines 258
Meyer Family Vineyards 282
Montakarn Winery 292
Nighthawk Vineyards 308

Noble Ridge Vineyard &
    Winery 312
Rigour & Whimsy 374
See Ya Later Ranch 412
Stag's Hollow Winery 438
Synchromesh Wines 450
Wild Goose Vineyards 498

SKAHA LAKE

Twisting but scenic, Eastside/Lakeside Road is the shortest route from Okanagan Falls to Penticton. It has recently been discovered by wine tourists, who usually drive the longer but faster Highway 97 between the two communities. Now that there are wineries in picturesque Kaleden, wine tourists need to plan a circle route around Skaha Lake. Those preferring to linger—the scenery again is beautiful—may wish to seek out one of the several interesting bed and breakfasts such as God's Mountain.

Currently, six wineries overlook Eastside and Lakeside Road. The vineyards here all have good western exposure and benefit from the effect of Skaha Lake. Even though the lake is relatively shallow (maximum depth is 55 metres) and small, with only 30 kilometres of shoreline, Skaha tempers the climate and extends the ripening season in late autumn.

In earlier times, one of Canada's larger peach orchards operated on the bench of land between the lake and the cliffs to the east. Peaches are notoriously tender. It is an axiom that grapes will flourish wherever peaches grow. The constraint to this viticulture region is the narrowness of the arable bench, which backs against silt and clay cliffs. The Skaha Bluffs southeast of Penticton are popular with rock climbers. Painted Rock Estate Winery helped pay to pave the road to the parking lot used by the climbers.

WINERIES

Black Dog Cellars 58

Blasted Church

  Vineyards 68

Crescent Hill Winery 120

Echo Bay Vineyard 144

Painted Rock Estate

  Winery 334

Pentâge Winery 338

KALEDEN

Kaleden is a village on the west side of Skaha Lake. During the past two or three decades, vineyards have gradually replaced the orchards that once covered the slopes. Given the location beside the highway and close to Penticton, it is surprising that most of the wineries here are recently established. Four were open or in development as this book was written (including Birch Block, which you'll find under "Virtual Wineries," page 27). Others are in the wings. There are attractions here in addition to wine. Linden Gardens has been described as the South Okanagan's best wedding venue. The Dominion Radio Astrophysical Observatory, nearby at White Lake, is open year-round and offers self-guided tours.

WINERIES

PENTICTON

With at least 10 wineries in the city limits, Penticton is the urban winery destination in the Okanagan. There is, in fact, an urban winery tradition begun here in 1966 when Evans Lougheed, a businessman, established Casabello Wines on Main Street. The winery's unofficial winery touring in the early 1970s was shut down in 1972 by the Liquor Control Board. The LCB reconsidered two years later, allowing winery tours and then, in 1977, tasting rooms. Casabello closed in 1994. Production moved to the Jackson-Triggs winery in Oliver, and the Casabello site was redeveloped as a shopping centre. The current Penticton wineries all benefit from the regulatory ground broken by Casabello, being able to host tours and tastings and to sell wines directly to consumers. The most unusual of Penticton's urban wineries is TIME Winery. The late Harry McWatters, TIME's founder, turned a former downtown movie theatre into a major winery, complete with a restaurant. It is perhaps no coincidence that Harry began his long career in wine as a salesman for Casabello.

WINERIES

Da Silva Vineyards and
    Winery 128
Evolve Cellars 152
Four Shadows Vineyard &
    Winery 166
Monster Vineyards 290
Perseus Winery 340

Play Estate Winery 348
Poplar Grove Winery 350
Roche Wines 382
TIME Winery 470
Upper Bench Winery &
    Creamery 476

NARAMATA BENCH

The number of wineries, thanks to the superb growing conditions for grapes and the remarkable landscape, makes Naramata Road the hottest winery address in British Columbia. Vineyards along the road have been selling for double the price of vineyards in, for example, California's long-established Mendocino County. Why? Well, first, there is not much land available. Second, it is easy for wine tourists to move from one superb winery to the next on what is the Okanagan's most concentrated route of fine wine.

Okanagan Lake tempers the climate. There are seldom vine-killing winter temperatures. The few late-spring frosts and a very long autumn bring grapes to optimal ripeness. Merlot and other Bordeaux reds grow well here, along with elegant Pinot Noir, peppery Syrah, and Pinot Gris, Sauvignon Blanc, Riesling, and Viognier. The bench on the eastern shore of the lake is a narrow strip of land that drops down from what's left of the Kettle Valley Railway (a good walking and biking trail) to the rugged lakeshore bluffs. The vines are bathed in sun from midmorning to the end of the day. The views from many tasting rooms take the breath away. Several wineries offer good bistro-style dining or fine dining for those who wish to linger in this superb setting.

SUMMERLAND AND PEACHLAND

When John Moore Robinson, a developer, founded Summerland in 1902, he advertised it as "Heaven on earth, with summer weather forever." That climate also accounts for Summerland's significant agricultural hinterland, seldom explored by visitors. Highway 97 sweeps by on the eastern side of Giants Head. This stubby extinct volcano overshadows the quaint town (population 11,600), whose Tudor-style architecture is mirrored in the Sumac Ridge winery.

For many years, Sumac Ridge was the community's only winery. Recently, numerous new wineries have opened, mostly on the western side of Giants Head, where there are good southeastern-facing slopes for grapes. The bucolic countryside, with twisting valley fingers extending deep into the mountains, is worth exploring (you might even find the buffalo farm). Between Summerland and Peachland, most of the vineyards cling to steep slopes running down toward Okanagan Lake, and are usually not visible from the highway. An exception is Fitzpatrick Family Vineyards, whose vineyards are on postcard-perfect plateaus just below the highway. There are also vineyards on the hillsides above Peachland (population 5,400) awaiting discovery by wine tourists who venture off the beaten path.

What most of the vineyards in this area have in common is cool-climate grape-growing conditions. Expect to find good Pinot Noir, Chardonnay, Pinot Gris, Pinot Blanc, and Gewürztraminer.

WINERIES

Back Door Winery 40
Dirty Laundry Vineyard 140
8th Generation Vineyard 148
Fitzpatrick Family
    Vineyards 160
Giant Head Estate Winery 178
Hainle Vineyards Estate
    Winery 188
Heaven's Gate Estate Winery
    194
Lightning Rock Winery 256
Lunessence Winery &
    Vineyard 268

Okanagan Crush Pad Winery
    (Free Form, Haywire, and
    Narrative) 316
Sage Hills Vineyard 392
Savard Vines 400
Saxon Estate Winery 402
Silkscarf Winery 418
Sleeping Giant Fruit Winery 428
Sumac Ridge Estate Winery 442
SummerGate Winery 444
TH Wines 460
Thornhaven Estates
    Winery 464

SLOPES OF MOUNT BOUCHERIE

Just a 20-minute drive southwest of Kelowna's urban sprawl, the Mount Boucherie wine region's best vineyards continue to hold off the pressure of land developers. Although many of the wineries here also have vineyards in the South Okanagan or the Similkameen, they husband these precious slopes. Bathed by the reflected light from Okanagan Lake, Mount Boucherie vineyards are well suited to delicate premium varieties like Pinot Noir and Riesling. Quails' Gate, which practises some of the best viticulture in the valley, even succeeds with Merlot and Cabernet Sauvignon.

The Stewart family, owners of Quails' Gate, have grown grapes here since the mid-1950s, having begun planting even before the floating bridge was built across the lake at Kelowna in 1958, replacing ferries and rail barges. The most mature vines at Quails' Gate include a block of Maréchal Foch planted in 1969.

Such old blocks are the exception; most vineyards on these slopes have been replanted since 1990 with premium varieties. Some of the steeper slopes have been given over to palatial homes, whose owners are drawn by stunning views over the lake. Arguably, the best lake view from any of the wineries belongs to the Mission Hill winery, perched on the brow of the mountain, some 130 metres above the surface of the lake.

WINERIES

Beaumont Family Estate
Winery   48
Black Swift Vineyards   64
Ciao Bella Winery   106
Crown & Thieves   122
The Dance Winery   130
Frind Estate Winery   174
Grizzli Winery   186
The Hatch   192
Indigenous World
Winery   210
Kalala Organic Estate
Winery   222

Little Straw Vineyards   264
Mission Hill Family
Estate   286
Mt. Boucherie Estate
Winery   300
Niche Wine Company   304
Off The Grid Organic
Winery   314
Quails' Gate Winery   358
Rollingdale Winery   384
Tender Hope Winery   456
Volcanic Hills Estate
Winery   490

KELOWNA AND LAKE COUNTRY

This is a region for history lovers. The Okanagan's first vines were planted in what is now East Kelowna, at an Oblate mission founded in 1859 by a French priest named Charles Pandosy. The restored mission buildings are now a heritage site on Kelowna's Benvoulin Road, worth a visit even though there never was a commercial vineyard (no vines remain today). Wine grapes have been cultivated on the nearby southwest-facing slopes since at least 1928.

Compared to the South Okanagan, the Kelowna area has cool growing conditions favourable to such white varieties as Riesling and Pinot Gris and reds such as Pinot Noir. Tantalus Vineyards and St. Hubertus have Riesling vines that were planted in the late 1970s; these now produce remarkably intense wines.

Another piece of history is the Calona Vineyards winery, which sprawls untidily near downtown Kelowna. This is British Columbia's oldest continually operating winery (established in 1932). Andrew Peller Ltd., which has owned Calona since 2005, has renovated the entire facility and added the vast Sandhill tasting room. The wine shop sells all the brands now made at this winery, including the Wayne Gretzky wines.

The Lake Country vineyards, which date from the 1970s, are about half an hour's drive north of Kelowna, on the eastern shore of Okanagan Lake. Several of the larger wineries operate excellent restaurants.

VERNON AND SALMON ARM

While this region is almost two hours north of the Okanagan wine trail, its position astride the Trans-Canada Highway helps attract visitors. The wine-touring signs that have gone up beside highways in recent years direct a burgeoning number of visitors to these northern wineries.

Grape growing this far north succeeds only where microclimates are unusually favourable or wine growers unusually determined. In Vernon, vineyards are planted on steep slopes whose southern pitch creates even more frost-free days than Black Sage Road. The northern arms of Okanagan Lake also help to moderate the climate. Closer to Salmon Arm, the vineyard at the Larch Hills Winery, with the highest elevation (700 metres) of any British Columbia vineyard, grows grapes on a steep, south-facing slope, but without a lake anywhere near, only the earliest grape varieties succeed. Winters are chilly at this elevation, but the heavy snowfall dumps an insulating blanket on the vines. There is enough precipitation in the Salmon Arm area that, generally, the vineyards are not irrigated. Several vineyards have been planted around the shores of Shuswap Lake. Nearly all northern wineries turn to Okanagan vineyards to source varieties, such as Merlot, that will not mature this far north.

WINERIES

Baccata Ridge Winery 38
Celista Estate Winery 98
Edge of the Earth
    Vineyards 146
Larch Hills Winery 244
Marionette Winery 272
OVINO Winery 332

Recline Ridge Vineyards &
    Winery 364
Sunnybrae Vineyards &
    Winery 448
Waterside Vineyard &
    Winery 492

BEYOND THE OKANAGAN

THOMPSON RIVER VALLEY

It is pushing the envelope to plant wine grapes around Kamloops, but that is not preventing some to risk vines in special microclimates. In 2005 Doug Wood, a physician, began planting the first commercial vineyard for his Sagewood Winery on the north side of the Thompson River about 23 kilometres east of Kamloops. Three years later, Ed Collett, a businessman, began developing a major vineyard for his Harper's Trail winery. In 2010, John and Debbie Woodward planted vines north of downtown Kamloops, on the banks of the North Thompson River. All of these vineyards are largely planted with vinifera varieties.

The perceived risk is that, in some winters, the temperatures are cold enough to freeze next season's fruiting buds and even kill vines. Monte Creek Ranch, with a winery beside the Trans-Canada Highway east of Kamloops, initially insured itself against hard winters by planting in 2010 hardy Minnesota hybrid vines in one of its two vineyards here. Vinifera were planted in the second vineyard, a steep south-facing slope. Both vineyards have succeeded. These pioneers have created a burgeoning wine region.

WINERIES

Harper's Trail Estate
Winery 190
Monte Creek Ranch
Winery 294

Privato Vineyard &
Winery 354
Sagewood Winery 394

LILLOOET

Fort Berens Estate Winery includes in its portfolio a wine called Camels White. The name is a nod to the community's rich history. In 1862, during a time of gold and silver exploration, a drover named John Galbreath brought a herd of camels for transporting freight among mining camps. His venture failed because the camels fought with the horses already providing transportation. The camels were turned loose in the wilderness. The tale was recalled as Fort Berens was establishing the first winery at Lillooet and researching the history to brand some of its wines. (The winery itself is named for a Hudson's Bay fort that operated briefly before the gold rush.)

Lillooet (population 2,300) was an attractive location because there was no question grapevines would flourish here. The community has some of the hottest days in British Columbia each summer, with a dry, sunbathed climate comparable to Osoyoos. With about 8 hectares (20 acres) of vineyard, Fort Berens is almost self-sufficient in grapes. The winery's success has encouraged the development of other vineyards in the area, as well as a second winery. The Lillooet area, located 240 kilometres northeast of Vancouver, has a rugged beauty that compensates for its location off the beaten track for wine touring.

WINERIES

THE KOOTENAYS

The clue that grapes can be grown in the Kootenays is the name of a small town just east of Trail: Fruitvale. There is a considerable history of successful tree-fruit production in the region with a climate in which early to midseason grape varieties will thrive. In the words of a provincial tourism brochure, "This is the warm side of the Rockies."

The word *Kootenay* has Indigenous roots. In the language of the Ktunaxa First Nation, *quthni* means to travel by water, a reference to the many rivers in the scenic region.

For the purposes of wine touring, this region extends from Grand Forks on the west to Creston on the east; and from the United States border north to the Arrow Lakes. There are microclimates throughout where grapes and other fruit are grown. Additional wineries are under consideration in the region.

WINERIES

Baillie-Grohman Estate
   Winery 42
Columbia Gardens Vineyard
   & Winery 112
Red Bird Estate Winery 366
Skimmerhorn Winery and
   Vineyard 426

Valley of the Springs
   Winery 478
William Tell Family Estate
   (no tasting room) 500
Wynnwood Cellars 504

VIRTUAL WINERIES

The term *virtual wineries* applies to producers that do not yet own a licensed winery. Typically, the vintners are young and ambitious but do not yet have the resources to buy vineyards of their own or build wineries. Thus, they make their wines at existing licensed wineries. Okanagan Crush Pad and BC Wine Studio provide formal custom crush services to virtual wineries. Other vintners make informal arrangements with other wineries. Virtual wineries are also required under the licences to sell their products where the wines are made. Regulations also prevent virtual wineries from selling wines through websites. None of the virtual wineries operate their own tasting rooms.

Perhaps because of such restrictions, virtual wineries strive to become licensed wineries once they have established their brands. Three licensed wineries in this book, Black Market, Nagging Doubt, and Winemaker's CUT, started several years earlier as virtual wineries. It is likely that some, if not all, the virtual wineries below will become licensed wineries one day. That is why they are included here.

WINERIES

WINERY PROFILES

ADEGA ON 45TH ESTATE WINERY

OSOYOOS

Ringing the church bells to communicate important village events was an art that Alex Nunes learned one summer in his native Portugal. He was 13 and home from a stint in the seminary. He immigrated to Canada two years later. The lingering memory of the two big bells inspired the addition of a bell tower to the winery's facade when it was built in 2011. Alex still considers adding a bell. "It is either buy one or go back to my hometown and steal one at midnight," he jokes.

The winery, whose warm butterscotch tones blend with the desert landscape of Osoyoos, was designed by Alex and his brother-in-law, Fred Farinha, who own the winery with their wives, Maria and Pamela. The winery sits high on the vineyard's west-facing slope. The tasting-room windows offer a grand view over the town and the lake. The 6,000-square-foot winery has thick concrete walls and a naturally cooled cellar for 400 barrels buried against the hillside. The interior's public areas acquired the instant patina of age by having walls finished with Italian clay and tiles on the floor.

The winery's European ambience reflects their Portuguese heritage (*adega* is Portuguese for "cellar"). Alex was born in Portugal in 1950, while Fred was born in Penticton in 1966. Their families were among the many Portuguese immigrants who came to Osoyoos at that time as tree-fruit growers. Both Alex and Fred operated orchards until about 2005, when vanishing returns from tree fruit left them with a stark choice: sell the land or plant grapes. "We decided to keep the land and build a winery," Alex says.

They planted three vineyards totalling 11.5 hectares (28½ acres), supporting 5,000 cases a year, with extra grapes for sale to other wineries. "Create our own future, you could call it," Alex says. Wine is in their blood. "We had wine on our tables

FRED FARINHA AND ALEX NUNES

and in our homes, always, since we were born," Alex remembers. "Your mom would ask you to go to the tavern in the village to get a litre of wine. It did not matter if you were five years old or ten years old. You would just go and get it." While they use a consulting winemaker, Alex and Fred, with years of experience as home winemakers, do almost everything themselves. "We are hands-on," Fred says. "We are in the field, and we are also in here."

MY PICKS

Viognier is the star among the white wines. The solid range of reds includes a peppery Syrah, a brambly Cabernet Franc, an elegant Cabernet Sauvignon, and a fine Meritage blend called Quarteto Tinto.

OPENED 2011

7311 45th Street
Osoyoos, BC V0H 1V6
T 250.495.6243
W adegaon45.com

ANCIENT HILL ESTATE WINERY

KELOWNA

This winery is the unabashed champion of Baco Noir, the dark hybrid grape created in 1902 by François Baco, a plant breeder in southwestern France. Because it is a winter-hardy grape producing full-bodied red wines, it was widely grown in the Okanagan until vineyards began switching to vinifera grapes. But in 2005, when Richard Kamphuys (pronounced *compass*) replaced fruit trees with vines, he chose Baco Noir for about a third of his 6-hectare (15-acre) vineyard.

Richard, who owns this winery with his wife, Jitske, planted varieties that tolerate the cold winters that can be expected at this site overlooking Kelowna International Airport, where grapes were first planted in the 1930s by the Rittich brothers. Natives of Hungary, Eugene and Virgil Rittich believed that vinifera grapes could succeed and wrote a book (British Columbia's first wine book) on how to grow grapes and make wine. Severe winters at the time doomed their pioneering trials, and fruit trees replaced vines.

Richard and Jitske came from the Netherlands in 1992 and bought an apple orchard. Richard, who was born in 1963, completed an advanced economics degree at the historic Erasmus University in Rotterdam before deciding he wanted a rural lifestyle for himself and his family.

He considered growing grapes as soon as he and Jitske, a former doctor's assistant, bought the orchard but was put off until 2005 by general pessimism at that time about the future of British Columbia's wineries. Since then, he has planted over 27,000 vines, choosing midseason-ripening varieties: Pinot Gris, Gewürztraminer, Lemberger, Zweigelt, Pinot Noir, and Baco Noir.

"I should have had more Baco Noir and less Zweigelt," Richard says now. "That hybrid seems suited to this area. It comes through in a lesser year as well as in a good year."

RICHARD AND JITSKE KAMPHUYS

To make the point, he pours a glass of Baco Noir from 2010, a cool year. The wine is full bodied with rich flavours of plum and chocolate. Invariably, it is the most popular wine at Ancient Hill, a baronial winery designed by Robert Mackenzie, the Okanagan's pre-eminent winery architect.

MY PICKS

Baco Noir leads a focused portfolio that includes Lazerus, a proprietary red made with Lemberger, a red grape the Rittich brothers once grew. Pinot Gris, Gewürztraminer, and rosé also are well made.

OPENED 2011

4918 Anderson Road
Kelowna, BC V1X 7V7
T   250.491.2766
W   ancienthillwinery.com

ANTHONY BUCHANAN WINES

VIRTUAL WINERY

Anthony Buchanan, who was born in 1970, was just 26 when he got so serious about wine that he joined the Opimian Society, a national wine-buying club. However, he did not set out immediately on a career in wine. "I was a hairdresser for 21 years," Anthony says. "I got into hairdressing right out of high school. I owned my own business for 11 years in Victoria."

He began considering a different career in 2001. "I have always loved food and wine," he says. "I like the social aspect of it as well." Initially, he set out to be a sommelier until he became more interested in winemaking. In 2007, he left the hair salon to work the harvest at Blue Mountain Vineyard, a winery specializing in Anthony's biggest passion, Pinot Noir. Then he took a job in the cellar at the Church & State winery at Brentwood Bay on Vancouver Island. There he met Nicole, now his wife and partner in the winery.

On the advice of Matt Mavety, the winemaker at Blue Mountain, Anthony enrolled in the University of Washington's enology program to qualify as a winemaker. In 2010, as he was finishing the course, he and Nicole moved to the Okanagan, where he made wine with several producers before becoming the senior winemaker at Desert Hills Estate Winery in 2016.

He had begun making wines for his own label in 2014 when he was with Eau Vivre Winery, a Pinot Noir specialist in the Similkameen Valley. "Pinot Noir has been a long-term passion of mine," he says. To avoid a conflict with his employers, Anthony focuses on different varieties, including Pinot Blanc. "I think it is extremely undervalued," he says. "There are not a lot of wineries that produce Pinot Blanc."

By 2019, he was making 1,500 cases for Anthony Buchanan Wines, which is now among the larger of the virtual wineries.

ANTHONY BUCHANAN

"The idea is to slowly establish the brand in the marketplace and get a really good following," Anthony says. "We will take each year, each vintage, as it comes. But there is the end goal of obtaining a small piece of property."

MY PICKS

Everything, including Pinot Blanc, Pinot Noir, Sémillon, and the bold Syrah.

OPENED 2016

T 778.931.2421

W anthonybuchananwines.ca
No tasting room

ARROWLEAF CELLARS

It was not a surprise in 2017 when Arrowleaf Cellars planted Arvine, a little-known Swiss white variety never before grown in the Okanagan. Arrowleaf is operated by Joe and Margrit Zuppiger and their family, Swiss immigrants who have lived in the Okanagan since 1997. "I always liked the wine," says their winemaker son, Manuel, of Arvine. "Of the Swiss wines, especially the varieties that are native to Switzerland, I always found that to be a standout."

When the family bought this 6.5-hectare (16-acre) North Okanagan vineyard, Manuel, who was born in 1976, was sent back to Switzerland to train in that country's top wine school. Now, Arrowleaf produces about 9,000 cases a year, a little more than half of which is white. In recent years, the Zuppigers have increased Pinot Noir plantings by converting a large Gewürztraminer block. Even though Arrowleaf's Gewürztraminer is one of its best wines, the popularity of the variety has declined while Pinot Noir has surged.

"It is fun to try something new," Manuel says. "Who knows? Arvine may take off in the future. It is always nice to have an alternative in case people get tired of Pinot Gris, or whatever."

Arrowleaf's attractive site adds to the winery's appeal. In 2014, Arrowleaf opened a tasting room and barrel cellar in a 5,000-square-foot building designed by Robert Mackenzie, one of the Okanagan's top winery architects. The tasting room is four times the size of the previous one and incorporates a restaurant. The windows provide a panoramic vineyard view.

MANUEL ZUPPIGER

OPENED 2003

1574 Camp Road
Lake Country, BC V4V 1K1
T   250.766.2992
W   arrowleafcellars.com

MY PICKS

The winery's excellent premium wines are now led by a red blend called Archive (formerly Solstice). Every wine here is well made and well priced. No other Bacchus can compare with this one.

BACCATA RIDGE WINERY

GRINDROD

Dave Robertson, a rancher and third-generation farmer, found himself in the wine business after approaching Sheldon Moore, the founder of Baccata Ridge, to make wine with Dave's blueberries. Ill health then prevented Sheldon from entering into a joint venture. Consequently, Dave bought the winery and moved it a few miles down the road. Daughter Samantha, mentored by Sheldon, now makes the wine, and her sister, Michelle, manages the wine shop.

For Dave, it is an agricultural sideline. He and Cathy, his wife, are shareholders in Blue Goose Cattle Company, an organic beef producer that runs 6,000 head of cattle on 24,300 hectares (60,000 acres). The couple also has a smaller ranch in Williams Lake with 1,000 head. In addition to this, Dave produces honey from 500 bee colonies at Cache Creek; and on 4 hectares (10 acres) at the home ranch, he has 20,000 hand-tended blueberry bushes. The blueberries and the honey provide raw materials for the winery's mead and fruit wines.

The Robertson family's organic ethic is likely what led to Sheldon considering a joint venture. Sheldon, an engineer and native of Fort St. John, spent many years with a technology firm in Southeast Asia. There, he absorbed Buddhist principles and wrote a book, *Remember Zen: Awaken the Buddha-Nature Within*. He applied those in running the Grindrod farm he purchased in 2001 and where he planted 4 hectares (10 acres) of grapes. "Zen is my approach to winemaking," he once said. "I try to be natural. I tell the pickers when they come here not to come in a bad mood and spoil the mood in the vineyard."

While Dave Robertson's blueberries are not certified organically, the management of the field is virtually organic. "It would be a lot cheaper to spray those blueberries than weed them by hand," Dave says. "But at the market, we get five dollars a pound

DAVE ROBERTSON

for our blueberries. I feel I can afford to do a little extra."

The Baccata Ridge wines are moderately priced. "Once wine gets over $20 a bottle, I struggle with it," Dave says. "I grew up poor."

MY PICKS

Current range not tasted.

OPENED 2012

184 Monk Road
Grindrod, BC V0E 1Y0
T   250.517.7051
W   baccataridgewinery.ca

BACK DOOR WINERY

Back Door Winery is nearly impossible to miss. The vineyard is surrounded by multicoloured lights at night, and the wine shop is decorated with lights and colours of all kinds. It is difficult to ignore when driving by on a rare straight stretch of Highway 97 through Summerland. Ironically, the winemaker and owner, Pieter Smits, keeps a low profile.

When Pieter bought the vineyard, it was overgrown, having been abandoned when the previous owner's winery project failed in 2007. The site, which is in the middle of an area of Summerland called Jones Flat, was very different from other Okanagan locations. For one thing, its high water table makes growing grapes relatively easy, with less need for irrigation.

The less easy part was the winery and wine-shop building, which was a derelict Depression-era house when it was purchased. "It took a lot more work than I think Pieter was expecting," explains Blake Allen, the general manager. Pieter's friends from Alberta told him that the only good thing about the building was the back door. Though it bothered him at the time, Pieter recalled it when he needed to come up with a name for the winery.

The first 2015 vintage was made at Pieter's parents' winery, Sonoran Estate in Summerland. Pieter grew up in the winery and is a self-taught winemaker. The portfolio at Back Door is extensive. There were 19 available during a recent visit, including coyly named wines like At First Blush and Behind Closed Doors. The winery has perhaps the only single-variety bottling of the rarely seen Oraniensteiner grape, an intriguingly aromatic wine.

The portfolio is likely to expand, pushing production to more than 9,000 cases. "We like having the broad portfolio," explains Blake. "We like trying to appeal to as many in the crowd as we can." The goal from the start was to appeal to locals in Summerland, often people who have never ventured into a wine shop before and who don't often purchase wines regularly. The tasting room has a welcoming casual and warm environment. It is open year-round.

The wine shop really comes alive in the summer when the two tasting bars in the shop get rolling and live music is playing on the patio. The winery hires local musicians whenever possible, and the events have drawn in crowds seeking a fun, informal, and entirely unpretentious wine-shop experience.

Always a community-minded winery, Back Door donates partial proceeds of individual wines to specific causes. The Nice Rack wines specify support of breast cancer research, and the Way Home (a blend of Pinot Noir, Pinot Meunier, and Merlot) contributes to the Red Cross to be allocated to the disaster preparedness fund to help deal with forest fires in BC.

MY PICKS
Current range not tasted.

OPENED 2015

9752 Jones Flat Road
Summerland, BC V0H 1Z6
T   250.800.1199
1.877.901.3667 (DOOR)
(toll-free)
W   backdoorwinery.com

BAILLIE-GROHMAN ESTATE WINERY
CRESTON

This Kootenay winery's success is due in some measure to its New Zealand connection. In 2009, when former Calgarians Bob Johnson and Petra Flaa needed to make Baillie-Grohman's first wines, they hired Dan Barker, the owner of the Moana Park Winery in Hawke's Bay and New Zealand's Young Winemaker of the Year in 2003. He travelled from New Zealand to make or advise on every Baillie-Grohman vintage through 2016. Meanwhile, Wes Johnson, Bob and Petra's son, went to New Zealand, and was mentored at Moana Park and other wineries while earning a degree in enology. He has now taken over as the winemaker at Baillie-Grohman.

Bob was born in 1958 in Red Deer. He was a reservoir engineer with Sproule Associates, a consulting firm he joined in 1984, until he retired in 2013 to focus on Baillie-Grohman's marketing. The winery now produces about 5,000 cases a year. The 7-hectare (17½-acre) estate vineyard is farmed by Petra, a former technology manager, with viticultural skills acquired from University of Washington correspondence courses. Pinot Noir makes up two-fifths of the vines. The rest of the vineyard is planted with Pinot Gris, Chardonnay, Sauvignon Blanc, Gewürztraminer, and Schönburger, along with 250 Kerner plants for occasional Icewine. The winery also farms its Creston Valley Vineyard and the newly planted St. Augustine Vineyard.

Bob and Petra had initially moved to a Creston cherry orchard because of their love of the Kootenays. Their decision to switch to growing grapes reflected a long-time love of wine. Both had been members of the Opimian wine club, and Bob once was a home winemaker.

Bob and Petra's winery is named for a legendary Kootenay-area pioneer, William Baillie-Grohman. He came in 1882 with Teddy Roosevelt to hunt trophy mountain goats. Impressed with

PETRA FLAA AND BOB JOHNSON

the area's farmland, he leased 19,200 hectares (47,500 acres). He organized a British syndicate to divert the Kootenay River and settle colonists on the drained land. The scheme ultimately stalled when a lawyer made off with investment funds, although remaining British settlers developed the area. Baillie-Grohman's colourful story lives on. Remains of the SS *Midge*, the steamboat he built to navigate the river, are in the Creston Museum.

MY PICKS

Everything, notably the full-flavoured Pinot Noirs.

OPENED 2010

1140 27th Avenue South
Creston, BC V0B 1G1

T 250.428.8768

W bailliegrohman.com

Picnic area

BARTIER BROS.

OLIVER

The wine-industry verity that "it's all about the dirt" is nowhere more obvious than at Bartier Bros. The winery's 5.9-hectare (14½-acre) Cerqueira Vineyard produces wines with complex flavours with a spine of minerality. The vineyard is on the Black Sage Bench's gravel bar where the last glacier, as it was retreating 10,000 years ago, laid down a calcium-rich layer of gravel. The vineyard was planted in the early to mid-2000s with Sémillon, Chardonnay, Merlot, Cabernet Franc, and Syrah. It began selling fruit to Township 7 when Michael Bartier was the winemaker there.

"I loved the grapes and coveted the property," Michael says. When the Cerqueira family's contract with Township 7 ended, they offered it to Michael and his older brother, Don, when Michael began making wine for the brothers' label in 2009. Subsequently, the brothers bought the vineyard.

They were both born in the Okanagan Valley, Don in 1958 and Michael in 1967, the sons of an accountant, and initially pursued careers outside of the valley. Don, an Alberta oil-industry executive, planted a small Gewürztraminer vineyard at Summerland in 2010. Michael, after getting a degree in recreational administration and working five years with a Victoria wine agency, returned to the Okanagan to start his winemaking career at Hawthorne Mountain Vineyards in 1995. Over the next two decades, he made wine at Township 7, Road 13, and Okanagan Crush Pad and provided consulting work with other wineries. The brothers began selling their wines in 2011 and established their winery and tasting room after buying the coveted Cerqueira Vineyard in 2015.

The vineyard's mineral content makes it singular. "All our rocks are crusted white [with calcium], and the small feeder

MICHAEL BARTIER

roots from the vines are 'hugging' those rocks," Michael says. "Every vintage, the wines are fresh, fruity, and minerally. . . . That limestone ends up in every glass of our wine."

MY PICKS

Everything. The Sémillon is a vivid expression of the minerality. The reds are bold and rich. The flagship Bordeaux blend is The Goal, named to recall the 1955 world hockey champions, the Penticton Vees.

OPENED 2009

4821 Ryegrass Road
Oliver, BC V0H 1T1
T   250.487.9667
W   bartierbros.com

BC WINE STUDIO
OKANAGAN FALLS

The winemaker Mark Simpson launched his Siren's Call wines in 2010 in what has been a successful effort to establish the credibility of the consulting company he had started three years earlier. "When I started my company, I was looking for consulting work as a winemaker," he recalls. "Nobody knew me as a winemaker. I was regarded as a beer guy from Vancouver. When I started making wine, I put my own skin in the game."

Mark, who was born in England in 1960, began his career in 1982 with the Molson breweries after earning a microbiology degree at the University of British Columbia. In 1992 he became the brewmaster for the Granville Island Brewing Company in Vancouver. He came to winemaking in 2001 as research director for RJ Spagnols Wine and Beer Making Products, which had just been acquired by Vincor International. "I got to buy grapes and juice from all over the world for the wine kits," he says. "And I was part of the Vincor winemaking team and got to hang out with the Vincor winemakers." In 2007 he set up his consultancy, Artisan Food and Beverage Group.

After making the initial vintages for Siren's Call at another winery, Mark settled BC Wine Studio on Hawk's Vineyard, an Okanagan Falls property acquired in 2012 by Steve Carter, one of the clients nurtured into winemaking by Mark, and now his business partner. Numerous other producers, including Nagging Doubt Winery and Black Market Wine Company, developed their brands with Mark before establishing wineries of their own. "BC Wine Studio is a collaborative place," Mark says. "We nurture people to start out in the industry."

Hawk's Vineyard is just 2.4 hectares (6 acres) in size. The estate fruit are dedicated to the Hawk's Vineyard brand. For BC Wine Studio's production, about 3,000 cases a year, Mark sources

MARK SIMPSON

grapes from growers—like Bordertown Vineyards in Osoyoos—that had previously used his consulting services. "I can source grapes from fantastic growers that I know and trust," he says.

"I have core wines I make every year," Mark says. Harmonious, the winery's flagship red blend, has been made every vintage since 2010, and has recently been joined by a white blend called Melodious. But his winemaking curiosity is such that he never passes up interesting varieties such as Grüner Veltliner, Viognier, and Petit Verdot. "If the brands get traction in the market, I keep making them," he says.

MY PICKS

Everything, especially Syrah and Harmonious, an iconic Bordeaux red blend.

OPENED 2013

2434 Oliver Ranch Road
Okanagan Falls, BC
V0H 1R2
T 604.862.3420
W bcwinestudio.ca

BEAUMONT FAMILY ESTATE WINERY

WEST KELOWNA

Now in her early 30s, winemaker Alana Lubchynski likely has more vineyard and winemaking experience than anyone else her age. She started driving tractors around the vineyard at age eight and has been making wine since she was legally able to consume it at 19. She took the winemaking program at Okanagan College in Penticton and worked vintages at other BC wineries. In the off-seasons, she worked at wineries in New Zealand and Australia for several years before bringing all that experience home to Beaumont's first wines.

Alana comes by the farming lifestyle naturally as her parents, Alex and Louise, both grew up on farms in Alberta. The family moved to the Okanagan in 1990 before she and her older brother, Scott, started school. Alex built houses for a few years while they searched for land to farm. It was the volcanic soil of Lakeview Heights on the eastern slope of Mount Boucherie that caught Alex's attention.

The first of three sites that he would purchase was an old cherry orchard with 50-year-old trees. It was purchased in 1995 and planted with grapes organically from the beginning. Growing organically was important to Alex and Louise, who did not want their kids around any farming chemicals when they were working in the vineyards. Both kids worked the vineyards growing up. "Our parents expected us to work and contribute," says Alana. The vineyard rows were marked out by Scott as a 10-year-old, who clearly had a good eye for details. "All these fields were all his eye, and they're not an inch out," recalls Louise.

The family grows Pinot Noir, Pinot Gris, Gamay Noir, Gewürztraminer, and Pinot Blanc on three different vineyard sites. From these, Alana selects the grapes that she wants to use for making wine before selling the rest to other wineries. With

ALANA LUBCHYNSKI

the growing demand for organic grapes in the Okanagan, the Lubchynskis were well ahead of the curve when they decided to farm organically. More than a few wineries have earned major awards for wines produced with grapes grown in Beaumont's vineyards. With all of the accolades, the temptation for many growers is to increase their own production, but the family has chosen to stay small, producing around 3,500 cases annually.

The wine-shop experience is always fun and casual. Most of the time, family members are the ones behind the bar, and they will welcome you like family. Musical instruments are everywhere, and Alex often serenades customers. Alex used to perform regularly in bands before moving to Kelowna and brings that performing spirit to the tasting room. Music has always been important to the family, which is why the front label on all of their wines is adorned with a beautiful treble clef.

MY PICKS

All wines are solid, but the Pinots all stand out here. The Pinot Noir is silky and complex, while the Pinot Gris is refreshing. The Pinot Noir Icewine is a rare treat.

OPENED 2006

2775 Boucherie Road
West Kelowna, BC
V1Z 2G4

T   250.769.1222

W   beaumontwinery.com

BELLA WINES

NARAMATA

An artisanal wine farmer from Dom Pérignon's time would be at home at Bella Wines, the only exclusive sparkling-wine producer in the Okanagan. The farmhouse and the postage-stamp organic vineyard, where pigs and chickens forage among the vines, seem transported from an 18th-century French countryside. So does winemaker Jay Drysdale's approach. Wines begin fermenting outside with wild yeast in neutral barrels. Most have the second ferment in bottle in the traditional Champagne method, with sugar and yeast added and then the mixture clarified after it becomes bubbly. But close to a quarter of Jay's wine is made in the older ancestral method, where still-fermenting wines are bottled to finish creating bubbles in those bottles. On release, ancestral sparkling wines might be a little cloudy and, well, funky—but always interesting and certainly authentic.

"My approach to this was to go back to basics, in that I really try and make wines that show a real honesty of where they come from," Jay says. The winery focuses on just Gamay Noir and Chardonnay, always vineyard designated. He transforms the varieties into at least a dozen sparkling wines in three different styles. "I like breaking the norm. I think BC has copied each other too long. I think it is time to shake things up a bit and try different things."

Born in Kamloops in 1972, Jay learned wine while paying his way through college by cooking in Vancouver restaurants. After taking a sommelier course, he began working in wine stores. He moved to the Okanagan in 2004 to run an Oliver restaurant and wine store. In 2010 Jay took a sales position with the Enotecca group of wineries. "That's when I fell in love with winemaking," he says. He began making wine for personal consumption while enrolling in Washington State University's winemaking program.

JAY DRYSDALE AND WENDY ROSE

Jay was already passionate about sparkling wine when he met Wendy Rose, now the other owner of Bella Wines. Her Californian father drank Champagne often. "When Jay first told me that he wanted his own brand of sparkling wine, I laughed," Wendy recalls. "I said, 'Dude, I have been drinking Alain Vesselle Champagne every day for the last 30 years.'"

Bella Wines launched as a virtual winery in 2012. It is now based on a somewhat remote farm north of Naramata. Jay and Wendy bought it in 2013, planted 1.2 hectares (3 acres) of Gamay Noir and Chardonnay vines in 2014, and opened a tasting room in 2015. "I was worried whether people would travel this far," Jay says. "But the people that find us really want to be here." Jay and Wendy preside in the boisterous tasting room—this is sparkling wine, after all—where visitors taste with vintage stemware from Jay's private collection.

MY PICKS

The reserve sparkling wines, which stack up well against grower Champagnes.

OPENED 2012

4320 Gulch Road
Naramata, BC V0H 1N1
T   778.996.1829
W   bellawines.ca

BENCH 1775

Bench 1775 offers an extensive selection of table wines and Icewines. "I am officially out of control," says Valeria Tait, the general manager and winemaker, with a laugh. "I make so many small lots to blend into the final wines. At times, something sticks out. I get excited and it ends up being a wine on its own." Such wines are first offered to Bench 1775's wine club, staying in the portfolio when they develop a following.

Valeria, who was born in 1964, is a renowned Okanagan viticulturist. She has an undergraduate degree in biochemistry and a master's in integrated pest management. She started working at the Summerland Research Station on plant viruses and then developed her independent consulting business with grape growers in the early 1990s as new vineyards were being planted. "I was lucky to get in on the industry when it was starting to grow," she says. She became Bench 1775's general manager in 2012 and remained after the winery was acquired in 2014 by Eric Liu, a China-born businessman. A wine lover, he once considered investing in France until he fell in love with the Okanagan's beauty, the rural lifestyle, and the quality wines. He also exports Okanagan wines to China.

The Bench 1775 property is a good example of the valley's beauty. The 7.5-hectare (18½-acre) vineyard's remarkable features include a lengthy private beach on Okanagan Lake. "There are very few wineries in the world that are on the water," Valeria says. "It's like we are working on a vacation site." The vineyard was planted initially to support a winery called Soaring Eagle, which was folded into Bench 1775 in 2011.

Under Eric's ownership, Bench 1775 also acquired two nearby vineyards on the Naramata Bench and, in 2019, began planting vines—mostly reds—in an 11.3-hectare (28-acre) former orchard

VALERIA TAIT

in the Similkameen Valley. The winery is largely self-sufficient in grapes, other than a long-standing grape-purchase agreement with the owners of Gold Hill Winery near Osoyoos. Valeria has been a consulting viticulturist there.

The other predecessor winery in the Bench 1775 history was Paradise Ranch Wines, formed in 1998 to make primarily Icewine. It was amalgamated with Soaring Eagle in 2011, emerging as Bench 1775. Icewine is about 20% of Bench 1775's production and significantly more of its revenues.

MY PICKS

Everything, especially the Sauvignon Blanc and the red wine blends.

OPENED 1998
(AS PARADISE
RANCH WINES)
1775 Naramata Road
Penticton, BC V2A 8T8
T 250.490.4965
W bench1775.com
icewines.com

BIRCH BLOCK VINEYARD
VIRTUAL WINERY

One of Murray Bancroft's treasured mementoes is a wineglass from a restaurant in Old Montreal. He was still an adolescent when his parents, during a business trip there, allowed him to taste the wine they were drinking. He was so impressed by the experience that he persuaded the restaurant to sell him the stemware.

"I think I have always had a bit of a passion for wine," says Murray, who was born in Vancouver in 1970. While backpacking in Greece after high school, he even developed a taste for Retsina. His university studies (in art history) included a year in Nice, where he acquired a love of rosé. His wine knowledge flourished when he began working in restaurants, notably the kitchens of some of Vancouver's top French restaurants, and continued in his career as a culinary consultant and a food stylist.

His wife, Sarah, who has a master's in political science and an extensive career in journalism, has come to share Murray's passion for food, wine, and France. In 2016, they bought 2 hectares (5 acres) of virgin land in Kaleden for an organic Pinot Noir vineyard. After planting, they spent a year in France, where Murray, who had begun studying winemaking and viticulture online from the University of California, worked harvests with a producer in Bordeaux and another in Champagne.

"Winemaking is similar to what I have learned in cooking," Murray has found. "There is definitely the technical side, and there is the other part that is creative. You need the technical side, but you also need passion."

The first Birch Block vintage, about 140 cases of 2018 Pinot Noir rosé, was made under the tutelage of winemaker Mark Simpson at BC Wine Studio, his custom crush facility. The Bancrofts, still busy with other careers, plan to continue that arrangement for several years. "I have a really good idea what style I like in wine,"

MURRAY AND SARAH BANCROFT

Murray says. "But I certainly need to employ people who have the technical experience [in] how to get there."

Birch Block, named for a grove of trees at the vineyard, currently has no wine shop, distributing its wines to select restaurants and over the Internet. "Things could change fairly quickly," Murray says. "We have an old barn that could be turned into a winery, and possibly we could do some tastings there. We are still planning out these next few years."

MY PICKS

Current range not tasted.

PROPOSED
OPENING 2022

236 Spruce Avenue
Kaleden, BC V0H 1K0
T   604.710.5057
W   birchblockvineyard.com
No tasting room

BLACK CLOUD

VIRTUAL WINERY

This winery results from the stubborn determination of winemaker Bradley Cooper and his wife and partner, Audralee Daum, to make great Pinot Noir on a shoestring. "It's becoming clear that the regulations for operating and licensing a winery favour those with substantial financial clout and basically keep people of modest means from playing any significant role," Brad complained in a 2011 blog posting. To be licensed independently, Black Cloud would need to spend thousands on a vineyard and small winery. With limited resources, Brad and Audralee have operated Black Cloud under the licence of various Naramata Bench wineries with which they have a relationship.

This is a common arrangement in the Okanagan for ambitious but impecunious winemakers. Black Cloud was born when one of Brad's clients, who later went bankrupt, compensated him with 80 cases of Pinot Noir that he had made in 2006. Audralee was unimpressed. "She said, 'Great, just as things get going, another black cloud comes over,'" Brad remembers. The winery's name was born, and they began hand-selling the wine. They make about 500 cases a year, all of it Pinot Noir.

Born in New Westminster in 1958, Brad is a journalism graduate from Langara College. After several years as a writer and photographer with community newspapers, he switched to restaurant jobs where he became wine savvy. In 1997 Brad started working in the wine shop at Hawthorne Mountain Vineyards, and then became a cellar technician and took Okanagan University College's first winery assistant course. He honed his skills by working the 1999 vintage at Vidal Estate in New Zealand and the 2000 Icewine harvest at Stonechurch in Ontario. In 2002, he left Hawthorne Mountain for the winemaking team at Mount Baker Vineyards in Washington State. He returned to the Okanagan to

BRAD COOPER

join Stag's Hollow Winery in 2003 and then Township 7 in 2005. He moved to Therapy Vineyards in 2018 while continuing the Black Cloud label.

Black Cloud sources Pinot Noir fruit from vineyards on the Naramata Bench and Okanagan Falls. Audralee, a children's counsellor who has worked in several Okanagan wine shops, helps market the wines. (The winery's website lists the wine shops that stock the wines.)

MY PICKS

The well-made Pinot Noirs are released in three tiers: Cumulus Nimbus, Altostratus, and entry-level Fleuvage. Red Sky Rosé is a recent addition to the portfolio.

OPENED 2009

T 250.490.7314
  250.488.2181
W blackcloud.ca
No tasting room

BLACK DOG CELLARS

OKANAGAN FALLS

Dave Rendina is a Winston Churchill buff, and that inspired the Black Dog name. Churchill suffered throughout his life from clinical depression, which he called his "black dog." Kate Durisek, Dave's daughter, explains: "For us, it is a bit of a metaphor for overcoming obstacles in life." Dave entertains other explanations as well for why the winery is called Black Dog. Skaha, the name of the nearby lake, is an Indigenous word meaning "dog."

If a black Churchillian mood ever bothers Dave, it is not obvious from his cheery demeanour in the wine shop. He is a retired engineer who, in his former career, was involved in the development of special materials for batteries and oil and gas catalysts. He also managed a portfolio of commercial and residential properties in Vancouver.

"I just love wine," he says. "I wanted to do something in my retirement that I enjoyed." In 2010, he and his partner, Beverlee Jones, bought this 4-hectare (10-acre) vineyard across the road from the Blasted Church winery. The vines—mainly Pinot Blanc and Pinot Noir—are more than 30 years old. There are smaller blocks of Cabernet Sauvignon and Merlot along with a recent planting of Pinot Gris. There also are apple trees that support the nearby Howling Moon cidery operated by Kate (and lavender being grown near the wine shop). Dave has made an Icewine-style apple wine. There are 88 apples in each small bottle, Dave notes.

Black Dog still sells most of its grapes to other wineries, keeping enough to allow Dave to make about 2,000 cases a year. "All of our wines are dry," he says.

DAVE RENDINA

MY PICKS

The Pinot Noir rosé and the refreshing frizzante rosé are examples of well-handled wines from the vineyard's Pinot Noir.

OPENED 2014

345 Parson Road

MAILING ADDRESS

385 Matheson Road
Okanagan Falls, BC
V0H 1R5

T 250.497.5991

W blackdogcellars.ca

BLACK HILLS ESTATE WINERY

OLIVER

Few Okanagan red wines are more iconic than Nota Bene, the Bordeaux blend made by Black Hills in every vintage since 1999. Even with production about 4,000 cases a year (and capped at that), most of this premium-priced wine is snapped up days after release.

The key to Nota Bene is the Cabernet Sauvignon that anchors the blend in most vintages. The winery has two Black Sage Road vineyards almost adjoining each other, totalling 15.8 hectares (39 acres) and both planted in 1996. Cabernet Sauvignon (four clones) makes up a third of the vines. The rest are Bordeaux red and white varieties, along with Syrah. In 2001, Black Hills was the first winery in Canada to plant Carménère, a rich and peppery red almost extinct in its native Bordeaux terroir but flourishing in Chile. About 1.7 hectares (4.1 acres) is growing here, including a block that was grafted onto Chardonnay vines to satisfy the demand for Carménère.

Black Hills was established by Senka and Bob Tennant (Senka created the Nota Bene blend) and Susan and Peter McCarrell, two business couples from Vancouver. When the McCarrells retired, Black Hills was acquired in 2007 by Vinequest Wine Partners, a group of investors. They expanded Black Hills by upgrading what was already a new winery, by buying the neighbouring vineyard and by opening the Wine Experience Centre, a million-dollar showcase for the wines in a vineyard setting. The "wine ambassadors" at Black Hills ensure a memorable experience.

In 2017 Andrew Peller Ltd., Canada's largest publicly traded wine company, acquired Black Hills and its portfolio of exceptional and interesting wines. Peller recruited New Zealand–born Ross Wise as the winemaker. He came to Canada to join Flat Rock Cellars in Ontario in 2009. He left there in 2012 and, for the

ROSS WISE

next four years, consulted with a number of Ontario wineries. He came to the Okanagan in 2016 to join Phantom Creek for three vintages before moving to Black Hills early in 2019. Ross, with his winemaking degree from Charles Sturt University in Australia, is expected to complete his Master of Wine studies in 2020.

Black Hills' second label, introduced in 2011, is called Cellar Hand. Second labels are traditional among Bordeaux's châteaux. The wines are by no means second-rate. Cellarhand is a home for the wines that remain after the major blends have been assembled.

MY PICKS

Everything. When Nota Bene is sold out, look for Addendum, a juicy red blend that is aged 12 months in barrel versus 16 months for Nota Bene. To get the exceptional Carménère, you need to join the Black Hills wine club.

OPENED 2001

4190 Black Sage Road

MAILING ADDRESS

4318 Black Sage Road

Oliver, BC V0H 1T1

250.498.6606 (tasting room)

T 250.498.0666

W blackhillswinery.com

Restaurant: Vineyard Kitchen, open 11–5

BLACK MARKET WINE COMPANY

KALEDEN

Rob Hammersley and Michelle Shewchuk, the owners of this winery, called this Kaleden property Conviction Ridge Vineyard when they bought it in 2018. "We finally have the conviction to do this," Rob says. They made Black Market's first vintages, beginning with 2012, at a custom crush winery while establishing their brand. Rob believes that "the best way to manage the risk of moving into a fairly crowded market is to get the market space first and work backwards."

Both were born in Winnipeg (Rob in 1971, Michelle in 1974), and they met at university where an informal tasting group fired an interest in wine. After university, they worked three years in Japan as English teachers and fostered a love of travel. Michelle went on to a career as an Air Canada flight attendant, while Rob became a corporate finance and strategy professional in the power and utilities industry in Alberta.

When they decided to start a winery, Rob enrolled in the highly regarded enology and viticulture courses offered by the University of Washington while also commuting regularly to the Okanagan to make wine. Ultimately, their search for vineyard property led them to Conviction Ridge, a 1.8-hectare (4½-acre) Kaleden vineyard growing Bacchus, Merlot, Pinot Gris, and Pinot Blanc.

The portfolio, which includes both red and white Bordeaux blends, is fleshed out with purchases of Sémillon, Sauvignon Blanc, Cabernet Sauvignon, Cabernet Franc, and Petit Verdot. "As far as reds go, Syrah is where my passion lies," Rob says. During his enology course, he did a research paper comparing growing conditions of Côte-Rôtie in the Rhône with the Okanagan. He concluded that Okanagan Syrah is distinctive because there is a wide temperature range between the hot days and the cool nights.

ROB HAMMERSLEY AND MICHELLE SHEWCHUK

Black Market has grown steadily from its first 200-case production in 2012. Production, which reached 1,600 cases in 2018, should rise substantially after the winery opens its own wine shop. "Our goal is that this facility would produce in the 5,000-to-6,000-case range," Rob says.

MY PICKS

Everything. The wines are complex and elegant.

SALES BEGAN 2015

198 Spruce Avenue
Kaleden, BC V0H 1K0
T 778.515.3311
W blackmarketwine.ca

BLACK SWIFT VINEYARDS

WEST KELOWNA

Until this winery opened, Black Swift Vineyards, along with Screaming Frenzy, the second label, were nurtured nearby at The Hatch winery. All are operated by Terrabella Wineries, a company established in 2010 to acquire or develop wineries in the Okanagan. In 2012 Terrabella acquired a vineyard on Boucherie Road just north of Quails' Gate. The Hatch was based here and became an incubator for several labels. The first Black Swift wines were released in 2015. Meanwhile, Terrabella bought a property farther along on Boucherie, planted 2.8 hectares (7 acres), and moved Black Swift there.

Jason Parkes, the winemaker for Black Swift, produces the ultra-premium wines in the Terrabella group. "The Black Swift wines are the showstoppers, the single-varietal wines," says Graham Dell, one of Terrabella's executives. All but one of the Black Swift wines are single-vineyard wines. The winery currently has contracts for fruit from 11 different vineyards between East Kelowna and Osoyoos and one in the Similkameen Valley. These are growers with whom Jason has worked during the past two decades that he has been making wine in the Okanagan.

"From North to South and East to West, we enjoy a multifaceted variety of soil types, topography, environments, and people," the winery says on its website. "We hope to celebrate these differences by farming numerous varietals in the localities that we feel suit them the most."

The leading varieties at Black Swift include Chardonnay—there are three in the portfolio—Cabernet Franc, and Syrah. The one Black Swift blend combines Cabernet Franc and Syrah. The red wines, except for Pinot Noir, are aged up to four years in barrel, with further bottle aging before release. The wines in the Screaming Frenzy portfolio are still premium but are more

WINEMAKER JASON PARKES

modestly priced. "Screaming Frenzy is driven more by value and approachability," Graham says.

The Black Swift name is inspired by a bird native to the Okanagan. "It is famous for its high-arching flight, slow and precise wing beat, and unique reliance on a single egg for each year's procreation," the winery says.

MY PICKS

Everything. The Chardonnays are bold, the Syrah and the Cabernet Franc even more so.

PROPOSED OPENING 2021

2345 Boucherie Road
West Kelowna, BC V1Z 2E7

T   250.317.1665

W   blackswiftvineyards.com

BLACK WIDOW WINERY

PENTICTON

It was a matter of celebration in 2011 when Shannon Lancaster joined Black Widow Winery, both in the vineyard and as a winemaker. She was later joined by brother James, giving a solid family foundation to the business that parents Dick and Shona had launched five years earlier.

It began in the summer of 2000 when the Lancasters, while looking for just a getaway cottage, bought this 2.8-hectare (7-acre) property, part of which had grapevines. "Classic upselling," Dick says of the realtor. "And as soon as we got a vineyard, the goal was to set up a winery." It was an easy step because Dick was already an award-winning home winemaker.

Dick was born in Toronto in 1953 but grew up in Montreal and acquired an interest in wine from his father, Graham, an Air Canada food services manager. Dick began making wine from wild grapes while still in high school. A three-month tour of European wine regions in 1976 sealed that interest. In Vancouver, where he and Shona lived from 1970 until moving to the Okanagan a few years ago, Dick was a home winemaker for more than 25 years.

You could call Dick a polymath, given all the skills he has acquired. Starting in biology, he earned a master's degree. Disillusioned by the lack of well-paying jobs, he took a real-estate course, and then sold cars and became district manager for a leasing company. Then he got a master's degree in business administration and finally qualified as an accountant. From 1992 until 2008, he was a vice-president with Imasco, western Canada's largest stucco manufacturer. Naturally, Black Widow's gravity-flow winery, which he designed, is finished in tawny-hued stucco. "How can I not use stucco?" he says, laughing.

The vineyard already had Gewürztraminer, Pinot Gris, and Schönburger when the Lancasters bought it. In 2001, they added

SHANNON, DICK, AND JAMES LANCASTER

Merlot and a bit of Cabernet Sauvignon, selling grapes until launching Black Widow in 2006. "We like wines that have some real flavour and character to them, and that comes from really ripe grapes," Dick says.

MY PICKS

Everything. The winery's signature red is Hourglass, a bold Merlot/Cabernet blend. The Gewürztraminer and the Pinot Gris, both finishing dry, are packed with flavour. Oasis is a lovely aromatic blend of Schönburger, Gewürztraminer, and Muscat. The winery's delicious dessert wines include a delightful dessert Schönburger, a fortified Schönburger called Mirage, and a port-style Merlot called Vintage One.

OPENED 2006

1630 Naramata Road
Penticton, BC V2A 8T7
T   250.487.2347
250.276.5396 (office)
W   blackwidowwinery.com
Picnic patio
Food service: Cheese, crackers, and other snacks
Accommodation: Beauvines Vacation Rental, cottage for two to four people

BLASTED CHURCH VINEYARDS

OKANAGAN FALLS

Blasted Church Vineyards succeeds both with the labels on its bottles and with what award-winning wines are in them. In 2002, when Chris and Evelyn Campbell—he was an investment dealer and she an accountant—bought what was then called Prpich Hills Winery, they hired the Vancouver marketing consultant Bernie Hadley-Beauregard to rebrand the winery. He hit a home run with the Blasted Church name and the labels. Since then, the labels have been redesigned twice. The first two generations were colourful caricatures, some of which were exhibited at the San Francisco Museum of Modern Art. The current labels draw their inspiration from the religious art of the Renaissance.

The Blasted Church name comes from how the movers took apart a church in 1929 when relocating it to Okanagan Falls from the abandoned mining town of Fairview. They loosened the nails in the heavy timbers with a small dynamite charge. The church still serves a congregation in Okanagan Falls. That story provided a narrative for many of the labels. The labels, in turn, have kept alive the conversations about the wines. The entire portfolio is an irreverent take on worship, from the label depictions of angels to premium wines called Cross to Bear, Holy Moly, Nothing Sacred, and OMG, the elegant sparkling wine. Blasted Church now produces more than 25,000 cases a year from its 17-hectare (42-acre) vineyard (and with purchased grapes).

For proof that labels are effective, just ask Evan Saunders, the winemaker at Blasted Church. "The first wine I started drinking consistently at University of Victoria was Hatfield's Fuse," Evan says, referring to a popular Blasted Church white blend. "I walked into a wine store. The colours [on the label] were bright, and it caught my eye. It is a funny coincidence that I ended up here." Born in Manitoba in 1984, Evan took a microbiology degree,

EVAN SAUNDERS

originally to prepare for medicine until an interest in wine took over. In 2011, he went to Brock University for a diploma in grape and wine technology. He returned immediately to the Okanagan and spent three years at Osoyoos Larose before moving to Blasted Church in 2014.

As the winery's vineyards have matured, Blasted Church has continually "premiumized" its wines. In 2016, Pascal Madevon, the former Osoyoos Larose winemaker, was engaged as a consultant to help make an iconic red blend. Predictably, the winery calls it Nectar of the Gods. "We want to really push and take the risks to make a wine like that, and do it in a larger volume," Evan said just before the wine was released. "There will be about 1,100 cases."

MY PICKS

Everything—and it is a remarkably long portfolio. A particular favourite is Nothing Sacred, a red Meritage that ages beautifully.

OPENED 2000
(AS PRPICH HILLS)

378 Parsons Road
Okanagan Falls, BC
V0H 1R5

T   250.497.1125
1.877.355.2686
(1.8.SPELLBOUND)
(toll-free)

W   blastedchurch.com

BLIND TIGER VINEYARDS

LAKE COUNTRY

This winery takes its name from one of the terms (*blind pig* is another) for illegal bars operated in the United States during, and even before, Prohibition. The operators tried to get around the law by charging customers to see performing pigs, tigers, or other animals while serving "free" drinks. It is a flight of fancy to apply the name to a perfectly legal winery in Lake Country. Jerry Wowchuk, who operates this winery with his wife, Charlene, and their daughter, Morgan, just wants to attach an aura of history to the winery. "Canada is very young," he explains. "It's hard to celebrate any history when there is none."

Running a winery is a long way from his roots in Winnipeg, where Jerry was born in 1966 and where he and Charlene met in high school. He started his career in the trucking industry, and moved on to manufacturing jobs, to plumbing, and then to the repair of restaurant equipment. That evolved into Kwik Auctions, a business in Burnaby specialized in auctioning restaurant equipment.

In 2007, the Wowchuks moved to the bucolic Lake Country property that had once been a goat and llama farm. "We fell in love with vineyards," Jerry says. Since 2010, they have planted 3.2 hectares (8 acres). The two largest blocks in the organic vineyard are Gewürztraminer and Riesling, with smaller blocks of Pinot Noir and Chardonnay. The winery, which opened in 2015, has extended its portfolio with fruit purchased from Osoyoos growers.

The closest Jerry has come to operating a blind tiger is presiding in his winery's charming tasting room. "I love working in the tasting room," he says. "I get people coming in from the Prairies. I like to talk. I am an auctioneer, so that is all I do, is talk. There is always a connection." The background music is drawn

CHARLENE AND JERRY WOWCHUK

from his vinyl collection because he believes that vinyl sounds better than digital music. The wines are served in generously sized Riedel stemware. "Even bad wine tastes good in that glass," he says. "I will never have cheap little glasses."

MY PICKS

Gewürztraminer, Riesling, and Pinot Gris wines all reflect the excellent Lake Country terroir. Hush Up Blush is a tasty Pinot Noir rosé. The aptly named Speakeasy Red is a good red blend anchored with Merlot.

OPENED 2015

11014 Bond Road
Lake Country, BC V4V 1J6

T   250.766.0622

W   blindtigervineyards.ca
Food service: Marno's
Woodfire Pizza

BLUE MOUNTAIN VINEYARD AND CELLARS

OKANAGAN FALLS

The term *estate winery* is used rather casually in the Okanagan. Strictly speaking, it should apply only to wineries self-sufficient from their own vineyards. Blue Mountain is a true estate winery. Ian and Jane Mavety have been growing grapes on this picturesque Okanagan Falls property since buying the land in 1971. Their intimate understanding of terroir and viticulture enable them to produce top-quality wines consistently. Blue Mountain marched to its own drummer by making dry French-style wines—the kind the Mavety family liked to drink—when most other Okanagan wineries were making off-dry German-style whites.

The winery's French tradition began when Ian and Jane travelled through France in the 1980s, doing the research supporting their decision to plant Burgundy and Alsace varieties. The late Raphael Brisebois, the consulting winemaker who helped make Blue Mountain's initial vintages, had grown up in Alsace and worked for Piper-Heidsieck in Reims. Champagne became the template for Blue Mountain's sparkling wines and remained so when Ian and Jane's son, Matt, took over the cellar in 1997 after graduating from Lincoln University in New Zealand. Matt's palate and style are influenced, however, by what he has learned during his own trips to France. Since 2001, in a quest for ever-more complex wines, he has fermented an increasing percentage of the wines with wild yeasts.

The flagship variety is Pinot Noir. At least five clones grow here, with multiple plantings of each on the various soils and aspects of the 32-hectare (79-acre) vineyard. This ensures that Matt has a palette of flavours with which to blend wines that are rich and complex.

Blue Mountain's annual production, about 16,000 cases, is focused and includes a reserve tier. About a quarter comprises

MATT AND CHRISTIE MAVETY

Champagne-method sparkling wines. The portfolio is completed with two reds (Pinot Noir and Gamay Noir) and four whites (Chardonnay, Pinot Gris, Pinot Blanc, and, since 2010, Sauvignon Blanc).

Prior to 2010, the Blue Mountain tasting room was open primarily by appointment. The family, after all, had its hands full looking after 150,000 vines and handling all the regulatory and customer paperwork that goes with a winery. However, a summer-long tasting season was established after Matt's sister, Christie, brought her marketing charm to this family-operated estate winery.

MY PICKS

Everything, including the elegant Pinot Noir and the remarkable sparkling wines.

OPENED 1992

2385 Allendale Road
Okanagan Falls, BC
V0H 1R2

T 250.497.8244

W bluemountainwinery.com

BLUE SKY ESTATE WINERY

OSOYOOS

Some wineries have hired big-city consultants to create a name. Harpreet Toor is not one to complicate such decisions, let alone farm them out. He and Navpreet, his wife, were discussing potential names while seated outside their home, surrounded by vineyards. It was one of those bright, clear South Okanagan days. The brilliant sky inspired the name. "As a small farmer, we don't have much money to spend on consultants," he explains.

Born in India in 1969, he spent nine months in a local police force before he and his parents immigrated to the Okanagan in 1998. Typically hard-working immigrants, they accumulated the down payment by 2002 to buy an orchard just outside Osoyoos. Harpreet soon discovered that "our fruit industry can't compete with the US." In 2004, he replaced the trees with 4.2 hectares (10½ acres) of vines that flourish on an ideal southeastern slope dropping toward Osoyoos Lake. He planted just four varieties: Cabernet Sauvignon, Cabernet Franc, Syrah, and Viognier.

While waiting for his vineyard to produce grapes, Harpreet earned a living by operating several service stations. "That's why we are surviving," he says. The lot of an independent grape grower can be tough. Harpreet had wineries offering the going average price for his varieties but, when harvest approached, finding a pretext to cut the price or even refuse the grapes. "What are we going to do?" he says. "We can't take these grapes and sell them on the fresh market."

In 2011, he took his fate in his own hands and got a winery licence. "The middlemen selling wine are making better money than farmers," he says of his decision. But as a businessman, he recognized that he had entered a long-term business. "Opening a winery is a many-year investment," Harpreet wrote on the winery's website. "You must have wine ready to sell before you

HARPREET TOOR

open your doors. Depending on the wine, it may take up to two years before you can sell that bottle to the consumer. That is why our first vintage was 2011 but we just opened in 2016."

This is a family-operated winery: the Toors have three growing children to help.

Blue Sky employs consulting winemakers to help Navpreet make the wines. "We let the grapes shape the wine and tell their own story," she writes. "We do not force the grapes to become the wine we want."

MY PICKS

The Viognier is full flavoured. Among the reds, Syrah, Cabernet Sauvignon, and Cabernet Franc stand out.

OPENED 2016

11621 87th Street
Osoyoos, BC V0H 1V2
T 250.495.1777
W blueskywinery.ca

BONAMICI CELLARS

OKANAGAN FALLS

Until planting its own vineyard on Rolling Hills Road, Bonamici Cellars operated as a "virtual" winery, making its wines at an existing licensed winery (as all virtual wineries must do). That did not deter Bonamici from making award-winning wines. It was, in fact, the only virtual winery to win a Lieutenant Governor's Award for Excellence.

The winery's name—Italian for "good friends"—was inspired by the long friendship of the owners, Philip Soo (the winemaker) and Mario Rodi. Mario, who was born in 1957 in Northern Ontario, was just 12 when he started helping his immigrant Italian father crush grapes for the family's wine. Philip was born in Vancouver in 1969, the son of immigrants from Hong Kong who were just discovering what little wine culture there was in Canada at the time. "We had family celebrations, but they never encouraged kids to drink," Philip remembers. "I was 12 or 13 when my first sip of alcohol, Baby Duck, was at a Christmas party."

It seems that was enough to get Philip interested. After getting degrees in microbiology and food engineering, he was offered jobs at a pharmaceutical firm and a company that produced gourmet salads, but having been a good amateur beer maker in college, he took a job with a manufacturer of beer kits "because it was in line with my hobby." Subsequently, Andrew Peller Ltd. bought this company along with a wine-kit company. Philip was then promoted to Peller's winery in Port Moody in 2000. When the winery closed five years later, he became one of the Okanagan's leading consulting winemakers after turning down an opportunity to work for Gallo in California.

Mario spent about 20 years in food and soft drink sales before joining Peller in 1995 as the general manager of Wine Experts, as the kit company was called. He and Philip, who reported to him,

PHILIP SOO

became close friends. Mario left Peller in 2009. Deciding to stay in the wine business, he proposed Bonamici to Philip. "He is a great winemaker," Mario says. "I focused on sales and marketing for my entire career. I thought this might be an opportunity for us to get together and build something great."

Bonamici's first vintage with grapes from contract growers was 2012. However, the partners went to work immediately on developing their own winery. In 2016, they bought a 4.2-hectare (10½-acre) property on Rolling Hills Road. "We have a wonderful southern-sloping aspect," Philip says. "It gets full sun from morning to night." They planted 0.4 hectare (an acre) each of Sauvignon Blanc and Pinot Gris in 2017. The following year, they planted another 0.8 hectare (2 more acres) with Chardonnay and Pinot Noir, as well as Sangiovese, which is destined to turn their Belviaggio wine into a Super Tuscan blend.

MY PICKS

Everything, including an Italian-styled Pinot Grigio, a Sauvignon Blanc/ Viognier blend, and especially Belviaggio, the flagship red blend currently based on Cabernet Franc, Syrah, and either Merlot or Malbec.

SALES BEGAN 2012

2385 Rolling Hills Road
Okanagan Falls, BC
V0H 1R2

T 250.486.8086
604.868.2356

W bonamicicellars.com

BORDERTOWN VINEYARDS & ESTATE WINERY

OSOYOOS

Mohan Gill summarizes his biography concisely. Born in India in 1976, he came to the Okanagan in 1993 with his immigrant parents. "I went to Oliver Secondary School," he recounts. "Then I started working."

Mohan has never stopped working. He bought his first orchard (with an older brother) in 1996. Today, he and his brother operate 45 hectares (110 acres) of vineyards and orchards in the Okanagan. They have their own fruit-packing house and, since 2018, a cidery attached to the winery.

Mohan dipped his toe into viticulture by planting less than a hectare (2 acres) of grapes in 2005. A quick study, he began increasing his vineyard area in 2007 and was soon selling grapes to both large and small wineries. One of his clients was Mark Simpson, who operates BC Wine Studio, a custom crush winery near Okanagan Falls. On Mark's urging, Mohan opened Bordertown in 2015, locating it strategically on the highway just north of Osoyoos. The expansive wine shop signalled Mohan's ambition that Bordertown become a substantial winery quickly. The winery produced 3,000 cases in 2013, its first vintage. That rose to 13,500 cases in 2017, and Mohan's goal is to reach 40,000 cases.

Bordertown established its credentials quickly, winning in 2016 a Lieutenant Governor's Award for Excellence in BC Wine for the debut vintage of its signature red blend, the 2013 Living Desert Red. The winery has developed an extensive portfolio because Mohan is growing at least 15 varieties, including even Grüner Veltliner, the Austrian white. With Mohan focused entirely on growing the best grapes he can, Bordertown has retained winemaking consultants Jason Parkes and Daniel Bontorin. Mark Simpson, a former beer maker, makes the cider.

MOHAN GILL

OPENED 2015

9140 92nd Avenue
Osoyoos, BC V0H 1V2

T   250.495.3332

W   bordertownwinery.com

MY PICKS

The reds—Merlot, Cabernet Franc, Cabernet Sauvignon, and Syrah—are particularly strong. Living Desert Red, now a blend of Cabernet Franc, Cabernet Sauvignon, and Merlot, is built to age. Among the whites, Grüner Veltliner and Muscat are excellent.

BOTTEGA WINE STUDIO (SEVEN DIRECTIONS)

VIRTUAL WINERY

Daniel Bontorin initially set out to carve a niche for himself by making only rosé for Seven Directions, a label owned by his partner, Kristine Witkowski. "We started out as a virtual winery with no brick-and-mortar building," he says. "We considered doing other reds and whites under the Seven Directions brand. But we were known for being the only rosé specialist in Canada, and we wanted to keep it that way. From day one we talked about making single-vineyard rosés exclusively. Rosé has always been one of my favourite wines to make."

Daniel's rosé-making pedigree goes back to the 2005 vintage when he made Vaïla, the outstanding rosé at Le Vieux Pin, a foundation for the current popularity of such wines.

Born in Surrey in 1976, Daniel pursued various careers, including importing motorcycle parts, until 2000, when he decided the real future was in wine. Since training at Okanagan University College, he has worked in several Okanagan wineries including Le Vieux and has done a vintage in northern Italy. Subsequently, he became a consulting winemaker for clients including Volcanic Hills Estate Winery and Bordertown Vineyards.

After Seven Directions was established, Daniel and Kristine folded it under Bottega Wine Studio. "Bottega isn't just a label," Daniel says. "I am looking to make higher-end wines from both red and white varieties." Bottega's initial releases included Viognier and Merlot. Because Bottega also was a virtual winery, Daniel and Kristine arranged to make the 2018 and subsequent vintages at Saxon Estate Winery in Summerland.

In another step to a winery of their own, the couple began planting a 1.4-hectare (3½-acre) vineyard in 2020 near Cawston. The varieties are Pinot Noir, Cabernet Franc, and Grenache, initially to support the winery's rosé portfolio. "With red grapes, I

DANIEL BONTORIN

have the flexibility in exceptional years to produce red wines and, with Pinot Noir, sparkling wine," Daniel says.

MY PICKS

The rosé wines are among BC's best, while the Bottega Merlot and Viognier display Daniel's bent for making bold wines.

SALES BEGAN 2013

665 Beecroft Avenue
Cawston, BC V0X 1C2

T   250.689.1439

W   bottegawinestudio.ca

No tasting room at the time of printing

BURNT TIMBER ESTATE WINERY

KELOWNA

Paul Bernard Lee, an inventor, holds at least 32 patents for oil-field tools and related products. As a consequence of that success, he has been able to create this winery on a spectacular property on the eastern shore of Okanagan Lake. From the tasting room, there is a view across the lake to Quails' Gate.

Bordering the 11.7-hectare (29-acre) property are charred trees, remnants of a 2003 forest fire that devastated vineyards, wineries, and the suburbs of Kelowna while leaving this property untouched. The winery recalls the fire in its name, as well as with one of its flagship reds, a Bordeaux blend called Bomberos, Spanish for "firefighters."

Paul was born in Calgary in 1960 and began working in the oil fields after high school. His father had a company selling drilling tools, some developed by a partner. That inspired Paul to unleash his own inventive abilities. "When I was 24 years old, I designed my first oil-field tool," he says. "I commercialized it in 1985." He formed his own company and did business internationally until selling the company in 2010.

Once a rum-and-Coke drinker, Paul developed his taste for wine while visiting Okanagan wineries. Eventually, he moved to Kelowna and, after selling his company, bought the Swick Road property. First, he built a nine-hole golf course and then, in 2016, he planted 1.6 hectares (4 acres) of Riesling, a variety suited to this comparatively cool site.

By then, he had already engaged consulting winemaker Jason Parkes to produce a series of bold red wines with South Okanagan grapes, starting with the 2012 vintage. Paul has installed the winery in what Jason calls a "dream cellar," with a capacity to do 10,000 cases a year. The winery opened with a 1,000-case inventory, but

PAUL BERNARD LEE

as the list of patents suggests, Paul is a man who thinks big. He also wants to do philanthropy with the winery, combining charity golf tournaments with wine tastings.

MY PICKS

The winery opened with its flagship red, Bomberos, and varietals of Syrah, Cabernet Sauvignon, Cabernet Franc, and Merlot. All are delicious and cellar-worthy.

OPENED 2018

180 Swick Road
Kelowna, BC V1W 4J5
T   250.609.1814
W   burnttimberwinery.com

BURROWING OWL ESTATE WINERY

OLIVER

In 1993, then a successful property developer, Jim Wyse was completing a 40-unit condominium project in Vernon when he spotted a "winery for sale" advertisement in a local newspaper. That winery turned out to be decrepit, but Jim's interest had been fired. He engaged a realtor and was introduced to the property on Black Sage Road where, several years later, the Burrowing Owl vineyards and winery were established in 1998. With Jim now in his 80s (but still playing hockey), the winery is now run by son Chris and daughter Kerri. The winery has 89 hectares (220 acres) of vineyard in the South Okanagan and the Similkameen.

Bill Dyer, a renowned Napa Valley winemaker, made Burrowing Owl's first eight vintages, beginning with 1997. His style—bold and generous wines—gave Burrowing Owl a cult following. Several winemakers later, that style still influences the Burrowing Owl portfolio, entirely made up of premium wines. The winery launched with four varietals: Pinot Gris, Chardonnay, Merlot, and Cabernet Franc. Other Bordeaux reds have since been planted, along with Pinot Noir, Syrah, and Viognier. One of the most popular wines is Athene, a co-fermented field blend of Syrah and Cabernet Sauvignon.

For budget-minded consumers, Burrowing Owl has a second label, Calliope, the name of an Okanagan hummingbird. After the original Calliope winery closed, Jim bought the brand, in part because of his intense love of birds. In 1993, when he named his vineyard after a cuddly burrow-dwelling owl then extinct in the Okanagan, Jim began to support the Burrowing Owl Conservation Society's breeding program to re-establish the owl population. More than $1 million of Burrowing Owl's tasting-room fees have gone to the successful breeding program.

The environmental ethic goes beyond saving owls. Visitors to the Tuscan-style winery are struck by the hundreds of

JIM WYSE

solar panels—even on a parking-lot structure. The winery and associated buildings, including a massive Oliver warehouse, rely almost entirely on solar power since the winery began installing solar panels in 2006. The eight electric-vehicle charging stations near the wine shop are available to visitors free of charge.

MY PICKS

Everything, including even a delicious fortified port-style wine called Coruja (Portuguese for "owl").

OPENED 1998

500 Burrowing Owl Place
Oliver, BC V0H 1T1

T 250.498.0620
1.877.498.0620
(toll-free)

W burrowingowlwine.ca
Restaurant: The Sonora
Room, closed during
winter
Accommodation: Guest
house with 10 luxurious
rooms and one large suite

CALONA VINEYARDS/
CONVICTION WINES

KELOWNA

The oldest name in British Columbia wine, Calona, is being replaced by Conviction Wines. The transition began in 2015 when Andrew Peller Ltd., which bought Calona in 2005, decided it was time to refresh both the winery name and its Artist label series. Conviction pays homage to the past with labels recounting major figures in the winery's history, as in The Industrialist Sovereign Opal.

Calona was launched in 1931 by Giuseppe Ghezzi, an Italian winemaker, backed by a group of Kelowna investors led by grocer Pasquale "Cap" Capozzi—who might be among the industrialists of the day. Another Conviction wine is The Priest Pinot Noir. It memorializes Monsignor W. B. McKenzie, the Kelowna priest who saved the struggling winery in the 1930s by having it make altar wine for the Catholic church.

It is fitting that this historic winery should be the exclusive producer of Sovereign Opal, the only wine grape developed at the Summerland Research Station that made it into commercial production. A single grower, John Casorso, has 3.6 hectares (9 acres) of it in his Kelowna-area vineyard. The variety, a perfumed and spicy cross of Golden Muscat and Maréchal Foch, developed a dedicated following since the first vintage in 1987.

More than labels have been refreshed since Peller took over the Calona winery, whose buildings have sprawled in downtown Kelowna since the 1940s. The former cramped wine shop has been replaced by a grand Sandhill tasting room with the ambience of a church (echoes of Monsignor McKenzie!). The shelves stock Conviction, Peller, Wayne Gretzky, and Sandhill, among Peller's major British Columbia wines. Since 2018, Peller has been engaged in a total renovation of the winery's processing facilities, providing cutting-edge winemaking tools for a crew led by Sandhill's Sandy Leier and Conviction's Sydney Valentino.

Sovereign Opal stands out as a unique white. Conviction wines, much like those in the Peller and Wayne Gretzky portfolios, deliver quality at attractive prices.

OPENED 1932

1125 Richter Street
Kelowna, BC V1Y 2K6

T   250.979.4211
    1.888.246.4472
    (toll-free)

W   convictionwines.ca
    andrewpeller.com/
    cascadia.php

CAMELOT VINEYARDS ESTATE WINERY

KELOWNA

Robert Young and Denise Brass opened this winery in 2009 with a mentorship that was the envy of their peers: the legendary Kelowna winemaker Ann Sperling made the initial vintages. Ann was consulting for Clos du Soleil winery and also launching her family's Sperling Vineyards. At the time, neither had their own processing facilities, while Camelot had space in its new building. Ann made the wines for all three while teaching Robert and Camelot's wine director, Julian Samoisette.

Robert's father, R.J., who died in 1996, once named a family home Camelot; Robert and Denise honoured his memory by calling the winery Camelot and then added touches from King Arthur's court. A sword embedded in a stone greets visitors. Inside the wine shop, there is a round table and replica suit of armour that Denise bought at auction for $650. "We had seen a genuine one from England," she says, a bit wistfully. "They were going for about £5,000 [about $8,500 Canadian]."

R.J. Young was ahead of his time when he planted a hectare (2½ acres) of Maréchal Foch vines on this property in 1974. Unable to get a winery contract, he soon pulled them out and planted apples. When Robert and Denise took over the farm, they continued to grow apples until 2006, when the price fell below the packing-house handling charges. Vines replaced the orchard in the next year: 1.6 hectares (4 acres) of Pinot Gris, Riesling, Gewürztraminer, and Pinot Noir. The original plan was just to sell the grapes, but, perhaps reflecting on R.J.'s experience, the couple chose to develop their own winery.

The venture is something of a retirement project, even if both are about 10 years from retiring. Robert, who was born in Quesnel, BC, in 1961; and Denise, who was born in Britain, are Air Canada flight attendants. They usually work together on the same

WINEMAKER
JULIAN SAMOISETTE

ROBERT YOUNG

international flights, on schedules that allow time to deal with the vineyard between flights. In 2018, nearing retirement, they brought in a partner to Camelot.

The winery has been producing about 1,200 cases a year from its fully planted vineyard and from purchased fruit.

MY PICKS

The wines are reliable across the range. My favourites are the Pinot Gris, the rosé, the Pinot Noir, and the Meritage.

OPENED 2009

3489 East Kelowna Road
Kelowna, BC V1W 4H1
T 250.862.8873
W camelotvineyards.ca

CASSINI CELLARS

OLIVER

This roadside winery's Tuscany-styled architecture has genuine roots. While Adrian Cassini, the owner, was born in Romania, his grandfather was Italian. Adrian's surname, in fact, was Capeneata. He changed it to Cassini after opening this winery.

His family in Romania had farmed grapes, but Adrian credits his interest in wine to restaurant jobs he had both in Romania and in Canada (he came here at the age of 30). "I had a chance to discover the food that goes with the wine," he recalls. "I discovered the taste and the romance of wine." When he moved to Vancouver, it was to sell and then manufacture and service equipment for fitness clubs. "I have that entrepreneur thing," he says. That led to making props for movie sets, and then building houses. After an Okanagan vacation about 2000, he wanted his own vineyard.

"I see myself in the vineyard," he says, waxing romantic during one interview. "I like the whole package. I like the Okanagan. I like the vineyards. I see myself walking the dog in that vineyard in a few years." Late in 2006, he purchased a lavender farm beside Highway 97, south of Oliver, now the site for his winery. After selling the lavender plants (another example of his entrepreneurism), he planted 2.2 hectares (5½ acres) of vines (Merlot, Cabernet Franc, and Pinot Gris) in the spring of 2007. He secured the consultant Philip Soo to mentor Adrian's evolution as a winemaker favouring bold, generous wines.

Adrian applied his *con brio* style to the winery's design, notably the grand wine shop. Visitors discover a 10-metre bar long enough to accommodate 25 or so tasters. "I can put in another bar on wheels, depending on the need, so that people are not frustrated from waiting," he says. Large windows on each side of the tasting room afford views of the barrel room and part of the winery's production area so that visitors can, as Adrian puts it, "see the magic."

ADRIAN CASSINI

MY PICKS

The Godfather is the winery's superb icon red, anchoring a family of powerful reds including Maximus, Nobilus (a Merlot), a Malbec, and a Syrah. The Pinot Noir is elegant. The equally satisfying range of whites includes two Chardonnays, a Viognier, a Sauvignon Blanc, and a delightful Pinot Gris called Mamma Mia.

OPENED 2009

4828 Highway 97
Oliver, BC

MAILING ADDRESS

PO Box 740
Osoyoos, BC V0H 1V0

T   250.485.4370
W   cassini.ca

CASTORO DE ORO ESTATE WINERY

OLIVER

In 2005, Calgarians Bruno Kelle and Stella Schmidt, on a wine-tasting vacation in the Okanagan, were asked at one tasting what they might be interested in. "Your entire winery," Bruno joked. That winery was not for sale, but nearby House of Rose Winery was. After an afternoon with Vern Rose, the winery's charismatic founder, the ambition to own a winery had a firm hold on Bruno and Stella. In 2006 they purchased Gersighel Wineberg, a small producer on a sweeping curve of Highway 97 south of Oliver. The only disadvantage of this highly visible location is that, on occasion, errant drivers fail to negotiate the curve. In the summer of 2017, a speeding truck shot off the road and took out 10 rows of vines before it stopped rolling.

On taking over the winery, Bruno and Stella changed the name to Golden Beaver, inspired by the success of Australian wines with animal labels. When some restaurateurs chafed at Golden Beaver, they dipped into the Latin languages to come up with Castoro de Oro and replaced the golden-garbed beaver on the label with a more dignified beaver in a top hat. "It sounds Old World with a New World look," Bruno explains. "We thought it would be a way to keep our story."

Bruno, a technical college graduate, grew up on a tobacco farm in Tillsonburg, Ontario. He helped his family diversify into culinary herbs and, after moving to Calgary in 1996 as a sales and marketing executive, even considered opening his own herb farm. Stella, a bookkeeper, grew up in a family that trained dogs. Predictably, the winery dogs are terriers. The current dog is Walnut; the predecessor was Cashew. Stella shares Bruno's passion for farming, and that drew them to the lifestyle of Okanagan wine growers.

The winery relies primarily on grapes from its 2.8-hectare

STELLA SCHMIDT AND BRUNO KELLE

(7-acre) vineyard, planted in 1980 and 1981. The original owner planted more than a dozen varieties, including Merlot, Vidal, Pinot Noir, Pinot Blanc, Riesling, Gewürztraminer, Viognier, and perhaps the Okanagan's only block of Siegfried, a German variety. Bruno, in fact, has so many varieties that he puts some into blends just so that the winery, now producing about 3,500 cases a year, has a manageable portfolio.

MY PICKS

Castoro de Oro was one of the earliest Okanagan wineries to produce a dry rosé. It is called Pinot Duetto because Pinot Noir and Pinot Blanc are "singing together." The winery's excellent Merlot is a frequent award winner.

OPENED 1995
(AS GERSIGHEL WINEBERG)

4004 Highway 97
Oliver, BC V0H 1T1
T 250.495.4991
W castorodeoro.com

C.C. JENTSCH CELLARS

OLIVER

On a Sunday afternoon in June 2010, the Testalinden Creek mudslide, triggered when an old dam broke, roared down the mountain. It destroyed Chris and Betty Jentsch's home and sent Betty and her daughter running for their lives. (Chris was not home.) But the slide missed the nearby Jentsch packing house, a modern building just beside the highway. That bit of good fortune enabled Chris to turn it into a winery in 2013.

A self-described entrepreneur, Chris, who was born in Kelowna in 1963, is a third-generation Okanagan fruit grower. He became an independent apple grower in the 1980s. He built his first packing house in 1989 and rebuilt it after fire destroyed it in 1991. When apple prices collapsed in the mid-1990s, he converted his orchards to cherries. "We were in a golden time for cherry exports, with a 63-cent Canadian dollar," Chris recalls. "Cherries were getting airfreighted to Taiwan."

In 1999, Chris planted his first vineyard, 7.7 hectares (19 acres) on the Golden Mile, just south of the Tinhorn Creek winery. He sold it five years later to pursue a much larger project—replacing his cherry trees with vines after overplanting led to a cherry surplus. "That was hard because we were ripping out highly productive cherry blocks that were picture perfect," Chris says.

In his usual style, Chris jumped in with both feet. Between 2005 and 2008, he planted 65,246 vines on a superb 19.4-hectare (48-acre) plateau on the Golden Mile. Once the vines produced, he sold grapes to several wineries, including Andrew Peller Ltd. He operated this vineyard for his own winery and his clients until 2018, when he sold it to the Phantom Creek Estates winery. He continues to farm three smaller vineyards in the South Okanagan.

The first C.C. Jentsch vintage was made in 2012 at Okanagan Crush Pad. Chris opened his winery with 300 cases of Viognier, 120

CHRIS JENTSCH

cases of Gewürztraminer, 550 cases of Syrah, and about 900 cases of a Meritage blend called The Chase. The winery's reputation is based on its Meritage, its Syrah, and an array of small-lot wines.

MY PICKS

Everything, especially the Syrah, The Chase, and the Viognier. The Small Lots wines are superb.

OPENED 2013

4522 Highway 97
Oliver, BC V0H 1T1

T   778.439.2091
W   ccjentschcellars.com

CEDARCREEK ESTATE WINERY

KELOWNA

This was a failing winery in 1986 when it was purchased by Okanagan-born Ross Fitzpatrick, a successful businessman and now a retired senator. A quarter century later, CedarCreek had become one of the valley's best wineries, twice winning Canadian Winery of the Year awards. Early in 2014, the winery attracted a friendly purchase offer from Mission Hill proprietor Anthony von Mandl.

"CedarCreek was not up for sale," the senator says. "However, when approached by Anthony von Mandl, the Fitzpatricks saw another family with a shared vision for the Okanagan Valley who would .continue their family legacy for generations to come. We have placed CedarCreek in very good hands."

While under new ownership, CedarCreek has continued to operate independently, producing a portfolio crowned by its Platinum series of reserve-quality wines. The mature plantings in the CedarCreek vineyards at the winery and near Osoyoos complement Mission Hill's extensive holdings. The oldest Pinot Noir blocks at the winery, Block 2 and Block 4, are just the length of a football field apart, but Block 2 yields a bright, feminine wine, while Block 4 yields a deep and powerful wine.

CedarCreek is one of a growing number of wineries operated by VMF (Von Mandl Family) Estates. "Each winery operates independently, with separate staffing and management, and its own hallmark and identity," Anthony says. "The common purpose is to produce wines that can stand alongside the best in the world." CedarCreek's Mediterranean architecture and the large tasting room and restaurant completed in 2019 make this a favourite destination winery for tourists.

The winemaker is Taylor Whelan, who joined CedarCreek in 2012. He was born in Campbell River in 1985; he initially set

out to be a marine biologist until an interest in wine proved more compelling. He completed a winemaking degree at Brock University in 2009 and, after working in wineries in Ontario, New Zealand, and Australia, came to the Okanagan in 2012. He followed his mentor, Darryl Brooker, with whom he had worked in Ontario and who had taken over at CedarCreek in 2010. After Anthony acquired CedarCreek, Darryl moved to Mission Hill, and Taylor was put in charge of the CedarCreek cellar.

MY PICKS

Everything, including the aromatic Ehrenfelser, which has a cult following; the German-style low-alcohol Riesling; and especially the nuanced Pinot Noirs.

OPENED 1980 (AS UNIACKE)

5445 Lakeshore Road
Kelowna, BC V1W 4S5

T 778.738.1027 (tasting room)
250.764.8866 (office)
1.800.730.9463 (toll-free)

W cedarcreek.bc.ca
Restaurant: Home Block
Restaurant, open daily
(except Tues.) noon–8

CELISTA ESTATE WINERY

CELISTA

Celista Estate Winery takes its name from the community on the north shore of Shuswap Lake. A scenic 30-kilometre drive from the Trans-Canada Highway, Celista was British Columbia's northernmost winery until the 2015 opening of Northern Lights Estate Winery in Prince George.

The winery is the latest career for Jake Ootes (pronounced O-tis, like the elevator company) and Margaret Baile-Ootes, his wife. Born in Holland in 1942, Jake came to Canada with his parents when he was eight and grew up in Renfrew, Ontario. After working as a journalist, he became a public information officer in Ottawa with the Department of Northern Affairs.

In 1967 he moved to Yellowknife as an executive assistant to Stuart Hodgson, the commissioner of the Northwest Territories. Three years later Jake took charge of public affairs and communications for the territorial government. In 1975 he bought a small newspaper in Fort Saskatchewan (near Edmonton), building this into a trio of community papers he sold eight years later to a large publisher. Returning to Yellowknife, he launched an in-flight airline magazine. "Then I decided I would go into politics," Jake says. He was elected to the territorial legislature in 1995, eventually becoming Minister of Education before retiring in 2003.

He and Margaret, the former owner of a Yellowknife art gallery, then moved to a 65-hectare (160-acre) farm at Celista that Margaret had acquired earlier. "This property was a bit of a wasteland," Jake remembers. "We thought we should plant grapes and get into wine." Beginning in 2002, he planted varieties already succeeding in other Shuswap vineyards, including Maréchal Foch, Ortega, Siegerrebe, Madeleine Sylvaner, Madeleine Angevine, and Gewürztraminer. Needing another red variety, he added Gamay

JAKE OOTES

Noir in a 2011 planting that has expanded the vineyard to about 2.8 hectares (about 7 acres). He has also purchased grapes from other vineyards in the region.

Jake relies on consultant Lee Holland (also a winemaker at Dirty Laundry Vineyard). "I have never made wine," Jake says. "First things first—perfect the grapes." The compact winery is in a spacious former garage. The tasting room, which opened in July 2010 and which features two wood-panelled bars, is on the ground floor of their home, with breathtaking views over the bucolic countryside.

Celista's wine labels are memorable by having sketches of Jake's visage beside Margaret's. These will become collector labels because, in 2019, Celista was being advertised for sale.

MY PICKS

Celista Cuvée and Ortega show off the vibrant flavours of this cool terroir. Marg's Rosé is a fine dry rosé, while the Oak Barrel Foch Reserve is a full-bodied red.

OPENED 2010

2319 Beguelin Road
Celista, BC V0E 1M6
T 250.955.8600
W celistawine.com
Picnic patio
Accommodation: Three cabins

CHAIN REACTION VINEYARDS

PENTICTON

Joel and Linda Chamaschuk, who own Chain Reaction, have come a long way in appreciating wine since they had a U-Brew make the wine for their wedding. "We didn't know anything about wine," Linda confesses. "We just knew if we liked it or if we didn't." Since 2017, when they bought a property on Naramata Road, Joel has taken the viticulture course at Okanagan College and worked in the cellar at Moraine Estate Winery with Dwight Sick, the winemaker. Both have completed level two in the Wine & Spirit Education Trust program, a sommelier-oriented course that has enriched their wine knowledge enormously.

The decision to commit to a winery developed gradually as Joel and Linda pursued successful business careers. Joel, who was born in New Westminster in 1967, has a science degree from Simon Fraser University. He has, at various times, been a business consultant, an IT manager, and a photographer. Linda, who was born in Powell River in 1968, continues to work as a business analyst at a health-care agency. Since 1989, she has been a business analyst and manager of technology projects in both the private and public sectors.

Neither grew up in families with much interest in wine. Their interest began in 1992 when they started camping in the Okanagan each summer and began visiting wineries. "I could not imagine a better job than to be the guy behind the tasting bar," Joel says. "Getting into the wine business has been in the back of our minds for decades. It always seemed a big dream because we did not have any formal training in that area."

Joel would bring it up from time to time with friends, one of whom advised him to think about Similkameen Valley, whose potential for growing wine was then overshadowed by the Okanagan. Joel and Linda ended up on the Naramata Bench. They

had become familiar with its concentration of wineries through volunteering for or competing in Penticton's renowned IRONMAN triathlon. Both are avid cyclists, a pursuit that inspired the name for their winery.

Beginning in 2018, they converted a former apple orchard to 1.6 hectares (4 acres) of vines. "We moved here to be involved in the wine industry," Joel says. "Even if apples were lucrative, we would have pulled them out." The largest block is Pinot Noir, followed by Riesling, Chardonnay, and Cabernet Franc. Chain Reaction's first modest vintage in 2019 was made with purchased Pinot Noir, Gewürztraminer, and Pinot Gris. Joel and Linda plan to open a tasting room in 2021 in their 2,000-square-foot winery, designed by Landform Architecture of Penticton. "We are targeting between 2,000 and 3,000 cases at full production," Linda says. "We hope to stay small and focus on quality, not to mention continue to enjoy a great quality of life, which is what brought us to the Okanagan."

MY PICKS

Current range not tasted.

PROPOSED
OPENING 2021

980 Naramata Road
Penticton, BC V2A 8V1

T 604.839.4088

W facebook.com/Chain-Reaction-Vineyards-Guest-Suite-600505640451332/
Accommodation: Vineyard cottage

CHECKMATE ARTISANAL WINERY

OLIVER

In 1994, Mission Hill Family Estate won a major award at a London wine competition for what the winery later described as "the best Chardonnay in the world." That wine was the cornerstone on which Anthony von Mandl built his Okanagan vineyards and wineries. In 2012, he bought the vineyard that grew the award-winning Chardonnay and transformed it, and a neighbouring property, into CheckMate Artisanal Winery, the producer of some of the world's best Chardonnays, along with equally fine Merlots.

The site has an unquestioned Chardonnay heritage. The original winery here was Domaine Combret (later called Antelope Ridge); it was the first Okanagan winery to win a gold medal at the Chardonnay du Monde competition in France. After it closed, Anthony acquired it and installed an intellectual Australian winemaker, Phil McGahan, to create CheckMate. Formerly a lawyer, Phil graduated in 2006 with a wine science degree from Charles Sturt University. His career took him to the Williams Selyem winery in Sonoma in 2010 and to CheckMate two years later.

Phil sources grapes from select blocks in the various vineyards Mission Hill's farming company owns throughout the Okanagan. (The checkerboard appearance of the vineyard blocks inspired the winery's name and the chess terms for the wines.) The object is to make wines that express individual terroirs, or blends that combine the strengths of the vineyard, which are farmed to Phil's direction. "These wines are all a little bit different," he says. "That is the challenge of making them. These are quite unique from each other."

His winemaking is elegantly simple. The Chardonnay grapes, for example, are picked at night and are pressed while still cool and fresh. Individual blocks are fermented separately with wild

PHIL MCGAHAN

yeast and aged about 18 months in French oak before being bottled. The Merlot, also fermented with wild yeast, is aged about 21 months in French oak, much of it new. Both wines are aged at least a year in bottle before release.

In 2017, CheckMate opened what it calls a "pop-up" tasting room, perched on a hilltop with a panoramic view of the Okanagan's Golden Mile appellation. Some may find the tasting fee steep until one realizes the wines retail between $75 and $125 a bottle.

MY PICKS

Everything, without question. The wines routinely score in the mid to high 90s. I awarded 100 points to the 2015 Little Pawn Chardonnay.

OPENED 2015

4799 Wild Rose Street
Oliver, BC V0H 1T1
T   250.707.2299
W   checkmatewinery.com

CHURCH & STATE WINES

OLIVER

While Church & State originated on Vancouver Island, it planted roots firmly in the Okanagan when it opened its Coyote Bowl winery in 2010. Crisply modern, gleaming with stainless steel and glass, this Robert Mackenzie–designed winery is set dramatically on a plateau commanding a panorama of vineyards and mountains. The real drama here is in the glass, with bold, ripe wines expressing the terroir of the South Okanagan.

The Brentwood Bay winery opened in 2002 as Victoria Estate and was near failure two years later when it was purchased by Kim Pullen, a former tax lawyer with a knack for turning businesses around. The key to putting Church & State back on its feet was securing good Okanagan grapes through developing or leasing 45 hectares (110 acres) south of Oliver. At first, grapes were transported to Vancouver Island for processing, until the winery moved production to a leased South Okanagan packing house, adding the Coyote Bowl facility for premium barrel-aged wines. Still open, the Brentwood Bay vineyard specializes in making sparkling wines.

Church & State's objective is to produce 10,000 to 12,000 cases a year, 65% of it red wine. The wine portfolio is built largely around the Bordeaux red varieties and the Rhône whites (Marsanne, Roussanne, and Viognier) that thrive in South Okanagan vineyards. By 2017, the winery's growth had outrun the initial objectives. Church & State was producing 35,000 cases, a volume that required it to scramble for exports as well as domestic sales. Finally, Kim and his son, John, decided to scale back. Church & State was sold to Sunocean Wineries and Estate, a Vancouver company operated by a Chinese businessman. The Pullens have opened a much smaller winery called Second Chapter.

Church & State also has chosen to focus more tightly

WINEMAKER ARNAUD THIERRY

on producing about 12,000 cases a year from its vineyards. Winemaker Arnaud Thierry, who was born in Normandy and trained in Champagne, had extensive experience in France before moving to the Okanagan in 2017 with his wife, also a winemaker.

MY PICKS

Everything, including the spectacular Roussanne and the intensely flavoured Syrah, Malbec, Petit Verdot, and Cabernet Franc.

OPENED 2002
(AS VICTORIA ESTATE WINERY)

4516 Ryegrass Road
Oliver, BC V0H 1T1

T   250.498.2700

W   churchandstatewines.com

CIAO BELLA WINERY

WEST KELOWNA

Take note of this winery's labels: they employ charming original photographs of Roberto Fiume's parents in their youth in Italy just before immigrating to Canada. Everything about this winery celebrates the Italian heritage of Roberto and his wife, Sharon. Among his winery peers, Roberto is better known as Robert, a partner in Kelowna-based Capri Insurance, which insures many wineries.

Roberto was born in 1969 in Yellowknife. He inherited a passion for wine from his parents, Luigi and Melina, who immigrated to Canada in 1956 from the Naples region of Italy. Luigi spent the next 25 years working in the Con gold mine, a Yellowknife landmark in production from 1938 to 2003. "In Yellowknife, the Italians there would get together and get grapes shipped up," Roberto recalls. "We grew up making wine in Yellowknife."

Luigi and Melina also operated Luigi's Pizzeria and Deli, still remembered fondly by Yellowknife old-timers. They sold the business to move to the Okanagan where the abundance of fruit and vegetables reminded them of Italy.

Roberto completed his education in Kelowna with an Okanagan College diploma in business management, which set him on the path to become a partner in the insurance agency in 2001. In parallel with that, he also became a grape grower. The Fiume family settled in West Kelowna's Glencoe district in 1983. Four years later, Roberto bought the property that had been the area's first vineyard. He pulled out the heritage hybrids in 1989 but did not begin replanting until 2000. Currently, he grows 2 hectares (5 acres) of Pinot Noir and a small block of Pinot Gris. Predictably, the wines bear the Italian varietal names: Pinot Nero and Pinot Grigio.

After selling grapes to other wineries, Ciao Bella debuted

(L TO R) SHARON, OLIVIA, ANTONIO, AND ROBERTO OF CIAO BELLA

with three wines from the 2014 vintage. The wines have been made by Jim Faulkner, the veteran winemaker formerly at Mt. Boucherie Estate Winery. The style of the wines emerged from Roberto's desire to mirror his interpretation of Italian wine. "We tried to keep it true to the Italian style," he says. "Italian wines keep a bit of their fruit, but they can also be dry at the same time. That is what I asked Jim to make."

MY PICKS

The Pinot Grigio has the lightness and freshness of an Italian wine. Pinot Nero grapes are used in the winery's excellent rosé and in a lightly oaked table wine.

OPENED 2015

3252 Glencoe Road
West Kelowna, BC
V4T 1M2

T 778.754.3443
W ciaobellawinery.com

CLIFF AND GORGE VINEYARDS

LILLOOET

The second winery in Lillooet, Cliff and Gorge is sited dramatically on a plateau 33.5 metres above the Fraser River gorge and bordered by mountains. The location inspired the name chosen by owner Eckhard Zeidler when the winery was launched after almost a decade of viticultural trials. It is 18 kilometres from Lillooet; the last half of Texas Creek Road is a well-maintained gravel road. Few other wineries boast such a spectacular location.

The 9-hectare (22-acre) vineyard, of which 3 hectares (7½ acres) are currently under vine, occupies part of the historic Texas Creek Ranch. The 67-hectare (165-acre) property, just a portion of the original ranch, is owned by the Zeidler family in partnership with Whistler photographer Brad Kasselman, who is not a partner in the winery. Born in North Vancouver in 1956, Eckhard had pursued a 25-year career as an investment banker in Canada and Europe. He ended that in 1999 to settle in Whistler, to follow a passion for skiing and for public service.

The thought of growing grapes in the region came to Eckhard when he was on the municipal council in Whistler and met Christ'l Roshard, then mayor of Lillooet. A small vineyard at the mayor's home had in 2004 spawned a multiyear, government-funded grape-growing trial. The encouraging results, in addition to attracting the development of the Fort Berens Estate Winery, led Eckhard to plant an experimental block of 37 varietals on Texas Creek Ranch in 2010.

Since then, he has begun to separate the winners from the losers. By 2018, when he made the initial 600 cases of wine for Cliff and Gorge, the promising varieties so far have been Auxerrois, Pinot Noir, Cabernet Franc, and Maréchal Foch. The latter variety has a long history in the Lillooet area, having first been planted in 1972 by Robert Roshard, Christ'l's father, who managed a test

ECKHARD ZEIDLER

vineyard for BC Electric for many years. In addition to these grapes, Eckhard also is growing four hybrids developed for hardiness and disease resistance by Swiss viticulturist Valentin Blattner.

Eckhard plans to make about 1,000 cases annually for several years while establishing the Cliff and Gorge brand. There is potential for growth, with another 6 hectares (15 acres) prepared for planting. The winemaking style avoids the use of oak, not because Eckhard is against barrels but because he does not want to mask the flavours of the grapes. "This is new terroir, and I figure folks that come to visit us deserve to taste what the grapes produce first and foremost," he says.

MY PICKS

Current range not tasted.

OPENED 2019

18450 Texas Creek Road
Lillooet, BC V0K 1V0
T   250.256.8000
    250.256.0051
W   cliffandgorge.com

CLOS DU SOLEIL

KEREMEOS

Michael Clark, the winemaker and managing director at Clos du Soleil, is a self-described worrier. "I consider it a strength," he says, chuckling. He worries about getting the details right to make the best wine possible. However, the Bordeaux-inspired wines at Clos are so well done that he actually has nothing to worry about.

The winery was launched in 2008 by four business couples led by Spencer Massie, a former naval officer who had developed a good palate both in his ship's mess and during various shore assignments near wine regions. Michael, who was born in Ontario in 1972, joined the partnership in 2012 following a wine passion nurtured since his youth. "I read *Champagne Is for Breakfast* when I was probably 10 years old," he says, referring to George Bain's classic Canadian wine book published in 1972. "I don't know other children who loved to read wine books."

Initially he pursued a career as an investment banker, latterly in Switzerland where he began formal studies in winemaking in 2010 and where he worked at Swiss and Bordeaux wineries. On returning to Canada, he completed the rigorous University of California enology program online while identifying Clos du Soleil as the winery where he could make his mark in British Columbia. "Winemaking is such a blend of science and art," he says. "That is what draws most people to it, including myself."

Clos du Soleil is focused on red and white wines from Bordeaux varieties. The initial 4-hectare (10-acre) vineyard was planted in 2007. In 2017 and 2018, the winery acquired neighbouring parcels. The property Les Collines (because of its hilly terrain) was planted with 2.2 hectares (5½ acres) of Sauvignon Blanc and Sémillon. The 4-hectare (10-acre) La Côte property had 2.9 hectares (7¼ acres) of mature vines, notably Malbec, and a cherry orchard since replaced with Merlot and Cabernet Franc.

MICHAEL CLARK

In the winery, which is well equipped with concrete and stainless steel fermenters, Michael ferments largely with indigenous yeasts. His winemaking style is minimalist.

"My philosophy is that our best wines demonstrate their quality in ways other than bigness or heaviness," he says. "A great wine has elegance and complexity, not huge, chewy fruit or aggressive tannins. To me, delicacy matters."

MY PICKS

Everything, notably Signature and Estate Reserve Red, both made with red Bordeaux varieties, and Estate Reserve White, an elegant Sauvignon Blanc/Sémillon blend.

OPENED 2008

2568 Upper Bench Road
Keremeos, BC V0X 1N4

T   250.499.2851

W   closdusoleil.ca

COLUMBIA GARDENS VINEYARD & WINERY

In 2006 Ben De Jager, a South African mining engineer, and his wife, Tersia, chose Canada among many opportunities when they decided to emigrate. They never regretted the choice, but after living six years in Timmins and Flin Flon, they tired of cold winters and began looking at vineyards and wineries in British Columbia. Before taking up engineering, Ben, who was born in 1962, had studied at Marlow Agricultural High School in South Africa, where students managed a vineyard and made wine.

The founders of Columbia Gardens, the first winery in the Kootenays, had listed the winery for sale. When the De Jagers came across the listing, they visited the Columbia Valley and, as Tersia puts it, "fell in love with the area." They purchased the winery in August 2013. "I wanted to go back to my roots in farming," says Ben. He grew up on a sheep farm and now raises between 30 and 40 sheep on the Columbia Gardens property.

Initially, Ben and Tersia contracted Lawrence Wallace to make the 2013 vintage for them. Lawrence, a veteran winemaker, is one of the former owners. He and the late Tom Bryden, his father-in-law, started planting grapes in the 1990s on a family farm 16 kilometres down the Columbia River Valley from Trail. The Bryden family had lived on this 20-hectare (50-acre) farm in the Columbia Valley since the 1930s, growing a range of products from vegetables to hay. They planted Maréchal Foch, Pinot Noir, Gewürztraminer, Auxerrois, and Chardonnay and small blocks of Kerner, Siegerrebe, and Schönburger.

While continuing to work as an engineer, Ben has taken over both viticulture and winemaking. He has increased the Siegerrebe block and planted Gamay Noir, bringing the vineyard size to almost 3.8 hectares (9½ acres). The winery, which produces about 1,900 cases a year, now has a portfolio of 13 wines, many of which,

TERSIA AND BEN DE JAGER

Ben says with pride, are award winners. Meanwhile, Tersia has renovated a house already on the property, turning it into a three-unit guest house with conference facilities.

The quiet charm of the Columbia Gardens wine shop delights first-time visitors, who do not expect a tasting room with sophisticated décor this far off the wine-touring route. The shop is a comfortably appointed log house with a patio deck for wine tasting and your picnic lunches in fine weather.

MY PICKS

Maréchal Foch is the backbone for several wines here—the premium Foch Private Reserve and Kootenay Red (a blend of several vintages of Foch). A bold port-style wine made with Syrah was recently added to the portfolio.

OPENED 2001

9340 Station Road
Trail, BC V1R 4W6
T   250.367.7493
W   cgwinery.com
Accommodation: Grape
Escape Guest House, with
three rooms

COOLSHANAGH VINEYARD

NARAMATA

Skip and Judy Stothert do not plan a winery at Coolshanagh Vineyard. By leaving the winemaking and distribution with professionals at Okanagan Crush Pad Winery, they are able to winter in a warmer climate. Each spring, however, they return to the vineyard that has become a consuming passion since they began planting vines in 2004.

The vineyard and winery began when Skip decided to retire and turn over his business, Green Roads Recycling, to his sons. "We moved here in 2003," Skip says, referring to the 21 hectares (52 acres) of forest that he and his wife bought at the north end Naramata Road, attracted by the seclusion and the stunning views over Okanagan Lake.

"My sons were taking over the business, and I got bored," Skip admits. "I researched grape varieties." He settled on Chardonnay and Pinot Noir, Burgundian varieties that suited his calcium-rich soil as well as his palate. "I grew up drinking Burgundian Chardonnays right from the get-go, when I was about 10 or 11," Skip says. "And there also was Burgundian Pinot Noir."

Trees were felled, land was prepared, and the first hectare (2½ acres) of Chardonnay was planted in 2004. Since then, the vineyard has been quadrupled with the planting of more Chardonnay and Pinot Noir. Between 2008 and 2011, Coolshanagh Chardonnay grapes were sold to Foxtrot Vineyards. Then, in 2012, Skip and Judy decided to launch their own label. The target, when Coolshanagh is at full production, is to release about 1,500 cases of Chardonnay and 300 cases of Pinot Noir annually.

Even without a tasting room, the hospitable Stotherts welcome visitors by appointment to the vineyard. After all, *Coolshanagh* is a Celtic word that translates as "a meeting place of friends." The name has been used by Judy's family, which has roots

JUDY AND SKIP STOTHERT

in Scotland and Ireland, for several generations to identify various homes. "When we decided on a name, we just liked 'meeting place of friends,'" Judy says.

MY PICKS

The Chardonnay, fruit forward with subtle oak and a mineral spine, is one of the most sophisticated in the Okanagan. The Pinot Noir shows great promise.

SALES BEGAN 2014

6301 North Naramata Road
Naramata, BC V0H 1N1
T 250.809.4695
W coolshanagh.ca
Visits and tastings by
appointment

CORCELETTES ESTATE WINERY

KEREMEOS

The name of this winery reflects the Swiss roots of the Baessler family. Before they moved to a Manitoba grain farm in 1978, Urs and Barbara Baessler had a family farm near Lake Neuchâtel in Switzerland called Domaine de Corcelettes. The name followed when they moved to a Similkameen Valley garlic farm in 2007 and planted vines in 2010. "The goal always was to have some grapes," Urs says.

The vineyard propelled their son, Charlie, into winemaking. Born in 1985, he took a job in the vineyard and cellar at Herder Winery and Vineyards after earning a science degree at the University of Lethbridge in 2007. Late the following year, he moved to the Burrowing Owl winery, where he became a vineyard manager and learned winemaking under the tutelage of Bertus Albertyn, then Burrowing Owl's winemaker. In 2013, the Baesslers opened their own winery on their 1-hectare (2½-acre) vineyard near Cawston, which grew just three white varieties.

Even with purchased grapes, the original Corcelettes could not support two families. Charlie and Jesce, his Nunavut-born wife, also worked at other Similkameen wineries, while Urs became a long-distance truck driver. Then Herder Winery, where Charlie had his start, came on the market in 2013 (the result of a divorce). The vineyard was larger and planted primarily with red varieties, and the winery was well equipped. Friends of the Baessler family, Brandon businessman Gordon Peters and his wife, Diane, partnered with the Baesslers to take over Herder early in 2015. Urs and Barbara sold the Cawston vineyard to move to a property adjacent to Herder, now rebranded as Corcelettes with a vineyard expanded to 8.5 hectares (21 acres).

The Corcelettes portfolio now supports the two Baessler families with five white wines and ten reds. Jesce says that Merlot,

JESCE AND CHARLIE BAESSLER

Cabernet Franc, and Syrah are the "three cheerleaders" in the uniquely sunbathed vineyard. The vines grow in mineral-rich soils bordered by a steep south-facing rocky hillside. Located halfway up the hill, the winery and the tasting room command a dramatic panorama over the Similkameen Valley.

MY PICKS

The flagship red is a Cabernet Sauvignon/ Syrah blend called Menhir (a term for stone obelisks in Switzerland). Pinot Noir, Meritage, Merlot, Cabernet Franc, and Syrah round out a solid red offering. The star of the white wines is Chasselas, made from the white variety widely grown in Switzerland.

OPENED 2013

2582 Upper Bench Road
Keremeos, BC V0X 1N4
T   250.499.5595
W   corceletteswine.ca

COVERT FARMS FAMILY ESTATE

OLIVER

Gene Covert, who operates this winery with Shelly, his wife, is the third-generation owner of Covert Farms. The Covert history in farming in the Okanagan started when his grandfather, George Covert, moved to Canada from California in 1959. George initially grew tomatoes and onions, the same crops that he had previously grown on his farm in the Central Valley. When it became clear that the Canadian market, with its marketing boards and difficult export conditions, was not going to allow him to grow only two crops, George diversified his crops to include grapes. That diversity remains fundamental to how Covert operates, as the family and staff explain during 90-minute farm tours.

Covert Farms is a 265-hectare (650-acre) property north of Oliver. Set on a plateau behind McIntyre Bluff, the organic farm produces numerous fruit and vegetable crops. There are also 140 hectares (350 acres) of vineyard, the majority leased by Andrew Peller Ltd., but with a significant block providing the fruit for the Covert winery.

Gene has spent his life around grapes. "I remember driving in the big truck delivering grapes to Casabello when I was little," says Gene, referring to the historic Penticton winery that operated between 1967 and 1994. Grapes fit the farm's diversity because they are harvested after the other vegetables and fruit are finished.

Crop diversity is a counter to monocropping—where a farm focuses on only one crop. This has led Gene to explore organic farming, and then biodynamics, and, more recently, regenerative farming. "The premise of regenerative farming is that the soil will always cover itself," explains Gene. "So just let it cover itself, but cover it with what you want it to be covered with." Since beginning these practices, Gene has reduced his weeding costs, which

GENE COVERT

can be significant with organic production, by 75%. "It made a significant difference, and we're seeing better vine health as well by not beating the soil up as much."

He believes that grapes grown this way more truly reflect the vintages. "Each vintage has its own nuances, so we just try to work it as seamlessly as possible," Gene says. "Every intervention in the winemaking process has a consequence. You'll have a benefit, but you'll also have a consequence to it. The least number of interventions you can make along the line, the [truer] the expression of the wine will be."

MY PICKS

The wines authentically reflect the vintages and the terroir. Amicitia is a Meritage blend based on Merlot, while the MDC is a dark blend of Cabernet Sauvignon, Zinfandel, and Syrah. Zinfandel is also used in a sparkling wine and as a rich red on its own that is worth seeking out.

OPENED 2006

300 Covert Place
Oliver, BC V0H 1T5
T   250.498.9463
W   covertfarms.ca

CRESCENT HILL WINERY

On its website, Crescent Hill Winery says it was established in 1980, even though it was not licensed until 2015. There is a story here.

The vineyard was started about 1980 by Glennallyn Murray, one of the great unsung characters in the early history of the British Columbia wine industry. A self-made man, he was born in Alberta and raised in Vancouver, and in the 1950s, he invested in 2 hectares (5 acres) of property in Port Moody. Subsequently, Andrés Wines (now Andrew Peller Ltd.) opened nearby, and Glenn, as he was known, became a close friend of Tom Hoenisch, the winemaker there and later at Casabello Wines in Penticton.

Glenn's interest in wine began there and really burgeoned when he travelled to Germany, discovered Gewürztraminer, and decided to plant some vines here. The sale of the Port Moody property gave him the resources to plant the first vineyard in Penticton. The Summerland Research Station told him that Gewürztraminer would grow in the Okanagan when pigs flew. He ignored them, smuggling in cuttings of Riesling and Gewürztraminer from Germany, and Orange Muscat from Hungary, and eventually began to make wine. There is a story, possibly apocryphal, that one year, Glenn even sold bulk wine to Casabello.

Before his death in 1999, he turned the vineyard over to his daughter, Teresa. For several years, she sold the fruit to various wineries until Russell Wiseman, her husband, learned winemaking at Okanagan College. With Russell backed by consulting winemakers, Crescent Hill finally realized itself by opening as a winery. "He would be really proud that we finally made it," Teresa says, "and we are legal."

TERESA MURRAY AND RUSSELL WISEMAN

She honours her father's colourful history on some of the wine labels. A dry Gewürztraminer—the variety dominates the 1.4-hectare (3½-acre) vineyard—is called Smugglers Daughter. A private-reserve Gewürztraminer is called Glennallyn.

MY PICKS

Obviously, the Gewürztraminer, made with fruit from old vines. Or the fun wine, a blush called Hissy Fit.

OPENED 2015

205 Spruce Road
Penticton, BC V2A 8V9
T   250.550.6861
     250.328.9363
W   crescenthillwinery.com

CROWN & THIEVES
WEST KELOWNA

From the exterior, the Crown & Thieves winery looks like a ruin. That is the deliberate intention of Jason Parkes, the owner and the winemaker. "When people come to Crown and Thieves, I want them to feel like it is a different experience," he says. "A lot of wineries are the same." The architects, Lake Monster Studio, have created a winery as memorable as Jason's wines.

Behind the false front is a three-floor winery with a 1,200-square-foot tasting room and a basement designed as a speakeasy. If the regulations allow it, musicians including Jason's band, Proper Man, will stage what he calls wine-and-music pairings here.

Jason was born in 1971 in Kitimat, the aluminum-smelting community and home to many amateur winemakers. "My dad always made wine with the Portuguese in Kitimat," Jason says. "I remember stomping grapes in my underwear." He dropped out of high school to pursue a career in music. Before he became a winemaker, he had a punk rock band called Glasshead. He started working in the cellars at Hainle Vineyards about 2000 when music wasn't paying the bills. Seized by a fascination for wine, he wound up Glasshead. "I stopped playing music because I was learning about wine," he says. When his winemaking career was solidly launched a decade or so later, Jason resumed writing music. He formed the new band and is its lead singer.

The Crown & Thieves label was created in the 2014 vintage. One of the first releases was a Syrah, which won a Lieutenant Governor's Award for Excellence. Jason has made the Crown & Thieves wines, along with wines for other producers, at First Estate Winery, a custom crush facility in Peachland. It was also there that Jason, when he was not making a prodigious number of labels for client wineries, resumed his music career.

OWNER AND WINEMAKER JASON PARKES

The Crown & Thieves portfolio is made with grapes from growers with whom Jason has tight relations. His own 2.6-hectare (6½-acre) vineyard is planted with Gamay Noir, Pinot Noir, Pinot Blanc, and Muscat.

MY PICKS

Jason has an especially good touch with Rhône varieties. The Roussanne/ Viognier and the Syrah are excellent.

PROPOSED

OPENING 2020

3930 Harding Road
West Kelowna, BC V4T 2J9

CROWSNEST VINEYARDS

CAWSTON

Crowsnest Vineyards is a rare example of a British Columbia winery where ownership has successfully transferred to the next generation. In 2017, Sascha and Ann Heinecke, who are brother and sister, purchased the winery from their parents, Olaf and Sabine Heinecke. "They were ready to sell a long time ago," Ann says. (The winery was first put on the market in 2013.) "It is a lot of work, and you get tired of it. They wanted to retire." The first change the brother and sister made was to convert the vineyard from overhead irrigation to drip irrigation.

The second-oldest winery in the Similkameen, Crowsnest was acquired in 1998 by the Heinecke family, immigrants from Germany. They rescued a struggling winery and stamped a European flavour all over it by adding a Bavarian-themed restaurant and a seven-room country inn. Sascha has put his diploma in hotel management to good use. He also became a skilled baker, making fresh bread daily for the restaurant and for sale in the tasting room. Future plans for Crowsnest include building a new bakery.

Ann, who has a diploma from the German winemaking school in Weinsberg, makes the focused portfolio exclusively from estate-grown grapes. The 6-hectare (15-acre) vineyard is planted primarily with Merlot, Pinot Noir, Chardonnay, Gewürztraminer, Riesling, Pinot Gris, and Auxerrois. The latter grape, a leading variety in Alsace, has struggled to find favour in British Columbia. "They don't know how to say it, so they don't want to buy it," Ann has concluded. She has a practical solution: she blends it with Gewürztraminer and Pinot Gris. The wine is called Cuvée #3, which sells easily.

Both the wines and the hospitality services here have earned Crowsnest very good reviews on such sites as TripAdvisor. Here is

SASCHA AND ANN HEINECKE

a typical 2018 review: "Gem hidden in the gardens of Similkameen Valley. Neat rooms, renovated in 'modern rustic' style, spacious but cosy. Awesome food made mostly of the farm products, including local bakery. Excellent wine. . . . Scenery landscape appealing to long walks after indulgent dinner. Friendly hostess and delicious homemade jams available along with local wine at the souvenir shop on the premises. The list goes on and on, but you got the idea."

MY PICKS

The four white wines here are crisp and dry. With the exception of the Family Reserve Merlot, the red wines are only lightly oaked.

OPENED 1995

2035 Surprise Drive
Cawston, BC V0X 1C0

T   250.499.5129

W   crowsnestvineyards.com
Restaurant: Open for breakfast, lunch, and dinner
Accommodation: Landgasthof Country Inn, with seven rooms

CULMINA FAMILY ESTATE WINERY

OLIVER

The winery name is simply explained: it is the culmination of a career in wine for Donald and Elaine Triggs and their daughter, Sara. At an age when most are retired, the parents created one of the South Okanagan's top vineyards and wineries.

Donald, who was born in Manitoba in 1944, began his career in 1972 with the winery arm of John Labatt. He left that a decade later to run the North American operations of a British fertilizer company. But in 1989, when Labatt sold its wineries, Donald led the team buying them (and co-founded the Jackson-Triggs winery). This became Vincor, which had grown to the world's 14th-largest wine company by the time Constellation Brands (the largest) took it over in 2006. A year later, he and Elaine began developing 22.7 hectares (56 acres) of densely planted vines on three mountainside benches on the Golden Mile.

They tapped the expertise of Alain Sutre, the same Bordeaux consultant they had worked with when Vincor (with a French partner) began the Osoyoos Larose vineyard and winery in 1999. Pascal Madevon, the initial Osoyoos Larose winemaker, joined Culmina for several vintages. In 2015, when Pascal opened his own consultancy, he was succeeded by another French-trained winemaker, Jean-Marc Enixon. It is hardly surprising there are Bordelaise fingerprints all over Hypothesis, Culmina's flagship red blend.

Alain assured them they could produce wines of even greater quality because the Okanagan terroir is much better understood. With that assurance, the Triggs family has set out to raise the bar again.

The three vineyard benches, each with differing soils and elevations, provide winemaking options. Merlot, Cabernet Franc, and Cabernet Sauvignon make up the largest blocks, followed by

ELAINE AND DONALD TRIGGS

Chardonnay, Riesling, Syrah, Malbec, and Petit Verdot. There is also 1 hectare (2½ acres) of Grüner Veltliner, the Austrian white.

The well-equipped winery is perched on the mountainside, allowing the winemakers to move gently with gravity. The design also affords superb views over the valley from the wine shop. Here, visitors also sit at an antique table that came from the barn of former Doukhobor leader Peter Verigin. The winery prefers to keep visitor groups small in order to offer in-depth tastings and personal vineyard tours.

In 2019, Donald and Elaine sold Culmina to Arterra Wines Canada, a national firm that already owned the former Vincor's Canadian wineries and run by proteges of Donald. Sara has become an Arterra marketing executive.

MY PICKS

Everything, including Hypothesis, Decora (a Riesling), and Unicus (the delicious Grüner Veltliner). Culmina's entry-level wines are released under the R&D label, featuring a charming childhood photo of Donald Triggs and his twin, Ron.

OPENED 2013

4790 Wild Rose Street
PO Box 1829
Oliver, BC V0H 1T0
T 250.498.0789
W culmina.ca

DA SILVA VINEYARDS AND WINERY

PENTICTON

If the name of this winery is not familiar to you, perhaps the original name is. Until 2018 the winery on Upper Bench Road just outside of Penticton was called Misconduct Wine Co. The change came about as an evolution of the vision by owners Richard and Twylla Da Silva.

When Misconduct was originally launched in 2008, it was one of BC's first virtual wineries. With no wine shop to promote the brand, it relied on online marketing and the help of a friend's wine agency for wholesaling. It was designed to be very low-key and off the radar. The branding, with 1920s Prohibition gangster-era themes, and the lack of a wine shop were both "a bit risqué" for the time, admits Richard. "I thought it was cool that in an industry that was all about personality and ego, we could actually go and counter that and do something in the shadows."

Even though the wines were all very good, it was still a tough sell. Richard quickly learned that his customers wanted to know that the wines came from somewhere specific and that someone was confident enough to stand behind it without being secretive about it. With a wine industry as small as BC's, staying in the shadows was not something the Da Silvas could do for long.

Richard and Twylla soon purchased an old house on Upper Bench Road that became the wine shop in 2011. Since customers wanted to know where the wines were coming from, Richard started promoting the vineyards that supplied the grapes for his wines. The concept of "wine from a place" has always been important to the Da Silvas even before starting Misconduct.

Richard, who was born and raised in Oliver, comes from a family that can trace their farming history back to the 18th century in Portugal. Extended family members worked in Okanagan orchards from the mid-1950s and then in vineyards once the

TWYLLA AND RICHARD DA SILVA

grape-growing industry got started in the late 1960s. The family's experience with soft fruit and grapes has given Richard access to a deep understanding of the many regions of the Okanagan. "That's where the family farming experience comes in," explains Richard, "because you have to know those nuances when you're growing soft fruits." The grapes for all of their wines come from specific vineyard sites throughout the Okanagan that tap into Richard's family knowledge of top-quality growing areas and sites.

As Misconduct evolved, a new line of wines called the Suspect Series was created and based on single varieties from single vineyards. With a slight tweak of the branding in 2018, the Suspect Series became Da Silva Vineyards, and Misconduct became a subbrand of Da Silva. The Kitchen, run by Abul Adame and located on the deck outside of the Da Silva wine shop since 2012, continues to be the perfect place for pairing Da Silva wines.

MY PICKS

Everything. The Chenin Blanc is beautifully crisp, the Chardonnay widely appealing. Do not miss the Syrah/Malbec. Though the Misconduct brand has been demoted somewhat, the Big Take is still a great wine and an excellent value.

OPENED 2008
(AS MISCONDUCT
WINE CO.)

375 Upper Bench Road North
Penticton, BC V2A 8T2
T   1.800.851.0903 (toll-free)
W dasilvavineyards.com
Restaurant: The Kitchen (thekitchen-dasilvavineyards.com), closed during winter

THE DANCE WINERY

WEST KELOWNA

Self-described "sisters in vine" Kirstin Wakal and Natasha Campbell, who own this winery, believe that their vineyard has the world's most northerly planting of Malbec. They also believe the terroir will produce wine that matches, if not surpasses, the renowned Malbecs of Argentina. The 10-hectare (25-acre) property, so far with an initial 2 hectares (5 acres) under vine, is a sunbathed south-facing slope nestled amid the suburbs of West Kelowna.

The property was acquired in 1980 by the Wakal family, who had moved earlier to the Okanagan from Winnipeg when the sisters were still schoolchildren. It remained undeveloped for years until Kirstin, a wedding planner, built her house there and created Sanctuary Gardens, a scenic venue for destination weddings. Then in 2015 the sisters planted vines for a winery, which would be strategically located on the Westside Wine Trail.

"We knew we wanted to farm something," says Natasha, an artist with a degree in fine arts from the University of Victoria. "Its location is perfect for grapes." It was not perfect initially: they spent four years filling in gullies to sculpt the land. The slope now reaches down almost to Okanagan Lake. The vineyard is tempered by the effect of the lake, one of the reasons the sisters are confident about Malbec. The other varieties in the vineyard are Riesling (the largest block), Ehrenfelser, and Orange Muscat.

The first wines were made in the 2018 vintage by consulting winemaker Daniel Bontorin and by a young Brock University graduate, Judah Campbell, a brother-in-law of the family who was working at another Okanagan winery. Despite the surname, he is not related to Natasha's husband, Roy, a building contractor who erected the winery for The Dance.

Natasha, who runs the vineyard, says the winery's name was

KIRSTIN WAKAL AND NATASHA CAMPBELL

inspired by watching the vines sway in the wind. "I think it just conveys the dance of life. This has been a bit of a dance for us, a bit of a learning curve—two steps forward, one step back at times."

"We hope to have some sparkling wine to serve the guests down at Sanctuary Gardens," Kirstin says. "A sparkling Ehrenfelser is a distinct possibility."

MY PICKS

Current range not tasted.

PROPOSED
OPENING 2020

Witt Road
West Kelowna, BC
V4T 2C5

T   250.878.2116
W   facebook.com/
     thedancewinery

D'ANGELO ESTATE WINERY

In 2004, Sal D'Angelo was the first in the Okanagan to plant Tempranillo, the Spanish red. Then, in 2018, he was the first to plant Montepulciano, the red native to the Abruzzo region in east-central Italy, where Sal was born in 1953. And he is considering planting more Spanish and Italian varieties.

His 3.6 hectares (9 acres) of vines are on a west-facing Naramata Bench plateau above Okanagan Lake. It has a million-dollar view, but Sal chose the site in 2001 because it has a long frost-free season. That sharply contrasts with the winery near Windsor, Ontario, that Sal sold in 2017. He had to drop the price by $500,000 after two very hard winters had killed half of the vines.

"I grew up with the smell of fermenting grapes," Sal says, recalling the home winemaking of his immigrant parents. He became a science teacher but began to plant grapes in 1983 in his Windsor-area property, opening that winery in 1989. By then, he had begun vacationing in the Okanagan each year, soon acquiring 70 years of weather data from the Summerland Research Station. That drew him to the Naramata Bench, where he became a friend of Vera and Bohumir Klokocka, the founders of Hillside Cellars (now Hillside Winery). Vera's Cabernet Sauvignon—she was the first to make this varietal in the Okanagan—convinced Sal it was easier to make big reds on the Naramata Bench than in the Windsor area. Beginning in 2001, he acquired adjoining farms totalling 11 hectares (27 acres), developing them as he disposed of his Ontario assets.

His son, Christopher, who had been running the Ontario winery until it was sold, subsequently has taken over winemaking at the Okanagan winery. Sal's daughter, Stephanie, handles business. Future plans call for a new winery with an underground

SAL D'ANGELO

cellar to reduce losses during the prolonged barrel aging of Sal's big reds. "We lose a litre per barrel per month," he says. "That is $36,000 a year in evaporation losses."

MY PICKS

The flagship wine is a red blend called Sette Coppa, which means "seven measures." The wine takes its name from the nickname of Sal's great-grandfather, Donato, who persuaded the local flour mill to take every seventh measure as payment for grinding his grain when others were being assessed every sixth measure.

OPENED 2007

979 Lochore Road
Penticton, BC V2A 8V1
T   250.493.1364
W dangelowinery.com
Picnic area
Food service: Food truck
Accommodation:
D'Angelo's Guest House,
with three suites

DAYDREAMER WINES

Shiraz is the signature variety at Daydreamer Wines. Shiraz practically runs in the veins of winemaker Marcus Ansems, the owner of this winery with his wife, Rachel. His family in Australia once owned a share of Mount Langi Ghiran, the legendary Shiraz producer in the state of Victoria, and his uncle, Trevor Mast, was a winemaker there.

"One of my favourite wines in the world was made at my family winery," Marcus says. "That wine was what inspired me to get involved with the industry." Born in 1974, he graduated in enology in 1996 from Adelaide University. He went abroad to gain experience, first with Simonsig in South Africa and then in Tuscany and the Rhône. He picked up his career in Australia briefly before a Canadian wine entrepreneur, Peter Jensen, recruited him in 1999 to run wineries in Ontario and Nova Scotia. In Niagara, before he returned to Australia in 2002 as a consulting winemaker, he met Rachel, an accountant with a talent in design and photography. In 2004 they moved to British Columbia where Marcus practised his craft at several wineries.

He became a Master of Wine (MW) in 2015. His 10,000-word thesis predictably involved his favourite variety: he studied the effect of fall frosts on Syrah when the grapes were still on the vine. (He found that good wine can be made from the frozen grapes.)

Daydreamer Wines opened in 2014, culminating Rachel and Marcus's shared dream of a family winery producing about 3,000 cases a year. The winery draws fruit from about 5 hectares (12 acres) of owned or contracted vineyard. Most of the acreage is on the Naramata Bench, but the cherished Shiraz is grown in a sunbathed Osoyoos vineyard.

Since earning his MW, Marcus has had many requests to take on consulting projects. "I turn down a lot," he says. "Any projects

MARCUS ANSEMS

I do tend to be based in the Okanagan. I don't really like to travel that much. I have three kids, and with the winery, it keeps me pretty busy."

MY PICKS

Everything, especially the reserve wines, which are released under the Marcus Ansems label.

OPENED 2014

1305 Smethurst Road
Naramata, BC V0H 1N1

T   778.514.0026

W   daydreamerwines.ca

DEEP ROOTS WINERY

NARAMATA

When Bryan Hardman began to build this family-owned winery, he presented a seven-year sales plan to his bank. Deep Roots, which sold about 1,000 cases in its first year, achieved Bryan's seven-year target within three years. For several years, the winery, sold out of wines by the end of summer, has scrambled to increase production. Most of the grapes are from the 8.5 hectares (21 acres) of Naramata Bench vineyard farmed by the Hardmans. Four generations of Hardmans have farmed near Naramata since 1919. The winery's name reflects their deep roots in the community.

Bryan, who was born in 1950, once owned 20 hectares (50 acres) of apple trees. He began switching to grapes in 1996 and stopped growing apples entirely in 2010 when, with his wife, Debra, and son, Will, he laid the plans for a winery. To learn winemaking, Will, born in 1983, did vintages in New Zealand and South Africa and then at a nearby Naramata winery, Van Westen Vineyards, where the first Deep Roots vintage was made in 2012 while the Deep Roots winery was under construction.

The Deep Roots vineyards, all planted on westward-facing slopes overlooking Okanagan Lake, grow an extensive selection of varieties. The signature red wines are Syrah and Gamay Noir; the signature whites are Chardonnay, Pinot Gris, and Sauvignon Blanc. The winery's two blends, Parentage White and Parentage Red, honour Bryan's mother, whose maiden name was Parent.

The winery's target is to stabilize production at 6,000 cases a year, limited only by the quantity of estate grapes and perhaps by the size of the cozy tasting room. Experience has shown that Deep Roots sells about three-quarters of its production from the wine shop.

BRYAN AND WILL HARDMAN

MY PICKS

Everything, especially the Syrah, the Gamay Noir, the Malbec, and the Cabernet Franc.

OPENED 2014

884 Tillar Road
Naramata, BC V0H 1N1
T   250.460.2390
W   deeprootswinery.com

DESERT HILLS ESTATE WINERY

OLIVER

Twin brothers Randy and Jessie Toor, born in 1964 in Punjab, spent their summers working in Okanagan vineyards after coming to Canada. In 1988, they bought a 10-hectare (25-acre) apple orchard on Black Sage Road, one of the Okanagan's best vineyard areas. When they discovered that apples of only middling quality can be grown on Black Sage, they switched to grapes (mostly Bordeaux reds and the first Syrah in the South Okanagan) in 1995. They named the vineyard Three Boys—their brother, Dave, is also a partner. Since 2005, they have added four other vineyards and now farm 34.5 hectares (85 acres).

"It was a little dream to start a small winery," Randy says. Successful beyond initial expectations, they now produce 12,000 cases while selling grapes to other wineries. The spacious tasting room and the bistro, opened in 2019 with both indoor and outdoor seating, are surrounded by vineyard.

Desert Hills is the Okanagan's largest producer of Gamay Noir, a red for which it has a stellar reputation. Anthony Buchanan, the winemaker who joined Desert Hills late in 2015, has refined the style. In his view, past vintages have been too bold. Under his hand, the Gamay has become an elegant wine with bright fruit, more in keeping with top-rated wines from Beaujolais.

Ursa Major is another label produced here. It is a small-lot premium-wine project developed by Randy's son, Rajen, who intends to transform it into a winery of his own in time.

JESSIE AND RANDY TOOR

Everything. The wine to ask for, if it is not sold out, is the award-winning Syrah, which is remarkable for intense nutmeg spice in both the aroma and the taste. Other notable wines are Mirage (an iconic blend), Malbec, Cabernet Sauvignon, Cabernet Franc, Merlot, Gamay Noir, Pinot Gris, Gewürztraminer, a blend of whites called Cactus, and the exceptional Viognier.

OPENED 2003

4078 Black Sage Road
Oliver, BC V0H 1T1

T 250.498.6664

W deserthills.ca

Restaurant: Black Sage
Bistro

DIRTY LAUNDRY VINEYARD

SUMMERLAND

No other winery is blessed with both a beautiful view and such a bumpy road as Dirty Laundry Vineyard. People who make the trek to the end of Fiske Street do it because they want to go there. More often than not, there are a lot of people who want to go there.

The Dirty Laundry experience is one of sights, sounds, and stories. The view over the Trout Creek ravine from the large patio is commandingly beautiful and, with no other winery in the immediate area, utterly unique to this one. Occasionally, the sound of a real steam locomotive on the only remaining functional section of the Kettle Valley Railway cuts through the otherwise peaceful scenery.

The story of Dirty Laundry has drawn people into the brand for well over a decade.

The property was originally planted by former Bavarian woodcarver Edgar Scherzinger, who named it Scherzinger Vineyards. After he retired in 2001, the new ownership hired the Vancouver marketing guru Bernie Hadley-Beauregard, who suggested rebranding it based on a local story from Summerland's history. According to that tale, a local laundry had fronted a brothel. It was ripe with branding possibilities for wine names, merchandise, and old-time chic. The new branding worked like a charm, and sales took off. Madame's Vines Gewürztraminer, a Girl in Every Port (a fortified wine), Bubble Entendre (a sparkling), and Bordello (a Meritage blend) are among the two dozen creatively named wines in the portfolio.

While the brand and wine-shop experience appealed to a particular demographic, the wines themselves were often overlooked by critics and more "serious" wine aficionados. The secret weapon beyond the branding is winemaker Mason Spink,

WINEMAKER MASON SPINK

who has been working below the radar to elevate the wines to a new, perhaps more respectable, level beyond the confines of the kitschy marketing. Most of the wines have seen a reduction in residual sugar. He has even been able to create a complex orange wine made from Gewürztraminer. "It's a real gateway wine to [appeal to the] wine nerds and wine trade," says Mason.

The large patio is a major draw to this winery, with its stunning views. There is an outdoor tasting bar if the indoor one is full. The extensive food options range from deli items to *al forno* pizzas. Beer is even available for those looking to refresh palates after wine tastings. The patio is shaded by grapevines, welcome on a hot summer's day.

MY PICKS

Gewürztraminer is a focus here, with a total of five different versions ranging from dry to sweet, white to orange, and even single-vineyard bottlings. The Hush rosé, which in years past was a simple sweet wine, has been slowly getting drier and more Provençal in style under Mason's watch.

OPENED 1995 (AS SCHERZINGER VINEYARDS)

7311 Fiske Street
Summerland, BC V0H 1Z2
T 250.494.8815
W dirtylaundry.ca
Food service: Pizza and deli, with a patio area
Accommodation:
The Parlour House
(250.328.8273), for up to eight people

EAU VIVRE WINERY

The vintage of 2017 was the first time that Sukh Bajwa had used the science from his civil engineering education since he had emigrated from India in 1997. He was working the harvest at Eau Vivre in preparation for taking over the winery that December. "Right away, as soon as I walked into the winery laboratory, I said, 'I know this stuff,'" Sukh says. "It is just a matter of learning the wine chemistry, but not chemistry itself."

Sukh and his wife, Neeta, purchased the winery from Dale Wright and Jeraldine Estin. They are Saskatchewan natives—Dale is a geologist, and Jeraldine is an educator—who had become fascinated with Similkameen wines as tourists. That led them to take over a small winery near Cawston when its ambitious founder, Lawrence Herder, moved to a larger property in 2008. Over the next decade, Eau Vivre made its name with Pinot Noir.

The winery was put on the market in 2017 so that Dale could refocus on his Saskatchewan business. The advertisement caught Sukh's eye, appealing both to his entrepreneurial nature and his burgeoning interest in wine. His civil engineering degree from an Indian university had not been recognized in Canada. In the typical hardscrabble immigrant's life, Sukh's first job was in a convenience store, followed by warehouse labour and fruit picking. In 2010, after eight years as a commercial trucker, he bought what he calls the only business in the village of Seton Portage, a combined grocery with a liquor store, and a pub with some hotel rooms. In 2014, he and his wife also purchased a motel in Enderby, which also had a liquor store.

The hospitality exposed them to wine. "I joke that I started drinking so much wine that it became worth buying a winery of my own," Sukh says. Working together in 2017, he and Dale produced about 950 cases of wine. In 2018, now working with a consultant,

SUKH BAJWA

Sukh made 1,600 cases. While that includes Pinot Noir rosé and table wine, the portfolio is moving strongly to Bordeaux varieties, matching Sukh's palate.

MY PICKS

The Gewürztraminer and the Riesling from the estate's 0.8 hectare (2 acres) are refreshing. The flagship red is the Bordeaux blend called Buddhafull.

OPENED 2009

716 Lowe Drive
Cawston, BC V0X 1C2

T   250.499.2655

W   eauvivrewinery.ca

ECHO BAY VINEYARD

OKANAGAN FALLS

The eye-catching hieroglyphics on Echo Bay's wine labels–meteorological symbols used to chart daily weather–symbolize the objective to make wine in tune with nature. "Echo Bay's wine," reads the explanation on the winery's website, "is a unique expression of time and place; the elements, terroir, and a family with their own approach to farming and winemaking."

The family is Mark and Kathy Rufiange and their daughter, Kelsey, the winemaker. They are descendants of the Kenyons, Penticton business leaders for over a century (including the founding of Greyback Construction in 1963). The vineyard, named for a Skaha Lake bay, is on a bucolic lakeside property where the extended Kenyon family has gathered since 1967.

Mark is an Edmonton-born engineer who ran his own engineered wood company until he retired in 2008. Bored by retirement, he and Kathy, a former nurse, decided in 2013 to plant 2 hectares (5 acres) of vines, all red varieties. That soon fired Kelsey's interest in making wine. Kelsey (born in 1988) already had a geography degree from McGill and a consumer's interest in wine. Now, she went to Lincoln University in New Zealand for a postgraduate degree in enology. She polished her skills by making wine in New Zealand, Australia, and California before making Echo Bay's first vintage in 2015.

Their viticulture follows organic and biodynamic practices. This carries on to the winemaking, where Kelsey ferments with indigenous yeast to enhance the sense of place in the wines. However, she keeps cultured yeast on hand just in case. The first two vintages were made at nearby Synchromesh Wines while Echo Bay built its own processing facility in a building modelled after a barn. To Kelsey's delight, the wild-yeast ferments proceeded without a problem in this virgin winery.

KELSEY, KATHY, AND MARK RUFIANGE

The style of the wines is well defined. "We don't like big, extracted wines," Kelsey says. "We are looking towards the more elegant style. Our alcohols, for the most part, have been in the low 13s." Using purchased grapes, Kelsey makes white wines that are released under a second label.

MY PICKS

Synoptic, the flagship red Bordeaux blend, is excellent. Keep an eye out for small-lot wines such as Cabernet Franc.

OPENED 2018

224 Eastside Road
Okanagan Falls, BC
V0H 1R5
T   250.490.6228
W   echobayvineyard.ca

EDGE OF THE EARTH VINEYARDS

ARMSTRONG

Although this winery, which Russ and Marni Niles opened in 2002, is only 6 kilometres from the highway, the scenic but twisty country roads create the perception that it is off the beaten path. Russ met that perception head-on in renaming the winery in 2009. "By the time people get here, they think they have gone off the edge of the earth," he says, laughing.

It is really not that remote. That explains why the winery tripled production between 2014 and 2019 and has just built a new winery nestled in the vineyard. "We are still small at 1,700 cases, and we probably won't go beyond 3,000, but that is a nice family business," Russ says.

Hunting Hawk Vineyards, as Russ called the winery originally, was sold along with Hunting Hawk's second winery, which Russ and Marni operated for four years at the O'Keefe Ranch near Vernon.

Russ was not disappointed that he no longer had to stretch himself between two wineries. "This has become fun," he says. "This has become a lot of fun." Born in Victoria in 1957, Russ is the former editor of both the *Vernon Daily Times* and *Vernon Daily News*, both of which are now defunct. He was drawn to wine as one of the original partners in Vernon's now-closed Bella Vista winery. He launched his own winery after the closure of the newspapers.

At the same time, the owner of the local flying club alerted him that an aviation website had posted a job offer. Russ began writing for AVweb.com and eventually became editor of what he says is the world's largest general aviation website, with 200,000 subscribers. He also edits *Canadian Aviator* magazine and pilots his Cessna 140 around the Okanagan.

RUSS NILES

Russ relies on purchased grapes (such as Merlot, Pinot Noir, Pinot Gris, and Gewürztraminer) as well as on his own 1.2-hectare (3-acre) vineyard. He is particularly enthusiastic about Maréchal Foch, grown both in his vineyards and by some neighbours. "I just happen to love the grape," he says. "It makes fabulous red wine."

MY PICKS

How can you not sample the Foch? The winery offers two—a dry version and an off-dry version called Smooth Foch. The winery rewards customers who come to this secluded location by offering substantial discounts for wines purchased there.

OPENED 2002
(AS HUNTING HAWK VINEYARDS)

4758 Gulch Road
Armstrong, BC V0E 1B4
T 250.546.2164
W edgeeearth.ca

8TH GENERATION VINEYARD

SUMMERLAND

The bold sign on this winery proclaims "8th Generation—winemakers since 1783." That celebrates the eight generations during which the family of winemaker and co-proprietor Bernd Schales have been wine growers. However, it could also be called 10th Generation. The Frank family of Stefanie Schales, Bernd's wife, recently learned that their wine-growing history in Germany goes back at least 92 years longer than that of the Schales family. They only confirmed that in 2009 after the Frank family went to church archives in Germany and found that the family had been growing grapes since 1691.

Bernd and Stefanie brought the family traditions to the Okanagan in 2003. Bernd, born in 1972 and trained at the winemaking school in Weinsberg, had spent nearly 10 years managing a vineyard for his family's Weingut Schales in Flörsheim-Dalsheim. With Bernd's father and two uncles already in the business in Germany, the young couple struck out on their own, canvassing opportunities in South Africa, New York State, and Ontario before being seduced, during a vacation, by the Okanagan's beauty. They bought a 4-hectare (10-acre) Okanagan Falls vineyard that had been planted in 1985 primarily with Riesling. Two subsequent purchases elsewhere in the valley have doubled their vineyards.

Bernd's family sent him off to Canada with his grandfather's antique wine press, which was a godsend in the 2007 vintage. That summer, Bernd and Stefanie shelved original plans to attach a winery to their Okanagan Falls home when they were able to buy the building previously housing the highway-side Adora winery just south of Summerland. The building was empty (Adora had moved its equipment elsewhere), and Bernd had an urgent need to order new equipment because the grapes were ripening quickly.

His grandfather's press, he discovered, was good for yet another vintage. That experience left him comfortable with venerable equipment, such as the 1961 mechanical filler for bottling the winery's two sparkling wines.

Given their Rheinhessen roots, pride of place in the 8th Generation portfolio is occupied by four different Rieslings, including a late-harvest version. The flagship wine, which is crisply dry, is Riesling Selection, which is released only from the best vintages.

MY PICKS

Everything, including the very fine Rieslings, the Chardonnay, and the Pinot Noir. The sparkling wines are called Integrity, based on Chardonnay, and Confidence, a festive pink sparkler based on Pinot Noir.

OPENED 2007

6807 Highway 97
Summerland, BC V0H 1Z9
T   250.494.1783
W 8thgeneration.com

ELEPHANT ISLAND WINERY

NARAMATA

Elephant Island raised the bar for fruit wines when Del and Miranda Halladay launched this winery. As winemaker, they retained Christine Leroux, whose entire training and experience had been in making grape wines. As a result, Elephant Island's fruit wines take the measure of grape wines any day. There are dry wines to go with food, sparkling wines for celebration, iced apple wines made just like Icewine, and fortified wines with cherries or currants as traditional as port. Most of the wines are made only with undiluted juice. "I know that it's a pretty common practice with fruit-wine production to use water," Del says. "What better way to dilute flavours and dilute wine? We're doing everything we can to use the pure fruit, and that's it."

This winery is tucked pleasantly amid the orchard that Miranda's grandparents bought years ago as a summer retreat on the Naramata Bench. The serene and shaded patio behind the wine shop is still a great spot for a picnic. The winery's singular name memorializes a family legend. When Catherine Chard Wisnicki, an architect and Miranda's grandmother, designed the house, her husband, Paul (an engineer), scoffed that it was designed purely "for the eye." Having already been told the property would be a white elephant, she responded by calling the house Elephant Eye-land.

Miranda, born in Powell River in 1973, is a geologist. Del, born in Victoria in 1972, went to Loyola College in Maryland on a lacrosse scholarship. He earned a marketing degree and a place on a professional American lacrosse team. Playing lacrosse, from which he retired in 2007, provided a "good part-time job" during the winter months as the winery became established.

Elephant Island's annual 6,000-case production was augmented several years ago with four grape wines, whose cheeky

DEL HALLADAY   MIRANDA HALLADAY

labels underline Del's winemaking confidence. The Viognier is
Told You So, while the Cabernet Franc is Naysayers. The Merlot is
Think Again, and the Chardonnay is the Other Way.

MY PICKS

The pear wine, light and delicate, is a favourite of mine with a salad course. The Little King is a crisply dry Champagne-method apple wine. The Pink Elephant is a sparkling apple wine with cassis dosage. The winery's tasty dessert products include the Stellaport, the Cassis, and an immensely popular Framboise. And don't miss the grape wines.

OPENED 2001

2730 Aikins Loop
Naramata, BC V0H 1N0
T 250.496.5522
W elephantislandwine.com
Picnic patio
Accommodation: The
Tree House rental suite

EVOLVE CELLARS

PENTICTON

Four years after opening at a lakefront location north of Summerland, Evolve Cellars moved to share quarters with TIME Winery in downtown Penticton. The original location, formerly a winery called Bonitas, was leased. When the lease expired in the summer of 2019, Christa-Lee McWatters, who was managing the winery, moved it to the urban winery started by the late Harry McWatters, her father.

"Evolve was founded under the principles of embracing change and moving ahead," Christa-Lee, who succeeded Harry as chief executive, said in a statement. "Every time a person reads one of the Evolve wine labels, they are reminded how important it is to take a step forward, to try to accomplish more and strive to achieve their best. Well, now we need to 'walk the talk' and keep changing and growing ourselves."

The winery's literature reflects the poetic logic behind the Evolve name. "To evolve means to change or develop slowly, step by step, one day at a time, into a more advanced state of being," the winery's marketing materials explain. "We believe that the Okanagan Valley has evolved to produce some of the best wines on the planet."

TIME Winery was developed in a former movie theatre in Penticton. What is called an Evolution Lounge has been added to give the Evolve wines their own tasting room. The wines are made by a team headed by Graham Pierce, the senior winemaker at TIME.

Evolve's wines all are value priced, usually under $20 a bottle, while the wines at TIME start at that price. It is part of a strategy to give each winery its own distinctive identity. "Our target consumer is different," Harry said of Evolve in a 2018 interview. "We are marketing a lot more to females between

CHRISTA-LEE MCWATTERS

25 and 45 years old. None of the white wines we produce see any oak. They are all varietally correct. They are not blended. They are all fruit forward. Even the red wines are all very fruit forward. Although they see some oak, it is neutral oak and for a shorter period of time."

MY PICKS

All the wines are well made, with a quality that overdelivers for the price.

OPENED 2015
(AS BONITAS WINERY)

361 Martin Street
Penticton, BC V2A 5K6
T   236.422.2556
W evolvecellars.com

EX NIHILO VINEYARDS

LAKE COUNTRY

Though the winery opened in 2008, the genesis of Ex Nihilo goes back to 1999 when founders Jeff and Decoa Harder were dating. "Within the first three months of dating," explains Decoa, "Jeff invited me to go to Napa Valley with him." A visit with Jeff's brother, James, who makes wine there, inspired them. Decoa needed little persuading since she had already marketed wines for both Quails' Gate and Mt. Boucherie wineries. "I woke up one morning and said, 'Jeff, we have to find land,'" she recalls.

A favourite sculpture called *Ex Nihilo* prompted the winery name. The Latin term literally means "out of nothing," and when the couple purchased a hillside orchard in Lake Country in 2004, they chose the term for their new winery. "It reminded us of what happens in the vineyard, in that every year, a new vintage is created," Decoa says.

Unlike other wineries in Lake Country, Ex Nihilo's wine portfolio contains a significant portion of big reds. Along with a bold Merlot, they also produce an iconic Bordeaux-style blend called Night. The portfolio is rounded out by a concise selection of varietals: Pinot Noir, Chardonnay, Pinot Gris, and Riesling. The Pinot Noir in particular has garnered acclaim after two consecutive vintages (2013 and 2014) won Lieutenant Governor's Awards for Excellence.

The winery, completed in 2009, includes an elegant tasting room, an art gallery, and a barrel cellar that is often used for tasting experiences. Visitors are surrounded by beautiful rows of vines the instant that they drive onto the property. This is an immersive aspect of the visitor experience, showing the amount of thought that the Harders have put into their design. Wine club members can even enjoy special tastings surrounded by these vines on the Privata Terrace, which is accessible from the wine shop.

Winemaker Marissa Neuner, from Fort St. John, who has been in the industry since 2013, joined the team in 2017 as winemaker and is now responsible for the winery's production of around 10,000 cases annually. She took over winemaking from former partner Jay Paulson, who sold his interest in 2017. New partners Mike and Janet Azhadi joined the Ex Nihilo team in 2018.

MY PICKS

Everything, notably the Riesling, Chardonnay, Pinot Gris, Pinot Noir, and the robust Night Bordeaux blend.

OPENED 2008

1525 Camp Road
Lake Country, BC V4V 1K1
T   250.766.5522
W   exnihilovineyards.com
Restaurant: Chaos Bistro,
open daily 11–7

FAIRVIEW CELLARS

OLIVER

At a recent party in the South Okanagan, Fairview Cellars owner Bill Eggert pulled out a 13-year-old bottle of his Cabernet Franc and quietly placed it on the table. Most other wine-industry people there had brought their recent vintages. Not Bill. He knows his wines and how they age. His Cabernet Franc was the first bottle to be finished.

Bill is a wine grower in the truest sense, and it shows in Fairview's portfolio, which is heavily weighted toward full-bodied reds. Ask Bill about what he does in the cellar, and he is forthcoming and often self-deprecating. He'll say things like "This wine did something I've never seen before" or "I don't know what this wine is doing this year, but it's really good." Ask about what he does in the vineyard, and he'll tell you about the three types of soil or the heat units in a typical season, but very little about how he manages the grapes or what influences his decisions. That type of information is more closely guarded.

Hints of his brilliance are often masked in the seemingly whimsical names for his wines, all of which originated with stories or suggestions. The Bear, Madcap Red, Obsequious, and Fumé Franc all have stories that make for interesting banter in the intimate wine-shop experience, which hasn't changed very much since he first opened his doors in 2000.

Bill, who was born in Ottawa in 1957, first learned about growing grapes and making wine in the Ontario wine industry. "Because my uncle had this nursery grapevine business, I met all these really cool people," Bill says. "They're the ones that really introduced me to good wines." One was the legendary Ontario winemaker Paul Bosc. Bill credits Paul's wife, Andrée, for suggesting he start his own winery. He moved to the Okanagan in 1983, working on construction and vineyards until he could

BILL EGGERT

realize his ambition. In 1993, he began planting his 2.4-hectare (6-acre) vineyard overlooking the Fairview Mountain Golf Club. Now, even after two decades in business, Bill still delivers his wines personally to customers on the coast.

Visiting the winery is the best way to enjoy Fairview Cellars. The wine shop has the feel of a cozy log cabin. The wine cellar is topped with a sundeck and pagoda that offer stunning southern views of the valley, the vineyards, and Mount Kobau to the west.

MY PICKS

Everything is grand cru level here. *The reds are notable for their complexity and depth of flavour, as well as their proven longevity. Sauvignon Blanc, Grüner Veltliner, and Chardonnay give the portfolio depth. Samples of the rare Iconoclast should not be refused if offered. The Bear and the Cabernet Franc are true treasures of the Okanagan.*

OPENED 2000

989 Cellar Road
Oliver, BC V0H 1T5
T   250.498.2211
W fairviewcellars.ca

50TH PARALLEL ESTATE

The 50th Parallel winery, near Carr's Landing north of Lake Country, is farther north than the actual 50th parallel. Operating a winery beyond the 50th is considered risky anywhere in the world since the accepted latitude range for wine production is between 30 and 50 degrees north or south. Founding owners Sheri-Lee Turner and Curtis Krouzel have accepted that risk, which is moderated by the sunbathed southern exposure of the vineyard and the influence of the lake.

The bright wine shop is surrounded by glass on three sides, which from the inside frames the vineyards, hillsides, and Okanagan Lake. "What we wanted to give people was the experience of not only the wine," explains Sheri-Lee. "We wanted to give people the experience of the Okanagan."

Curtis picks up on that point. "Anywhere you look, you're surrounded by the wine and you're surrounded by this amazing place that creates the wine."

The winery began humbly in a Quonset hut. The timbers from that were used for an elegantly curved tasting bar in an expanded wine shop. The grand winery was built subsequently and was joined in 2018 by the Block One restaurant. The architecture accentuates the winery's branding: the whole building is filled with parallel lines in the form of windows, columns, and steel beams. The culinary masterpieces in the restaurant are made using local ingredients, some grown on the property by the chef.

Curtis and Sheri-Lee respect the property's history. The property was a former vineyard site that only sold grapes until the pullout program in 1988 when the unwanted vines were ripped out. The land remained unused for nearly 20 years until Curtis and Sheri-Lee purchased it in 2008. They have planted a 27-hectare (67-acre) vineyard of precisely oriented rows on a long southward-

WINEMAKER MATTHEW FORTUNA

CURTIS KROUZEL AND
SHERI-LEE TURNER

facing slope. The journey is still in progress. Curtis says, "The vision that Sheri-Lee and I have had for the last 19 years—that's coming to fruition."

MY PICKS

Pinot Noir is the signature variety here, as Estate Pinot Noir and the higher-priced Unparalleled Pinot Noir. Both are exceptionally elegant, but the Unparalleled, which is produced only in the best vintages, is outstanding. The Pinot Gris takes on an aromatic finesse hard to find in more southern growing regions. All wines are complex, consistent vintage to vintage, and extremely well made by Matthew Fortuna, the winemaker.

OPENED 2013

17101 Terrace View Road
Lake Country, BC V4V 1B7
T   250.766.3408
W   50thparallel.com
Restaurant: Block One

FITZPATRICK FAMILY VINEYARDS

PEACHLAND

The visitor experience at this winery, where about 100,000 bottles of sparkling wine are maturing in vaulted underground cellars, is meant to be "luxury at play." The president, Gordon Fitzpatrick, or winemaker, Sarah Baine, often give personal tours and tastings. The resort-like winery has a bistro and a patio where visitors relax with a glass of wine while taking in views of the vineyard or Okanagan Lake.

This is the second winery established here by the Fitzpatrick family. Senator Ross Fitzpatrick, Gordon's father, purchased this lakeside property south of Peachland in 1994. Formerly a renowned orchard called Greata Ranch, it was redeveloped as a 16.2-hectare (40-acre) vineyard to supply the senator's CedarCreek Estate Winery across the lake. From 2003 until 2014, the Fitzpatricks also opened Greata Ranch Vineyards winery here. The sale of CedarCreek in 2014 led them to focus entirely on Greata Ranch.

"We had always bemoaned the fact that Greata did not get the attention we thought it deserved," says Gordon, who had also been CedarCreek's president. "My main focus was the brand at CedarCreek, and most of the [Greata Ranch] grapes went into CedarCreek wines. With our winemakers, we discussed what they thought Greata's best suit was. They came back with no reservations to say sparkling. We have all of this Chardonnay and Pinot Noir. Given the site and the acidity, that would be a natural."

The vineyard is a cool site planted to varieties well suited for the sparkling wines. The Greata Ranch winery was closed for three years to develop a new 8,000-case winery and to age an inventory of traditional bottle-aged sparkling wines. Gordon had begun the preparations in 2012 when he asked Darryl Brooker, then CedarCreek's winemaker, to make the 380 cases of sparkling wine with which the new winery opened in 2017.

GORDON FITZPATRICK

"It is not just a wine brand," Gordon says. "I want to create a little bit of a lifestyle brand as well. That is why there is emphasis on what we are going to be doing on site, and the restaurant and the food, and the way we present. I want to see if we can cross over and create what I call luxury at play."

MY PICKS

The sparkling wines, all crisply dry, rival Champagne at half the price. And the excellent still wines are as appealing for their flavours as for their whimsical labels.

OPENED 2017

697 Highway 97 South
Peachland, BC V0H 1X9

T 250.767.2768

W fitzwine.com

Restaurant: Fitz Bistro,
open daily (except Tues.)
11–4 for lunch, and at
4 for happy hour and
dinner on Fri.

FORBIDDEN FRUIT WINERY

CAWSTON

Half the farms in the Similkameen Valley are organic producers, with Steve Venables and Kim Brind'Amour among the pioneers. Their 57-hectare (141-acre) property, most of it still an untouched ecological sanctuary, has been farmed organically since 1977 and has been making organic wine since 2005.

Steve and Kim are self-described members of the "back to the land" generation. He was born in Victoria in 1952 and grew up in Indiana, where his father was deputy coroner. After two years studying science in college, Steve moved to the Okanagan to work in orchards. In 1977, he purchased the Sumac Road property, then raw land. Kim was born in Hull in 1963, the daughter of a market gardener; she formerly operated a health food store in Keremeos.

Their 9-hectare (22-acre) orchard is dedicated to tree fruit, including an astonishing 60 varieties of organic fruit that command premium prices. The winery was created initially to process so-called seconds (fruit with a less-than-perfect appearance). Steve and co-winemaker Nathan Venables (their son) now dip into all of the produce because the portfolio has quadrupled. It has about 20 products including fruit wines and ciders. The winery makes grape wines in its Earth Series and shares the proceeds with environmental causes. Other grape wines are made under the Dead End label, created by Nathan.

Only a kilometre or so from the highway, this winery is a refuge at the dead end of a narrow winding road down into the valley. The trees, including the majestic fir tree by the tasting room that Steve planted more than 35 years ago, provide shade on hot days. The tasting room is also the art gallery where Kim sells her attractive pottery, jewellery, and paintings. Nathan, who is a Red Seal carpenter by trade, also has begun making creative furnishings from wine barrels.

STEVE VENABLES

OPENED 2005

620 Sumac Road
Cawston, BC V0X 1C3

T   250.499.2649
     1.855.499.2649 (toll-free)
W   forbiddenfruitwines.com
Picnic area

MY PICKS

From dry to sweet, there are fruit wines for every palate. Pearsuasion, an oak-aged dry wine made from Asian pears, has delicious flavours of spice and ginger. Adam's Apple is a dry apple wine easily paired with main courses, while Pomme Desiree is a luscious dessert wine with six apple varieties. Crushed Innocence is a delicately pure expression of white peaches. The tour de force among the Mistelles (fortified wines) is Cerise d'Eve, a port-style cherry wine. The grape wines are equally well made, notably Cabernet Sauvignon, Merlot, and a Bordeaux blend called Redemption.

FORT BERENS ESTATE WINERY

LILLOOET

With a flair for history, Dutch immigrants Rolf de Bruin and Heleen Pannekoek named their winery after an 1859 Hudson's Bay Company trading post that was never completed. In contrast, their $7.5-million winery, completed in 2014, anchors one of British Columbia's newest wine regions.

Trained in economics and finance at the University of Groningen, the couple left high-powered careers in the Netherlands to become wine growers. "One of the primary reasons why we chose to start a vineyard was that we could not foresee ourselves working in a corporate environment and having kids," Rolf says. They arrived in the Okanagan in 2008 with two young children. They found the cost of Okanagan vineyard land prohibitive. On the advice of viticulturist Richard Cleave, they leased property at the edge of Lillooet and planted 8 hectares (20 acres) of vines in 2009.

The vineyard was not entirely a shot in the dark. BC Electric Company planted grapes in the late 1960s on its experimental farm near Lillooet, managed by Robert Roshard. In 2005 his daughter, Christ'l Roshard, then Lillooet's mayor, planted a small test plot of vines to kick-start economic diversification. Two years later, the provincial government and the BC Grapegrowers' Association launched a multiyear viticultural trial at five vineyards near Lillooet. With the encouraging results from this project, Rolf and Heleen undertook a large-scale planting of vinifera. When that succeeded, they doubled the vineyard in 2018 and 2019.

Fort Berens bottled wine from the 2007 and 2008 vintages they had purchased—the owners needed something to sell when the winery opened—and sourced grapes from both the Okanagan and Similkameen while waiting for their vineyard to produce. Lillooet has proven well suited for grapes. The growing season

HELEEN PANNEKOEK AND ROLF DE BRUIN

is as hot, if not hotter, than Osoyoos. The wide diurnal swings between hot days and cool nights result in full-flavoured grapes with good acidity. Merlot, Cabernet Franc, Pinot Noir, Pinot Gris, Chardonnay, Riesling, and even Cabernet Sauvignon and Grüner Veltliner are successful here.

With its excellent wines and its restaurant, Fort Berens is giving Lillooet the economic lift that Christ'l Roshard was seeking in 2005. Four other vineyards and a second winery have since been established in the Lillooet region. A two-hour drive north of Whistler, Lillooet (population 2,300), dramatically sited beside the Fraser River, no longer is too remote for wine touring.

MY PICKS

Everything, including the flagship reserves, White Gold Chardonnay, and Red Gold, a Bordeaux blend.

OPENED 2009

1881 Highway 99 North
PO Box 758
Lillooet, BC V0K 1V0
T   250.256.7788
1.877.956.7768 (toll-free)
W   fortberens.com
Restaurant: Ethical Table

FOUR SHADOWS VINEYARD & WINERY

PENTICTON

Wilbert and Joka Borren, both immigrants from the Netherlands, are nothing if not industrious. Wilbert was a 20-year-old graduate of an agriculture college when he arrived to work on an Alberta dairy farm. He met Joka in 1990, shortly after she arrived in Canada. In 1993, after the couple married, Wilbert concluded that the rising cost of milk quotas prevented him from realizing a dream of his own dairy. So he bought a hog farm near Lacombe, Alberta. "It took some persuading," Joka admits.

When they tired of hogs and hard winters, they moved to the Okanagan in 2011, now with four sons, to become grape growers. They bought the bankrupt Mistral Estate Winery and its 4.9 hectares (12 acres) of neglected vineyard on the eastern edge of Penticton. Wilbert made up for his lack of experience by engaging viticultural consultant Graham O'Rourke, co-owner of nearby Tightrope Winery. "I am a farmer," Wilbert says. "Stepping into the wine business is a new game."

Within a few years, Graham suggested that Wilbert did not need help anymore. Four Shadows Vineyard—a name inspired by the four Borren sons—was selling quality fruit to such top-flight wineries as Foxtrot Vineyards and Synchromesh Wines. "It was never our intention to start a winery," Wilbert says. "But then we were selling grapes [to wineries] that were all making good wines. People started to ask why we were not making our own wine." Once again, they overcame winemaking inexperience by turning to consultants. Tightrope's Lyndsay O'Rourke made the Four Shadows wines in 2017, and Pascal Madevon, formerly the Osoyoos Larose winemaker, took over in 2018.

The former Mistral tasting room, empty nearly a decade, was professionally renovated: one of their sons is a carpenter, while another, a welder, fashioned the winery's unique steel signage.

WILBERT AND JOKA BORREN

Four Shadows opened in May 2019 with five wines, well made and well priced. Cautiously, the vineyard continues to sell some grapes to other wineries. "We are starting small so we can just ease into it," Joka says. "And we can expand if it goes well."

MY PICKS

Everything, notably the Riesling, the Pinot Noir, and the refreshing rosé, made with Pinot Noir and Merlot.

OPENED 2019

250 Upper Bench Road
Penticton, BC V2A 8T1

T   250.493.3625

W   fourshadowsvineyard.com

Accommodation: The
Four Shadows Guest
House

FOXTROT VINEYARDS

NARAMATA

Burgundian in style and sophistication, Foxtrot Vineyards Pinot Noir has been sought out by collectors since the first vintages came to market. New Yorkers Douglas Barzelay and Nathan Todd bought the winery in 2018 from founder Torsten Allander, having tasted the wine with a private collector in Vancouver.

The winery was conceived after Torsten, a Swedish-born pulp and paper engineer, and his wife, Kicki, retired in 2002 to a 1.4-hectare (3½-acre) property on Naramata Road planted entirely with Clone 115 Pinot Noir. Two years later, they arranged to have the nearby Lake Breeze winery make wine with the grapes, in a trial that spanned three vintages. Convinced that the vineyard could produce world-class Pinot Noir, Torsten built a modest winery and engaged his son, Gustav, as winemaker. They also planted two adjoining vineyards to triple Foxtrot's size.

Inspired by their Vancouver tasting, Douglas, a retired lawyer, and his business partner in a wine brokerage, Nathan, bought a small peach orchard beside Foxtrot. When they engaged Gustav for viticultural advice, they discovered that Foxtrot itself was for sale. It was an opportunity they could not turn down. Nathan was born in Calgary and has family members living in the Okanagan. Douglas is an authority on, and collector of, Burgundy wines. He is co-author of *Burgundy Vintages: A History from 1845*, published in 2018. He was also an expert witness at the trial of Burgundy counterfeiter Rudy Kurniawan.

Gustav continues to make the Foxtrot wines. Douglas and Nathan also dipped into their Burgundy contacts to engage a consultant, Véronique Drouhin, the head winemaker of the renowned Maison Joseph Drouhin in Burgundy and Domaine

Drouhin in Oregon. Her involvement should ensure that Foxtrot Vineyards, producing 3,000 to 4,000 cases a year, gets the international recognition that the wines deserve.

MY PICKS

*Everything.
The winery's two Pinot
Noirs and its Chardonnay
are elegant and deeply
flavoured.*

OPENED 2007

1201 Gawne Road
Naramata, BC V0H 1N1
T   250.496.5082
W   foxtrotwine.com
Visits and tastings by
appointment

FRENCH DOOR ESTATE WINERY

OLIVER

The name of this winery comes from an insight Audra and Jason Shull once had while wine touring in Provence. "Why are we even here?" Jason said to his family. "We have Provence in our backyard." That led them to think of their winery on Black Sage Road as their door on French wine country. "The lavenders, the lake, the orchards, the vineyards . . . it is identical," Jason says.

The couple had grown up in Osoyoos where they had been high school sweethearts. They had pursued careers away from wine country but always with a desire to get back. Jason, who formerly ran a Vancouver-based firm called Golden Capital Securities, once put in a bid with some partners for Hester Creek Estate Winery when it was in a court auction.

Now, Jason can look across the Okanagan Valley at Hester Creek. In 2019, he and Audra took over the former Montakarn Winery on Black Sage Road. "I like this side of the valley better," he says. "The vineyard has a southern exposure."

After an extensive renovation of both the winery and the 2.8-hectare (7-acre) vineyard, the property is set to reopen in 2020 as French Door Estate Winery, with wines made by winemaker Pascal Madevon. He has become a legend in the Okanagan since coming from France in 2001 as the initial winemaker at Osoyoos Larose. He left there after 10 vintages and has consulted extensively. He was recommended to Jason by a friend, Vancouver wine merchant Jim Williamson, who interviewed 10 candidates for French Door.

"It is a lovely project," Pascal said in 2019. "I am totally involved in the winemaking and in the vineyard management of this winery." In his first vintage at French Door, Pascal made a rosé in the style of Provence. The vineyard grows four reds—Malbec, Merlot, Cabernet Franc, and Syrah—and three whites—Viognier,

AUDRA AND JASON SHULL

WINEMAKING CONSULTANT
PASCAL MADEVON

Chardonnay, and Sauvignon Blanc. Pascal fermented the whites in barrel and is aging the reds in oak. "We have a lot of diversity at this time, and that is interesting," the winemaker says.

MY PICKS

Current range not tasted.

PROPOSED
OPENING 2020

5462 Black Sage Road
Oliver, BC V0H 1T1

T TBA

W frenchdoorwinery.com

FREQUENCY WINERY

KELOWNA

This winery is operated by Anthony Lewis, a musician whose parents, Wyn and Marion, own the Vibrant Vine nearby. The distinguishing feature of Anthony's winery is that it is a recording studio, free to whatever artists wish to record there. He calls it a "sound infusion studio" because he infuses the wines with sound. Recently, Anthony and his father have been putting wines in cans. The Frequency brand is called "99 Bands in a Can."

Anthony was born in California in 1980. Frequency reflects his previous careers as a rock musician and music producer. A fan of both the Grateful Dead and the Beatles, he once had his own band. "It was called Storytime," he says. "The last show we played was the Ford Amphitheatre in Hollywood. Three sold-out nights." He moved from touring to producing music.

"I have recorded many albums for different people," he says. "I was a music producer, started up recording studios, and worked for record labels. In my last position before I moved to Kelowna, I was a music producer with a large facility in Colorado. We did radio acts, TV commercials. I got deep into that, and that is really where the winemaking comes from because it is totally the same thing." At his father's suggestion, he came to Kelowna to help develop the Vibrant Vine's vineyard. Soon, he was seduced by the challenge of winemaking, mentoring with the winemaking consultants retained by his parents' winery.

"We give you the whole sonic experience of wine," he says of Frequency. "It is designed to be fun. We are trying to provide memorable experiences for people who come to visit the Okanagan." Frequency, based on a 4.9-hectare (12-acre) vineyard, makes Pinot Noir and Gewürztraminer, as well as a sparkling wine.

Current range not tasted.

OPENED 2014

3210 Gulley Road
Kelowna, BC V1W 4E5

T 250.868.3737
W frequencywinery.com

FRIND ESTATE WINERY

WEST KELOWNA

The experience here begins with an arrow-straight tree-lined driveway, sweeping by a 2.4-hectare (6-acre) block of Maréchal Foch and leading to the rambling tasting room beside Okanagan Lake. This is a property with history. For more than 50 years, it belonged to the Bennett family: both W.A.C. Bennett and his son, Bill, served as premiers of British Columbia. In the fall of 2017, when Markus Frind began planning a major winery, he purchased the 5.5-hectare (13½-acre) Bennett property because it is strategically on the Westside Wine Trail, which is travelled by thousands of wine lovers each year. For several years, Markus expects to sell the Frind wines primarily from this wine shop.

This property is the tip of the iceberg of one of the Okanagan's most ambitious wineries. Markus also owns about 400 hectares (1,000 acres) of vineyard land that is being developed so that it can be farmed, in large measure, with self-driving machinery. If this succeeds, it will represent a breakthrough of precision agriculture amid Okanagan vineyards—by a winery owner whose initial success was in technology, with a dating website called Plenty of Fish.

Born in Germany in 1978, Markus was just four when his parents, descended from generations of farmers, moved to a 485-hectare (1,200-acre) farm at Hudson's Hope in northeastern British Columbia. After high school, Markus studied business and computer science at the British Columbia Institute of Technology. Then he had a series of technology jobs until, early in 2003, he created Plenty of Fish on his home computer. The website's success was explosive: by the second year, it was generating monthly revenues of $200,000 a month. Markus sold the site at its peak in 2015 for US$575 million.

By then, he already had a summer place near the Westside

WINEMAKER ERIC VON KROSIGK   MARKUS FRIND

Wine Trail and was a patron of the wineries. After reviewing wineries that might be for sale, he decided he had to start his own to achieve the scale of a major producer. Just before buying the Bennett property, he purchased 121 hectares (300 acres) of raw land on a hillside northeast of Kelowna. Advised that just 10% was suitable for vines, he deployed heavy equipment to fill in a gully and sculpt the slopes so that 80% could be planted. He also owns twice as much undeveloped land near Vernon, along with small vineyards in the south and central Okanagan.

The major varieties Frind is planting are Pinot Noir, Chardonnay, Riesling, Pinot Meunier, and Regent, a cool-climate German red hybrid new to the Okanagan. Typical of Markus, he is making a bold statement by planting 30 hectares (75 acres). Eric von Krosigk, Frind's veteran winemaker, suggests that Regent produces wines recalling full-bodied Italian reds.

MY PICKS

Frind debuted with excellent whites, including two Chardonnays, two Rieslings, a Viognier, and a well-made Pinot Noir.

OPENED 2019

3725 Boucherie Road
West Kelowna, BC V4T 0A8
T   778.754.7444 (tasting room)
    604.336.9850 (office)
W frindwinery.com

GEHRINGER BROTHERS ESTATE WINERY

OLIVER

There is a definite house style here, with wines that are youthfully vibrant and bursting with flavour. The winery releases both its white and red wines in the year after harvest, at their maximum freshness. For more than a decade now, all bottles have been flushed with nitrogen before being filled and then closed with screw caps that lock in the fresh flavours. Walter and Gordon Gehringer choose not to age their wines in oak barrels, again to preserve the pristine flavours. "These wines are better on their own," Walter says.

The brothers are Oliver-born sons of German immigrants. When their family conceived this winery in 1973, Walter, who had just completed high school, was sent to Geisenheim University, Germany's leading wine school, to become its first Canadian graduate. Gordon, his younger brother, also got his training in Germany, in Weinsberg. A generation later, Walter's son, Brendon, went to Australia for his winemaker training. He has worked for several years at Kellermeister winery in the Barossa Valley while deciding whether or not to return to the Gehringer cellar.

The winery's 10.5-hectare (26-acre) vineyard occupies a peninsula of glacial soil, sloping toward the east and the south. The shade from the mountains to the west shields the grapes from severe afternoon heat, allowing them to preserve fruity flavours and fresh acidity as they ripen. The terroir is especially suited to the winery's aromatic white wines, notably Riesling, Pinot Gris, Gewürztraminer, Schönburger, Auxerrois, and Sauvignon Blanc. The vineyard produces most of the grapes the Gehringers need to make about 30,000 cases each year.

For many years, the Gehringer whites usually had noticeable natural sweetness, much like many German whites. More recently, the wines have been finished dry or close to it, Walter

alertly having picked up changes in consumer preferences during his stints serving wine in the Gehringer tasting room. The house style consistently is attuned to popular tastes without any loss of finesse in the wines. The proof is in the winery's awards, particularly in a "Platinum" competition open only to wines of the Pacific Northwest that have already won gold in other competitions. Few wineries have as many Platinum awards (78 to the end of 2018) as Gehringer Brothers.

MY PICKS

All the wines are value priced. My favourite whites include the zesty Sauvignon Blanc, the peachy Chardonnay, and the elegant Pinot Gris. Flagship whites are the Rieslings (including the Icewine) and the Old Vines Auxerrois. The budget-priced red here is Summer Night, a soft, easy-drinking blend of Cabernet Franc and Pinot Noir.

OPENED 1986

876 Road 8
Oliver, BC V0H 1T1
T 250.498.3537
W gehringerwines.ca

GIANT HEAD ESTATE WINERY

SUMMERLAND

The impetus for Giant Head Estate Winery was several bottles of Gevrey-Chambertin, a Pinot Noir from the *premier cru* appellation of Clos Saint-Jacques that John Glavina and Jinny Lee enjoyed during a 1998 Burgundy vacation. As they were leaving Burgundy, John turned to his wife and said, "I have a strong feeling we are going to have a vineyard one day." In 2015, they opened this winery, which is named for the stubby extinct volcano that looms over Summerland.

John, who was born in Montreal in 1960, earned a computer science degree in 1985 from Simon Fraser University before starting a career with IBM. Eventually, he launched his own technology company, based for several years in Oregon where visits to Willamette Valley wineries nourished the affection for Pinot Noir that had started in Burgundy.

"Jinny likes to farm," John says of his wife, an electrical engineer whom he met at SFU. "We put an offer on a farm in 1995 before I went down to Portland, an organic farm near Pemberton. The deal fell through. It was always in the back of mind to find something for Jinny to farm." Finally, in 2002, the couple and their two children moved to the Okanagan and, two years later, bought an apple orchard near Summerland, which they converted to vineyard.

They grow Pinot Noir, Merlot, Gewürztraminer, and—for blending with the latter—about 100 vines of Riesling. They began selling grapes when their vineyard came into production. John began making Pinot Noir and Merlot for personal consumption in 2008. "It is hard to live in a vineyard and not make wine," he says. He made the first commercial vintage for Giant Head in 2014.

JOHN GLAVINA

MY PICKS

Everything, especially the Pinot Noir and the Blanc de Noir sparkling wine.

OPENED 2015

4307 Gartrell Road
Summerland, BC V0H 1Z4

T   250.460.0749

W   giantheadwinery.com

GOLD HILL WINERY

OSOYOOS

Gold Hill's first vintage was 2009. Cautiously, owners Sant and Gurbachan Gill sold all their grapes in 2010, making no wine as they awaited the consumer verdict on the wines before fully committing themselves to wine production. They realized that they had been overly cautious after their 2009 Cabernet Franc won a Lieutenant Governor's Award for Excellence, validating their winery and drawing a rush of consumers. Gold Hill's reputation was sealed a few years later with a second LG award for the 2012 Meritage.

Theirs is a heartwarming immigrant success story. They both grew up in the Indus Valley, a fruit-growing region in northwest India with a climate somewhat similar to the Okanagan. Sant, born in 1958, arrived in the Okanagan in 1984 with six dollars. Gurbachan, born in 1967, followed him in 1989. After a few years of orchard work, the brothers in 1991 began working in vineyards as well as farming an orchard they bought in 1995 beside the highway north of Osoyoos. When they had mastered grape growing, they converted their orchard to vineyards in 2007. Today, they farm more than 26 hectares (65 acres) throughout the Okanagan Valley.

To make the wines—for the Gill brothers do not drink—they recruited Philip Soo, a highly regarded Okanagan consulting winemaker. The Gold Hill wines, especially the reds, deliver bold flavours with robust alcohol levels. It reflects how the brothers farm their grapes on the steep vineyard behind the gold-hued adobe-style winery. The steep slope affords good sun exposure for the vines, with the rock-laden soil at the top also serving as a heat sink. The Gills get optimal ripeness by limiting the size of the crop and stressing the plants with sparse watering, so that the vines produce small, intensely flavoured grapes. "We really want to develop all the flavours that we can on the vine," says Navi Gill,

GURBACHAN AND SANT GILL

Gurbachan's son. "Phil makes the call. He will taste the grapes for the flavour. That's when we harvest. The sugars can be 27, 28 Brix. We don't pay attention to the sugars. We want the flavours."

Even the Cabernet Franc rosé reaches 15% alcohol in warm vintages. The winery developed a following for a deeply coloured rosé first made in 2011 after Gurbachan accidentally left a ton of grapes on the skins for two days instead of one. The consumer acceptance was so strong that, in 2012, the grapes were left on the skins for three days. Consumers loved the wine, but with dark rosés out of fashion, critics panned it, and Gold Hill has made a lighter, more mainstream rosé since 2016.

MY PICKS

Everything, including the lightly oaked Chardonnay, the flavour-packed rosé, and the reds—notably the Cabernet Franc and the elegant Grand Vin Meritage.

OPENED 2011

3502 Fruitvale Way
Osoyoos, BC V0H 1T1
T   250.495.8152
W goldhillwinery.com

GRANITE BLUFF ESTATE WINERY

OLIVER

Trevor Hammond's interest in plants began when, shortly after high school, he worked for the horticulture department at the University of Guelph. "I learned more there than I would have if I had spent thousands to be their student," he says. "All of the professors were my bosses." That set him on a path to succeed as a viticulturist and ultimately to launch Granite Bluff Estate Winery.

Born in Collingwood, Ontario, in 1978, he was still in high school when his mother moved the family to the Okanagan. When he returned to the valley after his stint in horticulture, the choice was working in orchards or in vineyards. Grapevines won out because there were no ladders to climb. In 1998, he began working in Tinhorn Creek's vineyards, starting a two-decade-long career in viticulture that ultimately had him teaching that program at Okanagan College.

His skills are not entirely self-taught. He studied viticulture at the college in 1999; a decade later, he took the college's winemaking course. He did not have a winery in mind at the time. He just wanted to communicate more effectively with the winemakers when they came to the vineyards where he worked. Along the way, Trevor has worked with such influential mentors as Bill Eggert at Fairview Cellars and winemaker Michael Bartier. Michael and he met at Road 13 Vineyards when Trevor worked there from 2005 to 2010. Granite Bluff made its debut 500 cases in 2018 at the Bartier Bros. winery under Michael's supervision.

The Granite Bluff winery is established on a property owned by Trevor's partner, Naomi Garrish. The previous owner had stabled horses there and left behind a barn, which Trevor, after teaching himself carpentry, renovated into a serviceable and rustically attractive winery. "Building a big fancy winery and a million-dollar tasting room is not what I envision," Trevor says.

TREVOR HAMMOND

"For me, that is not honest and genuine. The image I want to stick with here is natural—as natural as I can possibly be, by retaining what is already there."

The modest vineyard was planted in 2018 with Gamay Noir, Pinot Blanc, and Sauvignon Blanc. Trevor also has leased several other properties growing such varieties as Petite Sirah, Tempranillo, Merlot, Cabernet Franc, and Cabernet Sauvignon. With Trevor continuing to manage other vineyards, Granite Bluff's business plan is to remain small, producing sparkling wine and small-lot offerings that will vary from vintage to vintage.

MY PICKS

Current range not tasted.

PROPOSED
OPENING 2020

793 Secrest Hill Road
Oliver, BC V0H 1T5
T 250.689.1037
W facebook.com/
granitebluffestatewinery.ca

GRAY MONK ESTATE WINERY

LAKE COUNTRY

Gray Monk was one of the first estate wineries in BC when it released its first vintage in 1981. The tenacious efforts of founders George and Trudy Heiss in navigating the government bureaucracy, which was not always ready or able to deal with an industry as multifaceted as a winery, are truly the bedrock on which this winery's history sits. The Heisses prevailed, and Gray Monk has grown to become one of BC's most recognizable wine brands by breaking new ground within the province's wine and culinary scene.

George was the son of a hairdresser in Vienna and apprenticed with him before moving to Canada. Trudy came from Rostock in the former East Germany, which her parents fled in 1947 before settling in Edmonton in 1952. In 1961, Trudy met George while working as a model with pink hair at a hair colouring show at the Fairmont Hotel Macdonald in Edmonton. They worked at salons until moving to the Okanagan in 1971. They bought property to develop a vineyard next door to where Trudy's parents had bought three years earlier. They began planting the vineyard in 1972 and making wine in 1980.

The property has grown and evolved in the 40 years since. The Heisses' influence as a pioneering winery in BC helped to shape the modern industry. They were the first to plant major Alsatian grape varieties, Pinot Gris, Gewürztraminer, and Auxerrois. They contributed to the Becker Project, which was a significant large-scale trial of vinifera grape varieties in the Okanagan that finished in 1985.

Gray Monk's well-rehearsed hospitality experience includes a large tasting room, self-guided tours, and a restaurant called the Lookout Restaurant at Gray Monk, which features beautiful panoramic views of Okanagan Lake.

GRAY MONK ESTATE WINERY

In October of 2017, George and Trudy retired and sold Gray Monk to Andrew Peller Ltd. The new owners, recognizing how successful the winery has been, have maintained the portfolio.

MY PICKS

All of the wines here are well made. Standout varieties include Pinot Gris, Rotberger (a rare natural rosé grape), and Pinot Noir. The award-winning Odyssey sparkling wines are excellent value. The Latitude 50 series are affordable entry-level wines.

OPENED 1982

1055 Camp Road
Lake Country, BC
V4V 2H4

T   250.766.3168
    1.800.663.4205 (toll-free)

W   graymonk.com
    Restaurant: The Lookout
    (250.766.3168, option 3)

GRIZZLI WINERY

WEST KELOWNA

Alone among the wineries along busy Boucherie Road in West Kelowna, the imposing Grizzli Winery is visible from both that road and from Highway 97. The winery was located strategically to attract wine tourists—and they come by the busload.

Grizzli is owned by John Chang and Lan-Fed (Allison) Lu, who immigrated to Canada from Taiwan in 1995. They began making wine at home in 1996 from Fraser Valley berries, inspired by the fruit wines that John's grandmother had made. They opened Blossom Winery in a Richmond strip mall in 2001 with a portfolio of fruit wines. In 2008, they moved this to the much grander Lulu Island Winery, also in Richmond, and focused on Icewines for the export market. Amy Chang, the couple's daughter, has been at the helm of both wineries since 2016. The family also owns another winery in Ontario called Lailey Winery in Niagara-on-the-Lake.

Construction on the Grizzli winery started in 2014 with the winery opening in the fall of 2016. The sprawling complex includes both the production facilities and the extensive hospitality area. Current wines are produced both here and at Lulu Island, with most table wines and Icewines done here. The family farms 81 hectares (200 acres) in the Okanagan and Fraser Valleys.

Grizzli's 20,000-square-foot wine shop is one of the biggest in the valley. Bright and welcoming, it has large wine displays as well as displays of local art. The wine shop can easily accommodate up to 400 wine tourists at a time, not including the VIP area. The long tasting bar allows for a comfortable wine experience regardless of group size. The friendly multilingual staff can do tours in English, French, Mandarin, Cantonese, and German.

GRIZZLI WINERY

The Special Reserve Cabernet Franc stands out among the reds. The fruit wines are uniquely aromatic. Icewines are the real strength here, particularly the expressive Sauvignon Blanc and Gewürztraminer Icewines.

OPENED 2016

2550 Boucherie Road
West Kelowna, BC V1Z 2E6

T 250.769.6789

W grizzliwinery.com

HAINLE VINEYARDS ESTATE WINERY

PEACHLAND

Tucked against the side of a forested mountain, Hainle Vineyards has been threatened several times by forest fires. In September 2012, a raging fire damaged a vineyard, coming close enough to burn the roof and scorch the siding. "Someone asked me what I would do if the winery burns down," Walter Huber, the winemaker and former owner, remembers. "I would just rebuild."

Walter, who was born in Munich in 1959, began developing vineyards near Peachland in 1991, buying this winery in 2002 from the legendary Hainle family. The late Walter Hainle and his German-trained winemaker son, Tilman, began making Canada's first Icewines in the 1970s. Some of the inventory passed to Walter Huber when he bought the winery. When a bottle of the rare 1978 Icewine (the winery's first commercial production) was stolen from his truck, Walter considered insuring his remaining bottle for $1 million. He has retained Icewine as one of this winery's specialties.

It is hardly surprising that Walter is deeply influenced by traditional European methods. He puts sub-appellations, like "Appellation Peachland," on his labels even though they are not yet sanctioned in British Columbia. He makes wines in accordance with an 1856 wine-purity law that echoes the famous Bavarian beer-purity laws of 1516. And he prefers wines that are well aged.

"Because of the fire, we have to release some of the wines early for cash flow," Walter told me in the summer of 2013, as painters were restoring the winery's siding. "But I don't really like doing that. I like to release my whites when they are three to five years old, and my reds when they are seven to ten years old. What we are doing is old-style European wine aging. The excise officer said we have a bigger library of old wines than Mission Hill and Jackson-Triggs together." Destruction by fire would have been an incredible tragedy.

WALTER HUBER

In 2016 Walter sold the winery to Bella Craft, a company owned by Chinese businessmen. Ambitious to double production from the 15,000 cases made in 2019, the new owners are scouting the Okanagan for vineyard property. They also plan a new winery and tasting room.

MY PICKS

The Pinot Noirs are powerful, yet elegant. The blended reds, some with Bordeaux varieties and some based on Zweigelt, are bold. Lovers of older wines will be drawn to the library wines here, especially the mature dry Riesling.

OPENED 1988

5355 Trepanier Bench Road
Peachland, BC V0H 1X2

T 250.767.2525

W hainle.com

HARPER'S TRAIL ESTATE WINERY

KAMLOOPS

What makes this vineyard special is the same thing that has enabled Lafarge to operate a cement plant nearby since 1970: the underlying limestone in the area, which is quarried for cement but also benefits grape growing. Ed Collett, who owns Harper's Trail with his wife, Vicki, points to the cliff above the south-sloping vineyards. "That whole side hill is lime rock," he says.

This property on the north side of the Thompson River is about 16 kilometres east of Kamloops. Formerly, it grew hay and grazed cattle in what is quintessential British Columbia range country. The winery is named for Thaddeus Harper, the 19th-century American-born rancher who once owned the vast 15,569-hectare (38,472-acre) Gang Ranch, one of the first farms to use sturdy gang plows. Ed bought his modest slice of ranch country in 2007 after he had conceived the idea of developing a winery. He developed a taste for wine during travels to Chile on business for the mining-equipment company he established in 1987.

The desire for a winery emerged during Okanagan wine tours. Ed remembers relaxing at a bed and breakfast overlooking a vineyard and remarking, "I've got to get myself one of these." He began planting vines in 2008. He currently has 10.7 hectares (26½ acres) of vines and has plans for more in stages as he determines what varieties will succeed. "You have to take baby steps," Ed notes. "We are further north [than most vineyards], but obviously, it is not a deterrent for us." The cold winters led to the removal of Merlot, while a 2008 planting of Cabernet Franc succeeded so well that more was planted in 2012 and 2018, with 2.4 hectares (6 acres) of Pinot Noir and Gamay Noir in 2013. Riesling, Pinot Gris, and Chardonnay also are succeeding. Bacchus may also be planted. Wind machines combat early autumn frost.

ED AND VICKI COLLETT

Ginseng shade cloth on the vineyard's borders breaks the valley's constant winds. Propane cannons deter the birds.

The first several vintages, which included three different Rieslings, Chardonnay, Pinot Gris, Gewürztraminer, a white blend, a rosé, and a Cabernet Franc, were made for Harper's Trail at Okanagan Crush Pad in Summerland. A tasting room opened at the vineyard in the summer of 2013. The temporary winemaking facility used for that vintage was replaced in 2014 by a new production facility. There is a picnic patio, but plans for a restaurant remain on hold because, in 2019, the Colletts were entertaining offers to purchase their successful winery.

MY PICKS

The limestone terroir gives an elegant discipline to all the wines, especially the Rieslings. The delicious Silver Mane Block Riesling is an off-dry Mosel-style wine, while the Pioneer Block Riesling is austerely dry. The Cabernet Franc is a juicy, full-flavoured red.

OPENED 2012

2761 Shuswap Road East
Kamloops, BC V2H 1S9
T 250.573.5855
W harperstrail.com
Picnic patio

THE HATCH

The name The Hatch is appropriate for this winery: several wineries and brands have been hatched under this licence, including Black Swift, Screaming Frenzy, and Crown & Thieves. Black Swift and associated label Screaming Frenzy moved in 2016 to the new Black Swift winery, not far away on Boucherie Road. Crown & Thieves, owned by Jason Parkes, the winemaker who crafts all these brands, is scheduled to move to a new vineyard in West Kelowna.

Wine tourists need not fear that The Hatch will be hollowed out after this flock of labels leaves. The Hatch still produces an extensive portfolio under its Hobo, Talking Stories, and Gobsmacked series, and offers them with breezy informality in one of the least pretentious tasting rooms in the Okanagan. The tasting room has the décor of an old machine shop, with such items as historic wine bottles displayed casually to enhance the informality. There is even a small museum display of old blacksmithing tools in the corner. The barnwood chic is part of the branding image, as well as the charm, of The Hatch. The retro vibe of the wine shop, enhanced by the youthful enthusiasm of tasting-room staff, seems to attract a younger patronage than is found in more conventional wine shops.

The Hatch and its sister wineries, including Perseus in Penticton, are all owned by Terrabella Wineries, a holding company. The concept has been to create small and distinctive winery brands, with fruit from contracted growers throughout the Okanagan and Similkameen Valleys as well as from vineyards owned by the wineries. The Hatch is based on a mature vineyard acquired by Terrabella in 2013 from growers who were retiring. The 7.3-hectare (18-acre) property, formerly known as the Sunrise Vineyard, primarily grows Pinot Blanc and Gamay Noir. Early plans called for naming the winery Helios, the Greek god that carried the sun. Wiser heads prevailed in branding it The Hatch.

Jason Parkes, born in Kitimat in 1971, is the winemaker behind all of the labels and has one of the more colourful résumés in the industry. He led a "space punk" rock band called Glasshead and currently leads a New Wave band called Proper Man. Between bands, he took a vineyard job at Hainle Vineyards that led to a flourishing winemaking career, both with the Terrabella group and as a consultant for several other producers.

MY PICKS

All wines are solid and well made, though not always traditional in style. Life Cycle of a Hobo is an excellent white made from Müller-Thurgau, a variety being rescued from obscurity by The Hatch. The Dynasty blends, both white and red, are well crafted.

OPENED 2015

3225 Boucherie Road
West Kelowna, BC V1Z 4E4
T   778.755.6013
W   thehatchwines.com

HEAVEN'S GATE ESTATE WINERY

SUMMERLAND

"It started out as a family joke," says winemaker and co-owner Tyson Felt about how he came to be a winemaker at this beautiful Summerland winery. Originally grain farmers from Alberta, Tyson's parents had purchased a nearby property in 2015. They noticed that Heaven's Gate founders Andy and Diane Sarglepp had put the winery up for sale. They began suggesting purchasing the winery to their son, Tyson, whenever he visited the Okanagan for snowboarding, camping, or wine touring. Gradually the joke became a serious option. They looked at other wineries but in August 2017 purchased Heaven's Gate, and Tyson moved to Summerland from Edmonton. "What's the point of spending all this money going out there when I could spend money and live there?" recounts Tyson. "Except now I have no free time!"

Born in the Peace River region of Alberta, Tyson spent time in real estate before setting his sights on winemaking, which became an unexpected passion. He was a self-proclaimed "craft beer guy" before taking over Heaven's Gate but has quickly come to appreciate the art and science of winemaking. "I'm glad I went this direction because it's way more interesting than making beer," says Tyson. Taking over at Heaven's Gate meant that he didn't have to start from scratch. "This place is amazing! It needed some work on the business, but the property is great."

The business side needed an infusion of creativity. Although he had a new name picked out for the winery, Tyson wisely chose to retain the name Heaven's Gate, concluding that renaming would not be worth the cost of losing brand recognition. The new branding has changed only slightly while updating the labels quite elegantly.

The customer experience has also remained similar, with a large patio space with many umbrellas for shade. The wine shop

features the same Brazilian granite bar top, while outside the large water fountain is still a central feature for the winery experience. "They did a really good job setting this place up. They spent their money in the right places."

Tyson's quick study on winemaking paired with a fearless creativity has benefited the wine portfolio. For his second vintage in 2018, he produced a small batch of Gamay Noir in the *nouveau* style, which was released in early December. His Viognier and Gewürztraminer won major awards in the spring of 2019. His creativity doesn't stop there. He also has plans to create a wine that blends his interest in craft beer with his newfound love of winemaking.

MY PICKS

The award-winning Viognier is beautiful, and the Gamay Nouveau is worth a try.

OPENED 2011

8001 Happy Valley Road
Summerland, BC V0H 1Z4
T 778.516.5505
W heavensgatewinery.com

HERE'S THE THING VINEYARDS

OLIVER

Leah McDowell had been operating VQA wine stores for about 12 years when the British Columbia Wine Institute began transferring licences to Jim Pattison–owned Overwaitea Food Group's stores. "We'd never be able to compete with the Pattison Group," she remembers thinking. Earlier in her business career, she worked five years at one of those stores. Her manager then was Darrell Jones, who later became president of Overwaitea. Early in 2016, she telephoned him and sold her licences.

She and husband Jamie, a former distribution manager for a paper company, were looking for a business they could run together, when another vintner in the South Okanagan suggested they start a small winery. Fired up by the suggestion, she began sketching out winery names that evening on hotel stationery. Then she and Jamie engaged the help of winemaker Michael Bartier, who had worked at Road 13 Vineyards before opening the Bartier Bros. winery. Michael introduced them to the 4-hectare (10-acre) Rockpile Vineyard being sold by Road 13.

That gave the McDowell winery project a running start. Rockpile was originally planted in 2006, primarily with Cabernet Franc and Syrah, with smaller blocks of Gamay Noir, Viognier, and Roussanne. The property, which they took over after the 2016 harvest, has enough grapes to produce 3,000 cases a year. It also happens to be adjacent to the Bartier Bros. winery. Michael agreed to be winemaker for Here's The Thing and to process most of the fruit in his winery. Here's The Thing's two buildings, powered by solar panels, serve largely as a tasting room and barrel cellar.

Leah admires Viognier. "One of the first things I said to Michael is that I don't even know what Roussanne is. I am ripping it all out, and I am planting Viognier." The winemaker cautioned that they should first assess one vintage of Roussanne before

deciding whether to keep it. The wine proved to be excellent, and the vines remained. Experiences like that created a bond between the McDowells and their consultant. "Michael, Jamie, and I understand each other, and our goals are the same," Leah says. "It has been a great partnership for us, and we are proud to tell people that Michael is our winemaker."

The winery's name emerged from Leah's early jottings on hotel stationery. "We knew we would be a fairly small winery," she says. "What I was looking for was something fun and casual and laid back. I wanted to attract people with the name and the label—and then when they tasted the wine, they would know we are dead serious about good wine."

MY PICKS

Everything, notably the Roussanne, the Viognier, the Syrah, and the Cabernet/Merlot blend.

OPENED 2018

4740 Black Sage Road
Oliver, BC V0H 1T0
T 250.498.9712
W heresthethingvineyards.com

HESTER CREEK ESTATE WINERY

OLIVER

The winemakers at Hester Creek, Robert Summers and Mark Hopley, have a trick in blending The Judge, the flagship red since the first vintage in 2007. They add 15% of the previous vintage in each new vintage. In this way, they have a consistent house style "so our wine can be recognized as Hester Creek," Robert says.

The admirable consistency of Hester Creek wines begins in the 27-hectare (67-acre) vineyard, where some vines are more than 50 years old. Joe Busnardo, who immigrated to Canada in 1954 from Treviso in Italy and was the vineyard's original owner, planted only vinifera grapes. He was ahead of the times: second-rate hybrid varieties dominated Okanagan vineyards. When wineries refused to pay a premium for Joe's grapes, he opened his own Divino Estate Winery in 1983. When he sold the property in 1996 to move to Vancouver Island, the new owners renamed the winery after the creek on the south side of the vineyard.

Mismanagement drove Hester Creek into bankruptcy. The winery was purchased in 2004 by Curtis Garland, a Prince George businessman with the skill and resources to turn this into one of the valley's top wineries. He hired Robert, a veteran Ontario winemaker, and gave him the budget to design and equip a modern winery with the capacity to produce 60,000 cases a year.

Robert equipped the winery with 15 Ganimede fermenters from Italy, leading-edge technology for handling the red grapes gently. All of Hester Creek's reds are fermented in these vessels. That also accounts for the house style: fresh, fruit-driven wines with absolutely no harsh tannins.

The winemakers avoid the wild-yeast fermentation that has become fashionable elsewhere. "Rob and I prefer to know what we are getting," Mark says. "We have found some yeasts that we gravitate to and that work for us. I have done wild ferments. It is

ROB SUMMERS AND MARK HOPLEY

hard to get them dry. You can do it, but you never know what you are going to get. It is not the style we are going for here. We are just looking for food-driven wines and clean ferments."

The legacy of Joe Busnardo includes about one-seventh of a hectare (just over a third of an acre) of Trebbiano, an Italian white variety planted in 1968. Cuttings from those vines were used in 2005 to plant another 0.8 hectare (2 acres). So far, Hester Creek is the only Okanagan producer with Trebbiano in its portfolio. When another winery asked for vine cuttings, Hester Creek said no, determined to keep its monopoly on this exceptional wine as long as it can.

MY PICKS

Everything, especially The Judge and the Trebbiano. Value-conscious consumers should look for Character Red and Character White. Hester Creek wines sell out quickly. Good idea: join the 5,500-member wine club to get to the front of the line.

OPENED 1983 (AS DIVINO ESTATE WINERY)

877 Road 8
PO Box 1605
Oliver, BC V0H 1T1
T 250.498.4435
1.866.498.4435 (toll-free)
W hestercreek.com
Restaurant: Terrafina
(250.498.2229,
terrafinabyraudz.com)
Accommodation:
The Villa, with six
mountainside Tuscan-
style guest suites

HIDDEN CHAPEL WINERY

OLIVER

With wine names like White Wedding, Made of Honour, and Shotgun Wedding, the wines of Hidden Chapel appear to be marketed with kitschy matrimonial and religious symbols. It is not a gimmick. Weddings have been performed here for decades before the winery even existed.

The original owner, orchardist Bill Parsons, built the house and established gardens that became a setting for weddings. Parsons, with ties to the Summerland Research Station, had access to many different species of plants for the gardens. Though many of the trees and climbing vines that he planted were not native to the Okanagan, they are now firmly established and continue to grow successfully on the property.

The chapel at the back of the property was built by the second owner in the 1990s. Elizabeth Mengies was very religious and used the chapel for family services as well as weddings. The chapel has space for only six people comfortably in the pews (or eight uncomfortably) but is set back amongst the trees behind the garden. Hidden Chapel owner Deborah Wilde says that she meets people all of the time who got married on the property many years ago. "We had a couple renew their vows who were married here 20 years ago," Deborah says.

A savvy marketer, Deborah has been keenly interested in sales and marketing since opening her first business, a clothing store in Smithers, at the age of 21. In 1990, she moved to Kelowna, where she got into real estate, and slowly moved south through the Okanagan Valley. It was through working in real estate that she learned of the property that would become Hidden Chapel. It took four years from the moment she first saw the property until that deal was signed.

"It was the garden that attracted me," recalls Deborah, who has always enjoyed gardening. "It's a very peaceful place." Serenity in this part of the valley is not always available with Highway 97 not far away

DEBORAH WILDE

and a rifle range just around the corner, in addition to the mechanical sounds of agriculture in all directions. "There is a spiritual energy here," Deborah says. "People feel it. They sense it and they love it. And it's what drew me here too and kept me coming back."

Hidden Chapel's customers keep coming back too. The winery has a loyal following for its wines and many creative blends, which is apropos for the marriage theme. With small production and limited distribution, the winery's tasting room is the best way to get the wines. The wine shop has no tasting fees but accepts donations to South Okanagan Women in Need Society. One wine, Amazing Grace, is named after Deborah's sister, Grace, who passed away from cancer. The sales from that wine have been donated to the oncology department at the Penticton hospital, which recently expanded. "It's not all about making money," explains Deborah. "It's about giving back and being part of the community. As long as you can survive, everything's good."

MY PICKS

The whites are crisp, aromatic and approachable. The reds are all big and dark, being firmly rooted in Cabernet Sauvignon, which is the main variety grown on site. Look for Trilogy and Shotgun Wedding, which pairs Cab Sauvignon with Petit Verdot. The Holy Grail is a must-have for lovers of Cabernet Franc. The added bottle aging makes all of the reds appealingly smooth and vibrant.

OPENED 2010

482 Pinehill Road
Oliver, BC V0H 1T5
T 250.490.6000
W hiddenchapelwinery.com

HILLSIDE WINERY

PENTICTON

Among the delicious wines here, Duncan McCowan, the winery's president, singles out three flagship wines. There's Muscat Ottonel, the delicately spicy white wine, and Old Vines Gamay Noir, made with fruit from vines that were planted here in 1984 by Hillside's founders, Vera and Bohumir Klokocka. Mosaic is the elegant Bordeaux blend that was created in 2002 and, since the 2006 vintage, has been made only with Naramata Bench grapes.

Today, all of Hillside's wines are made with grapes grown in that sub-appellation. There is no stronger proponent of the Naramata Bench than Hillside winemaker Kathy Malone. Born in New York and with a chemistry degree from the University of Victoria, Kathy made wine at the giant Mission Hill for almost two dozen years before switching to Hillside in 2008 for a more "hands-on" cellar experience. Hillside owns or controls about 16 hectares (about 40 acres) of Naramata Bench vineyard, including a row of Cabernet Sauvignon planted by Vera in the 1980s. It is one of the first plantings of this variety in the Okanagan.

After Bohumir's death, Vera sold the winery, then operated from a heritage cottage, in 1996 to a Calgary businessman. In 1997, the new owner gave the Penticton architect Robert Mackenzie the first of his many commissions to design a winery. The winery's timber-frame design mirrors a gristmill, with a 22-metre tower looming over Naramata Road. When the winery went over budget, a large group of Alberta investors (as many as 95) took over in 1998 to complete the project and add the 160-seat bistro. Duncan, a wine-loving geologist and oil-industry entrepreneur and one of the 1998 investors, ultimately became the controlling shareholder.

Mosaic was first launched from the 2002 vintage. At a time when Bordeaux blends from Okanagan wineries still were rare, it was meant to burnish the winery's image. When Kathy took

DUNCAN MCCOWAN   KATHY MALONE

over as winemaker in 2008, the winery had already committed to using just Naramata grapes. "Before I came here, I would not have thought that was wise," Kathy says, having worked primarily with South Okanagan fruit at Mission Hill. She changed her mind at Hillside. "I love the type of ripeness we get on the Naramata Bench," she says. In the 2010 and 2011 vintages, Hillside lost one source of Naramata Bench Cabernet Franc. Rather than compromise on the winery's commitment to terroir, Kathy made those two vintages with no Cabernet Franc in the blend. That variety returned to the wine in 2012 when Hillside secured a new source.

MY PICKS

The Muscat Ottonel, the Gewürztraminer, and the Pinot Gris offer crisp and refreshing flavours. The winery's bold reds include the spicy Old Vines Gamay, the intense Reserve Merlot, and the peppery Syrah. The flagship Mosaic has a style quite reminiscent of fine Bordeaux.

OPENED 1990

1350 Naramata Road
Penticton, BC V2A 8T6

T   250.493.6274

W   hillsidewinery.ca
Restaurant: The Bistro at Hillside Winery, open for lunch and dinner mid-March through October

HOUSE OF ROSE WINERY

KELOWNA

House of Rose celebrated its 20th anniversary in 2013 by winning a double gold for its trademarked Winter Wine, judged the top dessert wine in the 2013 All Canadian Wine Championships. This medal, along with two golds, a silver, and a bronze at that spring's Northwest Wine Summit, indicates how much the wines have improved since Aura Rose and spouse Wouter van der Hall took charge in 2009.

The winery was founded by Aura's father, Vern Rose, a retired schoolteacher from Alberta. He bought this property in 1982 after a trip to New Zealand, where volunteering in a vineyard fired his interest in viticulture. He was one of very few Okanagan vintners who remained loyal to the heritage varieties that most others removed in the 1988 pullout. House of Rose still grows both Okanagan Riesling and De Chaunac in its 2.2-hectare (5½-acre) vineyard, along with Verdelet for Icewine and Maréchal Foch, almost the only red hybrid to make a comeback in British Columbia. Vern's winemaking style was eccentric; he often turned to creative blending to cover up the occasional oxidized wine. But he also was shrewd: when he began making Icewine, he could not use that term because he was not using VQA-eligible grapes. So he called it Winter Wine, promptly getting a trademark to keep the name exclusive to House of Rose.

His clientele loved him. Always garbed in a Tilley hat, Vern injected memorable enthusiasm into vineyard tours and marathon tastings. The summer of 2003, when Vern turned 76, sapped that enthusiasm after the Okanagan Mountain Park forest fire threatened his Rutland neighbourhood three times, forcing evacuation of the winery and sharply curtailing the usual number of visitors. He considered selling the winery, but before a buyer emerged, Vern was incapacitated by a stroke.

AURA ROSE

The winery stayed in the family when Aura stepped in. Aura, who ran her own health-care communications company, became involved with House of Rose in 1996 as the bookkeeper. She and Wouter, a Dutch-born child welfare consultant, refocused the sprawling wine portfolio at House of Rose and, as the medals show, brought a more settled style to the wines.

They have, however, not lost Vern's legendary panache for welcoming visitors. The anniversary celebrations included unveiling a 6-metre-high metal rose. Wouter maintains that it is the largest rose in Canada.

MY PICKS

The Maréchal Foch is one of the Okanagan's best. Many other wines here are still creative blends. Cool Splash is a fruity Riesling and Pinot Gris blend. Award-winning Hot Flash is a blend of Syrah, Maréchal Foch, and Pinot Gris sweet reserve. Sweet Mystery is an off-dry blend of Pinot Noir and Maréchal Foch. The varieties in Winter Wine White and Winter Wine Rosé are a winery secret.

OPENED 1993

2270 Garner Road
Kelowna, BC V1P 1E2
T 1.877.765.0802 (toll-free)
W houseofrose.ca
Picnic area

HOWLING BLUFF ESTATE WINES

PENTICTON

Others might rest on their oars after winning four Lieutenant Governor's Awards for Excellence, which is what Howling Bluff did during its first decade. Not proprietor Luke Smith. In 2018, he retained Pascal Madevon, a leading Okanagan consultant, for advice on viticulture and winery practices. "He is going to make us better at what we do," Luke explains. "In this industry, if you stand still, everybody is going to pass you."

Luke, whose mother, Lynda Smith, was secretary of the International Wine and Food Society's Vancouver chapter, became a stockbroker after getting a degree in economics. His interest in wine took him to the Okanagan in 2003 to convert a Naramata Bench orchard to vineyard by planting 15,000 vines. "Every single post put into the vineyard I have touched three times," he says. "I put the irrigation in. There is nothing here that I haven't done." He acquired winemaking knowledge by being mentored by consulting winemakers, notably Chris Carson, a Canadian trained in New Zealand, whose Pinot Noir passions soon rubbed off on Luke.

The initial plan was to make world-class wines with Bordeaux varieties. Luke did plant a small block of Pinot Noir just for the challenge of growing a variety reputed to be difficult. "There was never meant to be a Pinot here," he says. To his surprise, Howling Bluff's first major award was earned by his 2006 Pinot Noir. "Mother Nature was telling me that my vineyard makes a good Pinot Noir," he admits.

He replanted much of the 8-hectare (20-acre) vineyard. "Pinot Noir is one of the best wine [grapes] in the world," he says with a convert's conviction. "The most memorable wines I have ever had have been Pinot. What an incredible grape! You can make Champagne, table wine, and rosé. There is the magic and the versatility of the heartbreak grape."

LUKE SMITH

With his remaining varieties, Luke makes a small-lot Bordeaux red blend called Sin Cera, as well as Sauvignon Blanc and Sémillon. In the 2018 vintage, he also added a Pinot Gris from a three-year-old planting in his vineyard.

MY PICKS

Everything, especially the ultra-premium Century Block and Acta Vineyard Pinot Noirs.

OPENED 2007

1086 Three Mile Road
Penticton, BC V2A 8T7
T   250.490.3640
W   howlingbluff.ca

HUGGING TREE WINERY

CAWSTON

The bold red wines made here by Brad Makepeace reflect both his taste and the Similkameen terroir he works with. "There is so little space in Canada to ripen the big reds that it is a shame wasting the opportunity," he says. "It is not that I don't like lighter wines, but I have the ability to ripen Cabernet Sauvignon and Cabernet Franc here."

The winery is based on an 8-hectare (20-acre) vineyard planted entirely with Bordeaux reds, with a small block of Viognier. Syrah also was planted originally but failed because its location was too windblown. A Syrah planting is being considered on a more suitable site.

The winery was founded by Brad's parents, Walter and Cristine, both retired members of the RCMP. They bought this roadside organic fruit and vegetable farm in 2005, just before Walter retired, and added a vineyard.

Walter, who was born in Vancouver in 1953, joined the RCMP in 1975. When he retired, Walter was the staff sergeant in charge of the South Okanagan. Cristine, who joined the RCMP in 1990 and who had previously run the Keremeos detachment, retired in 2013 as a sergeant in the Vancouver headquarters.

Their interest in wine burgeoned after they were posted to Oliver in 1993. Walter says "the bug" was put in his ear by Randy Toor, one of the owners of Desert Hills Estate Winery, then an auxiliary RCMP constable. "He was just getting into grape growing, and he said, 'Walt, you should buy a vineyard,'" Walter remembers.

Hugging Tree started by producing 50 cases of Cabernet Sauvignon in 2011. Growth has been carefully controlled (2,000 cases in 2018), with the winery selling grapes while developing its sales. "My favourite wineries started around 2,000 cases and grew their demand," Brad says. "We are on the cusp of upping production."

BRAD MAKEPEACE

Both Walter and Brad have taken viticulture and winemaking courses at Okanagan College. Brad was a professional snowboarder, rock musician, and bartender in Whistler until he decided to move to the winery. "I wanted to support my dad's dreams," Brad says. "And when I spent time here, I got addicted to the lifestyle and the valley and the beauty. I always say it is not a get-rich lifestyle, but it is a rich lifestyle."

MY PICKS

The red wines stand out, especially the Cabernet Sauvignon, the Cabernet Franc, the Moonchild Merlot, and Telltale, the winery's Meritage blend.

OPENED 2014

1002 Highway 3
Cawston, BC V0X 1C3

T   250.499.2201

W   huggingtreewinery.com

INDIGENOUS WORLD WINERY

KELOWNA

Robert and Bernice Louie, members of the Okanagan Syilx people, proudly celebrated their heritage by calling their winery Indigenous World when they opened the elegant tasting room and restaurant in 2015. It is the Okanagan's second Indigenous winery and the only one with 100% Indigenous ownership. (Nk'Mip Cellars in Osoyoos is a joint venture.)

A remarkable entrepreneur, Robert was born in 1951 in a home on the reserve with neither running water nor electricity. "I learned to work at five years of age," he says. "I started working in the Chinese vegetable gardens, alongside my grandmother, my mother, and my uncle. We have always been hard workers." Robert, who has both business and law degrees, has been rewarded with considerable success. He has served twice as elected chief of the Westbank First Nation and has been the long-time chairman of Peace Hills Trust, the largest Indigenous financial institution in Canada.

Robert developed an appreciation of wine as he mixed with other business people nationally and internationally. The winery took shape after he met Jason Parkes, a sometime leader of a heavy metal band and also one of the Okanagan's best consulting winemakers. In 2014, they planted 1 hectare (2½ acres) of Muscat varieties on the reserve, qualifying Indigenous World's land-based status. The winery, with a capacity of 10,000 cases, buys most of its grapes throughout the Okanagan.

"I think wine is a good thing," Robert says, heading off the racist notion that alcohol and Indigenous people do not mix. "I know that Clarence Louie [the chief of the Osoyoos Indian Band] and his people are proud of what they have accomplished with Nk'Mip Cellars. Our intention is to be equally as proud. We do not see it as a negative thing whatsoever."

ROBERT LOUIE

Okanagan Syilx roots are celebrated. The menu at the Red Fox Club, the winery restaurant, includes traditional First Nations cuisine. The wine labels also reflect the heritage. Hee-Hee-Tel-Kin is the label for two blended wines (one red, one white). "It is a mystical stag, an alpine deer that is rarely seen," Jason explains. It is also the ceremonial name for Robert's son, Trenton, who is being coached in viticulture and winemaking. The winery's flagship red blend, with a stylized owl as a label, is called Simo. It was the Okanagan Syilx name given to Robert by his grandmother.

MY PICKS

Everything, especially Simo.

OPENED 2015

2218 Horizon Drive
Kelowna, BC V1Z 3L4
T 250.769.2824
W indigenousworldwinery.com
Restaurant: Red Fox Club
(778.755.6360), open
noon–8 Tues. to Sat.

INNISKILLIN OKANAGAN

OLIVER

Until 2014, Inniskillin Okanagan's winery and tasting room were in an antique facility next to its Dark Horse Vineyard. Production and the tasting room were then moved to the well-equipped Jackson-Triggs winery north of Oliver. However, the Dark Horse Vineyard in the Golden Mile sub-appellation still grows some of this winery's best wines.

The sunbathed 9-hectare (22-acre) vineyard, with rugged granitic soil, was planted with vinifera grapes in 1990 by Sandor Mayer, Inniskillin's Hungarian winemaker, who returned to his native land in 2014. "It is such a great vineyard, with the aspect and the soils, that things ripen very quickly there," says Derek Kontkanen, the winemaker succeeding Sandor. "It has an east-facing slope toward Osoyoos Lake, and it gets a lot of sun."

A remarkable range of varieties succeed here, from Cabernet Sauvignon to Chardonnay, Riesling, Pinot Gris, Marsanne, and Roussanne—and even Pinot Noir, a grape that usually prefers cooler sites. Gewürztraminer, however, became overripe. Those vines were grafted over to Tempranillo in 2005. In various vintages, Inniskillin has made a table wine with this Spanish red variety as well as a sparkling wine. In one vintage, Sandor even produced a Tempranillo Icewine.

Icewine is a major part of the heritage of Inniskillin Niagara, which acquired the Okanagan winery in 1994. The late Karl Kaiser, one of the founders of Inniskillin Niagara in 1974, pioneered Icewine production in Canada in the 1980s. Derek, who credits Karl as one of his mentors, did his master's thesis on Icewine fermentation when he was a student in Brock University's enology program. Inniskillin Okanagan's Icewines usually are made with Riesling, the variety most winemakers prefer for Icewine.

DEREK KONTKANEN

Inniskillin Okanagan's portfolio includes value-priced estate wines and a reserve series. The Discovery Series is for wines from varieties rarely found in the Okanagan, such as Zinfandel and Tempranillo. The Dark Horse Vineyard wines have a rising profile as single-vineyard wines showing off the distinctive flavours and qualities of this special vineyard.

MY PICKS

Everything, but especially Discovery Series wines and those from the Dark Horse Vineyard. Four exceptional limited production wines under the Dark Horse label—Chardonnay, Pinot Noir, Cabernet Franc, and Meritage—were released in 2019.

OPENED 1979 (AS VINITERA)

7857 Tucelnuit Drive
Oliver, BC V0H 1T2
T 250.498.4500
1.866.455.0559 (toll-free)
W inniskillin.com

INTERSECTION ESTATE WINERY

OLIVER

Bruce Schmidt describes sales and marketing as the "talent base" he has applied to pharmaceuticals, advertising, and financial consulting since earning a physics degree at the University of British Columbia in 1975. But his heart is in the wine business. "I have always been connected in some way to someone who is selling wine, making wine, or whatever," he says. "I have always been interested in a vineyard." The passion has come together at Intersection winery, so named because it is at the intersection of Road 8 and Highway 97.

A Kelowna native, Bruce began his wine career in 1978 with Nabisco Brands, the company that then owned Calona Vineyards. There, he put his formidable marketing talent behind Schloss Laderheim, the iconic Calona brand that became the top-selling white wine in Canada in the early 1980s. He left in 1985 to run an advertising agency for a couple of years and then moved on to consult with start-up companies, mostly in science, something he continues to do.

He also remained involved in wine, heading a group of investors that helped finance Blue Mountain Vineyard and Cellars in 1992. "Blue Mountain has been a great teacher of how you do things right," he says. In 2005, Bruce bought this highway-side 4-hectare (10-acre) orchard. Since then, he has planted 20,000 vines and has transformed a sturdy packing house into a winery. The 4-hectare (10-acre) vineyard is planted primarily with Merlot, along with small blocks of Riesling and Sauvignon Blanc. Dramatically different soil blocks in the vineyard enable the production of two distinctive Merlots—one called Silica, one called Alluvia.

Winemaker Melissa Smits, a native of Grimsby, Ontario, is a 2008 Niagara College graduate who has honed her considerable

BRUCE SCHMIDT   MELISSA SMITS

skills in both viticulture and enology by working at wineries in Ontario, Australia, and New Zealand before coming to the Okanagan in 2014. She joined Intersection in 2016 after several vintages in the vineyard and cellars at Burrowing Owl Estate Winery. "I really want to get a sparkling project under way here," she said in 2019. "When I graduated, I thought I would just make sparkling and aromatic wines."

MY PICKS

Everything. Silica and Alluvia are fascinating examples of terroir-driven Merlots. Viognier, Roussanne, Sauvignon Blanc, and Riesling are all well made.

OPENED 2012

450 Road 8
Oliver, BC V0H 1T1
T   250.498.4054
W   xwine.ca
Wine education classes
offered. See vinstitute.ca.

INTRIGUE WINES

This winery got its name after someone remarked to Roger Wong and Jillian, his wife, that wine is intriguing. This winery's growth is equally intriguing. Roger made 400 cases of wine in 2008, the first vintage, and 15,500 cases in 2018. Most of the wine is sold from the winery's tasting room, located just steps from busy Okanagan Centre Road, across the street from O'Rourke's Peak Cellars winery and a short drive from five other Lake Country wineries. "If we can bring more traffic to Lake Country, we all win," Roger says.

Roger, who was born in Vancouver in 1965 and has a geography degree, worked in a federal government job until he was 30. A home winemaker since he was 17, Roger then followed his passion. He volunteered at Tinhorn Creek for the 1995 crush. They hired him and encouraged him to take winemaking courses. He became winemaker for Pinot Reach Cellars in 1998 and, following an ownership change there, moved to Gray Monk in 2005 as a winemaker. He left that winery in 2019 to focus entirely on Intrigue.

Roger's first independent label was Focus Wines, concentrating on Riesling. The venture stalled in 2003 when smoke from the forest fires saturated Kelowna vineyards and ruined the grapes. The dream was reborn after Roger and Jillian partnered with Ross and Geri Davis to launch Intrigue. On their two properties near Wood Lake (near Oyama), the couples in 2008 planted 6.9 hectares (17 acres) of vines, the majority being Riesling.

The Davises turned half of their sprawling Lake Country home into a winery, with tanks outside and wine storage inside. It is a short drive to the spacious Intrigue tasting room to keep the shelves stocked. "It is only a matter of time before we build a winery here," Roger says.

ROGER WONG

MY PICKS

The affordably priced wines are easy-drinking, especially the four released under the Social label. Roger has a good touch with Riesling, Pinot Gris, and Gewürztraminer.

OPENED 2009

2291 Goldie Road
Lake Country, BC
V4V 1G5

T   250.980.3233
1.877.474.3754 (toll-free)

W   intriguewine.ca

Picnic area

JACKSON-TRIGGS OKANAGAN/ SUNROCK VINEYARDS

OLIVER

Jackson-Triggs has a large portfolio of award-winning wines available in the elegant hospitality centre that opened here in 2006. Behind the awards are some of Canada's best vineyards. Since 1998, Vincor Canada—now Arterra Wines Canada, the parent of Jackson-Triggs—has planted 525 hectares (1,300 acres) of vines, on Black Sage Road, on the Osoyoos Lake Bench, and near Okanagan Falls.

The *premier cru* is Sunrock Vineyards, a sunbathed 73-hectare (180-acre) vineyard on the Osoyoos Lake Bench that was planted in 1999. Since 2018, the wines, still made at the Jackson-Triggs plant by winemaker Dave Carson, have been elevated from the Jackson-Triggs portfolio to stand on their own, almost as if Sunrock were a separate winery.

"I started in the industry in 1982," Dave says. "I worked at Sumac Ridge for 23 years. I became the winemaker at See Ya Later Ranch for a few years. I did not start with Sunrock and that particular team until 2007. I still remember going up there with the team to taste the grapes. It was a beautiful October day. One of the bird bangers went off and echoed off the rocks. I felt a shiver go up my spine, and I said, 'Yes, I have arrived.'"

The vineyard had a similar impact on Troy Osborne, Arterra's director of viticulture.

"When I first drove into that vineyard, it was jaw-dropping," he recalls. "It is textbook viticulture. You have the massive granite face, a south-facing slope, and then a lake at the bottom of it. You get very good air movement through the vineyard. And it is just big. There are not a lot of sites in the South Okanagan where the heat units compare with that site." Cabernet Sauvignon, Merlot, Cabernet Franc, Shiraz, and Zinfandel are the varieties

DAVE CARSON

best adapted to Sunrock, which proved too hot for Pinot Noir and Chardonnay.

While the Sunrock wines all are single-vineyard wines, the other Jackson-Triggs wines draw fruit from the group's other vineyards. The wines in the Grand Reserve range rival the quality of Sunrock.

MY PICKS

Sunrock, of course, as well as the Reserve and Grand Reserve wines and the sparkling wine released under the Entourage label.

OPENED 1981 (AS BRIGHTS WINES)

7857 Tucelnuit Drive
Oliver, BC V0H 1T2

T 250.498.4500
1.866.455.0559 (toll-free)

W jacksontriggswinery.com
sunrockvineyards.com

JOIEFARM

Now producing about 15,000 cases a year, JoieFarm has been remarkably successful since it launched with just 840 cases from the 2004 vintage. Throughout its growth, JoieFarm has retained a tight focus on varieties and wines inspired by Alsace and Burgundy. "I work with aromatic German and Burgundian varietals because I think they thrive in our cool-climate, lake-moderated desert terroir," says proprietor Heidi Noble.

The Gewürztraminer-based wine called Noble Blend, now almost a third of JoieFarm's production, was inspired by the Edelzwicker blends of Alsace. A red blend called PTG is modelled on the Pinot Noir/Gamay Noir blend called Passe-Tout-Grains in Burgundy. Among the other wines are Pinot Noir and Chardonnay, the classics of Burgundy. The immensely successful Re-Think Pink! rosé, made with Pinot Noir and Gamay Noir, takes its inspiration from the pink wines of Anjou.

The winery was founded by Heidi and Michael Dinn, her former husband and now a Vancouver wine agent. After meeting at a sommelier school, they discovered a shared ambition to be wine growers. Heidi, born in Toronto in 1974, began cooking at 14. She has degrees in philosophy and literature but turned down an academic scholarship to enrol in a chef school. Before launching wine production in 2003, she worked in a top Vancouver restaurant. Connections in the restaurant trade paved the way for JoieFarm's success with well-made wines.

The JoieFarm winery was built in 2007 amid a 1-hectare (2½-acre) Naramata Bench vineyard. After operating for years without one, the winery has added an elegant tasting room, making the wines much more accessible to the fans of JoieFarm. The vineyard is entirely devoted to Moscato Giallo for the winery's delicate Muscat wine. For most of its grapes, JoieFarm relies on a group of

HEIDI NOBLE

"committed" growers. In 2013, when the winery added a reserve-wine tier, it termed the wines *En Famille* in tribute to its family of growers.

Beginning with the 2017 vintage, JoieFarm added a range of small-lot wines under the Chic Fille label, which Heidi describes as "tongue-in-cheek for 'cool girl.'" These are experimental wines with a serious underlying motive. "These are all 25- and 50-case projects," Heidi says. "They are meant to improve the core Joie portfolio. We have a changing climate, so it is very important to adapt. We have a very pronounced house style—an intense core of ripe fruit augmented by mouth-watering, juicy acidity. In hot vintages, you have to find different ways to preserve that natural acidity."

MY PICKS

Every Joie wine is quite simply delicious, with clean, fresh fruit flavours and vivid aromas, reflecting exceptional winemaking by Heidi and her team.

OPENED 2005

2825 Naramata Road
Naramata, BC V0H 1N1
T 250.496.0093
W joiefarm.com
Food service: Joie Picnique, open daily noon–4:30, May through early September

KALALA ORGANIC ESTATE WINERY

WEST KELOWNA

Kalala is the town in Punjab where Karnail Singh Sidhu, this winery's owner, was born in 1968. Translated, Kalala means "miracle place," and Karnail honours this on the winery's labels, which show a wolf and lamb with their heads together affectionately. Punjabi legend has it that these animals lived in serene harmony. Kalala's pastoral 6.9-hectare (17-acre) Glencoe Road property is similarly serene.

When Karnail came to Canada in 1993, his diploma in electrical engineering was not recognized, so he relied on his 25 years' experience as a farmer for employment in the Okanagan. In 1996, he joined the pruning crew at Summerhill Pyramid Winery. That was the beginning of a 10-year career there during which he emerged as a leader in organic viticulture in the Okanagan. The company he set up in 1997 with two brothers, Kalala Agriculture, has provided supplies and expertise for many organic grape growers in the valley. Kalala has done a number of research projects that have advanced organic farming in the Okanagan.

Karnail's winery gets fruit from his organic vineyards at Westbank and near Oliver in the South Okanagan. The south-facing Westbank property, one of the highest-elevation vineyards in this part of the Okanagan, is well suited to the cool-climate varieties planted here, including Pinot Noir, Pinot Gris, and Gewürztraminer. Karnail has a significant planting of Zweigelt, an Austrian red from which he has made table wine, Icewine, and, most recently, sparkling wine.

In a return to his roots, Karnail in 2013 began to export Kalala wines to India, culminating a marketing approach dating from a 1997 trip to explore the market there for Canadian Icewine. He even considered planting a Himalayan vineyard just for Icewine.

The winery is notable for the numerous charities and community events it supports. One of these practices could even foster more viticulture careers. In the fall, the winery welcomes busloads of students to tour the vineyard and the winery during vintage.

MY PICKS

The Pinot Gris and Gewürztraminer are refreshing whites. The Merlot, Pinot Noir, and Zweigelt, while aged in barrels, show attractive fruit flavours that are not submerged in oak. Premium single-vineyard wines are marketed under the Dostana label: the word means "friendship."

OPENED 2008

3361 Glencoe Road
West Kelowna, BC
V4T 1M1

T 250.768.9700
   1.866.942.1313 (toll-free)

W kalala.ca

KANAZAWA WINES

The rough-hewn wine shop here, as rustic as any on the Naramata Bench, reflects Richard Kanazawa's remarkable struggle to defeat one barrier after another in securing this winery licence in 2016. The winery, a modestly renovated tractor shed, is so unadorned that one regulator unkindly declared it an embarrassment. Wine consumers do not agree. Kanazawa wines can be found in restaurants and wine stores throughout British Columbia.

Richard was born and grew up in Langley, BC. He refreshed his heritage as a young man by going to Japan and playing rugby professionally. When he returned to Langley, a job delivering wine for the Chaberton winery fired his ambition to make wine.

In 2002 he enrolled in the renowned winemaking program at Charles Sturt University in Australia. Two years later, he returned to the Okanagan and launched his career at Red Rooster Winery. He moved on to Blasted Church Vineyards in 2008 and Lang Vineyards in 2012, and followed that with stints at Bench 1775, Kismet Estate Winery, and Serendipity Winery.

Soon after returning from Australia, Richard and Jennifer, his wife, had decided to start their label, debuting in 2010 with 900 cases. It was not easy—starting on a shoestring under the licences of the various wineries that employed Richard. Several of his employers actually objected to Richard's ambition. He had a stroke of luck in 2013 when he bought Pinot Noir grapes for rosé. The following year he took over the lease on that 1.6-hectare (4-acre) vineyard, which is at the corner of McMillan Avenue and Naramata Road, and then concluded he could turn one of the farm buildings into a winery and a tasting room. However, with one regulatory roadblock after another, he did not get his own winery licence until the summer of 2016.

"In what world do you have to be a millionaire four times over

to open up a winery?" Richard asks in frustration. "That is what I fought to get this licence. I like this shack. I like how small and old it is. And people seem to like this shack."

It also belies the sophistication of the wines and their evocative packaging, which echoes Richard's Japanese heritage. Each bottle bears a distinctive diamond-shaped flower (*hanabishi* in Japanese), which was the symbol, or *kamon*, that traditionally appeared on his mother's kimono. Several of the wines have Japanese names—notably Ronin, a red blend named for Richard's son.

MY PICKS

Everything, including Nomu (a white blend), Sakura (a rosé), and Raku and Ronin (both red blends).

SALES BEGAN 2010

1465 McMillan Avenue
Penticton, BC V2A 8T4

T   250.486.7424

W   facebook.com/
KanazawaWines

KETTLE VALLEY WINERY
NARAMATA

When they launched Kettle Valley, chartered accountant Bob Ferguson and geologist Tim Watts intended to limit production to three wines: Chardonnay, Pinot Noir, and a Bordeaux blend called Old Main Red (named for their Naramata vineyard where most of the grapes grow). And they believed they would never make more than 5,000 cases a year. However, they created a companion label, Great Northern Vineyards, after acquiring a 4.9-hectare (12-acre) Similkameen property in 2008, growing Zinfandel, Syrah, and Viognier. Production peaked at 11,000 cases before the owners rolled it back to 7,000 cases. "We are trying to pare it back a little and enjoy life a bit more," Bob says, reflecting on 28 vintages.

The extensive portfolio includes many single-vineyard wines expressing individual terroirs. One of Kettle Valley's best Pinot Noirs is grown in the Hayman Vineyard, which the partners planted in 1988. Production averages about 80 cases a year. The winery's legendary Barber Cabernet Sauvignon—again about 100 cases a year—comes from a 2-hectare (5-acre) vineyard that the partners have farmed since 2000 for businessman Dave Barber. While he died in 2010, his family still use the summer retreat while Kettle Valley manages the vineyard.

Wines like the Barber Cabernet are something of a labour of love, made from grapes cropped so sparingly that the selling price of the wine barely covers the costs. "It is because we enjoy doing it," Bob explains. "To make money on growing things like Cabernet Sauvignon and Petit Verdot in this region, you would have to be charging way more money than the market would bear."

The winery was named for the Kettle Valley Railway, whose railbed above the Naramata Bench now is a well-used hiking trail. Railway history and lore has been exploited in naming the wines. Adra Station, a reserve Chardonnay, takes its name from a station

TIM WATTS AND BOB FERGUSON

on the line. Naramata Bench Reserve Extra 4079, a red blend, is named for the last train over the Coquihalla Summit in November 1959 before a series of washouts closed the Kettle Valley service forever.

The Similkameen vineyard was named for the Great Northern Railway that once operated in that valley. There is a steam locomotive on the Great Northern labels, similar to Kettle Valley's labels.

MY PICKS

Everything. The bestseller is the deep-pink full-flavoured Pinot Gris, the result of three days of skin contact. The red wines are bold and age-worthy. The flagship is Old Main Red, a seamless blend of Merlot, Cabernet Sauvignon, Cabernet Franc, Malbec, and Petit Verdot. From the Great Northern portfolio, look for the Viognier, Syrah, and Zinfandel.

OPENED 1996

2988 Hayman Road
Naramata, BC V0H 1N1
T   250.496.5898
      1.888.496.8757 (toll-free)
W   kettlevalleywinery.com

KISMET ESTATE WINERY

OLIVER

Both the winery and some of the wines allude to the Dhaliwal family's rise from poverty in India, where they were among the poorest families in the village in Punjab. Moksha is a fine Syrah-based red; the name translates as "freedom" or "liberation." Kismet means fate or destiny, symbolizing the prosperity they found in the Okanagan.

Sukhwinder (Sukhi for short) Dhaliwal came to the Okanagan, where he had relatives, in 1989 at the age of 20. His brother, Balwinder, born in 1974, joined him in 1993. After a few years as vineyard and orchard labourers, they bought their first property in 1996 and planted grapes the following year. "After that, we never stopped," says Balwinder (who sometimes goes by the name of Bill). Now, they operate more than 140 hectares (350 acres) of South Okanagan vineyards and sell grapes or manage vineyards for well-known wineries.

Growing grapes introduced the brothers to wine. "We didn't drink wine when we were in India," Sukhi says. "As soon as we started dealing with those wineries, we starting getting some free wine." In time, that led them to open Kismet. Sukhi explains why: "The first thing is that we grow good-quality fruit; and we think if we make our own wine, we can make very good-quality wine. We have all the varieties. Secondly, I think we can make a little bit more money. And the third thing is that we really would like to have our own winery. That's our hobby."

It is a pretty serious hobby that is designed to grow to 10,000 cases a year, with a processing facility and a wine shop beside the highway. Consulting winemakers, primarily Mark Wendenburg, ensured that Kismet launched with good-quality wines. Dapinder Gill, a Dhaliwal relative, is being mentored by consultants. They have the luxury, as Sukhi says, to work with many varieties,

DAPINDER GILL

including rare blocks of Grenache and Mourvèdre.

Another meaning for *kismet* is luck. It seems appropriate since they have made their own luck for years.

MY PICKS

All the wines are interesting, including Saféd, a spicy white blend of Sauvignon Blanc, Muscat, and Sémillon. The red blends—Karma, Moksha, and Mantra—are full of flavour.

OPENED 2013

316 Road 20
Oliver, BC V0H 1T1

T 250.495.4462
   250.408.9800

W kismetestatewinery.com
   Restaurant: Masala
   Restaurant, open daily
   (except Wed.) 11–7

KITSCH WINES

KELOWNA

This is the winery launched by men's underwear. Owners Trent and Ria Kitsch, both Kelowna natives, began a business in 2006 to develop and market innovatively designed SAXX briefs. Five years later, when the business was proven, they sold it to a well-resourced manufacturer. "We had an exit strategy," says Ria, who has a business degree. "It was essential that if it was going to be big, it get into the hands of people that could make it big, because that wasn't us. So we sold the brand, and that allowed us to pursue our Okanagan dream of planting grapevines and starting the winery."

On property in northeast Kelowna owned by the Kitsch family, they planted 5.1 hectares (12⅔ acres) of vines. The largest planting is Riesling; the other varieties are Chardonnay, Pinot Gris, and Pinot Noir. The vineyard occupies a plateau, with a panoramic view to the south over the city and Okanagan Lake. In 2019, they acquired a nearby cherry orchard where they began planting 5.6 hectares (14 acres) of vines, primarily Pinot Noir, in 2020.

Grant Biggs, a rising young winemaker, began wine production in the Kitsch family's three-car garage. Grant was born in 1983 in Port Alberni. "My grandfather, I think, is the reason why I pursued a career in wine," Grant says, referring to Italian-born Elio Navé. "He used to order grapes from California—Zinfandel and Muscat—and we would make wine in the basement together when I was growing up." His interest in wine grew when he worked in Victoria restaurants, before becoming a cellar worker in the Okanagan, first at the Mt. Boucherie winery and then at Tantalus Vineyards. He came to Kitsch in 2015, armed with training from the University of California and a sure touch for making crisply refreshing wine.

"I look at wine as a form of art," Grant says. "I know wine

WINEMAKER GRANT BIGGS

is a blend of science and art, but to me it is a beautiful piece of art." By happy coincidence, Trent and Ria are art collectors. "We have art here that is [from] our collection," Ria says. "These are a little more contemporary in nature, a little more like street art. We are just trying to be true to who we are without having any type of gimmick. We are here to fuse things that don't go together all the time, like youthfulness and sophistication, or refinement but still approachability, in our wines. It is pretty authentic—hand touched, small batch, single-vineyard bottled."

MY PICKS

All the wines show remarkable purity, especially the Rieslings. Pinot Noir is impressive.

OPENED 2016

3330 Neid Road
Kelowna, BC V1W 4H5
T   250.864.6404
W   kitschwines.ca

LA CASA BIANCA WINERY

OLIVER

The vintage at La Casa Bianca begins in late April when Noël and Linda Berkland pick the dandelion flowers for wine. As their website proclaims, La Casa Bianca is the "home of unique wines."

They are South Africans (Noël was born in 1964) who travelled extensively around the globe before coming to the Okanagan in 2012. Noël worked in information technology and went wherever his contracts took him. "We have been all over the world these past 30 years," Linda says. "I think it was 35 places that we went to and none of them felt like home. And then we came here and felt instantly at home."

Noël has long desired to be a farmer but did not aspire to become a winemaker when he was globe hopping. Much of his wine education is from when he had a contract in the London office of Southcorp Wines, the Australian wine group that once owned major labels like Penfolds and Jacob's Creek. "Everyone who worked there had to take the wine courses, to understand all the wines, even if you were a consultant," he says. "It was a company where you were allowed to have a glass of wine at your desk."

One of Noël's subsequent contracts took him and his family to Calgary and employment with an oil company in 2007. A few years later, they vacationed in the Okanagan and were immediately enchanted with the scenic region. "We had always wanted a farm, and we started looking," Linda says. "We did not want to wait until we were too old to do something different, together. We have always loved working together as a family."

In 2012 they found a modest 2.4-hectare (6-acre) farm wedged between the highway and a creek, just north of Oliver. It came with almost a hectare (2½ acres) of vines, mostly Riesling. More varieties have been planted since. A few years ago, after

LINDA AND NOËL BERKLAND

Noël made wine for personal consumption, the couple decided to open a winery, naming it for their daughter. "With Noël's technical knowledge, he has always had a way of working it out," Linda says. "We do quite a bit of the winemaking together."

Noël has created a large portfolio of wines made with flowers, grapes, fruit, walnuts, and honey, with the recipes all recorded in his meticulous notebooks. The delicious dandelion wine is based on an old Nova Scotia recipe that Noël tweaked by adding dried Riesling grapes during fermentation. And they take particular pride in a wine made with haskap berries, renowned for their high antioxidant properties.

MY PICKS

Open-minded palates will revel in the flavours of Vin de Noix, the walnut wine; Dandy, the dandelion wine; and St. Nick, the white blend.

OPENED 2017

7249 Highway 97
Oliver, BC V0H 1T7
T   250.689.2790
W   lacasabianca.ca

LA FRENZ WINERY

When he conducts tours of the La Frenz vineyards, proprietor Jeff Martin is likely to have visitors smell a handful of earth. "That's alive," he exults. In 2012, before he planted vines on a new Naramata Road vineyard, he had livestock grazing on previously planted fall rye. The object was to get organic matter and bacteria into the soil. "The smell you get from the earth turns up in the fruit, and it is particularly noticeable in reds," Jeff says. "We're farming not only for the health of the vineyard but for the flavour of the soil."

That is how he farms all of La Frenz's 19.4 hectares (48 acres) of vineyards—all located on the Naramata Bench except one 4-hectare (10-acre) vineyard south of Oliver. Ninety-three percent of La Frenz's 12,000 cases of wine made annually is estate grown. "I am looking for vineyard-designated wines that totally reflect the effort that is going into the vineyard," Jeff says. "It is the French model."

At the age of 20, Jeff, who grew up on an Australian farm, started making wine in the McWilliam's winery in Australia. He and Niva, his wife, came to the Okanagan in 1994 as the winemaker at Quails' Gate Winery. After five vintages there, they opened La Frenz Winery on Naramata Road. (La Frenz is the surname of Jeff's paternal grandfather.) It is now well established as a family winery: their daughter, Elise, who was born in 1990 and has a business degree from the University of British Columbia, works with her father in the vineyards and with winemaker Dominic McCosker in the cellar. "She has been tasting wine since she was five years old," Jeff says with evident pride.

La Frenz wins so many awards for its wines that banners celebrating various winery-of-the-year honours fly almost permanently beside the winery. "I have come to the opinion [that]

JEFF MARTIN

DOMINIC MCCOSKER

there is just no place for average wine," Jeff has declared. "Why would I want to do average? It's way easier to sell the better wines."

Even with the demands of the winery, Jeff pursues a hobby that began in 1969 when he got his own show dog, a German shorthaired pointer, a breed he has owned ever since. "They are the Rolls-Royce of gun dogs," says Jeff, who now is one of North America's leading judges for the breed.

MY PICKS

Everything, from the exceptional whites, the delicious reds, and the extraordinary fortified wines. The flagship red, called Grand Total Reserve, deserves a place in every collector's cellar.

OPENED 2000

1525 Randolph Road

MAILING ADDRESS

740 Naramata Road
Penticton, BC V2A 8T5

T   250.492.6690

W   lafrenzwinery.com

LAKE BREEZE VINEYARDS

NARAMATA

One of the original half-dozen wineries on the Naramata Bench, Lake Breeze Vineyards was established by a Swiss-born South African businessman, Paul Moser, who came to the Okanagan in 1994 with his wife, Vereena, to buy a 10-year-old vineyard. As winemaker, he recruited Garron Elmes, then a recent graduate of Elsenburg College of Agriculture in Cape Town. Garron, who was born in 1972, has made every Lake Breeze vintage since 1995 and has also been the winery's president since 2013.

There have been several ownership changes throughout his career. The Mosers sold the winery in 1998 to Wayne and Joanne Finn, who, in turn, sold Lake Breeze in 2001 to two Alberta couples, including Drew MacIntyre, a Calgary investment banker, and his wife, Barbara. The MacIntyres have been sole owners since 2011 and have propelled several major expansions, capped by the 2016 introduction of two estate-grown premium wines under the MacIntyre Heritage Reserve label. The red, called Ardua, is a Merlot, and the white, called Astra, is a Chardonnay. The wines are a tribute to Drew's late father, William, a Royal Canadian Air Force veteran. The RCAF motto is *Per ardua ad astra*—"through adversity to the stars."

Merlot was chosen for the red because Drew, an enthusiastic wine collector, has the Bordeaux reds of Pomerol as a model. "I think Merlot is one of the varieties, especially around here, that we grow better than anything else," Garron says. Merlot also is an anchor variety in Tempest, the well-regarded red Meritage in the Lake Breeze portfolio.

The rare MacIntyre wines are limited to 150 to 200 cases a year. More abundant quantities are offered under the Lake Breeze label. "Pinot Blanc, Pinot Gris, and Sauvignon Blanc pay the bills," Garron says. "Our reputation is predominantly for whites." Lake

Breeze's annual production is about 14,000 cases a year.

The 3.6-hectare (9-acre) Lake Breeze vineyard affords a panoramic view over Okanagan Lake. To make the most of the view, a new wine shop and restaurant is to be built in 2020 at the highest point of the property.

MY PICKS

Everything, including Pinotage, made with grapes from the vineyard's postage-stamp-size block of that South African red variety. The MacIntyre Heritage wines are ultra-premium collector wines.

OPENED 1996

930 Sammet Road
PO Box 9
Naramata, BC V0H 1N0
T 250.496.5659
W lakebreeze.ca
macintyrewine.com
Restaurant: The Patio
Restaurant, open daily
11:30–3:30 April through
October

LAKEBOAT VINEYARD & WINERY

KALEDEN

Several years ago in the Kelowna airport, Calgarian Tara Whidden encountered a friend, Gordon Haskins, from her time studying law in Toronto. He was now, she discovered, a banker in Kazakhstan, and he was in the Okanagan to find a vineyard property for an eventual career change. She agreed to help by tasting wines from nearby producers every time he identified a possible vineyard. (He did find property on the Naramata Bench.) "I think that is how I got sucked into buying a winery," she laughs, referring to Lakeboat.

It is a little more complicated than that. She has travelled and tasted in many wine regions with her former husband, a developer with a love for food and wine. When she stopped practising law to raise her three daughters, she became involved in renovating houses through his business. In 2016, she purchased a century-old house in Kaleden to renovate. The house was surrounded by the vineyard of Topshelf Winery, a struggling property that was also for sale. Tara bought it in November 2017—and found she had taken on an even more challenging renovation job.

Topshelf Winery had been established by Leonard and Myra Kwiatkowski and got its name because two of their sons had played professional hockey. They bought the Kaleden property in 2008 as a retirement project (Leonard was 60) and opened the winery in 2011. They had taken on more than they had counted on and put the winery on the market soon after Tara bought the heritage house.

The vineyard, she discovered, was neglected. The mildewed grapes of the 2017 harvest had to be destroyed. She hired vineyard professionals to rejuvenate the 1.4-hectare (3½-acre) vineyard of Pinot Gris, Chardonnay, and Merlot. She has also begun to renovate both the winery and the tasting room, which she expects

TARA WHIDDEN

to open in 2022 after she takes up residence in the Okanagan.

The winery's new name reflects Tara's interest in the sternwheelers and sidewheelers that used to ply Okanagan lakes before there were railroads and highways. "They all had interesting stories," she says. "I find the history of the lake boats fascinating."

MY PICKS

Current range not tasted.

PROPOSED
OPENING 2022

236 Linden Avenue
Kaleden, BC V0H 1K0

LAKESIDE CELLARS

OSOYOOS

Harbans and Harkesh Dhaliwal and their son, Ricky, were considering building their winery near Oliver until they were able to purchase the Haynes Homestead in Osoyoos. Judge J. C. Haynes, the first customs agent and a major rancher in the South Okanagan, had built an elegant 10-room house here for his family in 1882.

The home, which commanded a view of Osoyoos Lake, was lived in almost until the Dhaliwals bought it along with a 5.6-hectare (14-acre) orchard where Cabernet Sauvignon and Sauvignon Blanc vines replaced fruit trees. While the house lacked heritage designation, the original plan was to use it as the Lakeside Cellars tasting room. Closer inspection showed this was not practical. Because of the high water table under the house, a sump pump struggled to keep the basement dry and free of mould. The house was demolished after historical artifacts were transferred to the Osoyoos Museum. Timbers from the home also have been used in the new wine shop.

The Dhaliwals are veteran orchardists and cherry growers in both the Okanagan and Creston, where Ricky was born in 1990. He developed an interest in grapes after the family, in 2009, began converting some of its South Okanagan orchards. After finishing high school, he began taking Okanagan College courses in viticulture and travelling to wine regions in Europe.

When a decision to develop a winery was made in 2015, Ricky turned to consulting winemaker Jason Parkes to make the wines. Jason's objective with most of his clients is to teach them to become their own winemakers. Lakeside's first vintage was sold in bulk to help finance the ambitious 9,000-square-foot production building at the far end of the vineyard. Now producing 3,000 to

RICKY DHALIWAL

4,000 cases a year, the winery has capacity to grow as Ricky's other vineyards mature.

"The end goal is to be growing my own fruit," says Ricky. In addition to Cabernet Sauvignon and Sauvignon Blanc, Lakeside now also grows Pinot Noir, Merlot, Cabernet Franc, Syrah, and Malbec. In 2019, Ricky planted just under a hectare (under 2½ acres) of Cinsault in the estate vineyard, having been inspired by the Cinsault rosé wines he tasted during a recent trip to Provence in France.

MY PICKS

Portage White and Portage Red are approachable blends. The Syrah, Cabernet Sauvignon, and Cabernet Franc are excellent.

OPENED 2019

5221 Lakeshore Drive
Osoyoos, BC V0H 1V6
T   250.535.0642
W   lakesidecellars.ca

LANG VINEYARDS

NARAMATA

Lang Vineyards is one of the two original wineries (Hillside is the other) on Naramata Road, now the Okanagan's most popular wine-touring destination. Guenther Lang founded the winery in 1990, a decade after emigrating from Germany. He and his wife, Kristina, were attracted by the property's spectacular setting high on the Naramata Bench. He opened a winery to exploit the Riesling and Maréchal Foch already growing there. He also planted Viognier. The winery built an excellent reputation with sound and creative winemaking.

He sold the vineyard in 2005 to Keith Holman, a local orchardist who was too aggressive in expanding into wine and went bankrupt in 2010. The venerable winery was acquired for about $2 million by Yong Wang, a Chinese entrepreneur. He was also attracted by the setting and stayed in the wine business because of the vineyard. Sensible to the prestige that still attached to the Lang name, he hired Guenther's nephew, Mike, who managed the winery until 2019.

While the wines had suffered during the Holman period, Lang returned to its former reliability in time to celebrate its 25th anniversary. One of the strengths of the property is vine age: some of the Riesling and Maréchal Foch vines are more than 60 years old, making them some of the oldest vines in the Okanagan. Older vines produce fruit with good acidity and deep flavours. Under winemakers Robert Thielicke and Duffy Driediger, Lang's Farm Reserve Riesling has regained the status of one of the Okanagan's collectible Rieslings.

Lang also purchases grapes from growers elsewhere in the Okanagan to extend its portfolio to include barrel-aged reds. "We are doing more with barrels," Mike Lang said in an interview before he left the winery. "My uncle never did too much with

ROBERT THIELICKE

barrels. We had limited space for barrels in the cellar, but after we built a warehouse, we could accommodate more barrels."

The wine shop at Lang, now one of the larger tasting rooms on the Naramata Bench, benefits from the same panoramic view that seduced both Guenther Lang and Yong Wang.

MY PICKS

The Farm Reserve Riesling, the Viognier, and Bravo White showcase the whites from this vineyard. Maréchal Foch is a heritage variety well worth tasting.

OPENED 1990

2493 Gammon Road
Naramata, BC V0H 1N1

T 778.514.5598
W langvineyards.ca

LARCH HILLS WINERY

SALMON ARM

The father and son team of Jack and Roman Manser have turned Larch Hills, which Jack bought in 2005, into a successful family winery. Born in eastern Switzerland in 1957, Jack had a 20-year career there as a forester before coming to Canada in 1992 when Roman was five. After operating a mixed farm in Alberta, Jack settled on wine growing as a farming business with more potential. Roman and Sasha, his wife, joined the winery in 2017. After 10 years working on oil rigs in Alberta, Roman also was ready for a career change.

Geographically, Larch Hills is just beyond the northern end of the Okanagan Valley. The non-irrigated 6-hectare (15-acre) vineyard (one of the highest-elevation vineyards in British Columbia at 700 metres) was developed by Hans and Hazel Nevrkla. Austrian-born Hans, a prizewinning home winemaker, cleared a south-facing slope on this forested property and planted early-ripening varieties. The three primary white varieties in the vineyard are Ortega, Siegerrebe, and Madeleine Angevine. After selling the winery, Hans tutored Jack through several vintages. "Hans made really nice wines," says Jack, who has continued to make wines that are popular and good value. "We just try to make something that people want," Jack says of the 6,000 cases the winery makes each year.

For Jack, managing the vineyard is the easy part of owning a winery. "Driving a tractor is nothing new to me. In forestry, I planted thousands and thousands of trees. Putting a plant in the ground does not scare me." He increased the vineyard's plantings of Ortega and Siegerrebe. The slope still has more than 25 hectares (62 acres) of land with vineyard potential, provided the forest is cleared.

JACK AND ROMAN MANSER

Because Agria is the only red variety grown here, Larch Hills buys red varieties, including Lemberger and Maréchal Foch, from Okanagan growers.

MY PICKS

I have always liked the dry Ortega, the fruity Siegerrebe, and the whimsically named Mad Angie (for those who cannot pronounce Madeleine Angevine). The Foch is a full-bodied, satisfying red.

OPENED 1997

110 Timms Road
Salmon Arm, BC V1E 2P5
T   250.832.0155
W   larchhillswinery.com

LARIANA CELLARS

OSOYOOS

The winery name is a tribute to Larry and Anna Franklin, the parents of Carol Scott, who owns this winery with her husband, Dan. Larry Franklin was a shareholder in Shannon Pacific Vineyards, a large Black Sage Road vineyard until it was broken up after the 1988 vine pullout. During one vintage, Carol was assigned to keep the starlings away from the grapes with a bird gun. In another vintage, she helped pick grapes. She also hauled grapes to the family home in Burnaby where her father made wine.

Those experiences planted the seed for this winery even as the Scotts, both born in 1963, pursued careers in Burnaby. Don is a millwright, while Carol has been a travel agent. They moved to Osoyoos in 1989, taking over a campground that her parents had established in 1968. The recreational-vehicle sites, which they still operate, take up the lakeside half of the 4-hectare (10-acre) property. The vineyard, which replaced apple and cherry trees in 2007, occupies the top half.

Planting vines was Carol's passion. "It took a few years to get Dan on board," she admits. "It was kind of a dream to plant grapes. I finally convinced Dan, and we cleared the land. It was a new tractor that convinced him." They planted Viognier, Cabernet Sauvignon, and Syrah. When the hard winters of 2008 and 2009 mortally damaged the Syrah, that variety was replaced with 2,500 Carménère vines. Now, they purchase Syrah for Lariana's red blend.

Lariana is the Okanagan's southernmost winery, tucked snugly against the 49th parallel, just east of the massive Canada-US customs post. The Scotts produce limited volumes (less than 1,200 cases a year) in a plain-Jane winery with a modest tasting room. They invested instead in top-flight equipment, including the California-made concrete eggs in which Carol and consulting

CAROL AND DAN SCOTT

winemaker Senka Tennant make Lariana's Viognier.

The winery's flagship red, usually anchored with the vineyard's ripe Cabernet Sauvignon, changes its name every year because the wine is named simply for the vintage. The first release was Twelve, succeeded by Thirteen, and so on. Adding 10 to the name should give you the year when the wine will be peaking.

MY PICKS

The exceptional Viognier, the companion red blend, the Carménère, and the occasionally released Cabernet Sauvignon.

OPENED 2013

9304 2nd Avenue
Osoyoos, BC V0H 1V1

T   250.498.9259

W   larianacellars.com

LASTELLA WINERY

OSOYOOS

Both in its architecture and in its portfolio, LaStella is inspired by Tuscany. Its organically farmed vineyards include Sangiovese, the great red varietal of Tuscany. Sangiovese is a significant portion of the blend in Fortissimo, a red wine whose style recalls the elegant reds of Tuscany. "It grows very well here," the winemaker Severine Pinte says. "It is a vibrant, fruity wine with natural acidity."

The Italian theme is also reflected in the winery's whites. Moscato d'Osoyoos, an aromatic lightly sparkling white, is inspired by Piedmont's Moscato d'Asti. The wine is a blend of three Muscat varieties, Muscat Blancs à Petits Grains, Muscat Ottonel, and Orange Muscat. LaStella's Vivace Pinot Grigio is made in the Italian style, which is why the wine is not called Pinot Gris. The crispy, refreshing Chardonnay, called Leggiero, is reminiscent of a northern Italian white. Of course, the southern Okanagan produces excellent Merlot, the grape used in two of LaStella's signature reds, Allegretto and Maestoso, wines that many Italian vintners must envy.

LaStella's secluded Tuscan-style wine shop is nestled at the bottom of a vineyard with 120 metres fronting Osoyoos Lake. Sean Salem, who owns the winery with wife Saeedeh, becomes lyrical when speaking of the birdsongs he has heard while relaxing here. The ambience makes this winery a favourite wedding venue in the South Okanagan. LaStella and its sister winery, Le Vieux Pin near Oliver, are operated by Enotecca Winery and Resorts, the Vancouver holding company set up by the Salems to make Okanagan wine.

"I like the challenge of having the two wineries," says Severine, who was trained in France and joined Enotecca in 2010. "I do have to think out of the hat, and really change my way to approaching the grapes and the final product. I joke that I turn my hat the

WINEMAKER SEVERINE PINTE

other way when I switch wineries. I do approach the grapes in a completely different way. I won't work the Merlot the same way I would work the Syrah."

MY PICKS

Everything, including Fortissimo, a good value, which is a Merlot-anchored wine with a Tuscan personality influenced by the Sangiovese, Cabernet Sauvignon, and Cabernet Franc in the blend. The ultra-premium Maestoso Solo Merlot is a tour de force.

OPENED 2008

8123 148th Avenue
Osoyoos, BC V0H 1V0
T 250.495.8180
W lastella.ca
enotecca.ca
Picnic patio

LAUGHING STOCK VINEYARDS

PENTICTON

In 2017, when David and Cynthia Enns solicited buyers for their Laughing Stock Vineyards, seven wine companies expressed interest. The successful bidder was Arterra Wines Canada, the national wine producer once known as Vincor International. Arterra already had seven wineries and extensive vineyards, all in the South Okanagan. With Laughing Stock, it gained a property on the Naramata Bench. "I have always been jealous that we were not involved in the Naramata Bench," Jay Wright, the president of Arterra, says. "It is one of the top sub-appellations in the Okanagan."

Laughing Stock, which David and Cynthia launched in 2003, now produces more than 12,500 cases of premium wine annually. The wines perennially sell out soon after release. Arterra's 485 hectares (1,200 acres) of vineyards give the winery considerable opportunity to expand production.

In their previous careers, David and Cynthia ran a company that consulted for mutual fund managers. The cheeky response to those who questioned their career switch was to call the winery Laughing Stock. Their financial background influenced some of the winery's branding: The flagship Bordeaux blend is called Portfolio. Two other blends in their line are Blind Trust Red and Blind Trust White. This niche marketing added to the winery's success. "I think our wine is the most corporately gifted wine in Canada, without a doubt," David says.

Arterra elevated David to executive winemaker and gave the founders a two-year contract to remain. As it happened, they cut ties with Laughing Stock in 18 months to pursue other business ventures, including a boutique Pinot Noir winery.

ARTERRA PRESIDENT JAY WRIGHT

Everything, especially Portfolio, an elegant blend that can be cellared for 10 to 15 years.

OPENED 2005

1548 Naramata Road
Penticton, BC V2A 8T7

T   250.493.8466

W   laughingstock.ca

Visits and tastings by appointment

LE VIEUX PIN WINERY

OLIVER

The Robert Mackenzie-designed winery is said to resemble a small French railroad station with its drooping overhang of a roof, shading the walls from the blistering Okanagan sun. The winery's French name was inspired by the old pine tree on the nearby ridge overlooking the town of Oliver. The compact winery was designed to produce about 3,500 cases a year. The owners believed it would be difficult to handcraft quality wines at much larger volumes. LaStella, its sister winery, was built for a similar capacity.

The owners had underestimated how well the wines would be received. A 2017 addition at Le Vieux Pin, blending elegantly with the original winery design, more than doubled capacity. Together, Le Vieux Pin and LaStella, which are supported by 32 hectares (80 acres) of estate vineyards, have the capacity to produce 20,000 cases a year.

French-trained winemaker Severine Pinte, who has been with the two wineries since 2010, produces distinctly different wines for each. She has no difficulty maintaining a high standard of quality. At Le Vieux Pin, the signature wines are Syrah and white Rhône varieties such as Viognier, Roussanne, and Marsanne. And each of the three Syrah wines differs from the others, reflecting both the vineyard sources and Severine's winemaking.

The top of the Syrah pyramid is the sophisticated and age-worthy Équinoxe Syrah. "Equinox means equal day, equal night," Severine says. "When I describe the wine, I tell people I am trying—and I insist on the verb *trying*—to reach perfection. Trying to bring into that one cuvée all the faces of the Syrah and to marry the components in a harmonious way around a long spinal cord of tannin that will let the wine stand on its own."

During its initial years, Le Vieux Pin produced exceptional Pinot Noirs. That varietal was dropped after the winery's

Syrah vineyards came into their own. Ironically, Severine was headhunted by another winery that specialized in Pinot Noir. "I would prefer to keep on making Syrah," she says. "I just love the aromas of Syrah and the way it evolves. And I like my wines to be a little bit structured. It is only possible because of all the work we do in the vineyard, making sure every plant is balanced."

MY PICKS

Everything. In addition to its Syrahs, the winery has excellent whites (Sauvignon Blanc, Chardonnay, and Rhône blends) and a top-flight rosé called Vaïla.

OPENED 2006

5496 Black Sage Road
Oliver, BC V0H 1T1

T   250.498.8388

W   levieuxpin.ca
enotecca.ca
Picnic patio

LIBER FARM & WINERY

CAWSTON

When Mike and Nicole Dowell opened the Liber Farm tasting room in July 2016, they realized a dream that had previously been snuffed out by the temperance-minded British Columbia regulators of the 1960s.

The Liber winery and its 2.8-hectare (7-acre) vineyard occupies a subdivided portion of the historic Mariposa Farm, which, in the early 1960s, was the first farm in British Columbia to be certified organic. Bob McFadyen, the original owner, acquired an interest in wine during wartime service in Italy. He planted 10 hectares (25 acres) of grapes, but when he applied for a winery licence, the government said the three wineries in BC were enough. The dream of a winery died, and in time, the vines were replaced with apples and vegetables—until 2007 when Craig Erickson, Bob's stepson, planted Chardonnay and Merlot and licensed Sleeping Lady Winery (named for a nearby mountain). Before sales began, however, he sold the property in 2015 and moved to Nova Scotia.

Enter the Dowells, whose interest had been fired during a 2005 winery tour in the Okanagan. Mike, born in 1974 just outside Edmonton, has been a manager with a heating and air-conditioning company. Nicole, born in 1977 in Edmonton, has a degree in chemistry. They are also importers of premium Colombian rum.

Changes in their personal lives, including a strong interest in organic food, led them to find this nascent winery in the Similkameen. "I remember being stuck in traffic, driving to work in the snow, and saying, 'Enough is enough,'" Mike says. They retained Pascal Madevon, a leading consulting winemaker, who helped finish 16,000 litres of 2015 wines that had come with the purchase and to guide them in subsequent vintages. "We wanted

MIKE DOWELL

to hire someone who could help us learn," Mike says. "We felt we needed to make sure our first vintage was good. We had to hire the best person we could."

Pascal assured them that their vineyard, not far from the Similkameen River, is top-rated terroir. "Here, everything is class one," Pascal confirms. "It could be very hot in the day, but at the end of the day, there is the river here and it cools the valley down fast. That is perfect for the Chardonnay and the Merlot. For me, this is an incredible spot for Chardonnay."

MY PICKS

Chardonnay and Reserve Merlot are standout wines. Good-value wines include Off Your Rocker, a whimsically named Merlot.

OPENED 2016

156 Sumac Road
Cawston, BC V0X 1C3
T 250.499.5305
W liberfarm.com

LIGHTNING ROCK WINERY

SUMMERLAND

The long valley stretching from Princeton to Summerland is a summertime conduit for thunderstorms. A bolt of lightning during one storm long ago is thought to have cracked a boulder in what is now this winery's vineyard. That inspired the name chosen by Jordan Kubek and Tyler Knight, the young couple running the winery.

Jordan was born in Victoria in 1990. Working in restaurants triggered her passion for wine—"I love to make wine," she says now. She came to the Okanagan in 2010 to finish sommelier studies but, after working the harvest there, was hired in 2011 by Okanagan Crush Pad Winery. She met Tyler, who was born in Prince George in 1986. A biology graduate, he began working in Crush Pad's vineyard. They discovered a shared passion for wine. Encouraged by Crush Pad, Jordan took Washington State University's winemaking course and began specializing in sparkling wine. She and Tyler added to their skills by working harvests in New Zealand, Australia, and Chile and travelling in Europe's leading wine regions.

Ron Kubek, Jordan's father and a retired realtor, decided to help them launch their winery by purchasing two vineyards, beginning in 2016 with the one with the cracked boulder, christened Elysia Vineyard, and then, in 2018, the Canyonview Vineyard. Both grow primarily Pinot Noir. Meanwhile, Jordan and Tyler bought and resuscitated a derelict Summerland vineyard, called St. Katharinas, where Pinot Noir was planted originally in 1968.

In 2017, Lightning Rock's first vintage, the couple made 1,100 cases of wine, doubling that in 2018. Some 40% is Pinot Noir; 30% is sparkling wine; the remainder is Chardonnay, Viognier, and a little Syrah.

JORDAN KUBEK AND TYLER KNIGHT   RON KUBEK

All vineyards are farmed organically. "On all the farms we are not using any synthetic chemicals," Jordan says. The winemaking style also is minimal intervention. The wines are fermented with indigenous yeast, with limited use of sulphur and, if possible, without fining (a clarification process) or filtering the wines. The goal is that the wines express the terroir with purity. "I am excited to compare the three single-vineyard sparkling Pinot Noirs, as they are all on very different soils but are all still in Summerland," Jordan says.

The winery itself perches at the top of the steep Elysia Vineyard, with a view over the vine-covered countryside and with Okanagan Lake in the distance. Add the occasional thunder and lightning storm, and it is hard to find a more dramatic location for a tasting room.

MY PICKS

The Pinot Noirs and the sparkling wines show that Jordan has mastered her craft.

OPENED 2018

6611 Giants Head Road
Summerland, BC V0H 1Z7
T 250.800.0175
W lightningrockwinery.com
Visits and tastings by appointment

LIQUIDITY WINES

OKANAGAN FALLS

Liquidity's founder Ian MacDonald's passions for both wine and art have come together at this Okanagan Falls winery. The tasting rooms and the public areas display art in exhibitions that change continually throughout the seasons, featuring international as well as Canadian artists. At the tasting bar, the wines are as sophisticated as the art. The most accomplished wines include Pinot Noirs and Chardonnays; the latter are frequent winners at the Chardonnay du Monde competition in France.

Liquidity was established when Ian, a Vancouver businessman and art collector, teamed up with wine-loving Albertans in 2008 to buy an ailing Okanagan Falls vineyard left over from a failed winery project. Initial vintages were made off site while they revived the vineyard. By 2013, a tasting room and bistro opened. A few years later, when Liquidity opened a separate premium tasting lounge for seated and tutored tastings, the walls displayed art from Ian's superb personal collection.

The vineyard had 4 hectares (10 acres) of mature vines, notably Pinot Noir; another four on the prime south-facing slope was planted with Viognier, Chardonnay, Pinot Gris, Merlot, Cabernet Franc, and a little Cabernet Sauvignon. In 2014 Liquidity added a contiguous 4 hectares (10 acres) of vines by taking over the neighbouring Lusitano Estate Winery, sold by the owners after just a year in business. These three blocks of vineyard mean that most of Liquidity's production, about 7,000 cases in 2018, is estate grown.

Liquidity's early vintages were made first by consulting winemakers and then by Matt Holmes, a young Australian. When he returned to his homeland, Liquidity recruited Ontario-born Alison Moyes. Working as a sommelier in Halifax fired an interest in winemaking. After training at Brock University, she came to

the Okanagan in 2008 to work at Osoyoos Larose, Stoneboat Vineyards, and, since 2015, Liquidity. Under her hand, the Liquidity portfolio has continually expanded to include the premium wines now offered to its exclusive wine clubs.

Her favourite grape? "Pinot Noir is my baby," she says. "Pinot Noir is where my heart is."

MY PICKS

Everything, including the Pinot Noirs, the Chardonnays, the Viognier, and the sparkling wines.

OPENED 2012

4720 Allendale Road
Okanagan Falls, BC
V0H 1R2

T 778.515.5500

W liquiditywines.com
Restaurant: Liquidity
Bistro, open daily noon–8,
and weekend brunch at 11

LITTLE ENGINE WINES

PENTICTON

The wines of Little Engine have three designated quality tiers: Silver, Gold, and Platinum. In the winery's first vintage, 2014, owners Steven and Nicole French elevated just 10% to Platinum and left 60% as entry-level Silvers. The intention, however, is to get to 60% Platinum as quickly as viticulture and winemaking can support that quality. "Our family motto is 'Dreams don't come true—dreams are made true,'" Steven says. After all, the winery's name was inspired by the 1930 children's story *The Little Engine That Could.*

For Steven and Nicole, Little Engine is a career change from the energy business in Alberta. Both were born in 1969: Nicole in London, Ontario, and Steven in Winnipeg. "We finished university [in London] and moved to Calgary and stayed there for over 20 years," Steven says. In 2011, they bought acreage near Penticton, where their sons attended hockey school. The following year, when the fruit trees were removed, they began planting Chardonnay, Pinot Noir, and Merlot.

Deciding to launch a winery, they made Little Engine's first two vintages at another winery until Little Engine's production facility was completed in 2016, amid about 2 hectares (about 5 acres) of vines right beside Naramata Road. To make the wine, they recruited Scott Robinson.

Scott, who was born in New Westminster, earned a degree in kinesiology and worked in that field for several years while his interest in wine grew. By 2005, he began juggling that with part-time work at Township 7. When he decided to commit to winemaking, he went to the University of Adelaide in 2008 and worked at leading wineries in New Zealand and Australia. He returned to the Okanagan to become the winemaker at La Frenz Winery and then, with a partner, to launch Stable Door Cellars in

STEVEN AND NICOLE FRENCH

2014. When that partnership ended, he was snapped up by Little Engine. The owners describe Scott as an "absolute perfectionist."

That fits Steven and Nicole's philosophy. "We won't compromise anything," Steven says. Perfectionism has its price. Little Engine wines are expensive, reflecting the cost of keeping yields very low to produce intensely flavoured wines. The big and bold house style, especially with the red wines, has found such a strong following that many are sold out by the end of the season. Little Engine will be challenged by its customers to increase the annual production beyond 6,000 cases.

MY PICKS

I am partial to the Silver and Gold tiers even if the Platinum wines are more elegant. However, if you own a Rolex, you insist on the best, and that is the Platinum tier.

OPENED 2016

851 Naramata Road
Penticton, BC V2A 8V1

T   250.493.0033

W littleenginewines.com

LITTLE FARM WINERY

CAWSTON

Little Farm Winery is one of the smallest wineries in British Columbia. "This is our tiny, tiny facility," the proprietor and winemaker Alishan Driediger says, standing in a building that would be a tight fit for a Volkswagen. "It is definitely a family affair," says the mother of two teenage daughters. "We pull help from family and children all the time."

The winery is based on a 2-hectare (5-acre) vineyard planted in 2008 with Riesling and Chardonnay. The first vintage, made in 2011, totalled just 56 cases of wine, wine that was well enough received to put Little Farm on restaurant wine lists in Vancouver. The winery has been operated by Alishan and her partner, Rhys Pender. They had moved to the Okanagan in 2003, operating a bakery and a catering business until moving to the Little Farm property. Rhys, who became a Master of Wine in 2010, is now active as a wine educator and consultant.

Winemaking seems to run in the Driediger family. Alishan's brother, Duffy, is a winemaker on the Naramata Bench. Armed with winemaking courses from the University of California, Alishan has developed a style that suits the tiny scale at Little Farm. "Our winemaking is pretty minimal," she says. "I want to do things as naturally as possible." Wines usually are fermented with indigenous yeast, often in neutral oak barrels. Wines are not moved much between fermentation and bottling.

The objective is to capture the flavours of the vineyard in the wines. That shows especially in her adoption of *pied de cuve* winemaking with Chardonnay. "I go out with a bucket, fill the bucket with grapes, stomp it, leave the juices there on the skins, and get a fermentation going," she explains. "We use that almost like a sourdough starter, in the tank as your inoculation. The theory is that, because [the grapes have] never come into the

winery and never touched anything in the winery, theoretically, there are no ambient yeasts on it at all. You are just getting the natural yeast from the vineyard. That is the purpose of doing it."

Alishan continues: "I love seeing natural things working and doing what they do. I love knowing that this is all something that has happened in our vineyard, created by our vineyard. The things that grow there, including our yeast, are all natural and part of the Similkameen."

MY PICKS

There is a fine purity of fruit in the Chardonnays and Rieslings from Little Farm's vineyard—as there is in the Cabernet Franc made with purchased fruit.

OPENED 2012

2155 Newton Road
Cawston, BC V0X 1C1

T 250.506.0096
(Alishan's cell)
250.317.8796 (Rhys's cell)

W littlefarmwinery.ca

LITTLE STRAW VINEYARDS

WEST KELOWNA

Little Straw is the consummate family winery: three generations of the Slamka family have worked here. "It's always just been our family," said the long-time winemaker Peter Slamka. "We have no relatives in this country. My parents were immigrants. There are seven kids, three of us, and my parents." Peter's father, Joe, came from the former Czechoslovakia to Canada in 1948. In 1962, Joe purchased an orchard on the eastern-facing slope of Mount Boucherie. Disappointed by poor returns from tree fruit, Joe began converting to grapes in 1969. Two decades later, the family decided to start a winery.

Peter, born in 1954, had been making wine in small volumes for family consumption. In 1993, he took off with his wife on a seven-month world tour that included a visit with winemaking cousins in Austria, and another visit with wineries in Australia's Barossa Valley. Then he threw himself into the business that consumed the family's efforts. "My first holiday was in 1993, before we started the winery," Peter says. "My next holiday was in 2010."

The family purchased land next door in 2000 to plant Pinot Noir, more Sauvignon Blanc, and Auxerrois, an increasingly rare Alsatian variety that has been Little Straw's flagship white from the beginning. The block here, planted by Joe in the early 1970s, is believed to be the oldest planting of this grape variety in the Okanagan.

In 2018, after both of Peter's parents had passed away, the family reduced production to refocus on the core wines and the wine shop. The vineyard that had been purchased in 2000 was sold, and the Barrel Top Grill, the restaurant that occupied the top floor of their winery, was put on hiatus. Peter retired as winemaker. He recruited Barbara Hall, a winemaker with a biochemistry degree. Born in Cambridge, Ontario, she developed

PETER SLAMKA AND BARBARA HALL

an interest in wine while working in Whistler restaurants and VQA wine stores. Since 2003, she has worked with several large wineries, including Quails' Gate and Chaberton. "It's a good thing to have sales experience when you're a winemaker," Barbara says. "The last part of winemaking is actually the selling and the presentation of the wine."

In that, she is in harmony with Peter, who is often in the wine shop, helping his nieces pour wine for his guests. "That's the best part of the business," Peter says.

"They're so good at what they do," Barbara says. "It is family, and it's a good family."

MY PICKS

Everything is well made, especially the complex Old Vines Auxerrois. The Tapestry, an excellent blend of five aromatic grapes, has a fiercely loyal following. Sauvignon Blanc and Pinot Noir are also noteworthy.

OPENED 1996 (AS SLAMKA CELLARS)

2815 Ourtoland Road
West Kelowna, BC
V1Z 2H7
T   250.769.0404
W   littlestraw.bc.ca

LOCK & WORTH WINERY

PENTICTON

In the spring of 2012, Lock & Worth moved into the buildings formerly occupied by Poplar Grove Winery after the latter had relocated to a larger winery overlooking Penticton. The partners are Ross Hackworth, the owner of Nichol Vineyard, and Matthew Sherlock, his sales director. The winery was launched as Clean Slate, but after a trademark conflict with a German wine brand, the partners switched to a name crafted from their surnames.

They took over the former Poplar Grove winery so that Ross could capture some of the wine tourists that never got to Nichol Vineyard at the far northern end of Naramata Road. "People are spent out, drunk out, and burned out by the time they hit the Naramata borderline," Ross says. "They have already hit 12 wineries. If people are only going to do the bench for one day, very few of them, unless they know Nichol, start there; just as few make it to the end."

There is another reason for Lock & Worth—it permits Ross to stretch his winemaking talents. Nichol Vineyard limits its production to just six varietals, with perhaps a few blends. "At Lock & Worth, I like to try different things," Ross says. "I don't want to encumber the Nichol brand with three or four new varietals. It confuses things."

From the vineyard of Gitta Pedersen (who operates the cheese company here), Lock & Worth is able to source well-grown Merlot and Cabernet Franc from mature vines. A rugged vineyard near Oliver supplies Sauvignon Blanc, and another in Kelowna grows Sémillon. The portfolio is primarily single-vineyard wines. The business approach is unpretentious. "We spend all of our money on our wines, not our marketing," the partners write on their website. "We eschew heavy bottles, advertising and fancy labels. In the winery we use old French Oak (not expensive) and

MATTHEW SHERLOCK

have very little in the way of technology (still use basket presses)."

Matthew Sherlock is also the sales director for Lock & Worth. He has a bachelor's degree in English and dramaturgy, but shortly after his 2006 graduation, he plunged into wine. While managing a large private wine store in Vancouver, he earned a diploma from the Wine & Spirit Education Trust, subsequently becoming a wine educator before joining Lock & Worth.

MY PICKS

Merlot and Cabernet Franc show the intensity of flavour that 20-year-old vines produce. Both the Sauvignon Blanc/Sémillon blend and the Sémillon are tasty.

OPENED 2012

1060 Poplar Grove Road
Penticton, BC V2A 8T6

T   250.492.4575
604.753.9646 (sales)

W   lockandworth.com
Food service: Poplar
Grove Cheese operates
from the same site, with
cheese available for
purchase

LUNESSENCE WINERY & VINEYARD

SUMMERLAND

The Lunessence wine shop feels like socializing during the entr'acte of an opera. The recorded classical music playing in the vineyard outside almost turns the wine shop into a concert hall lobby with bright white-painted walls and an expanse of patio windows. Music is an important part of the grape growing and winemaking process at Lunessence, where classical music also plays in the cellar. Live music is also performed on the patio and sometimes inside the wine shop. Wine-shop staff have been known to break into an aria now and then.

Lunessence opened in 2015 on the site of the former Sonoran Estate Winery after the latter had moved elsewhere. The property was purchased and renovated in 2014 by Zhizhong Si, an environmental consultant who was born in China and educated in Canada. Now based in Vancouver, Zhizhong hired an experienced team for the winery. The original winemaker and general manager, Michal Mosny, came to Canada in 2011 from Slovakia and stamped his musical passion on the winery. Michal left in 2019 to focus on his own winery, Winemaker's CUT.

His successor, Maxime Legris, who was born in Ottawa, has a winemaking degree from Brock University. After making wine in both Ontario and New Zealand, he came in 2014 to the Okanagan where he has worked previously at Pentâge and then CedarCreek. General manager Cameron Walker, an Australian who grew up in Singapore, worked in advertising on three continents before becoming a wine agent in Vancouver in 2012 and then moving to the Okanagan in early 2018 to join Lunessence. They are building the winemaking program with a goal of 5,000 cases produced annually.

The vineyard, transitioning to organic production, feels almost un-Okanagan-like in that there is a humidity unlike in

MAXIME LEGRIS   CAMERON WALKER

most other vineyards in the valley. The source of that unique microclimate is a stream located under the ground behind the winery, which eventually opens up into a ravine farther down the slope. The vine roots tap into this water source, which makes for very lush growth. The main 2.6-hectare (6½-acre) vineyard is planted with Riesling, Merlot, Pinot Blanc, Gewürztraminer, a little bit of Pinot Noir, and a rare white grape, Oraniensteiner, planted by the former owners. Oraniensteiner is a cross between two grapes—Riesling and Sylvaner—produced in 1985 at the research institute in Geisenheim. Canada likely has the world's largest acreage of this grape. Lunessence blends it with Pinot Blanc and also with three other grapes to produce the Quartet.

MY PICKS

All wines are unique and complex. The blends, such as the Duet and Quartet, are particularly interesting for their complexity and nuance. The chance to try the Pinot Blanc/ Oraniensteiner should not be missed. Excellent big reds—including Merlot and Cabernet Sauvignon—are made with purchased fruit.

OPENED 2004 (AS SONORAN ESTATE WINERY)

5716 Gartrell Road
Summerland, BC V0H 1Z7
T   778.516.3131 (tasting room)
W lunessencewinery.com

MARICHEL VINEYARD

NARAMATA

For viewing the extraordinary beauty of the Naramata Bench, few places are better than Richard Roskell's home, overlooking the 3 hectares (7½ acres) of Syrah and Viognier vines planted since 2000. The sculptured vineyard dips sharply down a slope, pauses for a rise, resumes on the top of the rise, and then disappears toward the lake. Richard, an excellent photographer, has posted his calendar-quality images of the vineyard on the winery's website.

Richard acquired this magical property after several years of searching Okanagan properties. It belonged to a pair of absentee German investors who were estranged from each other. Several purchase offers to their agent in British Columbia failed to get a reply. So Elisabeth Roskell, Richard's German-born wife (who died in 2015) searched German telephone listings until she located the reclusive owners. After six months of difficult negotiation, the Roskells finally bought the property late in 1999. This proved to be what the winery calls a "Goldilocks terroir: not too hot, and not too cold. . . . Ideally situated to capture the maximum amount of sunlight, and nurtured by the moderating influence of Okanagan Lake, 'The Bench' epitomizes the often claimed–but rarely realized–perfect terroir."

This was a new career for Richard. Born in North Vancouver in 1952, he was an Air Canada pilot until retiring early in 2005, fed up with jet lag. "The thought of doing another seven years of long-haul flying did not appeal to me," he says. "I really wanted to stretch out into something different."

Marichel (a contraction of several family names) makes only Syrah and Viognier. "I'll be surprised if we ever make it to 1,000 cases a year," Richard said in his first year. The wines were so well received that in his second year he said that Marichel would

RICHARD ROSKELL

expand. Production has since edged as high as 4,000 cases as Richard has been able to source grapes elsewhere in the bench as well. "We are not going to get big," he says. "We are going to stay personally focused on the vineyard and in the winery, and we will stay faithful to the terroir it comes from."

MY PICKS

The Viognier is vibrantly fresh, while the Syrah is rich and peppery, with a concentration that reflects Richard's decision to keep his tonnages low. The lower-priced Lone Wolf Syrah from purchased grapes is good value.

OPENED 2007

1016 Littlejohn Road
Naramata, BC V0H 1N1
T 250.496.4133
W marichel.ca

MARIONETTE WINERY

SALMON ARM

Jamie Smith's British accent belies the fact that he was born in Salmon Arm in 1973. The accent developed during his 11 years in Europe, where, after getting a degree in English literature, he went to Spain to teach because he was a fan of writer Ernest Hemingway. There he met his partner, Amanda Eastwood, also a teacher in the same language school in Cádiz.

When they discovered a shared passion for wine, they both enrolled in the highly regarded enology and viticulture program at the University of Brighton, near where Amanda had grown up. On graduating, they went to the Loire in 2009, apprenticing with winemaker Frédéric Brochet, a stern taskmaster with a passion for Pinot Noir. The following year, they worked at a Portuguese winery that specialized in red wines. Then, after working briefly with a small English winery, they moved to British Columbia in 2011 and did two vintages at Garry Oaks Winery on Salt Spring Island. "We learned a lot about how to manage a small winery," Jamie says.

In 2013, after a Christmas vacation in Salmon Arm, they were able to acquire a former orchard that they judged was well suited to grapes. After confirming that with a weather station (the growing degree days—a calculation that predicts when plants will ripen—compare with Burgundy), they began planting in 2014. Since then, they have planted about 8 hectares (20 acres) of varieties carefully chosen for the site: Pinot Noir, Zweigelt, Pinot Blanc, Pinot Gris, Chardonnay, Riesling, and Siegerrebe, all of them noble vinifera. "I am not a fan of Maréchal Foch," Jamie says of the hybrid widely planted elsewhere in the Shuswap.

Marionette's initial vintages have been made with grapes from Similkameen growers. Even after their vines are in full production, Jamie and Amanda intend to purchase varieties they

JAMIE SMITH AND AMANDA EASTWOOD

don't grow. "I feel a little defensive about [not having to follow] the estate-only model," Jamie says. "We are winemakers. We don't just want to make wine from four varieties. If, in my winemaking career, I was never able to make Cabernet Sauvignon because people thought I was buying grapes from somebody else, it would be a real shame."

MY PICKS

The wines here are fresh and fruit forward. Jamie and Amanda age the wines in polymer tanks, not barrels, so that oak does not suppress the fruit flavours.

OPENED 2014

2540 40th Street
Northeast
Salmon Arm, BC V1E 1Z3

T   250.832.7702

W   marionettewinery.com

MARTIN'S LANE WINERY

KELOWNA

The astonishing attention to detail at this winery telegraphs what to expect from the wines. The hues of the exterior of the cascading six-level winery pick up both the earth tones of this hillside and the scorched colour of nearby trees that survived the massive 2003 wildfire. The softly lit private dining room, in which owner Anthony von Mandl has hosted Prime Minister Justin Trudeau and his wife, Sophie Grégoire, is acoustically tuned so that guests at either end of the long table can converse with each other. The wines racked on the back wall include bottles of Domaine de la Romanée-Conti, announcing the winery's intent to make legendary wines. "That sets the stage of what this project is about," says Shane Munn, the New Zealand–born winemaker.

The winery, which was constructed between 2014 and 2017, is named for Martin von Mandl, Anthony's late father. He was still alive in 1981 when Anthony acquired the winery Mission Hill, back when it had dirt floors but a setting appealing to Anthony's imagination. Some years later, when Mission Hill was succeeding, Martin remarked to me that his son "has all of the ambition I never had." That ambition drives a winery like Martin's Lane to make some of the Okanagan's greatest Rieslings and Pinot Noirs.

Sebastian Farms, Anthony's viticulture company, owns vineyards throughout the Okanagan. Shane Munn has his pick when it comes to vineyard blocks. Each of the hand-picked lots is handled separately, from the crush pad through fermentation with wild yeast and aging in tank and barrels. He makes only single-vineyard wines that reveal the terroir of the finest blocks. The emerging *grand cru* Pinot Noir block is in Fritzi's Vineyard, on Mission Hill Road, named for Anthony's mother when she turned 100 in 2016.

Shane got his detail-oriented work ethic while completing

SHANE MUNN

his first university degree—in statistics. A year of travel in Europe fostered a love of wine. Returning to New Zealand in 2002, he enrolled in a three-year winemaking program while working at Esk Valley Estate winery near Hawke's Bay. A season at Malivoire Wine Company in Ontario in 2004 opened his eyes to biodynamic viticulture. Back in New Zealand, he worked with Millton Vineyards in Gisborne, a pioneering biodynamic winery. Shane's knowledge of organic and biodynamic winemaking was one reason that he was recruited for Martin's Lane and its superbly equipped winery. The Sebastian Farms vineyards are in transition to organic farming. Shane believes that "the only way we can make better wine is through growing grapes in a more sustainable, honest, and authentic way."

MY PICKS

At $50 to $100 a bottle, Martin's Lane wines are expensive but exceptional in every way.

OPENED 2017

5437 Lakeshore Road
Kelowna, BC V1W 4S5

T   250.707.2263

W   martinslanewinery.com

MAVERICK ESTATE WINERY

OLIVER

The origins of this winery go back to Uniondale, a small agriculture town in South Africa, and the friendship between the bank manager and the doctor. Schalk de Witt, the doctor, has a daughter, Elzaan. One of her playmates when she was five was Bertus Albertyn, the bank manager's seven-year-old son. She got her medical degree at Stellenbosch after her father moved to Canada in 1990. Meanwhile, Bertus had become a winemaker. They met again during a de Witt family vacation in South Africa, fell in love, and married.

Meanwhile, Schalk (rhymes with *skulk*) had invested in two Okanagan properties for vineyards. Having a winemaker in the family enabled the launch of Maverick. "When Bertus came into the picture, obviously, that was the way to go," Schalk says. "There is more profit in making wine than in selling grapes."

A 1976 medical graduate from Stellenbosch University, Schalk brought his family to Canada because they feared civil war in apartheid South Africa. He drove through the southern Okanagan on the way to a locum posting in Castlegar and was immediately attracted. "Even the natural vegetation—the sagebrush and the antelope brush—reminded me of the drier areas of South Africa," he says. Toward the end of a long career in general practice in Alberta, he began searching for property. In 2006 he purchased 19.4 hectares (48 acres) of raw land adjacent to the Osoyoos Larose vineyard near Osoyoos. Three years later, he purchased a former organic farm beside the highway, tapping his son-in-law's expertise to plant 3 hectares (7½ acres) of vines in 2011.

When Bertus, born in 1978, finished his enology degree at Stellenbosch University, he started at a large wine co-operative before joining family-owned Avondale (in South Africa) in 1994 as

BERTUS ALBERTYN

winemaker. He came to the Okanagan early in 2009 when Elzaan began her medical practice in Osoyoos.

The elegant Maverick wine shop, located just beside the highway, is an architectural echo of the Cape wineries where Bertus got his start. The vineyard on the slope behind the tasting room provides Sauvignon Blanc, Chardonnay, Pinot Noir, and Syrah. The latter are planted as bush vines, similar to Hermitage, where Bertus did a vintage before coming to Canada. "In Hermitage, I picked Syrah when it was snowing," Bertus says. "So I thought this might work in this valley, too."

MY PICKS

Everything, from the sparkling wine called Ella to the fortified wine called Fia, both named for Bertus's daughters. Origin is a delicious white blend, and Rubeus is a sophisticated red blend.

OPENED 2013

3947 Highway 97
Oliver, BC V0H 1T1
T   778.437.3133
W   maverickwine.ca

MAYHEM WINES

This winery emerged from a small virtual winery called Anarchist Mountain Vineyard, which was established near Osoyoos after Terry Meyer and partner Andrew Stone bought a 1.8-hectare (4½-acre) mountainside vineyard. She is the sister of JAK Meyer, owner of Meyer Family Vineyards at Okanagan Falls. Terry and Andrew, both Albertans, set down roots in the Okanagan after coming to help her brother in 2008 as he entered the wine industry.

Terry, who had her own daily television show in Edmonton for seven years, has had an extensive career in marketing and public relations. That included running the wine club for Tinhorn Creek. Andrew was born in 1972 in Fort Vermilion, Alberta. After a career working in the oil fields, he became a corporate systems analyst. He missed working outdoors, and after JAK invited him to the Okanagan, he took up viticulture and embraced the wine-industry lifestyle.

The Anarchist wines, a Chardonnay and a Pinot Noir, were made for them at the Meyer winery, which specialized in those very same varietals. "I was not really interested in supporting my sister to make more Chardonnay and Pinot Noir here, which was going to compete against us," JAK says. "That is why we launched the Mayhem brand, doing anything but Chardonnay and Pinot Noir." For copyright reasons, the Anarchist name was dropped in favour of Mayhem.

The business arrangement opens growth opportunities both for Meyer, which took over the Chardonnay and Pinot Noir grown on the Anarchist vineyard, and for Mayhem, which is no longer limited to the 500 cases that Terry and Andrew's vineyard could produce. Mayhem's flagship red is Merlot. The other wines in the portfolio, including Pinot Blanc, Pinot Gris, Sauvignon

TERRY MEYER

ANDREW STONE

Blanc, and Riesling, are made with grapes sourced from contract growers. "We are opportunistic," Terry says.

Mayhem has continued to make its wines at the Meyer winery but may eventually establish itself on a Meyer-owned vineyard in Kaleden.

MY PICKS

Everything. The Pinot Blanc, the Cabernet Franc, and the Merlot are excellent.

OPENED 2018

4287 McLean Creek Road
Okanagan Falls, BC
V0H 1R1

T 1.844.629.4361 (toll-free)

W mayhemwines.com

Tastings by appointment

MEADOW VISTA HONEY WINES

During Meadow Vista's first four years, founder Judith Barta operated the Okanagan's first meadery from a gritty industrial park in West Kelowna. The location did little for the visibility of this producer, even if it was on the busy Westside Wine Trail. But in 2013, backed by a silent partner, Meadow Vista moved to a 2-hectare (5-acre) farm in bucolic East Kelowna. Its fortunes have risen ever since.

Judith is also a massage therapist; her excursion into mead reflected an entrepreneurial bent that always defined her careers. In 2017, when she decided to focus on massage therapy, she sold the meadery to sisters Emily and Electra Vanderschee.

Born in Vancouver in 1971, Emily previously had a career in the food and beverage business, including six years at Summerhill Pyramid Winery. "I had known Judith for a number of years," Emily says. "I was working in the wine industry. Some years ago, when I decided I didn't want to work for other people anymore, I came and joined her in 2016." When Judith decided to sell the following year, Electra joined her sister in the meadery. Three years younger, Electra has a degree in social work and teaches mindfulness in Kelowna schools.

The division of responsibilities at Meadow Vista has Emily looking after selling the 3,000 or so cases of mead produced each year. Electra keeps a close eye on the 120 beehives kept on the Meadow Vista property (unless they are in nearby orchards so the bees can pollinate the fruit trees). She has taken apiary courses and works with Meadow Vista's apiarist.

Meadow Vista is believed to have made British Columbia's first sparkling mead, a bottle-fermented product called Joy. Subsequently, Meadow Vista added carbonated meads called Bliss—one infused with cherries and one with apples. New to

EMILY AND ELECTRA VANDERSCHEE

the portfolio is a braggot mead made with honey, malt, and hops in a crisp style appealing to beer fanciers. Meadow Vista tries to capture red-wine palates with Rubus, a mead made with the honey and fruit from the farm's thornless blackberries.

"We are making seven different styles of mead," Emily says. "We have three more we would love to put out: another Bliss; a wheat braggot; and something completely different. We are at a stage now where we are having a hard time keeping up to demand."

MY PICKS

Contrary to expectations, most honey wines are not sweet. The Bliss wines at Meadow Vista are crisply refreshing. Rubus, the blackberry mead, has a hint of tannin and a deep colour.

OPENED 2009

3975 June Springs Road
Kelowna, BC V1W 4E4
T   250.862.2337
W   meadowvista.ca
Restaurant: Meadow Vista Bistro, closed during winter

MEYER FAMILY VINEYARDS

OKANAGAN FALLS

Meyer Family Vineyards is among the Okanagan's foremost Pinot Noir and Chardonnay producers. The winery, operated by JAK Meyer and his partner, Janice Stevens, began as a hobby-scale Chardonnay producer with a 1.4-hectare (3½-acre) Naramata Bench vineyard planted in 1994. Born in Alberta in 1958, JAK had succeeded as an investment dealer and real-estate developer while becoming passionate about wine. Meyer's 2006 and 2007 vintages were made by a consulting winemaker, and the owners came to market in February 2008, with 600 cases.

Before long, they realized that this volume would not support a winery they had begun planning. Late in 2008, they purchased a 5.9-hectare (14½-acre) Okanagan Falls vineyard, the site of a stillborn winery, which became the Meyer Family winery. They replanted more than half of the vineyard with Pinot Noir, establishing the winery's direction. JAK also purchased a small Pinot Noir vineyard in Kaleden in 2018. The Meyer winery also purchases Chardonnay and Pinot Noir from contract growers, to support a production of at least 8,000 cases a year. "We are trying to raise the bar," JAK says. "There are not too many wineries that are specializing."

There are several tiers of wine made here, ranging from the value-priced Okanagan Valley tier. The top-tier wines are called Micro Cuvée, a selection of the best barrels of Chardonnay and Pinot Noir in each vintage.

Each year, the winery dedicates a Chardonnay in tribute to an individual or an institution, with a cheque paid to the appropriate charity. JAK and Janice's wide-ranging interests are displayed through that intriguing assortment of honourees, among them artist Bill Reid and hockey great Steve Yzerman. The 2009 Tribute Chardonnay was dedicated to Canadian rodeo champion Kenny

WINEMAKER CHRIS CARSON

JAK MEYER

McLean, whose family were Okanagan Falls pioneers.

Pinot Noir and Chardonnay are also the winemaking passions of Chris Carson, the winemaker who joined Meyer in 2008. Born in Edmonton, Chris was drawn to winemaking in 1997 while, as a backpacking student in New Zealand, he worked in a vineyard. That led to a winemaking degree from Lincoln University. Starting in 2001, he did Pinot Noir crushes in California, Burgundy, New Zealand, and the Okanagan before joining JAK's team.

MY PICKS

Everything. The wines are elegant and long lived. The traditional-method sparkling wine is a match to fine grower Champagne.

OPENED 2008

4287 McLean Creek Road
Okanagan Falls, BC
V0H 1R0
T   250.497.8553
W   mfvwines.com

MIRABEL VINEYARDS

KELOWNA

In 2005, Dawn and Doug Reimer moved to Kelowna in search of a site for their dream home. The property they bought overlooks a golf course and the city. But the apple trees on the slope spoiled the view for Doug until he planted Pinot Noir (and Chardonnay later). He decided to launch Mirabel Vineyards after several leading Okanagan wineries produced stunning wines from his grapes. "We were waiting to see what this terroir would really produce," Doug says. "If it produced something we were excited about, then we want to take ownership and put our name on it."

The Reimers are Winnipeg natives. Doug, who was born in 1955, is a member of a renowned trucking family. His father, Donald, started Reimer Express Lines in 1952 with one truck. A successor company, Reimer World Corporation, now employs 3,000 in Canada. "We have always loved wine, but that is not how I got interested in growing it," Doug says. "When we bought the property, we had such a beautiful piece of property, but we thought we could do more than grow apples and pears. They don't pay very much, and they don't look that good."

To make the wines, with 2015 the first vintage, the Reimers hired consulting winemaker Matt Dumayne and used the custom crush facilities at Okanagan Crush Pad Winery at Summerland. In 2018, when Mirabel licensed a production facility on its vineyard, David Paterson from nearby Tantalus Vineyards was engaged to make the Mirabel wines and direct work in the vineyard.

Doug has a singular focus. "We are trying to establish what will be a superior Pinot Noir in all of Canada, and knock down some doors in Oregon as well," Doug says. "I love Oregon Pinot Noir. I have done extensive travelling in the Pinot Noir areas in Oregon. Maybe that is where our love started. We love the

DOUG AND DAWN REIMER

Burgundians as well. I did not want it to taste like Okanagan. I wanted it to taste like 'world level,' although people talk of sense of place."

MY PICKS

The $70 Pinot Noir and the $40 Chardonnay are definitely worth the money. The winery also produces an elegantly packaged $30 Pinot Noir rosé and a pink sparkling wine.

SALES BEGAN 2016

3740 Hart Road
Kelowna, BC V1W 4G6

T   250.575.7000

W mirabelvineyards.com

Tastings by appointment

MISSION HILL FAMILY ESTATE

WEST KELOWNA

Seen from afar, the Mission Hill winery, with its 12-storey bell tower, could be taken for the crowning structure of a Tuscan hill town. It is hard to believe that this architectural extravaganza had dirt floors when Anthony von Mandl bought it in 1981. Today, thousands visit here, perhaps to see the original Marc Chagall tapestry in the entrance hall, or take in concerts in the 1,200-seat amphitheatre, or listen to the bells, the first ever cast for a winery by the 200-year-old Paccard Bell Foundry in France. They certainly visit to taste wines that more than measure up to spectacle.

Born in Vancouver in 1950 to European parents, Anthony started his own wine-importing agency in 1972 after getting an economics degree from the University of British Columbia. The idea of investing in the Okanagan emerged when a German winery commissioned a study but did not follow through with its own investment. The original Mission Hill, even though it was built on the Okanagan's most dramatic site, was in receivership for a third time when Anthony bought it. Determined and ambitious, Anthony turned Mission Hill into the anchor for the Okanagan's largest family-owned winery group supplied by 400 hectares (1,000 acres) of vineyards that are transitioning to organic.

Since 1992, the Mission Hill winemaking team has been led by experienced winemakers from either New Zealand or Australia. John Simes came from New Zealand in 1992 and retired in 2014. In his first vintage, he made a Chardonnay that won the first major award for an Okanagan winery in a London competition. The winery has won numerous awards since then. The current chief winemaker, Australian Ben Bryant, had been the chief winemaker for the Pernod Ricard group of wineries in Australia when Mission Hill's president (and former chief winemaker) Darryl Brooker recruited him in 2018.

WINEMAKER BEN BRYANT

ANTHONY VON MANDL

MY PICKS

Everything. Oculus, the Bordeaux blend made every vintage since 1997, is one of the Okanagan's top icon wines. The wines in Mission Hill's Terroir series are among the best single-vineyard wines in BC.

OPENED 1966

1730 Mission Hill Road
West Kelowna, BC
V4T 2E4

T 250.768.6400

W missionhillwinery.com
Restaurant: The Terrace
Restaurant (250.768.6467),
open daily for lunch May
to September, weather
permitting

MOCOJO WINES

NARAMATA

Kon Oh came to Canada from South Korea at 16 when his family moved to Alberta. It was his father's background in agriculture that brought Kon to wine (eventually). In Korea, his father was a leader in 4-H, an international agricultural youth movement. That brought him into contact with 4-H members in Alberta. "He got a taste of Western culture and lifestyle, and he decided to immigrate to Canada," Kon says.

The family settled in Lacombe. "When we were going to school, my father started a little vegetable garden and we were supplying mostly Korean stores in the city," Kon says. "We were growing radishes and cabbages, and stuff like that, for Korean people. We started with a little greenhouse in the early 1980s."

After a stint at retail employment, Kon picked up the family's bent for agriculture. "The farming life started with vegetables," he recalls. "I was not really thrilled to grow vegetables. It is a lot of work. I spent a year of research to develop the fresh-cut flower business in the greenhouse. We did that for 10 years, growing fresh-cut roses, competing with the South American cut-flower industry."

He and his wife, Dianne—she is of Dutch agricultural stock and grew up on a Nova Scotia blueberry farm—built a successful business, even with the disadvantage of heating a greenhouse in Alberta's winters. "We were working pretty much 24-7 cutting roses," Kon remembers. Ready for a change in lifestyle, they closed the flower business in 2008 and bought an established vineyard near Naramata. He also joined Naramata's volunteer fire department and is now its deputy chief.

In 2013, mentored by winemaker Richard Kanazawa, a neighbour, the couple decided to add value to their grapes by making wine. Starting with a debut production of 700 cases in

KON OH

2013, the winery is making almost 3,000 cases a year.

Kon made a significant change in his 1.8-hectare (4½-acre) vineyard, replacing 30-year-old Maréchal Foch vines with Malbec. "People either like Foch, or they don't," Kon has found. "Nobody sits on the fence." But it was not just consumer tastes that guided his decision. "I am not a fan of Foch," he says. "Maintaining the vines is a pain in the butt."

MY PICKS

The wines are all sound, with Malbec and Viognier standing out. Some will even lament that Foch was discontinued after the 2015 vintage.

OPENED 2014

1202 Gawne Road
Naramata, BC V0H 1N1
T 250.496.4063
W mocojowines.com

MONSTER VINEYARDS

PENTICTON

The Monster Vineyards winery makes wines that, with playful labels, celebrate the enduring myth of Ogopogo, the Okanagan's answer to the Loch Ness monster. There have been enough alleged sightings over the years to give a sliver of credibility that a prehistoric creature dwells in the dark vastness of Okanagan Lake.

Created in the 2006 vintage with sales beginning the following year, it is a sister label to Poplar Grove. Its value-priced portfolio complements Poplar Grove's premium portfolio. Both wineries draw almost entirely on grapes grown in the 30 hectares (75 acres) of vineyard owned by Barbara Holler, whose husband, Tony, is the majority partner in the wineries. As those vineyards approached full production, the Monster winery was built in 2011 on the site of a former Penticton apiary.

In contrast to the architectural showpiece Poplar Grove winery on the hillside above, the homely lines of the Monster facility hide the leading-edge winery under the metal skin. All of the Monster wines and most of the Poplar Grove wines are produced here. Stefan Arnason, the senior winemaker, has all of the tools a winemaker could want including a superbly equipped laboratory. Stefan, who was born in Port Moody in 1970, developed a keen appreciation of laboratories during three years at Andrés Wines and two at RJ Spagnols in New Westminster before he joined Poplar Grove in 2008.

Tony Holler has described the Monster wines as "fun wines that people can enjoy on a patio in the afternoon." The Monster concept was created by Vancouver marketer Bernie Hadley-Beauregard. "We did not want to refer to Ogopogo, but we wanted the wines to come in interesting bottles," Tony says. "We had

WINEMAKER STEFAN ARNASON

a graphic artist in London do all the images on the bottle. The images glow in the dark as well. It's a fun bottle, and the wine is very good."

MY PICKS

This portfolio does not break the bank; it just delivers flavour. Try the Riesling, the rosé, and Monster Cabs, an excellent Bordeaux blend.

OPENED 2007

1010 Tupper Avenue
Penticton, BC V2A 8S5

T   250.493.9463

W   monstervineyards.com

MONTAKARN WINERY

OKANAGAN FALLS

In an unusual move, Montakarn owner Gary Misson sold the original winery on Black Sage Road in 2019 to relocate the business to a virgin property near Okanagan Falls. It was strictly a practical financial decision. The sale allowed him to retire his mortgage and start off debt-free. "We will stay the same as we were before but without any bank pressure," Gary said in 2019 as he began planting a new vineyard.

He is a man of many careers and interests. Born in Campbell River in 1957, he spent 25 years sailing on tugboats and other coastal vessels. He still has a shaggy seaman's beard even though he tired of the sea years ago and earned a diploma in architectural technology in 2003. Between classes, he vacationed in Thailand where he met his wife, Monty, short for Montakarn, which inspired the winery's name.

When she found Vancouver's damp climate too cold after Thailand, they decided to put Gary's diploma to work on an Okanagan farm (he had a sister already living in the valley). In 2003, they bought a 4-hectare (10-acre) orchard near Oliver. After several years of growing peaches and apricots, his wine interest kicked in. "I have been making wine for myself since I was 20," he says. Since 2009, he planted about 3.6 hectares (9 acres) of Merlot, Malbec, Syrah, Cabernet Franc, and Chardonnay, along with blocks of Viognier, Tempranillo, and Sangiovese. The wines he made, initially with help from consultants, were often bold, reflecting the terroir of the Black Sage Bench. He still had an inventory of two years of wine when Montakarn was relocated to Okanagan Falls.

The move will lead to a profound change in Montakarn's portfolio because he is planting vines that suit the cooler terroir. Montakarn's new property is 5.6 hectares (14 acres) previously

GARY MISSON

occupied by a horse farm and by conifers. "We took nine logging trucks of timber out of here," Gary said in the spring of 2019 before developing the vineyard. He started with 1.2 hectares (3 acres) of vines, including Riesling, Chardonnay, Tempranillo, Albariño, and Muscat, along with small blocks of Merlot and Cabernet Franc on the hottest slope. Ultimately, Gary expects to plant a total of just over 4 hectares (10 acres).

MY PICKS

Current range was not available for tasting.

OPENED 2013

2356 Rolling Hills Road
Okanagan Falls, BC
V0H 1R2
T   250.498.7709
W   montakarn.ca

MONTE CREEK RANCH WINERY

Monte Creek Ranch Winery, set dramatically high above the Trans-Canada Highway, takes its name from a nearby community, now almost a ghost town, whose peak notoriety was in 1906 when the bandit Bill Miner held up a train for the last time. The winery has memorialized the event with two wines called Hands Up. Now the largest wine producer in the Thompson Valley sub-appellation, Monte Creek Ranch Winery has a capacity to make 54,000 cases a year. It all started in 2007 when Gurjit Sidhu, a Fraser Valley blueberry grower and nursery man, bought a 365-hectare (900-acre) ranch east of Kamloops for a new blueberry farm. When he learned blueberries do not thrive in the Thompson Valley's near desert, he decided to grow grapes.

Consultants advised against planting vinifera because the winters are colder here than in the Okanagan. So, beginning in 2010, Monte Creek planted British Columbia's first major block of winter-hardy Minnesota hybrid grapes. These include Marquette, Le Crescent, and three members of the Frontenac grape family, varieties that were unfamiliar to British Columbia consumers. Subsequently, Monte Creek concluded that the vinifera risk had been overstated and planted Riesling, Gewürztraminer, Chardonnay, and Pinot Noir. The vineyard blocks, which are on either side of the Thompson River, total 30 hectares (75 acres).

Monte Creek, which had its first vintage in 2013, also purchased grapes from the Okanagan. The increasingly tight supply of those grapes led Monte Creek in 2018 to acquire 37 hectares (92 acres) of raw land in the Similkameen Valley. The property is on the southwest flank of the Similkameen River, just east of Keremeos. It once was part of a ranch developed in the late 19th century by an English settler, Barrington Price. In recent years, it grew only hay.

ERIK FISHER

Monte Creek is taking advantage of the cool site's northeastern exposure to plant a significant block of Pinot Noir, a varietal of rising importance in the winery's portfolio. Pedro Parra, a Chilean viticultural consultant who has advised several Okanagan producers, helped Monte Creek explore the soil profile. "There is a considerable amount of limestone in some of those rocks, which we think will go a long way to producing premium-quality Pinot Noir," says Erik Fisher, the winery's general manager.

MY PICKS

Everything. In the Thompson River Valley, the Minnesota hybrids deliver riper-flavoured wines than in the northern US or Quebec, where they are also planted. The winery's Riesling, Chardonnay, and Pinot Noir are excellent as well.

OPENED 2014

2420 Miner's Bluff Road
PO Box 11
Monte Creek, BC
V0E 2M0

T   250.573.5399
1.855.633.9463 (WINE)
(toll-free)

W   montecreekranch.com
Restaurant: The Terrace
Restaurant, open daily in
season 11:30–6, weather
permitting

MOON CURSER VINEYARDS

OSOYOOS

Moon Curser Vineyards offers perhaps the most varietally diverse portfolio of any Okanagan winery. Chris Tolley, the winemaker and co-proprietor, is drawn to varieties beyond the popular mainstream vines. A Moon Curser wine list includes Arneis, Dolcetto, Tannat, Tempranillo, Touriga Nacional, Carménère, and Nebbiolo.

"I love the diversity," Chris says. "I love the affirmation that this valley is capable of doing a wide variety of wines. Maybe we do one of these varieties better than anywhere else in the world." Indeed, he would put up a Moon Curser Tannat against wines from Uruguay where that variety thrives. The flagship red at Moon Curser, Dead of Night, is an inspired blend of equal parts Tannat and Syrah.

Chris, who was born in 1966 in Montreal, is a former software engineer. Beata, his Polish-born wife, practised as a chartered accountant until the couple decided to change careers. "We were looking for something more, something better, and we decided to do a winery and vineyard," Chris says. Lacking a wine background, they went to New Zealand in 2003 for postgraduate degrees in enology and viticulture at Lincoln University. The following year, they bought an Osoyoos orchard where they planted their first vineyard and built the winery.

In both New Zealand and Australia, a small number of varietals dominate the wines. Chris and Beata concluded their winery was more likely to stand out if they did not merely echo what others were doing. That has not been taken to extremes: Moon Curser also offers Syrah, Cabernet Sauvignon, Malbec, and other Bordeaux varieties . A 4-hectare (10-acre) vineyard planted in west Osoyoos in 2018 grows Merlot, Cabernet Franc, and more Syrah.

BEATA AND CHRIS TOLLEY

In 2010, they decided that the winery's original name, Twisted Tree, was too bland and rebranded as Moon Curser. "Moon Curser is a synonym for a smuggler," Beata explains. "The whole idea is that the wine is all about the place. We picked Osoyoos for the sunshine and the heat. We wanted something that talked about the location, but we did not want to do it in the traditional way. There is a history of gold smuggling that took place here during the gold rush of the 1800s. The smugglers would curse at the moon because the border agents would catch them"—in its light. The labels echo this story: Dead of Night features a fox and an owl with a lantern.

MY PICKS

Everything, notably Dead of Night, a collectible red blend, and Afraid of the Dark, a blend of Viognier, Roussanne, and Marsanne.

OPENED 2006
(AS TWISTED TREE
VINEYARDS & WINERY)

3628 Highway 3 East
Osoyoos, BC V0H 1V6

T 250.495.5161

W mooncurser.com

Accommodation: The Hideout Guest House (a three-bedroom suite)

MORAINE ESTATE WINERY

PENTICTON

Oleg Aristarkhov crossed Canadian wine off his list after tasting his first in Edmonton ("The wine was awful," he remembers) when he and his wife, Svetlana, were new immigrants there in the 1990s. "I have liked wines all of my life," says Oleg, an oil-industry electrical engineer who was born in 1965 in western Siberia. He established a business involving instrumentation for the oil industry and came to Edmonton to enlist partners and technology to support his Russian business.

In time, they vacationed in the Okanagan, coming away impressed with the beauty of the valley and the rising quality of the wines. The Aristarkhovs bought a Naramata Bench property for a vacation home and then moved to the Okanagan after 15 years in Edmonton. "We asked ourselves, what is the reason for living in Edmonton?" Oleg says. "I can run my business from any place in the world." His neighbour was vintner Sal D'Angelo. Oleg tapped Sal's expertise and, by 2010, had planted 1.6 hectares (4 acres) of Pinot Noir on what he called the Sophia Vineyard, after one of his daughters.

That fall, the Holman Lang group of wineries went into receivership. One of the group's seven wineries, Zero Balance Vineyards, had just opened two years before. "After Holman went under, I thought it was a good business opportunity to pick up that winery," Oleg says. The winery is right on Naramata Road with a 2.8-hectare (7-acre) vineyard now named Anastasia, for his other daughter. Oleg bought the winery in 2011, renaming it Moraine for the glacial soil on the Naramata Bench.

Moraine's first winemaker, New Zealand–born Jacqueline Kemp, hired in 2012, made excellent wines through six vintages in what had been Zero Balance's dilapidated tractor shed. By 2017, when Moraine's production was 8,000 cases, she helped design

WINEMAKERS DWIGHT SICK
AND AMBER PRATT

SVETLANA AND
OLEG ARISTARKHOV

the current modern 15,000-case winery. When she left before the 2018 vintage (to join Therapy Vineyards), she was succeeded by Dwight Sick. Born in 1965 in Edson, Alberta, Dwight came to wine after 19 years as a flight attendant. He started in 2004 as a cellar hand at Township 7 Vineyards & Winery. After burnishing his winemaking skills with courses from the University of California, he joined Stag's Hollow Winery in 2008.

MY PICKS

Everything, especially Chardonnay, Viognier, Pinot Noir, and Malbec. The bread-and-butter value blends are Cliffhanger White and Cliffhanger Red.

OPENED 2012

1865 Naramata Road
Penticton, BC V2A 8T9
T   250.460.1836
    778.476.7688
W   morainewinery.com

MT. BOUCHERIE ESTATE WINERY

WEST KELOWNA

The dramatic new winery, tasting room, and restaurant that is Mt. Boucherie Estate Winery show that it has emerged with new ownership and new direction after a tumultuous recent past of family feuding.

When the winery opened in 2001, it was operated by three brothers: Sarwan, Nirmal, and Kaldep Gidda. Their father, Mehtab, brought his family to the Okanagan from India in 1958. The family began growing grapes in 1975, eventually owning significant vineyards in both the Okanagan and the Similkameen Valleys. Sarwan, the eldest brother, withdrew from the partnership in 2008 to establish his own family winery, Volcanic Hills. Several years later, an acrimonious split between the other brothers ultimately landed Mt. Boucherie in bankruptcy in 2014.

The winery attracted interest from several groups when the receiver put it on the market in 2015. The successful bidder, a group headed by Vancouver businessman Sonny Huang, took over Mt. Boucherie on March 30, 2016. Born in China, Sonny is a long-time resident of British Columbia and a self-made entrepreneur who started with a pizza shop and now is a real-estate developer as well as an importer/exporter of produce and wine.

Sonny has breathed fresh life into Mt. Boucherie; its future has never been brighter. The winery's 121 hectares (300 acres) of vineyards throughout the Okanagan and Similkameen Valleys have been rejuvenated; a quarter has been replanted, with better varieties such as Cabernet Franc and Cabernet Sauvignon replacing such unfortunate original choices as Dornfelder. The new winery has a capacity to produce 55,000 cases a year, double a previous high. The facilities include a 15,000-square-foot wine experience centre. It is located at the highest point on the property with a dramatic view of Okanagan Lake.

JEFF HUNDERTMARK

Winemaking was taken over in 2019 by Saskatoon-born Jeff Hundertmark. He started out in the hospitality industry, eventually becoming a sommelier; he was once the sommelier at the Château Laurier hotel in Ottawa. He then spent almost 20 years operating restaurants. "I fell in love with the whole aspect of wine," he says. "I decided in my 40s to go back to school and learn to be a winemaker. I was tired of wearing suits and ties." He worked with several Ontario wineries including Marynissen, Stoney Ridge, and Mike Weir Winery before he moved to the Okanagan in 2017, working initially at Rust Wine Co., which shares ownership with Mt. Boucherie.

MY PICKS

Pinot Gris, Riesling, and Gewürztraminer shine among the whites. Leading reds are Merlot, Cabernet Franc, and Syrah. Summit, always a good red Bordeaux blend, is better with the recent addition of Syrah to the blend. Contessa is a recently introduced luxury Bordeaux blend.

OPENED 2001

829 Douglas Road
West Kelowna, BC
V1Z 1N9
T 250.769.8803
W mtboucherie.com
Restaurant: To open Spring 2020

NAGGING DOUBT WINERY

KELOWNA

Searching for a wine name and a label, Rob Westbury turned to the Vancouver marketing guru Bernie Hadley-Beauregard, a creator of edgy labels. Rob recalls: "He said, 'You know, Rob, this is really your nagging doubt. This is that dream you have wanted to fulfill all your life, and it has been nagging at you.'"

A human relations executive, Rob launched Nagging Doubt as a virtual winery. With the help of a consultant, he made the first four vintages in a custom crush winery, starting with just 150 cases of wine in 2010. In the 2014 vintage, he established Nagging Doubt on a 5.6-hectare (14-acre) property in East Kelowna, turning an existing stable into a winery. Rob and his wife, Abbey, planted just over 2 hectares (about 5½ acres) of vines—Siegerrebe, Chardonnay, Pinot Noir, and Ortega, varieties suited to this cool site. A leased Naramata Bench vineyard grows Merlot for the winery.

Born in Edmonton in 1969, Rob has degrees in psychology and telecommunications management, leading to a career that took him all over North America with an international consulting firm. "I've always enjoyed wine, ever since I was legal to drink," he says. "The tipping point was I had an assignment in San Francisco. I remember going to Napa and Sonoma almost every weekend. I just woke up one morning and thought, 'I could definitely do this for a living.'" Starting as a virtual winery husbanded his limited resources. "The hardest thing about the BC wine industry is how much it costs to get into the business," Rob says. "I have had to be very creative in what I can accomplish."

Rob's target is to grow Nagging Doubt to 2,000 cases a year, tightly focused on The Pull, a Bordeaux blend, and the wines his vineyard gives him. "I have always wanted to stay boutique," Rob says. "My dream was to have a small, family-owned, hands-on

ROB WESTBURY

artisan winery." And that mirrors his approach to winemaking. "I am a big believer in terroir," he says. "Wines should taste like where they are grown. To me, the best way to achieve that is with minimal manipulation of the wine once it is picked."

MY PICKS

Everything, notably The Pull, a fine Merlot-anchored red blend; the Pinot Noir; and the Chardonnay. The Siegerrebe is a finely crafted aromatic white.

SALES BEGAN 2011

4513 Sallows Road
Kelowna, BC V1W 4C2

T 250.764.0610

W naggingdoubt.com

Visits and tastings by appointment

NICHE WINE COMPANY

WEST KELOWNA

The name Niche is appropriate as owners James and Joanna Schlosser are slowly carving out a wine career among their own busy lives. Since debuting with their first vintages in 2011, the pair have slowly grown their winery to producing 1,000 cases annually.

The key to their wines is their unique high-altitude vineyard, the Hugh and Mary Vineyard, which has been owned by James's parents Jerold and Kathleen Schlosser since 1978 and is named for James's grandparents. Jerold planted two clones of Pinot Noir in 1997. Other varieties planted since include Gewürztraminer, Pinot Blanc, Chardonnay, Maréchal Foch, and Riesling. Though the altitude is high, the southerly aspect ensures good sun exposure. The elevation also provides extreme diurnal temperature swings far exceeding those at lower elevations. In addition, the nearly constant wind keeps both mould and pests at bay. "Things don't stick," explains Joanna. "It definitely works for the Pinot Noir."

His parents encouraged James, who was born in 1975, to pursue enology at Brock University in Ontario after having completed a science degree at the University of Victoria. He began making wine while working as a technology development officer for the BC Cancer Agency. Joanna, who was born in North Vancouver, worked as a flight attendant while studying communications at Simon Fraser University. After leaving the airline industry, she studied graphic design at Emily Carr and spent six years with Lululemon's e-commerce platforms. Both James and Joanna worked full-time in Vancouver during the week and commuted to West Kelowna to work at Niche on weekends. Wines were sold largely through personal connections in Vancouver.

By 2014, they decided to move to the Okanagan to be close to the winery and to get to know other people in the industry. "The BC wine industry," says Joanna, "is one of the most friendly, co-

JOANNA AND JAMES
SCHLOSSER WITH SON HUGH

operative, supportive industries I've had the pleasure of working in." Because the Hugh and Mary Vineyard is too far off the beaten path for a wine shop, James and Joanna are actively looking for a new property with a vineyard and good access for a public tasting room.

MY PICKS

The Pinot Noirs, including the white Pinot Noir, are elegant. The whites and the sparkling wine are also well made.

OPENED 2011

1901 Bartley Road
West Kelowna, BC
V1Z 2M6
T   778.940.9463
W   nichewinecompany.com

NICHOL VINEYARD

NARAMATA

A few years ago, Ross Hackworth noticed an alarming trend with the winery's customer list. Wine-release announcements were bouncing back because long-time buyers, some on the list since the early 1990s, were dying just as he was increasing production. To attract younger consumers to the Nichol brand, he began in 2011 to sell wine in 20-litre steel kegs, one of the first wineries to do so. Wine-by-the-glass programs at restaurants target younger consumers. "The buzz was fantastic," Ross says. And he hired a sales director, Matt Sherlock, who was then an under-30s sommelier and wine educator. "We are finally seeing some younger traffic come to the winery," Ross said in 2012.

Ross inherited the aging customer list when he bought the winery from founders Alex and Kathleen Nichol, who retired in 2002. In fact, Ross probably was on the list. "I knew the Nichol wines," Ross says. "I'd been drinking them for years."

Born in California, Ross was 10 years old in 1973 when his parents bought the Penticton-area orchard where he grew up. A business graduate from the British Columbia Institute of Technology, Ross was previously a sales vice-president in the Vancouver office of a Japanese pulp and paper giant. Corporate entertaining educated his wine palate, but, tiring of the job's extensive travel, he was drawn back to Naramata.

Since taking over the winery, Ross has doubled production to about 3,500 cases, all with Naramata Bench grapes. The winery's 4-hectare (10-acre) vineyard has been supplemented with grapes from nearby vineyards, some planted with the same varieties Nichol already was growing: Syrah, Cabernet Franc, Pinot Gris, and Pinot Noir. "We are absolutely invested in Naramata," Ross says. "That has been my plan from day one. A lot has to do with the fact that I grew up out here. Every year, I appreciate the benefit of being out here."

ROSS HACKWORTH

MY PICKS

Everything. The Syrah can be a big, brooding South of France red in the best years and light and peppery in cooler years. The Cabernet Franc and the Pinot Noir are deep, concentrated wines. The pink-hued Pinot Gris, intense in flavour, is a deliciously eccentric take on this varietal.

OPENED 1993

1285 Smethurst Road
Naramata, BC V0H 1N1
T   250.496.5962
W   nicholvineyard.com

NIGHTHAWK VINEYARDS

OKANAGAN FALLS

On one occasion, Daniel Bibby arrived at the winery from his other job, garbed in a well-cut business suit, to host a late-afternoon tasting. The first thing he did was change into his casual winery garb. He is still general manager of Kelowna's leading hotel while also operating Nighthawk Vineyards with his wife, Christy, and their son, Dakota, the winemaker.

Born in Edmonton in 1968, Daniel came into the wine industry by way of the hospitality business. "I was an executive chef for a number of years," he says. "Then I became a director of food and beverage, then a director of operations, a hotel manager, and a general manager." However, the dream of operating a winery crystallized after he and Christy, a professional educator, spent a weekend luxuriating at the Burrowing Owl winery's guest house.

Initially with partners who have since left the business, Daniel and Christy in 2014 acquired a charming property with a log cabin home and a mature 4-hectare (10-acre) vineyard beside spring-fed Green Lake. Half the vines are Gewürztraminer, with Pinot Noir and Chardonnay making up the rest. They also contract grapes, including Bordeaux varieties, from Oliver vineyards.

Vintages from 2015 through 2017 were made under the direction of Matt Dumayne at Okanagan Crush Pad. Nighthawk gradually took control of the winemaking as Dakota completed enology courses and gained experience with other Okanagan producers. The objective is to involve the entire Bibby family during the course of the year. Dakota's three siblings join the family for blending sessions.

Nighthawk produces about 3,000 cases a year. "We always plan on remaining a farm-gate winery," Daniel says. "I always want to be in touch with our guests—to be able to walk the vineyard

DANIEL AND CHRISTY BIBBY

WINEMAKER DAKOTA BIBBY

with people and talk about what makes the grapes grow, and to taste them off the vines."

The winery's name was inspired by the nighthawks that nest in the Okanagan. "They are a unique bird to Canada, usually a warm-climate bird," Daniel recounts. "They come here because this is the northern tip of the Sonoran Desert. They usually come in the evening and circle around the vineyard. When they come in, we feel like they are guarding the winery at night."

MY PICKS

The Gewürztraminer and the Chardonnay are full of flavour. Pinot Noir and Cabernet Franc are well made. Nocturnus, a Bordeaux blend, is a collectible red.

OPENED 2015

2735 Green Lake Road
Okanagan Falls, BC
V0H 1R0

T   250.497.8874
    250.300.9161

W   nighthawkvineyards.com

NK'MIP CELLARS

OSOYOOS

In 1997, the Osoyoos Indian Band, having been refused a casino licence, regrouped around a more original idea: North America's first Indigenous winery in a joint venture with Vincor (now Arterra Wines Canada). Nk'Mip Cellars (pronounced EN-ka-meep) made its first vintage in 2000 and now produces 20,000 cases a year. The winery, a Santa Fe pueblo design by architect Robert Mackenzie, anchors a resort-like cluster of luxury condominiums, a golf course, and an interpretation centre overlooking Osoyoos Lake.

The entrepreneurial band operates a large business portfolio, of which the winery is the most prestigious. A significant number of the wines are released as the winery's top tier, called Qwam Qwmt (meaning "achieving excellence"). The winery has access to the best grapes grown in vineyards controlled by the band. "Grapes are not an issue for us," senior winemaker Randy Picton says. "The band has 1,500 acres [600 hectares] under production, and they will give us whatever we need."

Randy, born in 1968 in Saskatchewan, came to winemaking in 1996 after a career that included 10 years as a tree planter. He advanced rapidly in the cellar of CedarCreek Estate Winery, moving to Nk'Mip in 2002. Here he has developed a team that includes winemaker Justin Hall and cellar master Aaron Crey. "One of the things I am most proud about with our wines is the consistency across the portfolio," Randy says. "I think they are all good wines. There is a consistency there, and the fact that we have been a team for 15 years is one of the reasons."

The flagship wines, red and white, are both called Mer'r'iym, Salish for "marriage," since both wines are elegant blends. The red blend, usually anchored with the superb Cabernet Sauvignon from

RANDY PICTON

the vineyard around the winery, has been in the best vintages since 2008. White Mer'r'iym, a blend of about 70% Sauvignon Blanc and 30% Sémillon, was first made in 2016.

MY PICKS

Everything. The wines in the Winemaker's series, especially Dreamcatcher, Pinot Blanc, and Talon, are well priced. Every wine in the Qwam Qwmt tier shows sophistication and elegance. Mer'r'iym is an iconic wine for cellaring.

OPENED 2002

1400 Rancher Creek Road
Osoyoos, BC V0H 1V6

T   250.495.2985

W   nkmipcellars.com
Restaurant: The Patio Restaurant, open daily for lunch late April to early October, 11:30–3 (but extended to 4 pm July/August). Wine lounge, open April through October, 3–5 (extended to 7 pm July/August)

NOBLE RIDGE VINEYARD & WINERY

OKANAGAN FALLS

This winery took root in 1998 in Europe, where Jim and Leslie D'Andrea visited numerous wineries during a three-month family sabbatical. Jim was already a wine enthusiast with a growing library of viticulture books. In Châteauneuf-du-Pape, they met a former accountant who had switched careers to manage a winery and to live the appealing lifestyle. It inspired them.

Born in Welland, Ontario, in 1954, Jim moved to Calgary in 1982 to join the law firm Bennett Jones LLP. He headed the firm's employment practice group until retiring in 2016 to immerse himself entirely in the winery. Leslie, born in Toronto, has a master's in health administration and worked extensively in that field until switching her skills to the administration of Noble Ridge.

They looked at vineyard properties in France and Ontario before focusing on the Okanagan, a region that they believed held the promise for producing great red wines. In 2001 they purchased a 10-hectare (25-acre) hilltop property on Oliver Ranch Road with a small planting of Cabernet Sauvignon, Merlot, and Chardonnay. They filled out the vineyard with Pinot Noir and Pinot Gris. "We just love Champagne," Jim says. "That was what drove us when we started this." In time, the winery released a traditional-method sparkling wine called The One that mirrors very good Champagne.

They expanded in 2006 by purchasing a neighbouring vineyard on the east side of Oliver Ranch Road. "Being able to obtain some land in our area is of great importance to us," Jim says. "We are strongly of the view that the Okanagan Falls 'appellation' is a premier wine-growing region." The sturdy barn on the property became an excellent winery; its production capacity has since been doubled.

JIM AND LESLIE D'ANDREA

Noble Ridge is an estate producer relying exclusively on its own grapes. Its vineyards, when fully planted, will allow the winery to cap its annual production at about 6,000 cases. "Our goal was to make premium-quality wine," Jim says. "I have fallen in love with the reds."

The best wines of the vintage are released under the King's Ransom designation. This ultra-premium tier was launched in the 2006 vintage with a red Meritage. The King's Ransom wines are made only in exceptional vintages; the second one, also a Meritage, was produced in 2009. Subsequent wines in this tier have encompassed Chardonnay, Pinot Noir, and Cabernet Sauvignon. Good viticulture has ensured a King's Ransom in many vintages.

MY PICKS

Everything. Any wine under the King's Ransom label is world class, as are the more affordable tiers, including the elegant sparkling wine and the unpretentious Pinot Grigio.

OPENED 2005

2320 Oliver Ranch Road
Okanagan Falls, BC
V0H 1R2

T   250.497.7945
W nobleridge.com
Picnic area
Food service: Picnic foods
available

OFF THE GRID ORGANIC WINERY

WEST KELOWNA

It is unlikely that there is a winery in BC where the expression *family-run* means more than it does at Off The Grid winery in West Kelowna. The Paynter family's roots in the Okanagan go back to 1909 when Edwin and Margaret Paynter immigrated to Canada from England. They returned to Britain to serve in the First World War but returned to settle in West Kelowna in 1919. Their original property was quite large. Many of the parcels of land were subdivided over the years among the Paynter family.

The property where Off The Grid is located is surrounded by extended Paynter family and was purchased by Paynter brothers Nigel and Travis. Both married ambitious women who have largely spearheaded Off The Grid's winery operations. Travis's wife, Sheri, a chef by trade, is the winemaker, while Nigel's wife, Hayley, takes care of the wine shop and the marketing. Other members of the family help out when needed.

The determination to grow organically came from Sheri's late father-in-law, Geoffrey Paynter, who died in 2016 shortly after the winery had been established. While studying winemaking at Okanagan College, Sheri met others in the industry who reinforced that organic viticulture in the Okanagan was possible. The vineyard had been planted starting in 2005, and grapes were originally sold to other wineries.

People, animals, and vehicles mingle on this property. Cars are to drive slowly on the winery's gravel road to keep from stirring up dust but also to avoid animals that may be roaming free. "We've designed the farm so that people can interact with animals," explains Sheri. Two hectares (5 acres) on the site not suitable for planting are perfect for the goats, who were taken in as rescues from the SPCA. The goats are named after the characters in the television show *Friends* (Ross, Rachel, etc.).

They provide a unique farm experience for visitors along with fire control by eating the pine needles and bark trimmings from the trees. However, the goats also delayed the winery opening. Getting permits and licences for a commercial building with goats on the roof took so long that the winery missed a planned July 1, 2015, opening by four and a half months.

MY PICKS

The Rieslings (there are often more than one), Pinot Gris, and Zweigelt stand out in the portfolio.

OPENED 2015

3623 Glencoe Road
West Kelowna, BC
V4T 1L8

T 778.754.7562

W offthegridorganicwinery.com

OKANAGAN CRUSH PAD WINERY (FREE FORM, HAYWIRE, AND NARRATIVE)

SUMMERLAND

Wine trade publications often publish articles on the latest technology and trends in the industry. When a major wine magazine published an article about new egg-shaped concrete fermenters, it was no surprise that Okanagan Crush Pad took delivery of their own egg-shaped fermenters shortly afterward. They had clearly read the same publication and are equally enamoured with the latest wine trends and technology.

The winery was started by Christine Coletta and husband Steve Lornie in 2010 with a small selection of varietal wines branded as Haywire. Christine, born in 1955, was already a wine-industry veteran as the executive director of the BC Wine Institute through the critical 1990s when British Columbia wine started being taken seriously. Since that time, she has handled the marketing for many wineries throughout the province, and brought that acumen to OCP's three main brands—Haywire, Free Form, and Narrative.

Though each brand has a particular focus, they all start with grapes grown in the winery's three major vineyards: Switchback Vineyard next to the winery, Secrest Mountain Vineyard near Oliver, and Garnet Valley Ranch north of Summerland. When the planting at Garnet Valley is finished, OCP will have almost 53 hectares (130 acres) of vineyards, all of it organic. "What we're trying to do is be the masters and commanders of all of our own varieties, and planting everything that we need to be self-sufficient," Christine explains.

To test the limits of winemaking and viticulture, Christine has enlisted international expertise. Italian winemaking consultant Alberto Antonini and Chilean viticulturist Pedro Parra have guided the organic viticulture that Christine embraced. Farming with chemical fertilizers and pesticides is not judged beneficial.

STEVE LATCHFORD, JULIAN SCHOLEFIELD,
CHRISTINE COLETTA, AND MATT DUMAYNE

Christine believes that old vines in other parts of the world have survived for as long as they did because they weren't exposed to modern chemicals. "We need to step back from all of that stuff and just use some basic things." That philosophy includes a diversity of crops and animals near the vineyards. The Garnet Valley Ranch also grows vegetables, which are marketed and sold by Localmotive, operated by farmer Thomas Tumbach. Localmotive customers can add OCP wines to their orders of fresh vegetables.

Winemaker Matt Dumayne, who has been with OCP since 2014, has taken wine production in the direction that Christine wants, particularly with the use of concrete for fermentation and maturation. "I think we need to find our own style, and for me, part of that is not masking it with big oak," Christine says. "I personally don't think that we're going to be making British Columbia's calling card to the world with wines that emulate what everyone else is doing in Napa, Bordeaux, or anywhere else." Winemaker Steve Latchford, recruited in 2018, added more depth to the production team. Julian Scholefield holds the daily details together as operations manager.

MY PICKS

All of the wines show varietal character well, with a fresh and unique perspective that comes from the frequent use of concrete, which creates beautifully textured wines. Pinot Gris, Chardonnay, and Cabernet Franc are all standouts.

OPENED 2010

16576 Fosbery Road
Summerland, BC V0H 1Z6

T   250.494.4445

W   okanagancrushpad.com

OLIVER TWIST ESTATE WINERY

OLIVER

Gina Harfman, who purchased Oliver Twist in 2012 from founders Bruce and Denice Hagerman, decided to keep the winery name while creating a second label–Nostalgia–to put her own stamp on the business. The Nostalgia wines all have labels featuring pin-up girls created by Ralph Burch, a San Diego designer. "We have a lot of old things in here," Gina explains. "We go for the 1950s, 1960s theme. The baby boomers really like it."

Gina grew up around wine. Her maternal grandfather, Joe Fernandes, left Madeira in the 1960s to establish an orchard in Osoyoos. Her father, Fred, has 6 hectares (15 acres) of vineyard in Osoyoos. That sparked Gina's winemaking career, starting with the assistant winemaker course at Okanagan College in 2009 and a crush and a half at Cassini Cellars (until she went on maternity leave). She helped Denice and consultant Christine Leroux with the 2011 crush at Oliver Twist. "We were bottling one day," Gina remembers. "Bruce and Denice said, 'Why don't you buy the winery?'"

The offer was in character for the Hagermans, who had made a lifetime habit of moving to fresh adventures. "I like to do different things," Bruce said once. "I asked an old lady about the things she did in her life, and what it was she regretted. She said, 'Sonny, it is not the things I did in my life that I regret–it is the things I didn't do.'"

Denice continues to help Gina, now a single mother of two with a passion for winemaking. Gina has an extensive portfolio of small-lot wines, offered exclusively to members of the wine club that Oliver Twist established in 2013. The five or six wines in the Nostalgia series, along with the Kerner and Pinot Gris from Oliver Twist's 6.9-hectare (17-acre) vineyard, constitute the winery's major volume.

GINA HARFMAN

MY PICKS

Join the wine club for access to the small-lot wines. Meanwhile, explore the Nostalgia series, notably the excellent blend called Rockabilly Red. The taste is as seductive as the pin-up on the label.

OPENED 2007

398 Lupine Lane
Oliver, BC V0H 1T1
T   250.485.0227
W   olivertwistwinery.com

ONE FAITH VINEYARDS

When Bill Lui started this winery in the 2012 vintage, he set a very high bar. "First-growth [or *premier cru*] wines are what all my friends are used to," he said. "I hope I can be a first growth of the Okanagan in time."

His strategy for reaching that goal began with premium Black Sage Bench grapes and by retaining a distinguished consulting winemaker from Napa, Anne Vawter. She made the first four vintages for One Faith. After she left, Bill turned to other consultants, including Pascal Madevon, the initial winemaker at Osoyoos Larose. Bill also took courses in winemaking and viticulture to help him manage the 4-hectare (10-acre) vineyard that One Faith bought in 2016.

One Faith is a significant career change for Bill. He was born in Hong Kong in 1959 and grew up in Canada. After getting a degree in environmental science from Wilfrid Laurier University in Waterloo, he returned to Asia to work in merchant banking and manufacturing. In China, he managed a company that made medical instruments. After taking it public and selling his interest, he retired to Vancouver, in part to be with his school-aged children and to look after aging parents. And, with time on his hands, he decided to become an Okanagan wine grower.

He retained James Cluer, a wine educator and consultant with a Master of Wine, for guidance on grape sources and winemakers. The initial vintages were made with grapes from the Sundial and Saddle Ridge Vineyards on the Black Sage Bench. When those properties were sold, Bill bought One Faith's current vineyard, planted primarily with Merlot and Cabernet Franc, along with small blocks of Sauvignon Blanc and Sémillon. Other fruit is also purchased from Black Sage growers. Bill's target is to produce about 2,000 cases of premium wine annually.

WINEMAKER ANNE VAWTER

OWNER BILL LUI

The model is Bordeaux and the first-growth wines that Bill's friends drink. Grand Vin, the flagship blend, is priced accordingly. In the fashion of the leading Bordeaux estates, One Faith also releases an excellent but lower-priced second label, called Certitude. Nor does the winery miss a chance to add to its portfolio when it has a few barrels of well-made wine that does not fit into its blends, such as the Malbec/Petit Verdot blend in the 2016 vintage.

MY PICKS

Everything, especially the exquisite Grand Vin.

OPENED 2014

4644 Black Sage Road
Oliver, BC V0H 1T1

T   604.339.7070

W   onefaithvineyards.com

ORIGIN WINES

PENTICTON

Daiya and Blake Anderson typed potential winery names into their smartphones for several years before settling on Origin. The named clicked because both grew up in the Okanagan and pursued careers in Vancouver before rediscovering their roots in the valley to launch this winery.

Blake's parents planted and briefly operated a vineyard on Naramata Road, now the site of Moraine Estate Winery. Daiya met Blake at a vineyard party where, when offered a drink, she asked for a glass of wine and discovered they both were interested in wine. She had acquired the taste when working at Earls restaurants for 14 years. Born in 1982, she had grown up on Black Sage Road and in Penticton. "I actually started university in Kelowna," Daiya says. "I was studying political science and psychology, two interests of mine in daily life. Then I ended up working in a restaurant to pay for college. I got into management quickly."

In Vancouver, they furthered their knowledge of wine by studying sommelier courses in their spare time. "That's where we started to think maybe we would like to go back to the Okanagan. Maybe we will be able to do a vineyard or a winery one day, when we retired, or something along those lines."

In 2009, having decided to accelerate their plans, they developed a 2.8-hectare (7-acre) vineyard near Kaleden, planting Gewürztraminer, Pinot Noir, and Merlot. They soon realized that they needed to establish their winery where there was much more wine touring. That led to the Naramata Bench, the most concentrated cluster of wineries in the Okanagan. They purchased a secluded property with a million-dollar view of vineyards and Okanagan Lake. Here they planted 1.2 more hectares (3 acres) of grapes: Syrah, Cabernet Franc, Malbec, and a little Viognier. The previous owner, a woman, had lived here for 42 years and wanted

DAIYA AND BLAKE ANDERSON

new owners equally committed to the property. "We said our goal was to find a place where we are going to live forever," Daiya says. "Our goal is just to keep doing this."

They moved here in 2016, turning a well-built barn into a cozy wine shop. The landscaping at the winery, which also hosts weddings, carefully preserves the natural features on this bench. Natural except for the cactus garden, a nostalgic nod to Arizona where the couple were married.

Blake juggles vineyard work with a full-time job at a graphic arts studio in Kelowna. Daiya, who manages the wine shop with the professional charm of an ex-restaurateur, has taken the University of Washington winemaking course and makes the wines. "Winemaking is my big career shift," she says. "I absolutely love it."

MY PICKS

The winery started with four well-made wines: Gü, as the winery labels its Gewürztraminer; Chardonnay; Pinot Noir; and Farm House, a Merlot/ Cabernet Franc blend. Recently, an orange wine and a rosé joined the portfolio.

OPENED 2017

1278 Riddle Road
Penticton, BC V2A 8X2
T 250.328.2158
W originwines.ca
Picnic area

OROFINO WINERY

CAWSTON

Credit Orofino's John Weber for codifying sub-appellations in the Similkameen appellation. In 2018 he began naming on his wine labels regions where he gets grapes, including the Cawston Bench, the Keremeos Bench, and Olalla Gap. "Our tiny little valley, which is 24 kilometres long, has some fairly distinct growing areas," he says. "Consumers want to know about that."

This champion of the Similkameen, formerly a teacher, arrived in the valley in March 2001 from Saskatchewan with his wife, Virginia, a nurse. They took over a 1.8-hectare (4½-acre) vineyard near Cawston that had been planted in 1989. "We spent the first year on a huge learning curve," John remembers. Original thinkers, they used straw bales to build an energy-efficient winery and tasting room. Solar panels added in 2012 make Orofino largely energy self-sufficient.

John's unofficial sub-appellations extend the winery's practice of naming vineyards on the labels. Orofino, Hendsbee, and Passion Pit are all on the Cawston Bench, while the Scout Vineyard is on the South Cawston Bench. Comparative tastings of John's dry Rieslings from Hendsbee and Scout show the distinct flavours from terroirs just a few kilometres apart. The Hendsbee, John says, is "linear," while the Scout Riesling is "more friendly."

Orofino produces its wines entirely from Similkameen grapes. John no longer needs Okanagan fruit: the winery started by owning 3.6 hectares (9 acres) of vineyards, and John was contracting to farm another 8 hectares (20 acres). This included the Passion Pit Vineyard, a one-time spot for lovers' trysts, where the former owner planted a hectare (2½ acres) of Cabernet Sauvignon for Orofino in 2007. In 2018, Orofino bought the entire 4.2-hectare (10½-acre) property with plans to put vines on the rest.

Orofino's flagship wine is Beleza, a red blend anchored with Cabernet Sauvignon and Merlot. The original vintage in 2006 was simply labelled with the varietal names. The wine took the proprietary name in 2007. "It means 'beauty' in Portuguese," Virginia explains. "John spent some time in Brazil. It means a perfect moment, not just beauty. Some ask, 'How are you?' and the reply will be 'Beleza.'"

MY PICKS

Everything, including the fine Rieslings, the Moscato frizzante, and the Syrah. Beleza is built to be cellared.

OPENED 2005

2152 Barcelo Road
Cawston, BC V0X 1C2
T   250.499.0068
W orofinovineyards.com
Accommodation: Two
vineyard suites

O'ROURKE FAMILY VINEYARDS

This is the showpiece partner to O'Rourke's Peak Cellars, which primarily makes bright, fresh aromatic whites. O'Rourke Family Vineyards specializes in premium Pinot Noir and Chardonnay. The O'Rourke winery perches at the top of a long, sloping 40-hectare (100-acre) vineyard, situated so that guests have a view down the length of Okanagan Lake to the Bennett Bridge, 30 kilometres to the south. The architecturally designed gravity-flow winery is above a barrel cellar—280 metres of tunnels bored into a hard granite outcrop. The ambient year-round temperature is expected to be about 10°C (50°F), ideal for wine storage.

The man behind this showcase winery is Edmonton businessman Dennis O'Rourke. Sureway Construction Group, which he founded in 1973, is one of Alberta's largest construction contractors. He had had a second home in Lake Country for almost 30 years before he decided to invest in wine production in the area.

And he decided to make an impact. He bought a 57-hectare (140-acre) property that was part derelict orchard and part a stand of conifers, mostly killed by pine beetles. The property is a few kilometres south of 50th Parallel Estate, another showcase Lake Country winery that opened in 2013, the year when planting began at the O'Rourke vineyard. There are 6.5 hectares (16 acres) of conifer forest at the back of the property. "Our main entrance comes in through that forest," says Adrian Baker, the New Zealand–born winemaker and general manager. "The driveway which comes through the forest has curves in it, so you can't see the entrance and the exit at the same time. When you come through this way, you have the big reveal of the vineyards and the lake. The whole theatre of it is that the Okanagan is so bright, with the lake and the skies."

NIKKI CALLAWAY   DENNIS O'ROURKE

As grand as the winery is, Dennis is determined that it will be a family winery. "The vision for the owner is that people in his family . . . be it his grandchildren or his nieces and nephews—will be involved in the business as it goes on," Adrian says.

In 2019, Nikki Callaway, a winemaker with extensive Pinot Noir experience, joined this winery. She had previously been chief winemaker at Quails' Gate and Laughing Stock Vineyards.

MY PICKS

The polished Chardonnay and the Pinot Noir are very elegant and age-worthy.

PROPOSED OPENING 2020

14551 Carrs Landing Road
Lake Country, BC
V4V 1A8
T   250.766.9922

O'ROURKE'S PEAK CELLARS

This is one of two wineries developed by Dennis O'Rourke, an Edmonton businessman, and both managed by Adrian Baker, a New Zealand–born winemaker. O'Rourke Family Vineyards makes just premium Chardonnay and Pinot Noir. O'Rourke's Peak Cellars produces wines that are fresh and aromatic, offering them in an elegant wine shop and bistro.

Adrian, who was born in Wellington, had made wine in New Zealand for a decade before coming to the Okanagan in 2010. The intention was a family adventure—he is the father of four home-schooled children—but he liked the winemaking opportunity here. After two years helping launch 50th Parallel Estate, he joined the nearby O'Rourke project in 2013 to develop the 45-hectare (110-acre) vineyard and plan the associated wineries.

He made the 2016 vintage for O'Rourke's Peak Cellars in a winery building still under construction. It was sited beside busy Okanagan Centre Road in Lake Country. Open year-round, the tasting room (with a modest and refundable tasting fee) is designed to be as accessible as the wines.

One of the specialties at O'Rourke's Peak Cellars is Grüner Veltliner, the great Austrian white varietal. Adrian planted a few acres to assess the vines. Initial success led him to plant 4 hectares (10 acres), one of the larger plantings in the Okanagan. Another specialty at O'Rourke's Peak Cellars is Gewürztraminer, an aromatic white that often does not get the attention it deserves. "I love making Gewürz," says Adrian, who ferments a portion in barrel, a portion in tank, and a portion on skins in order to craft a complex wine. "You don't go halfway with Gewürztraminer—or it is like getting half a tattoo."

ADRIAN BAKER

MY PICKS

Everything. The winery excels with white wines, including Riesling and Grüner Veltliner.

OPENED 2017 (AS THE CHASE WINES)

2290 Goldie Road
Lake Country, BC
V4V 1G5

T 250.766.9922
W orourkespeakcellars.com
Restaurant: Garden
Bistro, open daily noon–8

OSOYOOS LAROSE

OSOYOOS

Almost two decades after Osoyoos Larose made its first vintage in 2001, the winery finally expects to open a tasting room of its own in 2020. That arises from the winery's unusual history. It was launched in 1999 as a joint venture between Groupe Taillan, a Bordeaux wine company, and Vincor International, the parent of Jackson-Triggs vintners and other Canadian wineries. Donald Triggs, then president of Vincor, had proposed the venture as a means for transferring expertise from historic Bordeaux to the emerging Okanagan wine region.

The partners planted just red Bordeaux varieties in a 32-hectare (80-acre) vineyard a few kilometres northwest of Osoyoos, on the western side of the Okanagan Valley. The first in a series of veteran French winemakers arrived to manage the vineyard. A large area of the Jackson-Triggs winery north of Oliver was partitioned off as the Osoyoos Larose winery, but the wines were never made available in the elegant Jackson-Triggs wine shop.

Vincor was taken over in 2006 by Constellation Brands, a large American producer with no ongoing commitment to the Osoyoos Larose joint venture. To end the brand's drifting, Groupe Taillan acquired Constellation's stake in 2013, taking full ownership of Osoyoos Larose. That triggered the search for a location to build a new winery and a tasting room. A number of potential sites were canvassed before the winery decided to build in the vineyard, despite an initial lack of services. The vineyard affords magnificent views over the South Okanagan.

The winemaking style is definitely French. The winemaker from 2001 through 2012 was Pascal Madevon, the grandson of a Burgundy wine grower and a graduate of Bordeaux's top winemaking school. When he left, he was succeeded by Mathieu

WINEMAKER CAROLINE SCHALLER

Mercier and then, in 2017, by Caroline Schaller, both also trained in leading French wine schools but with experience as well in California and South America.

Only two wines are made at Osoyoos Larose each vintage, although there is consideration to releasing small lots of individual varietals. The flagship is Le Grand Vin, an age-worthy blend built around Merlot plus the four other Bordeaux reds. In the 2004 vintage, the winery launched its second label, Pétales d'Osoyoos, a softer, earlier-drinking red blend.

MY PICKS

Le Grand Vin is structured to age 10 or 15 years. While you wait for the wine to reach maturity, you drink the more accessible Pétales.

OPENED 2004

17808 103rd Street
Osoyoos, BC V0H 1V2
T   250.495.4027
W   osoyooslarose.com

OVINO WINERY

SALMON ARM

Legend has it that Yankee Flats Road, not far west of Salmon Arm, was named for the Vietnam-era draft dodgers who once lived in this bucolic farm country between the Salmon River and the Fly Hills. John Koopmans considered it as a name for his winery but decided against it, concerned about attracting anti-American sentiment. He settled on OVINO, Italian for "sheep," alluding to the farm's flock of sheep. He jokes that he will just hang an N in front of the name when he is sold out.

Born in the Netherlands in 1956, he became interested in wine as a student at a Dutch agricultural college that organized several field trips to French vineyards. "My chemistry professor was fascinated with wine and used it a lot as examples," John remembers. "He had a bit of a club there, messing about with smaller batches of wine."

Discouraged by a perceived lack of opportunity to farm in the Netherlands, he joined an uncle in Canada in 1977. A muscular, sturdily built man, John spent many years both in forestry and in dairy farming before he and Catherine, his wife, bought this 12.5-hectare (31-acre) Yankee Flats farm in 1992 for a dairy herd of their own. Fourteen years later, deciding it was time to do something new, he replaced the cows with the small herd of sheep. That gave him time to concentrate on the 1.6-hectare (4-acre) vineyard planted mostly in 2007. His winery is large enough to make about 1,000 cases a year. "We will stay small," he says. "I sell most of the wine from the shop. Local support is good, but there are only so many wine drinkers."

While a consultant helped him with the 2009 vintage, John has taken over making the wines since. His preference is for dry wines, but for those with a sweeter palate, he makes an off-dry white called Entice and a dessert wine called After 5.

JOHN KOOPMANS

The domed vineyard has exposures to "all sides of the compass," he notes. He grows Pinot Gris, Gewürztraminer, Pinot Meunier, and Maréchal Foch, along with small blocks of Petit Milo (a white hybrid created by Swiss breeder Valentin Blattner), L'Acadie Blanc (a hybrid grown in Nova Scotia), and Traminette (a white American hybrid). He also has Regent, a winter-hardy German red. John blends it with Pinot Meunier to make what he calls Black Riesling because a German synonym of Pinot Meunier is *Schwarzriesling*.

The wines at OVINO are among the most affordable in British Columbia. Most prices have hardly been increased in a decade. "We were thinking we should charge a bit more, but because we are off the beaten path, we get a lot of repeat customers because the price point is good," John says. "I'd rather sell the wines from here."

MY PICKS

Pinot Grigio is made in the light, refreshing Italian style. Sauvage Blanc is a fruity white from the Petit Milo grape. Black Riesling is a dry, fruity red, while Momento is a well-made Maréchal Foch.

OPENED 2010

1577 Yankee Flats Road
Salmon Arm, BC V1E 3J4
T   250.832.8463
W   ovinowinery.com

PAINTED ROCK ESTATE WINERY

A former Vancouver investment dealer, John Skinner—who owns this winery with his family—shrewdly has relied on Bordeaux wine consultant Alain Sutre since 2006. Alain, who consults for several leading Okanagan wineries on viticulture and winemaking, has helped shape exceptional premium wines.

The 10-hectare (25-acre) vineyard and the winery occupy a southwestward-sloping bench above Skaha Lake. The property formerly grew apricots before John, after an extensive search in the Okanagan, bought it in 2004. It has been transformed into one of the great vineyards of the Okanagan.

"When I started Painted Rock, we actually spent a year studying the site with a weather station in the middle of it," John says. "We also augered a hole every three metres. We know the depth of the alluvial silt layer everywhere on the vineyard. We have a map of it."

The first vintage was 2007, enabling John to realize his dream of moving from trading stocks to growing wine by the time he was 50. With each new vintage, Alain schooled his client in the art of wine growing by, among other things, assessing the quality of grapes by eating them as they ripened. After several vintages, they noticed an increasing intensity of flavours. Trenches were dug beside some vines; John and Alain discovered the roots were penetrating the silt to reach the underlying gravels, to produce grapes with vivid flavours. Since the 2014 vintage, the varietal wines have been made entirely from the named variety so as not to obscure the flavours through blending.

John had signalled his confidence from the start by naming his flagship wine Red Icon. Pretentious at the time, it has become an iconic Okanagan wine, the leader in an excellent portfolio. The winery won so many awards when it debuted at the 2009 Fall

JOHN SKINNER

Okanagan Wine Festival that it was named the BC new winery of the year. To date, four Painted Rock wines have won Lieutenant Governor's Awards for Excellence, among many other awards. In recent years, Painted Rock wines have been exported to some of Europe's most sophisticated markets.

The best place to taste the wines, however, is the elegant tasting lounge that opened in 2013, overlooking the vineyard and the lake. It is one of the most popular wedding venues in the valley.

MY PICKS

Everything. The Chardonnay's intense fruit is subtly framed by oak. The standouts among the varietal reds are Cabernet Franc and Syrah. Red Icon is a sophisticated blend that can be aged 10 to 15 years in a good cellar.

OPENED 2009

400 Smythe Drive
Penticton, BC V2A 8W6

T   250.493.6809

W paintedrock.ca

PELLER ESTATES

KELOWNA

The Peller wines have been available in the Sandhill boutique on Richter Street in Kelowna since 2005. That was when Andrew Peller Ltd. took over Calona Vineyards and Sandhill.

Now a national company, Peller was launched in British Columbia in 1961 as Andrés Wines by Andrew Peller, a Hungarian-born brewer whose winery application had been thwarted in Ontario. Development-hungry British Columbia welcomed him with a low-priced winery site in the Vancouver suburb of Port Moody. Andrés, which is now called Peller, achieved national stature, in no small measure with the amazing success of its grapey Baby Duck sparkling wine that was created in Port Moody in 1971. Baby Duck still has a following, but the Port Moody winery closed at the end of 2005 when the business, now run by Andrew Peller's grandson John, moved into the Richter Street winery.

Once a sponsor of the Inkameep Vineyard, Peller now is British Columbia's third-largest grape grower. It owns the 28-hectare (70-acre) Rocky Ridge Vineyards in the Similkameen Valley, the 81-hectare (200-acre) Sandhill Vineyard, and a 121-hectare (298-acre) vineyard at Covert Farm near Oliver. It also buys grapes from the 42-hectare (105-acre) Vanessa Vineyard in the Similkameen, which grows only red varieties.

The Peller wines are made by the same team, including winemaker Stephanie Van Dyk, that looks after the other brands here. The Peller management has chosen to position Sandhill and Wayne Gretzky as the premium brands. The Peller wines are moderately priced and include both VQA wines and blends that combine BC wines with imported international wines.

STEPHANIE VAN DYK

MY PICKS

The Raven Conspiracy white and Raven Conspiracy red are good value.

OPENED 1961 (AS ANDRÉS WINES)

1125 Richter Street
Kelowna, BC V1Y 2K6

T 250.979.4211
1.888.246.4472 (toll-free)

W peller.com

PENTÂGE WINERY

Pentâge Winery opened its tasting room only in 2011, eight years after opening the winery. The reason: it took Paul Gardner 11 years to plan and dig the massive 5,500-square-foot cave from the crown of hard rock commanding this vineyard's million-dollar view of Skaha Lake. Cool and spacious, this cave accommodates barrels and tanks of wine in a feat of engineering unlike anything else in the Okanagan, except perhaps the Mission Hill cellar. Tours are offered, but you can even appreciate the ambience just by peering through the gigantic glass doors at the front of the cave.

This was a derelict orchard when Paul and Julie Rennie, his wife, were so enchanted with the property in 1996 that they bought it and began planting vines three years later. Julie, the Scots-born daughter of a marine engineer, was executive assistant to a well-known Vancouver financier. Paul, born in Singapore in 1961, spent 20 years as a marine engineer before tiring of going to sea. "I got caught up in winemaking in the early '90s," he remembers.

Now, he spends most of his time in the winery's two Skaha Bench vineyards, which total 6.5 hectares (16 acres), growing so many varieties—including even Zinfandel—that one vineyard is called the Dirty Dozen. "I would still rather make small lots of interesting wine than big tanks full of wine," he says. An example of an eccentric but delicious wine was the 2011 Appassimento Style Cabernet Franc, where he mimicked Amarone by drying the grapes 58 days before crushing them.

Paul is very much hands-on, both in the vineyard and in the winery. In 2019, he even found partners to launch a bottling-line business. "I decided it would be a good idea to try to have a bit more control over every aspect of our winemaking," Paul says. "We can now literally bottle whenever we want—and I know we are using the best equipment we can get."

PAUL GARDNER AND JULIE RENNIE

The winery now produces about 5,000 cases a year. It is a remarkable kaleidoscope of wines from entry level (under the label Hiatus) to premium. The winery's 3-litre bag-in-the-box Pinot Gris is especially popular with restaurants.

The winery name, a play on the Latin word for "five," was chosen after Paul planted five red varieties to make his flagship red, also called Pentâge. The wine is built primarily with Merlot and Cabernet Sauvignon; small amounts of Cabernet Franc, Syrah, and Gamay Noir add complexity and personality.

MY PICKS

Everything, including the Pentâge red, the Syrah, the Cabernet Franc, the Gamay Noir, the Merlot, and the Hiatus blends. The Rhône red, called GSM, and the Rhône white are expressive wines. The portfolio is rounded out with sparkling wines, Icewines, and a port-style red.

OPENED 2003

4551 Valleyview Road

MAILING ADDRESS

4400 Lakeside Road
Penticton, BC V2A 8W3

T   250.493.4008

W pentage.com

PERSEUS WINERY

This is a rare find: an urban winery in a 60-year-old house that is within walking distance of downtown Penticton. Perseus is so optimistic about its accessibility that it even installed a bike rack. And it takes pride in being the gateway winery to Naramata Bench.

The winery, which released its first wine in 2009 under the Synergy label, opened its wine shop in 2010 in a residential neighbourhood. It has been positioned as an urban winery, with a tasting-room patio looking out over the city. There is a glimpse of the country, however: Perseus's Lower Bench Vineyard, a 2-hectare (5-acre) Pinot Gris planting, is just beyond the parking lot at the rear of the winery. The winery was renamed soon after it opened for the Perseus constellation, which is said to hover over the estate vineyard during harvest.

The winery was launched initially by three Penticton businessmen. Larry Lund is a hockey professional who trained young players at the Okanagan Hockey Camps and Academy from 1963 to 2004. Ron Bell, a developer and hotelier, planted the 2.6-hectare (6½-acre) Old Station Vineyard near Skaha Lake with Syrah and Sauvignon Blanc. In 2009, he and Larry planted 22.3 hectares (55 acres) of grapes at what they call the Blind Creek Vineyard near Cawston in the Similkameen Valley. Their third partner, Jim Morrison, ran a construction company.

In 2011, this trio sold the majority interest in Perseus to Terrabella Wineries, a company headed by Bob Hole, a Vancouver businessman. The winemaker of record—here he is called the constellation commander—is Jason Parkes, the winemaker for other wineries in the Terrabella group. Those properties are all clustered in West Kelowna, making Perseus an outlier to the group. For that reason, Perseus was for sale in 2019.

CONSTELLATION COMMANDER JASON PARKES

MY PICKS

*Invictus, the flagship
Bordeaux blend, and
Cabernet Sauvignon lead
the red wines here. The
Sauvignon Blanc and the
Pinot Gris are crisp and
appealing.*

OPENED 2010
(AS SYNERGY)

134 Lower Bench Road
Penticton, BC V2A 1A8

I   250.490.8829

W perseuswinery.com

PHANTOM CREEK ESTATES

OLIVER

Perched high amid vines of the Black Sage Bench, the architecturally stunning Phantom Creek Estates became one of the Okanagan's finest destination wineries the day it opened in the spring of 2020. Richter Bai, the Chinese-born owner, is said to have invested $100 million in the project. "My goal is to produce outstanding wine in Canada," he has said.

He has spared nothing in pursuing that objective. He was formerly a successful mining owner in China and had worked on a farm as a youth. After immigrating to Canada with his family, he identified wine growing as a prestige agriculture opportunity here. He started in 2014 by retaining wine educator James Cluer, MW (Master of Wine). They spent much of 2015 visiting top wineries in France and California until Mr. Bai, as his colleagues call him, understood how to achieve his goal.

He has invested in the best of everything. In 2016, he bought two of the best vineyards on the Black Sage Bench. The Becker Vineyard, as it is now called, was planted in 1993. The nearby Phantom Creek Vineyard was planted a few years later. The vineyards, in total about 26 hectares (65 acres), had long produced award-winning wines. Subsequently, Mr. Bai added more prime vineyard property on Black Sage, on the Golden Mile, and in the Similkameen Valley. And he recruited Alsace winemaker Olivier Humbrecht, MW, to lead Phantom Creek's transition to organic and, in time, biodynamic grape growing.

The Becker Vineyard already had a winery under construction. Harry McWatters, the previous owner, had started to build a substantial cellar before selling the property. Mr. Bai brought leading winery architects from California. Their design more than doubled Harry's cellar, topping it with several tasting rooms and a restaurant with breathtaking views of South Okanagan vineyards.

WINEMAKER OLIVIER HUMBRECHT, MW

RICHTER BAI

WINEMAKER FRANCIS HUTT

Mr. Bai reached out to the Napa Valley for expert winemakers. He retained Anne Vawter and her husband, Cameron, both respected consulting winemakers. Anne, who had grown up in Washington State wine country, got her winemaking training at the University of California. When Mr. Bai hired her, she was already familiar with Okanagan fruit after making several vintages for One Faith Vineyards. In 2016, Phantom Creek's first vintage, she and her team made about 6,000 cases of wine, working in a well-equipped temporary winery as construction progressed on the showpiece winery.

While she continues to consult for Phantom Creek, Mr. Bai has staffed the cellar with a team of experienced resident winemakers led by New Zealand–trained winemaker Francis Hutt. "I had a big corporation in China," he says. "I understand if you want to do something that is the best, you must have the best team."

MY PICKS

Absolutely everything, including the Riesling, the Pinot Gris, the Cabernet Sauvignon, and exceptional red blends.

OPENED 2020

4315 Black Sage Road
Oliver, BC V0H 1T1

T 250.498.8367

W phantomcreekestates.com
Restaurant: To open
Spring 2020

PIPE' DREAMS WINERY

OLIVER

The name of this winery comes from a question that John Ness, the owner, asked himself when launching the project: Is it a big dream, or just a pipe dream? The quality of the wines answers the question. When the tasting room opened in 2016, the offerings included one of the best Grüner Veltliner wines made in BC.

Pipe' Dreams, which offers four other wines, is a short drive north of Oliver and west from Highway 97. Sportsmens Bowl Road dead-ends at a shooting range. If you have gone too far, turn around and look for a flat vineyard on the north side of the road.

A big man with a friendly personality, John was born in 1947 in Winnipegosis and grew up in Vancouver. His family usually vacationed in the Okanagan every summer with friends who lived there. "I would spend a week cliff diving with the other kids," he remembers. "I always loved it here. I always thought we should move here, but we never did."

When he finished Grade 12, his main interests were skiing and surveying. "Around 1968, I was offered a job at Jasper on a professional ski patrol," he says. "I was in the Canadian National Ski Patrol, going every weekend." Then he found employment as a surveyor, his other passion. "I surveyed from 1968 to 1975," John continues. "Then I started with Nova Corp., surveying pipelines. About 1980 I went into construction management in the pipeline area. That's what I have been doing ever since: construction management, looking after quality specifications, inspection staff—that kind of business."

While he earned his living in Alberta, he could not escape the allure of the Okanagan. He returned to ski in the winter and to explore on his motorcycle in summer.

In 2009 he bought the Sportsmens Bowl property. Nothing was being cultivated there at the time. "I thought I will do some

grapes," John says. After engaging consulting winemaker Mark Wendenburg, John planted 1.4 hectares (3½ acres) in 2011. He chose varieties outside the mainstream of Okanagan plantings: Grüner Veltliner, Kerner, Gamay Noir, and Zweigelt. "I did not want to have the same kind of grapes as everybody else," John says. "I didn't want to do Merlot because everyone does Merlot." As it happens, he now leases a 0.4-hectare (1-acre) block of Merlot from a neighbour.

MY PICKS

Everything in this small portfolio is well made, especially the Grüner Veltliner and the Gamay Noir.

OPENED 2016

168 Sportsmens Bowl Road
Oliver, BC V0H 1T5
T 250.485.4192
W pipedreamswinery.com

PLATINUM BENCH ESTATE WINERY

OLIVER

The seed for this winery was planted a decade earlier when Murray Jones and Fiona Duncan took a cycling vacation through the vineyards of Bordeaux. "It was one of those aha moments when we were out in the vineyards," Fiona remembers. "What an incredible reality that somebody has this as their lifestyle!" But they returned to their fast-paced business lives in Winnipeg. It took an Okanagan vacation seven or eight years later to germinate the seed.

Murray, who was born in Winnipeg in 1954, became a chartered accountant to pursue a successful career in manufacturing (buses, garments, and tents for the military). Fiona, who was born in 1962 and grew up in West Vancouver, met Murray after she went to Winnipeg in 1988. She spent a number of years as vice-president of production development for Nygård International, a major garment designer and manufacturer.

"We've always had a keen interest in wine," Fiona says. "We started talking to the people who owned the wineries in the Okanagan. Here were people who had taken this on as a second career. We started thinking maybe this could be our reality as well." Early in 2011, they purchased a 5.6-hectare (14-acre) vineyard on Black Sage Road with 15-year-old vines—of Chardonnay, Pinot Gris, Merlot, Cabernet Sauvignon, and Merlot. Richard Cleave, the legendary viticulturist, lent his vineyard expertise to Murray and helped the couple find experienced winemakers.

A few years of wine growing led Murray to conclude that Platinum Bench should concentrate on red wines, particularly when the winery was challenged to sell its well-made Chardonnay because of the variety's unpopularity. "Even my mother wouldn't drink Chardonnay," Murray laments. He replaced 1.2 hectares (3 acres) of Chardonnay with Cabernet Franc, Syrah, Petit Verdot, and Malbec.

MURRAY JONES

The winery is also well known for the bread that Fiona bakes and sells in the wine shop. She began taking baking lessons at the San Francisco Baking Institute when she was a high-powered fashion executive in Winnipeg. "It was part of a stress-management program that she had," Murray says. At least 300 loaves are baked daily, using a sourdough starter kept alive since Fiona's first trip to San Francisco more than 25 years ago.

MY PICKS

Everything. The Pinot Gris, Gamay Noir, and rosé are delicious. The flagship wines here include Block 28 Gamay Noir, Cabernet Sauvignon, Merlot, and Meritage.

OPENED 2012

4120 Black Sage Road
Oliver, BC V0H 1T1

T 250.535.1165

W platinumbench.com

Food service: Artisan bread, local cheeses, and cold cuts

PLAY ESTATE WINERY

PENTICTON

Everything about Play Estate Winery is theatrical, from its perch on a hillside overlooking Skaha Lake to wines with names such as Improv and Ad Lib. The winery is owned by Calgary hotelier Stagewest Hospitality, which includes dinner theatres in many of its hotels. The company is managed by Jason and David Pechet, third-generation members of a family that got into the business by building hotels along the Alaska Highway. Both are graduates of Cornell University's renowned hotel management school.

Both are also wine lovers. The winery was conceived by Jason and Mohamed Awad, a former hotelier and winery manager in the Okanagan. On land leased from the Penticton Indian Band, they arranged to plant a 4.9-hectare (12-acre) vineyard and build the winery on a slope surrounded by an elegant residential development and close to Penticton's airport. The winery, which opened with wines from the 2014 vintage, now produces about 5,000 cases a year, with triple that capacity. The winery also includes a bistro, in line with the Stagewest philosophy of including multiple attractions in its properties.

The estate vineyard is planted with Merlot, Cabernet Franc, Cabernet Sauvignon, Viognier, Sauvignon Blanc, Sémillon, Orange Muscat, and Muscat Ottonel. Play also leases a 3.2-hectare (8-acre) vineyard in Kaleden, which has Merlot, Cabernet Franc, Cabernet Sauvignon, Viognier, and Muscat Blanc à Petits Grains.

The style of Play's wines is still emerging. The original vintages were made by Mohamad and Marina Zarrillo, a California-trained winemaker. After both left Play, the winery early in 2019 recruited Stephanie Bryers, formerly the assistant winemaker at Culmina Family Estate Winery. Born in Ontario in 1988, she acquired a passion for wines while working in a wine shop and taking sommelier training.

"I decided I did not want to work in restaurants and pour wine," Stephanie says. "I liked the idea of making it. We always had a couple of days [in sommelier training] where we would go to a winery and do a couple of punch-downs for the fun of it, or help on the bottling line. I liked that so much more, so I went to school." A 2015 graduate of Niagara College, she made wine in New Zealand, Portugal, and Ontario before coming to the Okanagan.

MY PICKS

The Moscato is a crisp, refreshing wine made with three Muscat clones. The winery has launched a number of small-lot wines, including Viognier, Gewürztraminer, Syrah, and Merlot, that are delicious.

OPENED 2016

507 Skaha Hills Drive
Penticton, BC V2A 0A9

T 236.422.2675

W playwinery.com

Visits and tastings by appointment

Restaurant: Bistro, open 11–8 Wed. through Sat., and 11–4 on Sun., closed during winter

POPLAR GROVE WINERY

PENTICTON

From its perch on the side of Munson Mountain, Poplar Grove Winery commands a breathtaking view of Penticton and its two lakes. It is a far cry from founder Ian Sutherland's tiny original Poplar Grove winery, about the size of a pickers' cabin beside a vineyard off Naramata Road. One of the first five wineries in the area, Poplar Grove was a highly regarded boutique winery in 2007 when Tony Holler invested in the winery.

Tony is a doctor who was born in Summerland in 1951 and who has run several successful pharmaceutical companies. A Napa Valley vacation in 2004 spurred him to build a lakefront home near Poplar Grove and to plant a vineyard, which Ian agreed to manage. It was the beginning of a friendship that proved crucial for Poplar Grove. Tony was used to thinking long term in business, and it was no different with wine. "I am not looking for a return on my investment tomorrow," Tony says. "Maybe the real returns come not for me but for my children and my family."

Poplar Grove was producing about 4,000 cases a year when Tony invested in the winery. It is now on the way to producing 25,000 cases a year, almost all with estate-grown fruit. Tony's wife, Barbara, manages the 40 hectares (100 acres) of Poplar Grove vineyards. Their four sons, one with enology training from Lincoln University in New Zealand, are all involved with Poplar Grove.

As a collector of fine international wines, Tony believes that Poplar Grove wines can play in the big leagues. The portfolio has a disciplined focus primarily on six or seven mainstream varietals, crowned with two collectible red blends—Benchmark and Legacy. "This valley can produce world-class wines," Tony says. "That's what got me excited about going into the wine business."

He believes that Okanagan wines now attract an international

TONY HOLLER

clientele. He plans to build a luxury 10-unit inn beside the winery. "When I grew up here in the 1960s, the Okanagan was a place where families came in the summer for ultra-cheap vacations," Tony recalls. "Over time, the Okanagan—and it is mainly because of the wine industry—has attracted a more and more affluent clientele," he says, making his case. "Now you have people flying from all over the world, some in their own planes."

MY PICKS

Everything, especially Pinot Gris and Legacy; the latter blend is anchored with Merlot, Malbec, and Cabernet Franc and is a cornerstone wine for collectors.

OPENED 1997

425 Middle Bench Road North
Penticton, BC V2A 8S5
T 250.493.9463
W poplargrove.ca
Restaurant: The Restaurant at Poplar Grove Winery

PRIEST CREEK FAMILY ESTATE WINERY

KELOWNA

Jane Sawin once called husband Darren a "winery stalker." He began researching the wine business by parking at wineries and counting the tasting-room traffic, including how many bottles of wine guests carried when they departed. His interest in opening his own winery came after an unsatisfactory year of selling table grapes from their property in East Kelowna.

Aside from home winemaking, Darren was then a wine novice. Born in 1970, he had grown up on a family farm near Big Beaver, a tiny village in southern Saskatchewan. "I had always dreamt of having a ranch," he says. While he worked as a ranch hand, the dream was financially out of reach. He moved to Calgary, tried selling real estate, and then began renovating houses for a portfolio of rental properties. Jane, with an arts degree from the University of Saskatchewan and a diploma in architectural design, applied her project-management skills to the rental portfolio.

In 2010 they moved to the Okanagan, where they had previously vacationed, and once again began building and selling houses. "We always wanted to get back to our farming roots and to raising our four kids on the farm," Darren says. In 2015 they purchased a Southeast Kelowna wine-trail property with just under a hectare (2 acres) of mature Gewürztraminer and about 3 hectares (7½ acres) of table grapes. Two years later, having been told they could not grow Pinot Noir, they offered to sell the farm in order to finance another vineyard purchase.

Winemaker Jason Parkes was one of the first potential buyers to look at the Sawin property. Subsequently, he bought elsewhere for his own project, but he assured the Sawins that they could grow Pinot Noir. (Neighbouring SpearHead Winery specializes in Pinot Noir.) Darren replaced the table grapes, while Jason agreed to make the Priest Creek wines and mentor Darren in winemaking.

The winery is named for a creek at the back of the property. It is believed the creek took its name from the Oblate mission established nearby in 1859 by Father Charles Pandosy, credited with planting the Okanagan's first vineyard (for sacramental wine).

MY PICKS

Current range not tasted— but Jason Parkes makes excellent wines for his clients.

PROPOSED
OPENING 2020

2555 Saucier Road
Kelowna, BC V1W 4B7

T   250.801.7355

W   priestcreekwinery.com

PRIVATO VINEYARD & WINERY

KAMLOOPS

John and Debbie Woodward know that their vineyard is challenging, even with its sunbathed slope facing southeast toward the North Thompson River. The property, a half-hour drive north of downtown Kamloops, is one of the more northerly vineyards in British Columbia planted to vinifera (Pinot Noir and Chardonnay).

"Debbie has always wanted a vineyard," says John, who was born in Kamloops in 1954. John, a professional forester, and Debbie, a certified general accountant, met when they worked for the same forestry company. Preferring to work independently, they bought their 32-hectare (80-acre) farm in 1987. Here, they established a tree nursery now growing 30,000 Christmas trees and deciduous trees for landscaping needs.

Early in his forestry career, John, encouraged by his employer, began making wine at home from kits. He liked the wine until he moved it to storage that was too hot over the summer and the wine fell apart. That ended his winemaking until he and Debbie vacationed among Italian wineries during crush some years ago. Seeing tiny wineries harvesting and processing grapes inspired them. "It was just the fuel we needed to get going," Debbie says.

They figured there was nothing holding them back: they had land for vines and farm buildings readily convertible to winemaking. And they had finished putting their children through school. "Before, we were running a business with the purpose of supporting the family," Debbie says. "Now we are doing it because we are passionate to make a really good glass of wine."

In 2010, they planted 1.2 hectares (3 acres) of vines—Pinot Noir, Chardonnay, and one row of Maréchal Foch. He also reacquainted himself with winemaking by making two barrels of wine in 2010 with consultant Gustav Allander of Foxtrot Vineyards. The first

ADAM, DEBBIE, AND JOHN WOODWARD

commercial vintage in 2011 comprised about 600 cases of Pinot Noir, Chardonnay, and Cabernet Franc. In 2013, when Gustav stopped consulting, the Woodwards turned to New Zealand-trained Jacqueline Kemp for guidance on sourcing Okanagan grapes and making wine, at least until John had become adept at making award-winning wines. Privato has since emerged as a family winery, with son Adam, a civil engineer, having become the winery's operations manager.

The Woodwards sell their wines through restaurants and directly to consumers. Initially, they did not plan to open a tasting room, considering their farm too far off the beaten path. They changed their minds in 2013, opening a charmingly rustic tasting room, creating gardens, and making the picturesque vineyard available for weddings.

MY PICKS

Both the Chardonnay and the several Pinot Noirs are elegantly polished. Woodward Cider Co, Adam's firm, sells excellent craft ciders here as well.

OPENED 2012

5505 Westsyde Road
Kamloops, BC V2B 8N5
T   250.579.8739
W   privato.ca

PROSPECT OF THE OKANAGAN

VIRTUAL WINERY

This is the largest of the Okanagan's virtual wineries, which is why there is no tasting room. Prospect is a brand produced in the Mission Hill winery but not sold in Mission Hill's wine shop. Here, winemaker Corrie Krehbiel takes advantage of Mission Hill's excellent vineyards and winemaking technology to produce astonishing quality wines, considering the price. As this book was written, the most expensive wine was a $16.50 Pinot Noir. The strategy here is to overdeliver. "We are trying to make approachable wines that you will want to enjoy with what the Okanagan or Canada has to offer," Corrie says. "Like having a glass of Pinot Grigio out on the deck after a day of boating."

The winery was originally called Ganton & Larsen Prospect Winery, named for two growers then associated with Mission Hill vineyards, with the labels inspired by Okanagan history. The idea was to give historical grounding and a sense of place since there was no separate winery or tasting room. Mission Hill has always let this brand stand on its own. The wines are widely distributed but are not available in the Mission Hill tasting room. A separate winery might be built one day, but nothing is imminent.

In a 2018 rebranding, the winery dropped the Ganton & Larsen prefix and refreshed the labels, with references drawn from the vineyards. For example, the Shiraz is called The Sage because that plant grows widely in the Okanagan. The only label that is fanciful is Ogopogo's Lair Pinot Grigio, inspired by Rattlesnake Island offshore from one of the vineyards that supply fruit for Prospect. The underwater caves are said to be a habitat of the legendary monster of Okanagan Lake.

"My great-aunt claims she saw Ogopogo come out of the water and onto a beach," Corrie says. Born in Kelowna in 1975, Corrie was drawn to winemaking through a casual bottling-line

job at CedarCreek Estate Winery when she was still in high school. She went on to get a food sciences degree at the University of British Columbia and enology training at Lincoln University in New Zealand. She came back to the Okanagan, working primarily at CedarCreek and, since 2014, with Prospect. "I never left the industry," she says.

MY PICKS

Everything. The flawless wines, widely available in wine stores, are priced to be affordable for daily consumption.

OPENED 2007

PO Box 474
Oliver, BC V0H 1T0
T 604.264.4020
W prospectwinery.com
No tasting room

QUAILS' GATE WINERY
WEST KELOWNA

Quails' Gate is owned by one of the Okanagan's great pioneer farming families. Richard Stewart Sr. emigrated from Ireland in 1906 and established a nursery business that the family operated for more than a century before selling it. His son, also Richard, became a grape grower, planting vines as early as 1961. When the vines thrived on what Quails' Gate now calls its Home Block, Richard's son Ben, who had been a banker, joined the family business in 1979 and, a decade later, launched the winery. In 1992, his younger brother, Tony, left his career as a stockbroker to become the winery's business manager. He took over as president when Ben left for a career in politics.

From its start as a farm-gate winery making 2,000 cases a year, Quails' Gate now flirts with 100,000 cases a year and anchors a growing wine empire. The Stewart family operate Lake Sonoma Winery in California, which they acquired in 2012. And in 2022, they plan to do the first crush in a new winery (yet to be named) in East Kelowna established on the former nursery property. Much of the 85 hectares (210 acres) have been planted, making it the largest single vineyard in East Kelowna.

It is triggering replanting in the Home Block, a sunbathed 20-degree slope on the flank of Mount Boucherie. Here the Stewarts planted the Okanagan's first Pinot Noir in 1975. That is now the flagship varietal at Quails' Gate. The white varieties on the Home Block—Chasselas, Sauvignon Blanc, Pinot Blanc, Riesling, and Optima—have joined Chenin Blanc in the cooler East Kelowna vineyard. The Home Block is being converted entirely to red varieties.

A significant block of Pinot Noir has also been planted in East Kelowna, primarily to support making premium sparkling wine under the direction of Quails' Gate's senior

TONY STEWART

winemaker, Susan Doyle. A native of Tasmania in Australia, she worked a dozen years in California before joining Quails' Gate in 2018. She is the latest in the long line of Australian- or New Zealand–trained winemakers to put their stamp on Quails' Gate wines. She is supported by Ross Baker, a Kelowna native with a biochemistry degree, who joined the winemaking team in 2013.

MY PICKS

Everything. The premium wines are released as Stewart Family Reserve or with labels (like Richard's Block) commemorating Stewart family members. Not to be missed is the iconic Old Vines Foch, made in the rich style of Australian Shiraz.

OPENED 1989

3303 Boucherie Road
West Kelowna, BC
VIZ 2H3
T 250.769.4451
   1.800.420.9463 (toll-free)
W quailsgate.com
Restaurant: Old Vines
Restaurant (250.769.2500),
open daily at 11 for lunch
and dinner; Sun. brunch
10–2:30; high tea Sat./Sun.
at 2 and 3:30
Accommodation: A luxury
vacation home for up to 14
people, and a cabin for up
to 7 people

QUINTA FERREIRA ESTATE WINERY

OLIVER

Without a doubt, Maria and John Ferreira, owners of Quinta Ferreira, have the Okanagan wineries' most enduring love story. Both were born in Portugal but came to Canada as children a few years apart. John's family came first in 1961 when he was six years old. They first met a few years later on the day that Maria and her family first arrived in Canada. They both grew up in Oliver and attended Southern Okanagan Secondary School. One evening in Grade 11, Maria called John's house to speak with her sister, and John answered the phone. He asked her out during that conversation. "And the rest is history," Maria says, smiling. "John was very shy." They were married in 1974.

Quinta Ferreira is perched on the ridge overlooking the town of Oliver on a property that had been farmed by John's parents. When they retired in 1979, they asked if John and Maria wanted to buy the property. Both knew the farming lifestyle, but both were also well into other careers. After refusing initially, the couple tried it out for a year by leasing the property and then relented by purchasing it in 1980. They grew apples, peaches, and cherries for the next 20 years and raised their family.

With the growth of the wine industry in the late 1990s, they converted to growing grapes. In 1999, the apples came out, followed by the peaches in 2000 and finally the cherries a year later. They turned their packing house into a winery to help produce wine for another winery that was just starting up. This became an opportunity for their son Michael to learn about winemaking as he worked with the other winery's winemaker. When that winery bought its own property and moved out, the Ferreiras began making their own wine in the 2005 vintage.

The wine shop's large horseshoe bar easily accommodates the summer crowds and makes for a sociable atmosphere. Along with

JOHN FERREIRA

wine, the shop is filled with art created by Maria's sister Carmen Tomé, an accomplished painter and photographer. Special events are often held outside on the spacious patio featuring food and live music. The amazing view of the valley and McIntyre Bluff to the north make even parking the car spectacular.

Sadly, Maria Ferreira passed away suddenly in December of 2019.

MY PICKS

Most are single varieties— Merlot, Syrah, Malbec, Zinfandel, Chardonnay, Viognier, and Pinot Blanc. The Malbec and Zinfandel small lots are particularly worth exploring. The blends pay tribute to their Portuguese heritage: Mistura Branca, Mistura Tinto, and Obra-Prima— their most prestigious red.

OPENED 2007

6094 Black Sage Road
Oliver, BC V0H 1T8

T   250.498.4756

W   quintaferreira.com

RAMIFICATION CELLARS

OKANAGAN. FALLS

The staff at Ramification Cellars have considered providing binoculars for visitors who are birders as well as wine lovers. The winery and its 2-hectare (5-acre) vineyard nestle beside Vaseux Lake, a bucolic site rich in flora and fauna. McIntyre Bluff towers over the valley south of the lake, while Mount Hawthorne rises from its western shore. The bighorn mountain sheep resident in the nearby wilderness inspired both the winery's name and the bold ram's head on the labels.

The winery has been developed by Don Lloyd and his daughter, Rachel. Through a company called C21 Development Group, Don has developed residential and commercial real estate in the Okanagan since 1973. He also operates a number of KFC franchises in Canada and the United States. "The family loves wine," says Jeff Parkinson, Ramification's chief operating officer. "Rachel has a passion for wine and for the industry. The idea of having a beautiful property like this, right on the lake, met a family desire."

The Lloyds purchased the lakeside property in 2006. In 2013, Pinot Gris and Pinot Noir were planted in a vineyard managed by a professional viticulturist. Consulting winemaker Robert Thielicke began making the Ramification wines in 2015, starting with 140 cases of a reserve Pinot Noir that was aged in French oak barrels for 21 months. The portfolio has been extended in subsequent vintages with more Pinot Noir, a Pinot Noir rosé, and a Pinot Gris, all estate grown.

The vineyard enables the winery to produce between 1,200 and 1,500 cases a year. It is likely that much of that will be sold from the wine shop at this appealing location overlooking the lake. Visitors who are not birders will want to linger in this peaceful setting or launch kayaks onto the lake. A ban on motorized vessels protects the charm of Vaseux Lake that attracted the Lloyd family.

WINEMAKER ROBERT THIELICKE

MY PICKS

Everything, especially the Pinot Noirs.

OPENED 2019

3500 Highway 97
Okanagan Falls, BC V0H 1T2
T   250.498.4884
W ramwine.com

RECLINE RIDGE VINEYARDS & WINERY

TAPPEN

Listed for sale in 2018, Recline Ridge may be operated by its third owner in 20 years when this book appears. Mike Smith, the first owner, sold in 2010 when he tired of the wine business. For Graydon and Maureen Ratzlaff, the sale was a logical step for a couple who have enjoyed variety in their business careers. The general improvement in Recline Ridge's wine portfolio had added value to the business.

Recline Ridge is one of British Columbia's northernmost wineries, 14 kilometres west of Salmon Arm in the pastoral Tappen valley, just off the Trans-Canada Highway. The quiet countryside appealed to the Ratzlaffs after 25 years in Greater Vancouver, where Graydon held senior positions with various food-processing firms. "We were looking for a lifestyle improvement," he says. "We viewed the wine industry as a happy industry."

Born in New Westminster in 1952, Graydon grew up in Summerland. After graduating from the University of British Columbia's food sciences program, he began his career with Kelowna's Sun-Rype Products. In 1985 he and Maureen, a retail specialist, moved to Vancouver to experience big-city living. Graydon became a specialist in setting up and managing processing plants. He worked at various times with snack food manufacturers, producers of food for aquaculture, a poultry processor, and, ultimately, for Vincor Canada's RJ Spagnols division. A home winemaker himself, Graydon set up a plant to make kits and other supplies for home vintners. Here, he discovered that the wine industry was "a community of folks that just love the products." At Recline Ridge, he and Maureen joined that community.

Recline Ridge's 2.4-hectare (6-acre) vineyard grows Maréchal Foch, Siegerrebe, Optima, Madeleine Sylvaner, Madeleine

GRAYDON RATZLAFF

Angevine, and Ortega. The winery also buys grapes, including Zweigelt and Blaufränkisch, from the nearby vineyards. Graydon and Maureen came up with creative branding for these tongue-twisting varietals. For example, the wine made with Blaufränkisch (also known as Lemberger) is called Just Being Frank.

The winemaker and vineyard manager since early 2015 has been Alberta-born Jaime Flemke, a Brock University graduate with experience in Ontario and in the Okanagan. Her broad taste in wines is reflected by the Recline Ridge portfolio, which runs the gamut from dry wine to dessert wine. "As a winemaker, I enjoy almost all wines, and as a result, I'm always keen to try my hand at new styles," she has said.

MY PICKS

All the wines are clean and fresh. The wine called Hummingbird's Kiss, made with botrytis-affected Optima, is as delightful as its name.

OPENED 1999

2640 Skimikin Road
Tappen, BC V0E 2X3
T   250.835.2212
W   reclineridgewinery.com

RED BIRD ESTATE WINERY

CRESTON

Not having a background in wine growing, Red Bird founders Remi and Shannon Cardinal canvassed the other Creston wineries before deciding, in 2015, what to plant. The two largest blocks in their 1.2-hectare (3-acre) vineyard are Pinot Gris and Gewürztraminer; and there are small blocks of Schönburger and Kerner. All had already proven themselves in other vineyards.

Remi and Shannon also have taken a flyer on six rows of a red called Gamaret (pronounced *gamma-ray*), from which they made 20 cases of rosé from their first harvest in 2018. The early-ripening hardy variety is a red developed in a Swiss research station from a 1970 cross of Gamay Noir and Reichensteiner and released commercially in 1990. There are at least 400 hectares (1,000 acres) of Gamaret in Swiss vineyards. There also are smaller plantings in northern Italy, Beaujolais, and Belgium—and now six rows in British Columbia. And more if the wine succeeds, which seems likely.

The couple began their journey to wine growing in 2009 when Shannon took the viticulture course at Okanagan College. "When I took the course, we were semi-serious," she says. Born in Red Deer in 1981, Shannon is an environmental consultant specializing in oil-well remediation. Remi, who was born in 1980 near Montreal, is a forester. He and Shannon met in 2003 while working on a forest inventory in northern Saskatchewan. International travel fired their decision to become wine growers.

They spent six years looking at properties from Nova Scotia to British Columbia. They concluded that Creston was an "up-and-coming" wine community with land considerably more affordable than in the Okanagan. The Creston lifestyle, with access to skiing and hiking, also appealed to them. They converted a neglected orchard near Baillie-Grohman (Creston's largest winery) to vineyard.

REMI AND SHANNON CARDINAL

Red Bird's first vintage was 2017, with a production of 340 cases, some with Okanagan grapes. Remi and Shannon's eventual goal is to produce 2,000 cases a year, all of it with Creston-area grapes. The 2017 wines were made at BC Wine Studio in Okanagan Falls, whose owner, Mark Simpson, also acts as Red Bird's consultant. Remi and Shannon converted a building at their property for winemaking in 2018. They intend to build a new winery there and open a tasting room by 2021, replacing the informal tasting arrangements that have greeted visitors so far.

MY PICKS

The debut wines, Pinot Gris, Gewürztraminer, and Meritage—all are a good start.

OPENED 2018

1046 Lamont Road
Creston, BC V0B 1G1
T   250.254.8885
W   redbirdwine.com

RED HORSES VINEYARD

Red Horses Vineyard is perhaps the most focused small winery in the Okanagan. The vineyard is planted exclusively with Cabernet Sauvignon. The winery opened with just Cabernet Sauvignon and Merlot, the latter made with purchased grapes. "There is a possibility in the future we might plant something other than Cabernet Sauvignon," says Tim Fortin, one of the partners. "Now, I just want to make the best Cabernet I can make."

The winery is owned by Tim and Eileen Fortin and Tim's parents, Rod and Pat Fortin. It represents a circuitous journey to wine by both couples. Rod was born in northern Saskatchewan in 1940. He was 12 when his family moved to Oliver. "I started working in the orchards when I was 13, and I pretty well had my fill by the time I left here in 1959," he remembers. After high school, he pursued several successful business careers in Vancouver, including modular housing for resource communities in the 1960s, followed by gravel production. After he sold that business, he and his wife retired in 2008 to the Okanagan, which he maintains has the best climate in Canada.

In 2009 they bought a 1.1-hectare (2¾-acre) orchard with 70-year-old trees near Tuc-el-Nuit Lake, at the outskirts of Oliver. Rod had no desire to begin growing tree fruit. "It was perfect for growing grapes," he says. "I have always had an interest in wine. I drink wine every day, at least a couple of glasses." His favourite wine is Cabernet Sauvignon. For several years, he sold the grapes, keeping enough to make wine for personal consumption.

Then Tim and Eileen bought an adjoining property, also planted Cabernet Sauvignon, and proposed a winery. Born in Vancouver in 1966, Tim met Eileen at cooking school there. Their love of wine developed in restaurants (Eileen's Winnipeg family had operated a restaurant). After cooking school, they started

EILEEN AND TIM FORTIN

their own catering company. That business led Tim to film-industry catering and then to a 30-year career managing logistics in that industry. When he retired, Tim and Eileen also moved to Oliver, to a vineyard and the management of Red Horses. The winery, which displays two life-sized metal horse sculptures, takes its name from a family interest in horses and western lore.

Consulting winemaker Philip Soo makes the wine for Red Horses, which will launch with 100 cases of 2017 Cabernet Sauvignon, 450 cases from the 2018 vintage, and close to 1,000 cases in 2019. "And I don't think we will go above 1,000 cases," Tim says. "We will try to keep the quality up and the volume down."

MY PICKS

These are among the Okanagan's best Cabernet Sauvignons.

PROPOSED
OPENING 2020

365 Zinfandel Avenue
Oliver, BC V0H 1T4

T   250.689.0332

W   redhorsesvineyard.ca

RED ROOSTER WINERY

PENTICTON

Perhaps no Red Rooster fans are more pampered that the 100 or so members of the winery's Adopt-A-Row club. They get to prune and harvest their rows in the 0.8-hectare (2-acre) Malbec block at the front door of the winery. The annual case of wine that comes with the membership includes several bottles of Malbec. There also are tastings and dinners with Red Rooster winemakers Karen Gillis and Elaine Vickers. Unfortunately, there is a waiting list to join, but a good alternative is the winery's Rare Bird Club. Among its attractions is preferred treatment in the tasting rooms of the other four Okanagan wineries owned by Andrew Peller Ltd.

Swiss immigrants Beat and Prudence Mahrer opened Red Rooster in 1997. They sold it to Peller in 2005 after relocating from the modest original winery near Naramata to the palatial Robert Mackenzie–designed buildings on Naramata Road. The Mahrer imprint remains in the art displayed around the winery, including the nude sculpture near the Malbec block called *Frank the Baggage Handler*.

"I like interesting wines, and I want to make interesting wines," Karen Gillis says. Born in Vancouver, she grew up in a family of chefs. She initially had that career in mind when she completed a diploma in food technology at the British Columbia Institute of Technology in 1996. But after three years developing food products, she zeroed in on wine and joined Peller. She has been at Red Rooster since 2007.

One of the rarest of the interesting wines Karen makes is a blend called the Golden Egg, rare because Grenache and Mourvèdre, blended here with Syrah, are difficult to grow and are not widely planted in the Okanagan. Karen's enthusiasms extend to varietals like Riesling, Viognier, and Merlot and blends like Meritage. "I am a believer that Meritage should be the best of the best," she says.

ELAINE VICKERS   KAREN GILLIS

Red Rooster also has added sparkling wines to its portfolio. "I have always wanted to be a sparkling-wine person," Karen says. "I like to drink sparkling wine. That is originally why I came to Red Rooster. They had sparkling before I came, and it disappeared off the table for a while."

When Karen was promoted within the Peller group in 2019, Elaine Vickers was added to the Red Rooster cellar. Elaine, who grew up in Abbotsford, has a master's degree in molecular biology. She once considered playing Ultimate Frisbee professionally. She became interested in wine while working in a wine store when she was a student. That led her to get an enology degree from the University of Adelaide in Australia. She returned to Canada in 2010 to make wine at Jackson-Triggs, Blasted Church Vineyards, and Black Hills Estate Winery before coming to Red Rooster.

MY PICKS

Everything. The wines never disappoint. The upper-tier wines are released under the Rare Bird Series label.

OPENED 1997

891 Naramata Road
Penticton, BC V2A 8T5
T   250.492.2424
W redroosterwinery.com
Restaurant: Smugglers
Smoke House (seasonal
hours)

RICCO BAMBINO/CROOKED CROWN VINEYARD

KELOWNA/OLIVER

In 2017, Kelowna native Jason Alton returned to his hometown after 20 years in Australia to sink all of his resources into Ricco Bambino. The winery, focused on low-intervention and natural wines, deviates significantly from the usual template for Okanagan wineries.

To begin with, Ricco Bambino has two tasting rooms. The first, an urban winery, opened in August 2017 on Pandosy Street, where it has become a popular downtown wine bar with evening hours. It is also a functioning winery with three 1,600-litre concrete eggs for fermenting and aging wines. There are, in fact, no barrels here nor at Ricco Bambino's Crooked Crown Vineyard near Oliver. The wines are all fermented and aged in concrete or stainless steel. Ricco Bambino's 2017 and 2018 vintages were made at Okanagan Crush Pad Winery, where the cooperage is almost exclusively concrete.

The Crooked Crown Vineyard north of Oliver, where the second tasting room is located, was planted in 2019. The 3.6-hectare (9-acre) organically farmed vineyard is designed to produce most of the fruit Ricco Bambino will need for a targeted production of about 3,000 cases a year. The vineyard grows Pinot Noir, Chenin Blanc, Chardonnay, Syrah, and Grenache. There are plans to add some Nebbiolo to the mix.

Winemaker Sebastien Hotte employs primarily natural winemaking techniques to make pure artisanal wines expressing terroir. "I was looking to make more low-intervention wines," he says, explaining his move from the Desert Hills winery in 2018 where he had been assistant winemaker. "And it was important for me to get into organic farming." Sebastien, born in Quebec, initially became a sommelier and worked in restaurants around the world before switching to winemaking in 2014.

JASON ALTON

SEBASTIEN HOTTE

Ricco Bambino has enabled Sebastien to explore the emerging world of natural wine, including what is called *pét-nat*, or *méthode ancestrale*, an ancient method of making sparkling wine. "Making this style of wine is hard," says Sebastien, who also produces Charmat-method and traditional-method bubblies. "I like drinking sparkling wines, and so does Jason."

MY PICKS

The portfolio is invariably interesting. The white wines are crisp; the red wines are light and quaffable. The sparkling wines are my favourites.

OPENED 2018

101 – 1630 Pandosy Street
Kelowna, BC V1Y 1P7
T 236.420.2203

CROOKED CROWN VINEYARD

8977 Highway 97
Oliver, BC V0H 1T2
T 250.498.4546
W riccobambino.com

RIGOUR & WHIMSY

OKANAGAN FALLS

The Rigour & Whimsy portfolio is daring, consisting primarily of skin-fermented, barrel-aged white wines, known in the trade as orange wines. "There are other styles that I like," says winemaker Costa Gavaris, owner of this winery with his partner, Jody Wright. "I love Chablis, Jody loves Chablis. When we were planning this winery in 2015, there were few offerings of orange wine in BC. We love to drink it. It is one of the wine styles that we couldn't get whenever we wanted, so we decided, 'Let's make it.'"

Costa and Jody first tasted an orange wine several years earlier in Paris. It is surprising it took that long, considering his infatuation with wine. The grandson of Greek immigrants, Costa was born in 1982 in St. John's, Newfoundland. He and Jody both grew up in St. Andrews, New Brunswick. Their early careers took them in different directions. He got a university business degree, joined a technology company in Edmonton, and then, in 2008, moved to Kelowna to work for a health-care technology company. Jody, meanwhile, earned a doctorate in marine microbiology at the University of British Columbia. They rekindled a childhood friendship during an Okanagan skiing vacation that led to romance and marriage.

By this time, Costa had begun reading extensively about wine. Then he immersed himself in the Wine & Spirit Education Trust program, graduating in 2013 with top marks and a diploma qualifying him as a wine professional. Asked if he wanted to move to the Master of Wine studies, Costa said no. "That's when I said, 'I want to make wine.'"

In 2016, the couple bought a ton of Pinot Blanc grapes and made wine at Okanagan Crush Pad. The success of that trial triggered Costa's decision to become a wine grower. In 2017 they bought a 2-hectare (5-acre) property on McLean Creek Road

COSTA GAVARIS, JODY WRIGHT, AND THEIR SON, STRATOS

and, after leaving sites for a winery and a home, planted Gamay Noir and Chenin Blanc. In the meantime, they arranged to make the Rigour & Whimsy wines at the nearby Echo Bay Vineyard. In 2018, Costa made 800 cases of wine and laid plans to get his production to 2,000 cases as quickly as he could. They also left jobs in Vancouver to move to the Okanagan with their young son.

"Living in the city was not working for us," Costa says. "We wanted to be connected to a piece of land. We wanted to experience time differently."

MY PICKS

Orange wine is not for everyone's palate, but these are well-made examples of what is an emerging style globally.

SALES BEGAN 2018

4112 McLean Creek Road
Okanagan Falls, BC
V0H 1R1

T 604.363.5775
W rigourandwhimsy.ca

RIVER STONE ESTATE WINERY

OLIVER

What makes River Stone unique is the vineyard. Visitors drive up a steep and narrow vine-hugged road to the wine shop on the hilltop. The hill that driveway climbs, and on which the vines are planted, is a mound of gravel deposited in a former geological time by the postglacial flow of the Okanagan River. This is what River Stone has in common with some of the *grand cru* châteaux of Bordeaux, which are also located on top of river-strewn gravel deposits.

The winery is owned by Ted and Lorraine Kane. Ted, who's from Edmonton and was born in 1962, was so focused on wine growing that he grew grapes in a greenhouse there just to learn how. He and Lorraine, now a family physician, moved to Oliver in 2002 to plant a 2.8-hectare (7-acre) vineyard on land that, for all of its excellent viticultural qualities, had been fallow for 30 years.

Emulating Bordeaux wineries, Ted planted grape varieties needed for blending. The aspect of the vineyard—rows descend down the hill in three directions—enabled Ted to plant each variety on the most advantageous slope. The wine that Ted envisioned is called Corner Stone and debuted with the 2009 vintage. It was dominated by Merlot for the first four vintages, peaking at 59% of the blend in 2010. Since 2014, Cabernet Sauvignon and Cabernet Franc have taken over the lead roles in Corner Stone.

That change reflects the ongoing refinement of the wines. "For me, the most fun is to think about a new experiment that I'm going to try," Ted says. That sense of discovery led to two additional wines: Stones Throw, a Merlot-dominated blend, and Milestone, an exclusive small-lot blend of equal parts Cabernet Franc and Merlot inspired by Bordeaux's Château Cheval Blanc. Milestone is produced only in exceptional years and in very limited volume.

TED KANE

The hilltop is crowned with the Kane family's home and the garage that functioned as a winery until 2015. Production was moved in that vintage to a new building at the bottom of the property's eastern slope. The expansion freed up Ted's garage for the first time. But, he notes, "it just fills up with stuff, like everyone's garage." The wine shop, however, still occupies the basement of the house. It leads to an expansive picnic area and a beautiful garden that is surrounded by vines.

MY PICKS

All wines are top quality, with nuances and complexity showcasing well-grown varieties. Corner Stone is the iconic wine showing the best of each vintage. The Pinot Gris is dry, elegant, and a standout among that variety in the Okanagan. The excellent rosé is made with Malbec, a variety rarely used for rosé.

OPENED 2011

143 Buchanan Drive
Oliver, BC V0H 1T2
T   250.498.0043
W   riverstoneestatewinery.ca

ROAD 13 VINEYARDS

OLIVER

It may have been the castle that caught the eye of Mission Hill's Anthony von Mandl, who bought this winery late in 2018. More likely, it was the old vines of Chenin Blanc, a variety not grown in the Mission Hill vineyards; or it was simply the strength of the Road 13 brand. In each of the previous six years, the National Wine Awards competition placed the winery among Canada's 10 best wineries. In the 2018 competition, it was the number one winery.

The original owners of the winery, Peter and Helga Serwo, erected a replica Bavarian castle for the first winery and tasting room because it reminded them of their European roots. The winery, struggling to sell 1,000 cases a year, was acquired in 2003 by Mick Luckhurst, a hard-charging entrepreneur from Port Alberni who was attracted to wine growing after he and Pam, his wife, spent a summer in the Okanagan. With a succession of first-rate winemakers, production and sales grew rapidly. Major growth came after the winery changed its name to Road 13 in 2008, a decision that later paved the way for Golden Mile, historically a geographical term, to become the Okanagan's first sub-appellation several years later.

The wines that set Road 13 apart from von Mandl's other wineries are its Chenin Blanc, including a superb sparkling wine, and the winery's family of Rhône wines. Seldom grown in the Okanagan, Chenin Blanc vines now more than 50 years old were in the vineyard when the Luckhursts bought the property.

The Luckhursts chose purposely to champion Rhône varieties, which, with the exception of Syrah, had not been embraced by many other wineries. "It happens that I am really passionate about Rhône varieties," general manager Joe Luckhurst says. "Consistently, those were the best grapes coming off our vineyards. I wanted to be the valley's Rhône specialist."

JOE LUCKHURST

Everything. The reds— including the GSM and the Syrah—are bold in flavour. The Chenin Blanc and other whites (Viognier, Marsanne, and especially Roussanne) are outstanding. The Honest John's blends overdeliver.

OPENED 1998 (AS GOLDEN MILE CELLARS)

799 Ponderosa Road, Road 13

Oliver, BC V0H 1T1

T 250.498.8330

1.866.498.8330 (toll-free)

W road13vineyards.com

ROBIN RIDGE WINERY

KEREMEOS

After more than a decade of marketing the wines of their Robin Ridge Winery, owners Tim and Caroline Cottrill still have modest prices for their very sound wines. Many of their peers began asking aggressive prices as the reputation of British Columbia wines soared. Robin Ridge might be leaving money on the table, perhaps because it has maintained a low profile. "You have to earn prices, I think, not just demand them in the marketplace," Tim says. The buyers of the 2,000 or so cases of wine he makes every year clearly benefit from that modesty.

The son of a carpenter, Tim was born in Kelowna in 1966 and grew up in Summerland, where he helped his father build houses. When they tired of the construction industry's boom-and-bust cycles, Tim and Caroline (who grew up on a peach orchard) moved to the Similkameen Valley in 1996, purchasing a 4-hectare (10-acre) hayfield near the Grist Mill, where they began planting vines after clearing the stony terrain. They were drawn to grapes because both had made wines at home.

While Tim studied winemaking and viticulture at Okanagan University College, they started by planting a 1.2-hectare (3-acre) block of Chardonnay in 1998, adding Gamay Noir in 1999, Merlot in 2001, and Pinot Noir in 2004. As well, there are small plots of Gewürztraminer, Cabernet Sauvignon, St. Laurent, and Rougeon (a rustic French hybrid since replaced in the vineyard with Cabernet Franc), along with half a hectare (1¼ acres) of Sovereign Coronation table grapes. When Tim made Robin Ridge's first commercial vintage in 2006, he took the precaution of getting professional guidance from Lawrence Herder, then the owner of a neighbouring winery.

Robin Ridge now has a total of 7.3 hectares (18 acres) under vine. It has been farmed organically since the purchase of a nearby

TIM COTTRILL

property in 2012. There are plantings of Riesling, Petit Verdot, and Malbec, and more Cabernet Sauvignon, Cabernet Franc, and Gamay. While Tim continues to sell grapes to other wineries, he has been increasing the Robin Ridge portfolio as well. Notably, the winery's Meritage now includes five Bordeaux varieties.

Tim and Caroline are a community-minded couple. He is a member of the Keremeos fire department, while Caroline manages the town's pharmacy. Their four children have grown up on the vineyard and also have been involved in both viticulture and winemaking.

MY PICKS

The flagship red is the Gamay Noir, but the Pinot Noir, the Merlot, and the Cabernet Franc are excellent, while the Meritage is more complex with each passing vintage. The lightly oaked Chardonnay is crisp and fresh. The most unusual wine is a rosé called Flamingo, a grapey wine from the Sovereign Coronation grapes.

OPENED 2008

2686 Middle Bench Road
Keremeos, BC V0X 1N2

T   250.499.5504

W   robinridgewinery.com

ROCHE WINES

In France, where Dylan Roche and Pénélope Furt-Roche, his partner, began making wine, they never had the opportunity to work with Zweigelt, an Austrian red, or Schönburger, a German white grape. In 2014, they almost turned down the 2-hectare (5-acre) Upper Bench vineyard, now home to their winery, because it was planted mostly with those varieties. "We hesitated," Dylan says. "Then a few months later, we said this is the perfect location, the perfect exposure, the perfect soil. It is just the two varieties that we were sticking on." The Zweigelt has been turned into a fine rosé, while the spicy Schönburger now makes an excellent table wine. And they planted small blocks of Chardonnay and Pinot Noir.

Dylan was born in Vancouver in 1976, the son of a lawyer and a nurse. After getting a University of British Columbia degree in urban geography, he went to Burgundy in 2000 as a bike mechanic and cycling guide and developed his interest in wine there. By 2003, he was enrolled in enology studies in Beaune. Pénélope had five generations of winemaking and viticulture behind her at the family estate, Château Les Carmes Haut-Brion. It was sold just before the couple came to the Okanagan in 2010, where they worked initially as consulting winemakers.

In 2012, they launched the Roche label with 85 cases of Chardonnay. Beginning in 2013, Dylan and Pénélope began to extend their portfolio by purchasing Pinot Noir and Pinot Gris from the 6-hectare (15-acre) Kozier Organic Vineyard nearby on the Naramata Bench. In 2016, they took over the farming of the vineyard, which also grows Merlot, Gewürztraminer, and Viognier, a solid foundation for their portfolio.

The metal-clad winery, which they built in 2017, fronts on busy Upper Bench Road. It is a practical, well-designed building,

PÉNÉLOPE FURT-ROCHE AND DYLAN ROCHE

double-insulated to reduce energy consumption, and designed for a capacity of 6,000 to 10,000 cases. The compact tasting room is tucked into a corner with windows looking over the vineyard.

MY PICKS

Everything. The Pinot Noirs and the Chardonnay recall Burgundy. The Pinot Gris is remarkably complex. And don't overlook Arôme, as the winery calls its dry Schönburger.

OPENED 2017

60 Upper Bench Road South
Penticton, BC V2A 8T1

T   236.422.2722

W   rterroir.ca

ROLLINGDALE WINERY

WEST KELOWNA

Rollingdale Winery was the first Okanagan winery to secure organic certification for its vineyard. Steve and Kirsty Dale, the owners, have maintained an organic focus since their first vintage in 2004. "We drink a lot of our own wines," Kirsty says, "so we don't want to consume all those things that we don't think are safe."

Steve, who was born in 1971, and Kirsty started dating in high school before they moved from London, Ontario, to Vancouver. Their roots in organics took hold at a garden shop that they ran in Port Moody for three years. Then they moved to Switzerland to work as horticultural consultants. They took advantage of their European base to explore many wine regions before coming back to Canada and settling in the Okanagan in August 2003.

Steve enrolled in the winery assistant program at Okanagan University College in Penticton. On his practicum, he was assigned to a new vineyard on Hayman Road in West Kelowna that had been leased by the Hainle winery. As soon as he arrived, he was smitten with the vineyard. "I thought, 'It is a perfect opportunity because it is a really great location for a winery,'" Steve says. "I thought, 'This is what I have been looking for.'" He took over the lease for 2004 and bought the property the next year.

Rollingdale built its reputation with organic viticulture in BC. They would now be considered "early adopters" of these practices, now becoming widespread in the Okanagan. The people who joined Rollingdale were attracted to the commitment to organic wine. Brendan Smith, the winemaker, was hired in 2013 as a vineyard worker and quickly progressed to the cellar. He started doing "more of everything" and by 2017 was taking care of the winemaking. "It's not just one person that makes this stuff—it's a whole production," Brendan says. "We're all involved. I wouldn't

be able to do what I do without everybody else."

The wine shop, open year-round, is at the front entrance of the metal-clad winery building, allowing visitors to watch cellar activities. Just standing at the tasting bar is an immersive winery experience in the sights, sounds, and smells of a working winery.

MY PICKS

There is a large portfolio of small-lot wines; if something catches your attention, purchase it immediately as it may be sold out by your next visit. The Estate Maréchal Foch, which the winery calls a "quaffable" red, is usually available. The Icewines are always star attractions.

OPENED 2006

2306 Hayman Road
West Kelowna, BC V1Z 1Z5
T   250.769.9224
W   rollingdale.ca

RUBY BLUES WINERY

PENTICTON

The effervescent personality of Prudence Mahrer, one of the proprietors, informs everything about this winery, including the bohemian artwork, the red stiletto shoes sold in the wine shop, and the endless peals of laughter in the tasting room.

Did we mention the irresistible house style of the wines? "It is a Ruby Blues style: you open it, you can just keep drinking it," says Blair Gillingham, the winemaker. "You don't have to have food; you don't have to do anything. You can just open it and enjoy it with your friends and family."

Prudence and Beat, her husband, ran fitness centres in Switzerland before immigrating to the Okanagan. Here, they opened Red Rooster Winery in 1997. They sold it in 2005 to Andrew Peller Ltd. They soon found they missed the wine industry, returning to it in 2009 with what was then called Ruby Tuesday Winery. The name was inspired by a Rolling Stones song, "Ruby Tuesday," a favourite of Prudence's because it is about a free-spirited young woman following her dream. A trademark dispute led the winery to be renamed Ruby Blues, which apparently also alludes to a Beatles song. "Some of the songs from the '60s have so much meaning," Prudence says.

Unlike the baronial Red Rooster Winery next door, Ruby Blues operates as a boutique. "I want to do what I really loved the most—producing wine, quality wine of course, and then selling it myself to customers," Prudence says. The consistently friendly wines are offered in a tasting room where the only fee is a smile.

If you are not smiling, Prudence will tease one out of you, perhaps by trying to sell a pair of red stiletto shoes that she first ordered in 2011 from a cobbler in Vietnam. "They are very high-heeled, very feminine, probably nothing to walk in the vineyard

WINEMAKER BLAIR GILLINGHAM

PRUDENCE MAHRER

with," Prudence says, laughing. "They are meant to walk from home to the car and to the restaurant and then back. They look extremely fancy."

MY PICKS

Everything, notably the Viognier, a consistent award winner. Red Stiletto and White Stiletto are well-made easy-drinking wines, while Black Stiletto is a Syrah-based blend that can be cellared.

OPENED 2009 (AS RUBY TUESDAY WINERY)

917 Naramata Road
Penticton, BC V2A 8V1

T   250.276.5311

W   rubyblueswinery.com

RUST WINE CO.

Look closely at the continually changing labels of this winery. Each has sprung from a photo taken by a consumer of a rusty object. Or look at the winery's exterior, clad in steel specially manufactured to weather quickly. It supports the image of a winery with a colourful history.

The original 1.2-hectare (3-acre) vineyard was begun in 1964 by Hungarian immigrant John Tokias, who formerly worked at a mine in the BC interior. To house his family, he moved a mining camp bunkhouse, log by log. He added a sod roof, adorning it bizarrely with sun-bleached skulls of game and livestock scavenged from nearby hills. He retired from grape growing in 2004, selling the property to a former Bowen Island brewer named Don Bradley.

Don built a 4,000-case-capacity winery, intending to call it Antelope Brush, before selling in 2007 and moving to Vancouver Island, where his wife, an emergency room nurse, had a job. The new operator was Bruce Fuller, a former Vancouver marketing executive who, undeterred by a lack of capital, had already promoted three or four conceptual wineries. This time, he enlisted the Gidda brothers, then owners of Mt. Boucherie Estate Winery, as silent partners. Bruce moved into the bunkhouse, took off some of the skulls, and, with wines made by Mt. Boucherie, launched Rustico Farm & Cellars.

A horse-loving thespian who favoured cowboy hats, Bruce was inspired by the area's mining history in labelling the wines. The iconic Zinfandel was called Bonanza; a red blend was Last Chance; and a Pinot Gris was provocatively called Isabella's Poke. And the tasting room, filled with antiques, did a roaring business—until a family dispute led to the Gidda brothers losing their properties in 2016.

RYAN DE WITTE

In 2017 the owners who had taken over Mt. Boucherie rebranded Rustico as Rust, and they have crafted a distinctive portfolio. The winery's Golden Mile vineyard, now 4 hectares (10 acres), continues to grow the Zinfandel that made the property famous. Cabernet Sauvignon has replaced Chancellor, a heritage French hybrid. And there is a small block of Gewürztraminer that is more than 50 years old. Ryan de Witte, a young winemaker who worked previously at a small Niagara winery, took over in the Rust cellar in 2019.

With access to the 121 hectares (300 acres) of vineyards owned by Mt. Boucherie, Rust also specializes in making small lots of the same varietals from different terroirs. The main focus of the winery is single-vineyard, single-variety wines. This allows the tasting-room staff to let visitors compare, for example, three different Merlots or four different Syrahs. It is a rare education in how different terroirs are reflected in the wines.

MY PICKS

Red wines have pride of place in this portfolio, notably the Old Vine Zinfandel, which, in most vintages, is a bold and age-worthy wine.

OPENED 2009
(AS RUSTICO)

4444 Golden Mile Drive
Oliver, BC V0H 1T1
T   250.498.3276
W rustwine.com

RUSTIC ROOTS WINERY

CAWSTON

"It was one of our goals to make wines that would surprise people," says Sara Harker, a co-owner and the winemaker here. She challenged the perception that fruit wines are sweet by producing wines that range from dry to sweet to sparkling. She also builds complexity into the wines through blending and creative winemaking. For example, she blends about 30% Santa Rosa plum wine with 70% Fameuse apple wine to create a lively pink sparkling wine. Fameuse, also called Snow Apple, is a heritage variety produced by a tree planted on this farm in 1916. All the wine labels include an image of the immensely rooted Snow Apple tree.

The winery, making about 3,000 cases of organic wines a year, is incorporated into the highway-side organic fruit stand operated since the late 1950s by the Harker family, which has very deep roots in the Similkameen Valley. The patriarch of the family, Bruce Harker, has farmed here since 1975. His maternal great-grandfather was Sam Manery, the fourth settler baby born in the valley after Sam's parents came there in 1888.

Bruce and Kathy, his wife, developed a flourishing business with organic fruit. As they reached their 60s, they were thinking of retirement, when Troy, their son, and his wife, Sara, returned to the farm and the business. This brought a fifth generation into Harker's Organics, with a sixth in the wings.

That was the incentive to develop the winery with Sara as the winemaker. Born in Oliver in 1982, Sara is a member of a family that emigrated from Hungary in 1956. She comes to wine through the restaurant business. After studying science for a year at Langara College and then business administration at Okanagan University College, she spent eight years working at various positions at the Fairview Mountain Golf Club. Sara equipped herself for the winery

SARA HARKER

KATHY AND BRUCE HARKER

by taking Okanagan College's winery assistant program and being mentored by consultant Christine Leroux. After refining the fruit-wine portfolio, Sara added four ciders in 2012.

MY PICKS

Everything, starting with the refreshing peach-nectarine wine and the spicy apple pear. There are several sparkling wines: Pippin, a dry wine from apples and nectarines, and Fameuse, a tangy apple and plum rosé. Iced Ambrosia is a delicately sparkling dessert wine made from Ambrosia apples.

OPENED 2008

2238 Highway 3
Cawston, BC V0X 1C2

T   250.499.2751

W   harkersorganicsrusticroots.com
Restaurant: Barn Door Bistro,
open for breakfast and lunch

SAGE HILLS VINEYARD

SUMMERLAND

The road to Sage Hills from Highway 97 is not fully paved and at one point more closely resembles a goat trail. "You can't turn around till you get here!" owner Rick Thrussell says. The surprise is to find a sophisticated winery and its elegant wine shop at the end of the road.

Rick developed his winery and vineyard here for many reasons, one of which is the stunning view over Okanagan Lake. He hired a French consultant to select the most suitable grape varieties to plant—Pinot Noir, Pinot Gris, and Gewürztraminer—which form the foundation of Sage Hills' portfolio. "We only do straight varietals," explains Rick. "We don't do any blending at all. I just think that you get a better product." The vineyard was planted starting in 2007 with the first vintage produced in 2012.

Rick developed an appreciation for wine early. From the age of six, he helped his grandfather make wine in his basement in south Burnaby from grapes grown in his backyard. When he was old enough, wine became his beverage of choice. "To me, wine had a history," says Rick. "It had a geographical significance. It paired with foods. And there was a story behind it." A trip in his 20s to Uniacke Cellars, an early estate winery that is now CedarCreek, cemented the image of what living in wine country could be like. Rick wanted his own winery. He worked in the communications industry and then built homes until 2006 when he bought this property, then an orchard, near Summerland.

Though Sage Hills' wines respect a rustic traditional history, they are most definitely modern in style. The wine shop is both beautiful and functional, with comfortable seating for everyone tasting at the wraparound bar. There is a more intimate tasting table set against the windows for small groups or families. Without a bad seat in the house, nobody misses out on the view.

RICK THRUSSELL

MY PICKS

Everything in this creative lineup is superb. Pinot Gris is used for three different wines—Brut Sauvage (a natural-method sparkling wine), Rhymes with Orange (an orange wine), and a table wine. The Syrah is made as a rosé, and there is a fortified Merlot in addition to traditional table-wine versions of both. The iconic Pinot Noir is only produced as a table wine, often limited to two bottles per person.

OPENED 2013

18555 Matsu Drive
Summerland, BC V0H 1Z6
T 250.276.4344
W sagehillswine.com

SAGEWOOD WINERY

A black Labrador named Kayla once was Doug Wood's constant companion in the Sagewood vineyard. Kayla died just before Doug and Shelley, his wife, opened Sagewood Winery in 2014. They have commemorated their pet dog, however. The gnarled branch that Kayla played with was incorporated into the winery logo. And the Sagewood sparkling wine is called Kayla.

The 1.4-hectare (3½-acre) vineyard, planted in 2005, was the first commercial vineyard in the Kamloops area. Seventeen varieties are grown in this rugged soil. There are so many different varieties because when Doug, a doctor, was taking viticulture courses at Okanagan College, some of his fellow students gave him extra vine cuttings. Doug planted them all to see what would flourish. Most of the varieties did flourish, and he sold grapes to established wineries. In 2013, when a wine made with his grapes won double gold at competition, Doug decided it was time to launch his own winery.

Born in Kamloops, Doug started a military career after high school. "On my dad's side of the family, every male served in the armed forces," Doug says. He started in the navy as a radio operator and then, after a university degree in physics, became a communications engineer in a signals regiment where, he recalls, the mess wine was Schloss Laderheim. When he became interested in medicine, the Canadian Forces sponsored the training because they needed doctors. Eventually, he became the base surgeon at Canadian Forces Base Shilo, with the rank of major. But he then met Shelley, who was in Kamloops, and he left the military in 1997 to establish his own medical practice in that community.

Doug had begun making wine when he was still in his teens but a serious interest only flourished after he left the military. He spent several years canvassing properties around Kamloops until

SHELLEY AND DOUG WOOD

he settled on this site. As is often the case with vineyards, the rocky site seems inhospitable to anything but sage. Yet to Doug, when he needs a break from medicine, the vineyard is therapeutic. "You go out in the vineyard, and it is relaxing," he reflects.

MY PICKS

Ortega, Kerner, and Siegerrebe among the white wines; and Cabernet Franc and Maréchal Foch among the reds.

OPENED 2014

589 Meadow Lark Road
Kamloops, BC V2H 1S9

T   250.573.1921

W   sagewoodwinery.ca

ST. HUBERTUS & OAK BAY ESTATE WINERY

KELOWNA

In the spring of 2012, Leo and Andy Gebert, owners of this winery, more than doubled their Chasselas plantings. The 4 hectares (10 acres) of Chasselas in this winery's 32-hectare (80-acre) vineyard almost certainly is the largest block of that white variety in Canada. It speaks to their heritage. Chasselas, which yields a soft, easy wine, is the leading white in the vineyards of Switzerland where the brothers grew up.

Born in 1958 in the wine-growing town of Rapperswil, Leo is a banker by training but a farmer at heart. He came to the Okanagan in 1984 and bought the historic Beau Séjour Vineyard that has grown grapes since 1928. His younger brother, Andy, who had skippered yachts in the Caribbean, joined Leo in 1990 in developing this family winery. Their wives, who are sisters, are involved in the business. Leo's son, Reto, has taken on vineyard duties after graduating from Niagara College's winery program.

The varieties grown here have changed several times with different owners and new consumer tastes. Chasselas is a sentimental favourite, but the most important white variety here is Riesling, including one of the three blocks of Clone 21B Riesling planted in 1978. The other two are at Tantalus and Sperling. All of these wineries release deeply flavoured Old Vines Riesling. The St. Hubertus version is released under the Family Reserve label. Part of the wine portfolio is released under the Oak Bay label, reflecting that portion of the vineyard called Oak Bay.

The Gebert family brings a strong environmental ethic to wine growing. The vineyard is farmed sustainably and, in 2017, began to transition to organic methods. Most of the energy used in the winery buildings is supplied by solar panels. "Our goal," Andy says, "is to be carbon neutral."

ANDY AND LEO GEBERT

St. Hubertus has the unwanted distinction of being the only Okanagan winery destroyed by a wildfire. The 2003 Okanagan Mountain Park fire destroyed 239 buildings in Kelowna, including the original St. Hubertus winery and Leo's heritage home. Fortunately for St. Hubertus, the fire did not destroy the warehouse in which nearly all the wine was stored. Since then, the winery has produced a wine called FireMan's Red whose sales support fire rescue services.

MY PICKS

St. Hubertus has crisp and fruity whites, notably Riesling, Gewürztraminer, Schönburger, Pinot Blanc, and Chasselas. The winery's top reds include Maréchal Foch, Gamay Noir, and Pinot Noir. A white blend called Great White North, at $12.50 a bottle, is one of the best-value wines in the valley.

OPENED 1992

5205 Lakeshore Road
Kelowna, BC V1W 4J1
T 250.764.7888
W st-hubertus.bc.ca
Picnic area

SANDHILL

Sandhill's first vintage in 1997 and every vintage since have been made in the sprawling Calona winery in downtown Kelowna. Sandhill was conceived in a deliberate decision to make premium wines that would stand apart from the pedestrian image that Calona wines earned over the years when it did not control its own vineyards. Then in the late 1990s, the Sandhill estate vineyard was planted on Black Sage Road in a joint venture with Burrowing Owl Estate Winery.

Burrowing Owl went on to build its own winery. However, plans for a Sandhill winery on Black Sage Road were delayed and then shelved. Andrew Peller Ltd., which purchased both Calona Vineyards and Sandhill in 2005, opted instead for a major rebuild of the Calona winery. That included the large and elegant Sandhill tasting room, which also sells other wines made by the Peller winemakers in this winery.

Howard Soon, Sandhill's winemaker until he retired in 2017, decided to make just single-vineyard wines—wines expressing each vineyard's individual terroir. "In my early career, a lot of our wines did taste the same," Howard said in one interview before he retired. "They were not distinct." He worked with Sandhill's viticulturists and with selected other vineyards to assure that the grapes coming to the winery did express individuality.

Sandy Leier, who succeeded Howard, carries on his philosophy. She has also added wines branded as "terroir driven," which are blended from several of the vineyards supplying Sandhill. Sandy was born in Vancouver and grew up in Kelowna, where she prepared for a winemaking career with a degree in chemistry from the University of British Columbia Okanagan. She joined the Andrew Peller winemaking team in 2006. Before taking over Sandhill, she was the lead winemaker for both Calona Vineyards and Wayne Gretzky Okanagan.

SANDY LEIER

Sandhill's estate vineyard, at 70 hectares (174 acres), planted in the 1990s on Black Sage Road, is one of the largest. The nearby Osprey Ridge Vineyard (4.9 hectares/12 acres) is a source of Viognier. The winery gets Pinot Gris from the 17.4-hectare (43-acre) King Family Vineyard near Penticton, and Pinot Gris, Chardonnay, and Sauvignon Blanc from the 119-hectare (294-acre) Hidden Terrace Vineyard at Covert Farms, near Oliver. Sandhill's Cabernet/Merlot blend is made with grapes from the 42-hectare (104½-acre) Vanessa Vineyard in the Similkameen Valley.

Sandhill's premium wines are released in the winery's Small Lots tier. Depending on the vintage, there are at least a dozen Small Lots wines, including Sangiovese and Barbera, two Italian red varieties rarely seen in the Okanagan. These are usually single-vineyard wines, reflecting the founding philosophy of the winery. The terroir-driven blends usually are released as more moderately priced wines.

MY PICKS

The Sandhill Small Lots wines are exceptional. The flagship wines are Sandhill One, a Bordeaux blend built to age; Sandhill Two, also a Bordeaux blend; and Sandhill Three, a blend of Cabernet Sauvignon, Barbera, and Sangiovese—the Okanagan version of a Super Tuscan blend.

OPENED 1999

1125 Richter Street
Kelowna, BC V1Y 2K6
T 250.979.4211
   1.888.246.4472 (toll-free)
W sandhillwines.ca

SAVARD VINES

SUMMERLAND

The sign on Highway 97 coming from Summerland indicates a right-hand turn to get to Savard Vines. In reality, the arrow should be pointing almost straight down. From the access road, the driveway contains five complete switchbacks to reach the wine shop far down the slope. Those switchbacks give the name "5 Turns" to the winery's Pinot Noir and Gamay Noir blend.

Owners Lori and Michael Savard purchased the site in 2003 as a recreational property to get away from their medical careers in Edmonton. Lori worked as a nurse practitioner in cardiology at the University of Alberta and Michael as an emergency room physician, which he continues to do with time off from tending the vines. Michael grew up on a mixed cattle and grain farm in Alberta, and it did not take long for him to want to start planting crops on the property. A few fruit trees were already planted but were a lot of work to maintain. He experimented first with garlic and then ryegrass, but it was hard to ignore their property's potential for grapes. In 2008, they planted Pinot Noir and Pinot Gris, along with small amounts of Malbec and Cabernet Franc.

While Michael looked after the grape growing, Lori quickly took an interest in the winemaking. While in Edmonton, she became a sommelier with ISG (International Sommelier Guild) and then took a two-year program through the University of California, Davis. "I love the fermentations," says Lori, "because to me, it's almost a composite of everything that I've learned in my life: biology, chemistry, microbiology, and sanitation." Daughter Heather Savard, who was studying at the Nova Scotia College of Art and Design at the time the first vintages were ready for bottling, contributed her artwork to the wine labels.

The first vintages were made at other wineries, but by 2015 they were making wine in their own winery even though it was

LORI SAVARD

not fully completed at the time and did not yet have electricity. "We were running power cords from the house," recounts Lori. Pascal Madevon helped out with winemaking decisions for these vintages and remains an adviser. After a few vintages, the winery is producing consistent wines. Of special note is the Riesling, a beautifully balanced New World-style Riesling that is a focus of Lori's attention. "I love Riesling," she says. "I always say that my next husband is going to be a Riesling."

MY PICKS

All wines are strong and show great potential. The Beards, Horns, & Hooves Riesling is beautiful with a long finish. 5 Turns is an excellent blend of Pinot Noir and Gamay. The Pinot Noir is complex and refined.

OPENED 2017

25200 Callan Road
Summerland, BC V0H 1Z6
T 250.494.1926
W savardvines.ca

SAXON ESTATE WINERY

SUMMERLAND

If launching flaming pumpkins skyward with a trebuchet seems entertaining, Saxon Estate Winery will appeal to you. "We call them victims, not customers," says Paul Graydon, co-owner along with his wife, Jayne, of Saxon Estate Winery. He specifies that they are "victims of our humour" rather than of the organic wines. "We have a lot of fun with them," Paul says. Wine names like Drunken Knight, English Rose, and Crown Jewel take their cue from the British culture of these Londoners who purchased the small Summerland winery (formerly known as Hollywood & Wine) in 2015.

Paul had an international sales career in information technology, while Jayne sold Piper-Heidsieck Champagne in Britain before the couple had children. They immigrated to North America in 2003, settling in Calgary. In 2011, searching for opportunities in the wine industry, they started their own import agency in Alberta. In seeking out British Columbia wineries to represent, they became more interested in making their own wine than in selling other people's wines. A year later, they purchased Hollywood & Wine in Summerland's bucolic Prairie Valley area. They renamed it Saxon, after the Saxony region of England where they come from, which provided branding opportunities around the name.

In addition to the memorable name, the wine labels were designed entirely with the consumer in mind. "We've done this based on a European model, but we enhanced it and made it our own," explains Paul. The colourful plasticized labels do not ripple or come off in water but easily peel off if people want to save the labels. The back labels feature wine descriptors, including flavour profiles and food-pairing ideas that help customers and sommeliers to serve the wine. "We feel like we're different, being

PAUL AND JAYNE GRAYDON

Europeans," Paul says. "We grew up with wine in supermarkets."

At one point, Saxon boasted the smallest wine shop in the Okanagan, with room for only one small group at a time. The intimacy of the room worked, and guests often left charmed and with more than a few bottles of wine as well. Plans are under way for an expanded guest experience.

OPENED 2007 (AS HOLLYWOOD & WINE)

9819 Lumsden Avenue
Summerland, BC V0H 1Z8

T   250.494.0311

W   saxonwinery.com

MY PICKS

All wines, fruit forward and accessible, are made with organic grapes, are low in sulphites, and are vegan-friendly. The hybrid Léon Millot, now rare in Okanagan vineyards, produces bold and dark reds. Look for the English Rose, Gewürztraminer, and Four Play.

SCHELL WINES

VIRTUAL WINERY

For the past decade or two, Chardonnay has been unfashionable–but it had a champion in Jennifer Schell. "I am a huge Chardonnay-crazed person; always have been," she says. "I have never left its side through the bad times." In 2016, when she enlisted her brothers, Jonathan and Jamie, as partners in Schell Wines, the first wine they made was a Chardonnay.

The Schells grew up in East Kelowna, where the family have been orchardists for several generations. Jennifer and her brothers, who operate a dental laboratory, no longer are directly involved in agriculture. Jennifer, however, remained indirectly involved through her careers as editor of *Food & Wine Trails Magazine* and as the author of four regional cookbooks. Her first book in 2012 was *The Butcher, the Baker, the Wine & Cheese Maker: An Okanagan Cookbook*. An award-winning celebration of the valley's food and wine artisans, it established her reputation.

"I learned from writing about wine for so long," Jennifer says. "But being on the winemaking side has been an education. It is quite an undertaking, but it is also the most wonderful, exciting experience."

She is a founder of the Garagiste North wine festival. This annual event is open just to small wineries–producers making no more than 2,000 cases of wine a year. Jennifer engaged one of the *garagistes*, Rob Westbury, to help the Schells make their wines at his Nagging Doubt Winery in East Kelowna. They produced just 300 cases of Chardonnay in 2016, making Jennifer an eminently qualified *garagiste*. More Chardonnay has been made in subsequent vintages, along with several red blends. The fruit comes from premium growers that Jennifer identified during a decade of wine writing in the Okanagan.

JAMIE, JENNIFER, AND JONATHAN SCHELL

The wines all have touches of the Schell family. When Jennifer was a little girl, her nickname was Jenny Wren; that is why there is a wren on the Chardonnay label. One of the red blends is called Xeferius. It was the given name of her great-grandfather, an immigrant from Bessarabia. The Schells have yet to buy land for a vineyard and winery. It could happen: there is an orchard in the family currently leased to a cherry grower.

MY PICKS

There is a reason why restaurants snap up Schell's Chardonnays and red blends: the wines are very well made.

OPENED 2017

T   250.469.4549

W   jenniferschell.com/
     schell-wines

No tasting room

SCORCHED EARTH WINERY

KELOWNA

This winery and its hillside vineyard are surrounded by Okanagan Mountain Park. The landscape is still bleak with dead blackened trees from the 2003 fires that destroyed homes and the forests in this area. That prompted the name for the winery that Anita and Peter Pazdernik opened on the 4.9-hectare (12-acre) property, which they bought in 2004.

The previous owner had planted a vineyard in 1989, primarily growing table grapes with a little Auxerrois. The vineyard, along with the lakeshore home, escaped destruction because fire retardants and water were dumped liberally on the property. However, that so damaged the vines that the Pazderniks pulled them all out.

"We rebuilt the vineyard from the ground up," Peter says. "When we removed the table grapes, we ripped out the trellis system and the irrigation system. We then resculpted the land to gain better exposure. Then we put in over 400 dump-truck loads of compost to renourish the soil. The previous owners were conventional farmers, not organic. And we let the land lie fallow for a year." Beginning in 2009, Peter and Anita, together with son Shae and daughter Kiana, planted about 7,000 vines—four clones of organically grown Pinot Noir.

They come by their love of wine from a European heritage. Peter was born in Prague, growing up there and in Toronto when his parents immigrated to Canada in 1976. He has a commerce degree from the University of Toronto and has had careers in sales and marketing. Anita is a Winnipeg native who grew up in the Okanagan, which is why she and Peter moved back to the valley after a brief business stint in Calgary. "We have friends who own wineries in different places around the world," Anita says, explaining their decision to develop one. "Everyone said it is a great opportunity."

PETER AND ANITA PAZDERNIK

In 2011, with help from consultants, they made their first barrel of Pinot Noir, a trial so successful that friends and family had consumed it all within months of bottling the wine. The first commercial release was three barrels of Pinot Noir from the 2012 vintage. Production now averages about 500 cases a year, with a target to reach 2,500 cases. The challenge may be protecting the grapes from bears. In 2017, a female bear and two cubs ate an estimated five tons of grapes. Peter salvaged enough to make 175 cases of Pinot Noir rosé, which was released as Bearly Blushing Rosé.

MY PICKS

Everything, including the estate Pinot Noirs and a Merlot from purchased fruit.

OPENED 2014

6006 Lakeshore Road
Kelowna, BC V1W 4J5

T 250.717.7994

W scorchedearthwinery.ca

No tasting room

SCOUT VINEYARD

CAWSTON

Scout Vineyard opened with an advantage: the name was well known because, for several years, Orofino Winery made acclaimed vineyard-designated wines from this vineyard, which is farmed by Murray Fonteyne and his wife, Maggie.

Former Albertans, Murray and Maggie moved to the Similkameen Valley to farm a highway-side property south of Cawston. After growing apples for several years, they converted to a 2.4-hectare (6-acre) vineyard with roughly equal plantings of Riesling, Syrah, and Pinot Gris, plus a small block of Cabernet Sauvignon. When the vines began producing fruit, Murray sold them primarily to Orofino, an established winery north of Cawston.

The partners in the Scout Vineyard winery are Saskatchewan natives Aaron Godard and his wife, Carly, a flight attendant whom he met at university. Aaron, born in Saskatoon in 1983, has a fine arts degree from the University of Saskatchewan, an education financed by planting trees each summer. His interest in wine was triggered by working in restaurants. "I wanted to do some harvests and at least dip my feet and see if that was what I wanted to do," he says. He worked the 2010 vintage at Orofino, was offered a full-time job, and stayed there for nine years. After working with Scout's grapes, he and Murray discovered a shared ambition to make wine and decided to work together.

A former apple-packing house on Murray's farm was turned into a winery, with Scout's first vintage of 750 cases made here in 2018 while renovations were under way. The completed winery is designed with capacity for Scout (1,500 cases made in 2019) and for custom crush winemaking for other small growers in the Similkameen.

Scout is the first winery in the valley to ferment some of

AARON GODARD

its wines in *kvevris*, beeswax-lined clay vessels imported from Georgia. For centuries, vintners in that nation have fermented and stored wine in these vessels, which are traditionally buried so that wine is kept at a cool, stable temperature. Scout, which also uses stainless steel tanks and barrels, also buries its kvevris.

Expect Scout's wines to be similar to those that Aaron made with Scout grapes at Orofino, but with a personality gained from the kvevris and other practices. The vineyard, while not yet certified, is farmed organically. The grapes are all fermented with indigenous yeasts. "We don't want to have any commercial yeasts in here," Aaron says. "The goal will be to not filter or fine the wines. It is a means to achieve making the wines we want to make—hopefully, pure expressions of the Similkameen."

MY PICKS

Current range not tasted.

OPENED 2019

761 Highway 3
Cawston, BC V0X 1C3
T   250.599.9103
W scoutvineyard.com
Tastings by appointment

SECOND CHAPTER WINE COMPANY

OLIVER

This winery takes its name from a Black Sage Road vineyard, but it also speaks to the career in wine by the owners. This is the second time Kim Pullen and his son, John, have launched a winery.

Victoria-born Kim is a former tax lawyer and entrepreneur who got into the wine business in 2004 by buying the failing Victoria Estate Winery on Vancouver Island. He intended it to be an investment, but after dumping the inventory of unacceptable wine, he was forced to be a hands-on operator. He renamed the winery Church & State. By 2008 he had vineyards and a processing facility in the South Okanagan. The winery was making 35,000 cases of highly regarded wine by 2017 when it was acquired by Sunocean Wineries and Estate, a Vancouver company owned by a Chinese businessman and his daughter.

To remain wine producers, the Pullens kept two vineyards and planted a third, totalling 8 hectares (20 acres), enough to make about 4,000 cases of premium wine each year. "The goal is to focus on those 20 acres and make them as best as we can; we are trying to be high end and boutique," John Pullen says. He was still at university when he started working with Church & State. "Second Chapter is a distillation of what we were doing before, not starting over again."

A temporary processing facility and tasting room operated in 2019 at John's home on Tinhorn Creek Road, where a small block of Cabernet Franc was planted. The permanent facilities are expected to be completed in 2020 on the Second Chapter vineyard on Black Sage Road. For the new winery, the Pullens kept two top vineyards, including the Rattlesnake Vineyard on the Golden Mile. This vineyard consistently grows award-winning Merlot and Malbec. The other varieties grown for the winery include Cabernet Sauvignon, Syrah, Viognier, and Roussanne. And they continue to get the exceptional

JOHN PULLEN   KIM PULLEN   PHIL GLAZEBROOK

Chardonnay from Joseph Boutin's Gravelbourg Vineyard on Black Sage Road.

The Pullens have chosen a completely different marketing strategy for Second Chapter. They plan to sell all their wines to the Second Chapter wine club and at the winery's tasting bar. "We want people to come and spend time with us," John says. "Taste some wines, hang out on the patio, have a chat with the winemaker, and really connect with us. That is how we intend to promote wines that are not cheap."

The winemaker is Phil Glazebrook, a native of Guelph who came to wine from a career in restaurants. A graduate of Niagara College, he started working in the Okanagan at the Summerhill Pyramid Winery restaurant and then moved into the cellar there. Subsequently, he made wine at Church & State and Road 13 wineries before rejoining the Pullens during the 2018 vintage.

MY PICKS

Viognier and Roussanne among the whites and the reds, including Merlot, Malbec, Cabernet Sauvignon, Cabernet Franc, and Syrah.

OPENED 2018

FOR 2020:
> 510 Tinhorn Creek Road
> Oliver, BC V0H 1T1

BEGINNING 2021:
> 4576 Black Sage Road
> Oliver, BC V0H 1T0

T   250.486.5524
W   scwines.ca

SEE YA LATER RANCH

OKANAGAN FALLS

The portfolio at See Ya Later Ranch includes wines named Ping, Rover, Jimmy My Pal, and Nelly. These were four of the 12 dogs owned by Major Hugh Fraser, a veteran of the First World War who lived at the ranch from 1919 to 1966. Such was his affection for his dogs that all were buried under headstones that have now been gathered at the base of a tree in front of the tasting room. The name of this winery was inspired by the major's breezy "See ya later" signature on the many letters he wrote.

This is the third name for this winery. An entrepreneur named Albert LeComte launched the winery in 1986 under his own name. It became Hawthorne Mountain Vineyards when the founder of Sumac Ridge, Harry McWatters, bought it in 1995. A few years after Vincor (now Arterra Wines Canada) purchased the winery in 2000, it was rechristened to take advantage of the canine legacy. The winery honours that legacy by welcoming visitors with dogs and by contributing to the major's favourite charity, the Society for the Prevention of Cruelty to Animals.

This 40-hectare (98-acre) property is the highest-elevation vineyard in the South Okanagan, rising to 536 metres and sloping to the northeast, an unusual exposure for a northern-hemisphere vineyard. However, this cool location makes it one of the Okanagan's best sites for Gewürztraminer, Pinot Gris, Chardonnay, and Pinot Noir. Its Gewürztraminer blocks, totalling 18 hectares (44½ acres), may make up the single largest planting of this aromatic variety in North America.

David Saysomsack, the winemaker at SYL since 2015, has taken advantage of the quality fruit delivered by the vineyard to develop a Legacy tier, starting with Chardonnay and Pinot Noir. Born in Laos in 1976 but raised in Abbotsford, he was a home winemaker for a decade while working in health care. His wife,

DAVID SAYSOMSACK

Shari, suggested he turn his hobby into a career. David took an enology degree at Brock University and, after two vintages in Ontario, returned to British Columbia to work at Pacific Breeze, Burrowing Owl, and then See Ya Later. And he no longer makes wine at home now that his hobby has blossomed into full-time work.

MY PICKS

Everything, but especially the Chardonnay, one of the SYL vineyard's most expressive wines. Among the reds, Ping is a solid Meritage, and Rover is a tasty Shiraz.

OPENED 1986 (AS LECOMTE ESTATE WINERY)

2575 Green Lake Road
PO Box 480
Okanagan Falls, BC
V0H 1R0
T   250.497.8267
W   sylranch.com
Restaurant: Major Fraser Room and Patio Lounge, open daily (except Tues.) 11:30–3:30

SERENDIPITY WINERY

NARAMATA

Judy Kingston found it daunting to show her wines to restaurateurs and consumers when the winery opened in 2011. "For me, it was like I was in the bottle," she says. "It was because I planted the grapes. I have seen them all the way through and then helped put them in the bottle. It was a funny experience to sit there and watch others taste."

You have to appreciate that, in her previous career, she spent 25 years practising computer law in Toronto. "I have never sold anything in my life because I've been a lawyer," she explains. "I never had to."

An automobile accident triggered her decision to do something completely different. Passionate about food, she thought about running a bed and breakfast. In the fall of 2005, during an Okanagan vacation, she looked for retirement property and, charmed by Naramata, bought an apple and cherry orchard next to Therapy Vineyards. By 2007, the property had been contoured and the fruit trees were replaced with 4.2 hectares (10½ acres) of vines, including Merlot, Cabernet Franc, Malbec, Syrah, Pinot Noir, Sauvignon Blanc, and Viognier.

Embracing her project with enthusiasm, Judy enrolled in both the viticulture and winemaking programs at Okanagan College and then did a crush in 2009 in New Zealand. Her enthusiasm rubbed off on her daughter, Katie O'Kell, now the winemaker. Armed with a biology degree, Katie set out initially to be a cancer researcher and then to study law before coming to the winery to help her mother. She qualified as a winemaker after getting 100% in a final exam from the University of California, Davis, and also doing a crush in New Zealand. She took over as winemaker in 2017, succeeding a series of consultants.

JUDY KINGSTON AND KATIE O'KELL

MY PICKS

Start with Devil's Advocate, a red blend; and then proceed through the Private Reserve red varietals; and end with Serenata, an elegant Bordeaux blend that is aged five years in oak. I also like the rosé, the traditional-method sparkling wines, the Sauvignon Blanc, and the Viognier.

OPENED 2011

990 Lower Debeck Road
Naramata, BC V0H 1N1
T 250.486.5290
W serendipitywinery.com
Restaurant: Bongo Bistro,
open during summer for
lunch and dinner

SEVEN STONES WINERY

CAWSTON

George Hanson likes to keep his wines so close at hand that a short tunnel runs from the basement of his house to the underground cellar that he built in 2013. At 3,000 square feet, the cellar accommodates 300 barrels, a small waterfall (for good humidity), a commercial kitchen, and a special-events table with seating for more than 30. Visitors, of course, need not use George's tunnel. There is a spiral staircase from the winery's tasting room.

The man who once described himself as the Yukon's best amateur winemaker has come a long way since leaving his telephone company job there to plant an 8-hectare (20-acre) vineyard in the Similkameen Valley in 2001. "The reason I planted this vineyard was to make a Meritage blend," he says. That's why he grows Cabernet Sauvignon, Cabernet Franc, Merlot, Petit Verdot, and Malbec, along with a little Pinot Noir and Syrah. Acknowledging a demand for white wine, he also planted 1 hectare (2½ acres) of Chardonnay.

"The Legend is my top priority," George says of his iconic red blend with Bordeaux varieties. The Legend—only 100 cases are made each year—crowns the winery's entire production, now approaching 4,000 cases a year. George selects his favourite barrels for The Legend, then makes another selection for his Meritage blend. The remaining wines are released as varietals. That requires George to grow everything to the quality that can produce The Legend. "This is an exceptional place to grow grapes," George says.

The vineyard is called Harmony One. George considered that name for the winery as well until his wife, Vivianne, dipped into the Similkameen's Indigenous history. The winery is named for seven massive rocks that are freighted with Indigenous lore. Speaking Rock, for example, was a First Nations meeting place,

GEORGE HANSON

while Standing Rock–Highway 3 jogs around it–is associated with a tale of a woman who rode her horse to the top. These and other stories are celebrated on the wine labels and in the tasting-room mural. Vivianne, a vivacious Quebecer who once operated a Prince George health foods store, died in 2012. The Seven Stones Pinot Noir from that vintage has a tribute label for her.

Besides building the barrel cellar in 2013, George also launched a Seven Stones Wine Club, hoping to enrol about 50 members that year. To his surprise, the club had 52 members by the end of its first month. "What I learned from that," he says, "is that our brand has some traction."

In 2019, George advertised the winery for sale. The $8 million asking price reflects how much value he believes he has added to it since opening.

MY PICKS

Everything, including the Chardonnay, the rosé, the Pinot Noir, the Cabernet Franc, the Meritage, the Syrah, and the Row 128 Merlot. Of course, The Legend is the wine for your bucket list.

OPENED 2007

1143 Highway 3
Cawston, BC V0X 1C3
T   250.499.2144
W sevenstones.ca

SILKSCARF WINERY

SUMMERLAND

"I cannot do just one thing," explains Silkscarf owner Roie Manoff. "My experience as a pilot flying airplanes—it was multitasking. I need to do a few things simultaneously." It follows that Roie would be drawn to the many tasks needed to own and operate a winery.

Born in Argentina in 1951 but raised in Israel, Roie had a 26-year career in the Israeli Air Force before moving on to starting technology companies. His passion for wine developed after he retired from the military and dreamed of running his own winery. He considered many countries to start his winery, including Argentina and Israel, but chose the Okanagan Valley after visiting in 2003. It was the personal experiences that customers enjoyed with the wineries here that appealed to him. "I like the interaction with the customer; that's the reason we got into wine—to engage people about wine, about the love of wine, the passion of wine," Roie says.

Part of that experience involved food, always an important part of his family's experience with wine. In the early years, Silkscarf also ran a kitchen on weekends, preparing food to pair specifically with each wine. It was so successful that the third year's summer season was fully booked a year in advance. The kitchen was shut down when the Manoff family decided it was taking away from the family's winemaking time. As Roie said, "We have to focus on wine." The experience had been innovative and appealed to foodies, who continue to remain loyal to Silkscarf's wine.

The winery's grapes are grown in the 4-hectare (10-acre) vineyard, including varieties usually not found this far north. It grows Gewürztraminer, Chardonnay, Riesling, Muscat, Viognier, Pinot Gris, Malbec, Merlot, Cabernet Franc, Cabernet Sauvignon, Pinot Noir, and Syrah on the crest of the hill on Gartrell Road.

ROIE MANOFF

"It's crazy!" says Roie. "It takes us about a month-plus to harvest, because that one is ready now and that one is ready later." Since the beginning, the winery has also purchased grapes from an Oliver vineyard to supplement the blends and the volume.

As for a possible return to flying, Roie says he has not flown for over 15 years, and unless he can fly jets, he's not interested. Most small planes available here are simply "too slow," he says.

MY PICKS

Everything. Viognier and Cabernet Sauvignon are standouts, and the Saignée rosé, when available, is beautiful.

OPENED 2005

4917 Gartrell Road
Summerland, BC V0H 1Z4

T   250.494.7455

W   silkscarf-winery.com

SILVER SAGE WINERY

Each November, about 80,000 festive lights are strung on the grounds of Silver Sage Winery, welcoming guests to the year-round tasting room. "Do you know how many people get engaged in the snow?" Anna Manola, the winery proprietor, says. "I put a bottle of wine in the snow with two glasses." Touches like that make Silver Sage's friendly tasting room one of the most popular in the Okanagan. There is no tasting fee; voluntary contributions are given to local charities.

The winery was launched by Anna and Victor Manola, who had managed vineyards and made wine in Romania before coming to Canada around 1980. After successful careers, the couple returned to their roots in 1996, purchasing a 10-hectare (25-acre) property beautifully situated beside the meandering Okanagan River. The winery stands peacefully amid vineyards with the aplomb of a French château, a testament to Victor's skills as a builder. Victor died in a winery accident in 2002 as the building neared completion. It was completed by their son Cornelius, who has continued to help Anna run the winery.

The production here is about 70% grape wines and 30% fruit wines. There is some overlap: Anna makes highly original wines including blends of fruit with grape wines. Sage Grand Reserve is a unique wine: Gewürztraminer turbocharged by fermenting the wine with sage harvested from a South Okanagan mountainside. The wine, with herbal aromas and flavours of rosemary, is reminiscent of Retsina, the intensely flavoured wine from Greece. Another singular offering is The Flame, a dessert wine made with Gewürztraminer, peach and apricot, and a red pepper tingling in each bottle.

ANNA MANOLA

Anna, a former mathematics teacher with a sure touch with fruit wines, has maintained a stable portfolio over the winery's history. In recent years, she has considered adding sparkling wine, Silver Sage having become a popular wedding venue.

MY PICKS

The Pinot Noir and the Pinot Blanc are tasty. Sage Grand Reserve and The Flame are memorable for their originality. A warning: the longer The Flame is cellared, the fiercer the red pepper bite becomes. Reset the palate with the fruit wines, all with room-filling aromas and intense flavours, and with the blends of grape-and-fruit wines.

OPENED 2001

4852 Ryegrass Road
PO Box 293
Oliver, BC V0H 1T0
T   250.498.0310
W   silversagewinery.com
Accommodation: Three
guest suites

SINGLETREE WINERY

In 2018, when the Etsell family purchased the year-old Ledlin Family Vineyards on the Naramata Bench, Singletree became just the second British Columbia winery with tasting rooms in the Okanagan and in the Fraser Valley. The other is Township 7 Vineyards & Winery.

The original Singletree opened a wine shop near Abbotsford in 2015. Singletree is run by Andrew Etsell, his wife, Laura Preckel, and Andrew's parents, turkey farmers Garnet and Debbie. They began planting a vineyard, now 5.3 hectares (13 acres), in 2010 after the study of horticulture led Andrew to choose wine growing as a career. Beginning in 2013, Singletree made its first five vintages at Okanagan Crush Pad Winery in Summerland, under the hand of winemaker Matt Dumayne, Andrew's mentor.

Singletree's production reached 3,500 cases in 2017 when the Etsell family began planning their own production facility in Abbotsford. Faced with ever-rising estimates for construction costs, they decided to buy Ledlin. Singletree gets about half of its grapes from contracted growers on the Naramata Bench; and Ledlin already had a small winemaking facility with a 1.4-hectare (3½-acre) vineyard. Fred and Erica Ledlin had purchased the property several years earlier as a home in the country and had been seduced by the vineyard to open a winery. After a season, the seduction wore off and they sold it to the Etsells.

"It was an easy decision to choose Naramata," Andrew says. He doubled the size of the Naramata winery, enabling him to bring Fraser Valley grapes here at winemaking season. The wine shop here offers a full selection of estate-grown wine from the Abbotsford vineyard along with wines from Okanagan grapes. And that is mirrored in the Abbotsford wine shop.

ANDREW ETSELL

Andrew has continued to use Matt Dumayne's consulting services. "We work really well together," Andrew says. "It is nice to have someone who knows the ins and outs of winemaking and has a similar style to how I like to make wine."

MY PICKS

Everything, but especially Siegerrebe, the aromatic white that does so well in the Fraser Valley, and the crisp Grüner Veltliner. The best of the Okanagan is reflected in Harness, the winery's Bordeaux blend. Merryfield, a sparkling wine made from Chardonnay and Pinot Noir, joined the portfolio in 2019.

NARAMATA LOCATION OPENED 2019

1435 Naramata Road
Penticton, BC V2A 8X2

T   604.381.1788
W   singletreewinery.com

SKAHA VINEYARD @ KRĀZĒ LEGZ VINEYARD AND WINERY

Since 2014, this winery's labels have evolved from Krāzē Legz, the winery's original branding, to SKAHA Vineyard, a name that is inspired by the nearby lake and more adaptable to restaurant wine lists. The original brand worked primarily in the tasting room, where owners Sue and Gerry Thygesen sometimes even wore period dress to accentuate the Roaring Twenties theme they had chosen for the winery. That decade was a golden era of the Charleston, a provocative dance whose high-kicking steps inspired the Krāzē (*crazy*) Legz name.

The wines in the early vintages, with jazz-dancer labels, were branded around the musical terms or colloquial language of the 1920s. The Charleston was the era's most popular dance. Other favourites included the Cakewalk, the Lindy Hop, and the Black Bottom Stomp (the latter from a Jelly Roll Morton song). The Bee's Knees was slang for excellence, inspired perhaps by the knees of Bee Jackson, a world champion Charleston dancer in the '20s. Unfortunately, the theme did not resonate with restaurateurs as much as it did with the owners.

Gerry Thygesen was a marketer of food products in his previous career. Born in Bonnyville, Alberta, in 1957, Gerry began his career in 1980 with Okanagan Dried Fruits, a Penticton company that became a national success. He joined a similar company in Seattle in 1996, got a marketing degree there, and was a marketing vice-president for several American food companies before returning to the Okanagan in 2007 to plant the Krāzē Legz vineyard at Kaleden. He and Sue, an equestrian as well as an equine photographer, bought this 5.6-hectare (14-acre) orchard in 1995. It now grows Merlot (the major block), Cabernet Franc, Chardonnay, and Pinot Blanc.

SKAHA @ Krāzē Legz was the first winery in Kaleden, an attractive village laid out in 1909 on the western shore of Skaha Lake. According to *A Traveller's Guide to Historic British Columbia* by Rosemary Neering, the town's name celebrates the site's pastoral beauty. The name combines the first syllable of *kalos*, Greek for "beautiful," with *Eden*. There have been vineyards here at least since the 1970s but, despite the easy access from the highway, no winery until Krāzē Legz opened in the fall of 2010. Another has since opened, and several are under development.

The SKAHA labels communicate the names of the wines crisply and cleanly. The Roaring Twenties imagery has given way to a stylized horse. *Skaha* means "horse" in an Indigenous language.

MY PICKS

Everything. The red wines have aged in oak for 24 months. The whites are crisp, especially the Pinot Blanc. The port-style wines are among the best in the Okanagan.

OPENED 2010

141 Fir Avenue
PO Box 108
Kaleden, BC V0H 1K0
T 250.497.6957
250.490.6606
W krazelegz.com

SKIMMERHORN WINERY AND VINEYARD

CRESTON

When Calgary bankers Ryan Burgis and Janek Guminski took over Skimmerhorn in mid-2017, they believed that Autumn Tryst, the winery's white blend, was too sweet. But they left the style alone because it is their bestselling wine. "We're trying to let the clients tell us where we should take the business," Ryan said in 2019. "That has proven successful in our first two years here."

Skimmerhorn was founded by one-time orchardists Al and Marleen Hoag. Beginning in 2003, they planted 6.9 hectares (17 acres) of vines on a sunny slope at the south edge of Creston, intelligently choosing varieties that would ripen here (Pinot Gris, Gewürztraminer, Ortega, Pinot Noir, and a large block of Maréchal Foch). Knowing it would be difficult to attract Okanagan expertise to Creston, the Hoags went to New Zealand and hired Geisenheim-trained Mark Rattray. The solid quality of the wines helped them succeed and helped again when they were selling the winery.

"I loved the wines and I loved the property," Ryan said after a site visit in 2016. "I got very excited. Before this, I didn't actually know there was a wine region in the Kootenays. And I have been drinking BC wine for 20 years." Born in Ontario in 1976, he joined the Canadian Imperial Bank of Commerce after university and transferred to Calgary in 2005, conveniently closer to skiing and wine touring in the Okanagan, where a brother lives.

His business partner, Janek, born in 1969, grew up in Vancouver and worked in restaurants before also becoming a banker. Janek grew up in a wine-loving home (his Polish father collected wines). The spark that set off the Skimmerhorn purchase was an email from Janek's Calgary wine merchant announcing the winery was for sale that Janek forwarded to Ryan. "Let's do this," Ryan responded.

JANEK GUMINSKI

Needing expert advice before buying the winery, Janek asked Will Coleman, a long-time golfing friend, to look at Skimmerhorn. Will had started Township 7 Vineyards & Winery in 2001 and sold it in 2006 to become a consultant. When he agreed to manage the winery for at least three years, Ryan and Janek bought Skimmerhorn, a successful winery producing 4,000 to 4,500 cases a year and selling it all from the wine shop and in the Kootenays.

"There is a great opportunity for the Creston Valley to have three or four more wineries," Janek says. "And we are on the lookout for more land so we can grow."

MY PICKS

Current range not tasted.

OPENED 2006

1218 27th Avenue South
Creston, BC V0B 1G1

T   250.428.4911

W   skimmerhorn.ca
Restaurant: Bistro, open daily 11–4 during high season, with dinner service on Fri./Sat. in July and August, closed during winter

SLEEPING GIANT FRUIT WINERY

SUMMERLAND

Thousands visit Summerland Sweets each year, attracted by the fruit products and, in summer, by the generous ice cream parlour. The fruit winery, which opened here in 2008, was a logical addition to the business started in 1962 by the legendary Dr. Ted Atkinson.

He was one of the Okanagan's leading scientists, head of food processing at what was then called the Summerland Research Station. When he was near retirement, he created a line of fruit candies for a Rotary Club fundraiser. Frustrated that no company would take on the product, he set up Summerland Sweets to commercialize a range of fruit-based products that has grown to include syrups and jams for domestic and export markets.

Ted Atkinson's family still operates Summerland Sweets. His granddaughter's husband, Len Filek, was a young commerce graduate when he joined the company in 1984. Today, he is the general manager. He spearheaded the addition of a fruit winery with a tasting room inside the Summerland Sweets store. "It had been a thought in the family for quite a while," he says. "With the other projects we had, we just kept putting it off." The winery went ahead after Sumac Ridge founder Harry McWatters urged Len to give the stream of visitors to Summerland Sweets another reason to visit.

Len retained Ron Taylor, a veteran winemaker already working with numerous fruit wineries in British Columbia. "My dad was a home winemaker, but I am not interested in making wine," Len admits frankly. "I am interested in *wine*, and I am interested in a good product. That's why we have someone making it for us."

LEN FILEK

MY PICKS

Almost two dozen fruit wines are available here, including dry examples from pear and apple and delicious off-dry wines from cherry and raspberry. Recent additions (there's a waiting list for them) are a pumpkin table wine and "pumpkin pie" dessert wine. All wines are remarkable for aromas and flavours that could be fresh from the tree.

OPENED 2008

6206 Canyon View Road
Summerland, BC V0H 1Z7

T 250.494.0377
1.800.577.1277 (toll-free)

W sleepinggiantfruitwinery.ca

SONORA DESERT WINERY

OSOYOOS

Brothers Paul and Herman Gill both have business degrees and careers with financial institutions. Nevertheless, they launched the Sonora Desert Winery to maintain the agriculture tradition they grew up with. Their mother and father, Manjit and Chamkaur, emigrated from India in the 1970s to work in Okanagan orchards. They bought their first orchard in 1989.

"We were born and raised in the orchards," says Herman, who was born in 1990 (brother Paul was born in 1984). "We have done everything from picking and pruning, all the harvesting and planting. We have held jobs in the packing house. We knew this is our history. We did not want to let go of it. We want to carry it forward to our future generations."

Over the years, the orchards were converted to vines. The Gill family now farms about 10 hectares (25 acres) of vineyards, all near Osoyoos and largely dedicated to red varieties. They grow Cabernet Franc, Syrah, Tempranillo, and Viognier—and so much Merlot that the winery's portfolio includes both a Merlot rosé and a white Merlot.

The inspiration for the winery came from Desert Hills Estate Winery. The Toor brothers who own that winery are uncles to the Gill brothers. "We worked in the cellar and tasting room at Desert Hills before we got started," Herman says.

As you might expect, the brothers exercise considerable financial discipline by initially using the Desert Hills equipment and winemaking team to get started. "As you are aware," Herman says, "the start-up costs of a winery are large. We try to be cost efficient. For now, it is working out for us to lease out some crushing time. Eventually, we will work towards our own crushing equipment."

HERMAN AND PAUL GILL

The target is to produce 4,000 to 5,000 cases a year. "That is the maximum we will produce," Herman said in 2019. "We expect that it will take five years to get there."

MY PICKS
Current range not tasted.

OPENED 2018

10238 160th Avenue
Osoyoos, BC V0H 1V2
T   250.801.3001
    250.408.8586
W   sonoradesertwinery.ca
Accommodation: Five
bed-and-breakfast suites

SPEARHEAD WINERY

KELOWNA

Located in bucolic East Kelowna, SpearHead specializes in Pinot Noir even though it debuted in 2010 with well-received Bordeaux reds called Vanguard and Pursuit. Made with grapes purchased from a Black Sage Road vineyard, they established the SpearHead brand while the winery awaited fruit from the estate vineyard, planted in 2008. They were discontinued after the 2013 vintage.

"We don't grow Merlot or Cabernet Sauvignon, and I don't think it would make sense to plant those varietals in our area," the proprietor, Bill Knutson, says. "I think a wiser course is to focus on Pinot Noir and do a good job with it. The Kelowna area is emerging as a pretty strong region for Pinot Noir."

SpearHead had three founders. The instigator was Kelowna photographer Brian Sprout (who subsequently left the partnership). He enlisted a high school classmate, Vancouver lawyer Bill Knutson, and a semi-retired investment dealer, Bruce Hirtle. Knutson, who still has a busy law practice, and his wife, Marina, now are majority owners. The partners planted vines in a former apple orchard on Spiers Road, which inspired the winery's original name, SpierHead. It was changed in 2018 to avoid a trademark dispute with Spier Wine Farm in South Africa, founded in 1692.

SpearHead's 6-hectare (15-acre) Gentleman Farmer Vineyard grows multiple clones of Pinot Noir, along with small blocks of Riesling and Chardonnay. "I hope we can develop a niche with a significant variety of Pinot Noir clones for different bottlings," Bill says. In 2017, to carry out that strategy, he recruited Grant Stanley as SpearHead's general manager and winemaker.

Born in Vancouver in 1967 and trained in New Zealand, Grant previously spent 10 years at Quails' Gate Winery and four at

MARINA AND BILL KNUTSON

50th Parallel Estate. Both specialize in Pinot Noir. Grant, who has his own Pinot Noir vineyard in West Kelowna, once said, "I think about Pinot Noir 80 percent of the time."

MY PICKS

Everything, including the rare White Pinot Noir. The flagship Cuvée is a powerful, concentrated Pinot Noir built for long aging while also delicious on release. Club Consensus is the name of a Pinot Noir blended by members of the winery's wine club from Pinot Noirs in the cellar. It has won numerous awards.

OPENED 2010

3950 Spiers Road
Kelowna, BC V1W 4B3
T   250.763.7777
W   spearheadwinery.com

SPERLING VINEYARDS

KELOWNA

The history of North Okanagan grape growing and winemaking lives here. This winery has been launched by the Sperling family whose Casorso ancestors planted Kelowna's first vineyard in 1925 and who were among the original investors in what is now Calona Vineyards.

The story began when Giovanni Casorso came from Italy in 1883 to work at Father Pandosy's mission before striking out on his own (he was once the Okanagan's largest tobacco grower). His sons planted several vineyards. Formerly known as Pioneer Ranch, the 18.2-hectare (45-acre) Sperling Vineyards was planted initially in 1931 with grapes and apples by Louis and Pete Casorso. When Pete retired in 1960, Bert Sperling, his son-in-law, switched the entire property to vines, both wine grapes and table grapes. The grapes here include a 56-year-old planting of Maréchal Foch, a 43-year-old planting of Riesling, and a planting of indefinite age of Pearl of Csaba, a Muscat variety once grown widely in the Okanagan. Recent plantings include Pinot Gris, Pinot Noir, and Chardonnay. The vineyard is farmed organically and biodynamically.

Undoubtedly, the Sperling family has been thinking about a winery of its own ever since Bert's daughter Ann, who was born in 1962, began her winemaking career in 1984, first with Andrés Wines (now Andrew Peller Ltd.) and then with CedarCreek Estate Winery. She moved to Ontario in 1995 where she helped launch several stellar wineries. She and Peter Gamble, her husband, consult internationally and own a premium boutique vineyard in Argentina.

As busy as her career has been, one thing had been missing in Ann's life. "I have always wanted to make wine with my parents' vineyard," she says. "I got to make wine with some of the grapes when I was at CedarCreek, but not anything extensive."

ANN SPERLING

The Casorso story came full circle with this premium winery in 2013 when a production facility with a 10,000-case capacity was completed in the middle of the vineyard. Because the wine shop is on a separate small vineyard with the Sperling licence, a different licence was required for this facility. It is licensed as Magpie Cellars, named for a flock (or murder) of magpies that have lived here a long time. "They have watched over us and criticized our work for generations," Ann says. "It seemed fitting to acknowledge their role." The vineyard is not convenient for wine touring.

MY PICKS

Everything, including the Old Vines Riesling, the Chardonnay, the Pinot Noir, the Old Vines Foch, the Pinot Gris, the affordable Icewine, and exceptional sparkling wines. One of the most popular wines here is the aromatic Market White.

OPENED 2008

1405 Pioneer Road
Kelowna, BC V1W 4M6

T 778.478.0260

W sperlingvineyards.com

SQUEEZED WINES

OLIVER

The personality of Squeezed Wines is captured in the name that Christina, Michael, and Nicole Ferreira chose for the winery. "We wanted a name that portrays a fun atmosphere, passion for winemaking and marketing and most of all the celebration of grapes to wine," they explain on the website. They were schooled in wine before they started Squeezed. John and Maria Ferreira, their parents, operate Quinta Ferreira on Black Sage Road near Oliver. From the debut vintage in 2011, Squeezed was a virtual winery until June 2019 when it opened at this physical location on Tucelnuit Drive just north of Oliver.

The three siblings have complementary skills in winery management. Michael, born in 1984, has made wine at Quinta Ferreira since 2005. His wines have won major awards, notably a Lieutenant Governor's Award for Excellence in BC Wine in 2011 for the Quinta Ferreira 2008 Syrah. Michael also handles the online wine sales. Christina is a marketing specialist with her own event-planning company in Kelowna. As an early adopter of social media, Christina promoted Squeezed's production online. It sustained the winery's sales before the wine shop opened in 2019. She handles the sales in BC's interior, while Nicole, an accountant in Vancouver, looks after sales there and does administration for Squeezed.

A still installed in the new facility produces spirits to make fortified wines. There are plans to add a full line of spirits to the portfolio. "We will be producing grape spirits for fortified wines and brandy, and also grain spirits for our vodka, gin, and whiskies," Michael says. He has already been making a fortified port-style wine at Quinta Ferreira.

Because Tucelnuit Drive connects to Black Sage Road, popular with wine tourists, Squeezed is well located. The wine shop, with

NICOLE, MICHAEL, AND CHRISTINA FERREIRA

a tasting bar accommodating large numbers of visitors, is set back amid the vines. The 2-hectare (5-acre) property grows Merlot, Syrah, Cabernet Franc, Cabernet Sauvignon, Gewürztraminer, and Sangiovese. Michael also has another 2-hectare (5-acre) vineyard nearby.

MY PICKS

The whites, particularly the Gewürztraminer, are the strength here. The reds show promise.

SALES BEGAN 2012

7315 Tucelnuit Drive
Oliver, BC V0H 1T2
T 250.485.4309
W squeezedwines.com
Visits and tastings by appointment

STAG'S HOLLOW WINERY

OKANAGAN FALLS

In the spring of 2018, Stag's Hollow founders Linda Pruegger and Larry Gerelus were invited to bring their Dolcetto, a red wine, to Italy, for an international Dolcetto tasting. It was a tribute to the pioneering work they have done with interesting varieties not among the Okanagan's mainstream wine grapes. They first planted Dolcetto, a juicy Italian red grape, in 2011. More recently, they have released Teroldego, an Italian red made by just one other Okanagan winery. They also grow Tempranillo and Albariño, two Spanish varieties.

In 2019, the winery, now producing 5,500 cases a year, caught the eye of Eric Liu, a low-profile Chinese immigrant investor who had purchased the Bench 1775 winery five years earlier. Expanding his holdings, he purchased vineyard property in the Similkameen Valley in 2018 and then Stag's Hollow. Linda and Larry have remained as winery managers, and Keira LeFranc continues as winemaker.

They entered the wine industry in 1992 when they moved from Calgary to buy a 4-hectare (10-acre) Okanagan Falls vineyard. The property was growing Chasselas and Vidal. They converted it to Chardonnay, Riesling, and Pinot Noir but kept just enough Vidal to release a wine called Tragically Vidal because so little remained in the Okanagan. The wine developed such a cult following that Larry had to plant more.

The winery's 6.5-hectare (16-acre) Shuttleworth Creek Vineyard, a former pasture just south of Okanagan Falls, was purchased in 2011, with planting beginning the following year. This is where Stag's Hollow grows its Italian reds and its Spanish white, along with multiple clones of Pinot Noir, now a core variety for Stag's Hollow. While the winery contracts grapes from the South Okanagan, most of its grapes are estate grown, enabling the winery to craft wines expressing the local terroir.

WINEMAKER KEIRA LEFRANC

MY PICKS

Everything, including the reserve wines released under the Renaissance label.

OPENED 1996

2237 Sun Valley Way
Okanagan Falls, BC
V0H 1R2

T 250.497.6162
1.877.746.5569 (toll-free)

W stagshollowwinery.com

STONEBOAT VINEYARDS

OLIVER

This charming family winery operated by Julie and Lanny Martiniuk evolved from the vine nursery they started in 1983. The nursery has supplied vines to more growers than Lanny can remember. "That's a couple of million plants ago," he says now when someone speaks about a vineyard with vines that Lanny started.

Lanny, who was born in Vancouver in 1949, has pursued numerous careers (electrician, stonemason, prospector, nuclear medicine technician). He is a farmer by avocation. The Martiniuks launched Stoneboat to ensure a market for the grapes grown on their own 19.8 hectares (49 acres) of vineyards.

He has propagated numerous obscure varieties, keeping some for his own vineyard. After propagating Pinotage, the South African red, he nurtured his own 2.8-hectare (7-acre) block of Pinotage, now one of Stoneboat's bestselling reds. He also nurtured such German whites as Kerner and Müller-Thurgau, the cornerstone of Gravelbar Chorus, Stoneboat's popular white blend. Lanny retains a rare planting of Oraniensteiner, an aromatic, high-acid German white, to produce Verglas, Stoneboat's dessert wine.

Stoneboat has also become a significant sparkling-wine producer since 2013, when it revived in the Okanagan a technique for making sparkling wine called the Charmat process. It takes its name from a French scientist, Eugène Charmat, who in 1907 perfected a method of fermenting wines in bulk to make Prosecco.

Lanny and Julie were early to recognize how the recent enthusiasm for Prosecco had become the rising tide lifting all boats: consumers no longer keep sparkling wines just for special occasions. Stoneboat now makes three different sparkling wines. "We worked hard to dispel that myth," Julie says. "It doesn't have to be a special occasion. You can have it with popcorn while you are watching a movie."

JULIE AND LANNY MARTINIUK

MY PICKS

Everything here is well made. Pinot Noir and Pinotage—branded Rock Opera—are the red wine stars. Alessio is the proprietary name for the winery's fine Pinot Blanc.

OPENED 2007

356 Orchard Grove Lane
Oliver, BC V0H 1T1

T   250.498.2226

W   stoneboatvineyards.com

SUMAC RIDGE ESTATE WINERY

SUMMERLAND

The oldest continually operating estate winery in the Okanagan, Sumac Ridge is among the most popular visits for wine tourists. The attractions include the winery's premium table wines under the Black Sage Vineyard brand, its Steller's Jay sparkling wines, and its value-priced table wines under the Sumac Ridge brand.

Steller's Jay Mountain Jay Brut is the iconic sparkling wine originated by Sumac Ridge in 1987. Made in the traditional Champagne method, the wine is a blend of Chardonnay, Pinot Noir, and Pinot Blanc. Named for British Columbia's official bird, Steller's Jay has now spawned a family of sparkling wines. These include a sparkling Gewürztraminer, a sparkling Shiraz, and a sparkling rosé made with Gamay Noir and Merlot.

The passion for sparkling wine began with Harry McWatters, who founded the winery in 1979 with Lloyd Schmidt. Harry quipped that sparkling wine was what he drank while deciding what wine to have for dinner. Harry moved on to establish TIME Winery, leaving the sparkling-wine culture to be carried on by winemaker Jason James. "We'd like consumers to drink [sparkling wine] at least once every two weeks," Jason says.

A native of North Bay, Ontario, Jason has an honours biology degree from the University of Guelph and a Brock University diploma in winemaking. He has been at Sumac Ridge since 2005.

The Black Sage Vineyard wines (along with Steller's Jay) were spun off as premium brands in 2012, but they remain available in the Sumac Ridge wine shop. The Black Sage family of wines initially were varietals just from that legendary vineyard, planted in 1993 and 1994 with Bordeaux reds. With access to the other vineyards farmed by Arterra Wines Canada, Black Sage's parent company, Jason also produces Zinfandel, Chardonnay, and Viognier. The portfolio is crowned with a fine Meritage and a fortified red.

WINEMAKER JASON JAMES

MY PICKS

Everything. The sparkling wines never disappoint. Among the Black Sage wines, the stars are Merlot, Cabernet Franc, Chardonnay, and Viognier.

OPENED 1980

17403 Highway 97 North
PO Box 307
Summerland, BC V0H 1Z0
T   250.494.0451
W   sumacridge.com
blacksagevineyard.ca
stellersjaywines.com

SUMMERGATE WINERY

SUMMERLAND

The Kerner grape has no greater champions in the Okanagan than Mike and Gillian Stohler, the owners of SummerGate. "I love Kerner," Mike says. While at a German wine-industry trade show some years ago, he and Gillian researched the origins of the grape. It is a 1929 cross of Riesling and Trollinger, named for some obscure reason after a poet called Justinus Kerner. The variety is well suited, Mike believes, to the bucolic Prairie Valley vineyards that supply SummerGate.

The Stohlers bought the property in 2007 and moved their family from Vancouver. Mike (born in Ontario in 1972) was managing a Vancouver call centre, and Gillian, trained in accounting, was also working there when they decided in 2003 to move to the Okanagan for a different lifestyle. "We realized, as some people do, when you are climbing up the corporate ladder, that sometimes it is leaning against the wrong wall," Mike says. "We were young enough to make a change."

The 3.6-hectare (8.8-acre) vineyard had been planted by the previous owner with Riesling, Muscat Ottonel, and Kerner, the particular favourite with Mike and Gillian. Recently, they have planted an additional 2 hectares (5 acres) of Kerner.

The SummerGate portfolio consisted entirely of white wines until 2018, when the first harvest came from a neighbouring vineyard with 1.2 hectares (3 acres) of Pinot Noir and 0.4 hectare (1 acre) of Siegerrebe. The decision to make only white wines for the first eight vintages was not for lack of interest in red wine. Mike says, "We could have bought Pinot Noir grapes, or any red wine grapes in fact, even organic ones, but I didn't want to because I want the wines that we have here to represent this little corner of Summerland. We're the only winery in little Prairie Valley, and I want my wines to represent this area." The first non-white wine,

GILLIAN AND MIKE STOHLER

a rosé, was released in the spring of 2019. A Pinot Noir table wine is expected from the 2020 or 2021 vintage.

The Prairie Valley terroir is complex. The new Kerner vineyard is higher up the slope from the winery. "It's turned out to be much hotter up there, even though it's higher in elevation, but it's got quite a lot more slope, and it's a very rocky soil," Gillian says. "So if you can imagine, this was at one time a lake. This [the winery vineyard] is the bottom of the lake, so there is really heavy clay here." The higher vineyard would have been the shore. "It has lots of rocks, and it just holds the heat in up there. We'll be harvesting those grapes a week or two before we harvest the rest of our grapes. It's that much of a difference!"

Gillian—she pronounces her name with a hard *g*—is the winemaker, having taken Okanagan College winemaking courses while being mentored by a consultant. Her small-batch winemaking involves cool fermentation and the liberal use of dry ice to protect the delicately aromatic wines from air. This reductive winemaking yields fresh, clean, and focused wines.

MY PICKS

Everything is beautifully aromatic, especially the Moscato frizzante, which is made with Muscat Ottonel grapes. The occasional late-harvest wines are always interesting.

OPENED 2011

11612 Morrow Avenue
Summerland, BC V0H 1Z8
T   250.583.9973
W   summergate.ca

SUMMERHILL PYRAMID WINERY

KELOWNA

Summerhill founder Stephen Cipes and his family pioneered organic wine growing in the Okanagan, an industry-wide trend there and in the Similkameen Valley. His son Ezra, the winery's president, says that his parents began working toward organic certification as long ago as 1988. "Organic certification is important because it provides transparency for the way we farm and make our wine," he says. The winery in 2019 took this to yet another level by achieving the status of a certified B Corporation, a relatively new designation for companies dedicated to ethical business practices.

The idealism of the Cipes family is evident to all visitors to this winery. There is a so-called World Peace Park in front of the winery. Towering over a globe encircled with flowers is Summerhill's Peace Pole. Inscriptions exhort May Peace Prevail on Earth in 16 languages.

The family's spiritual side is represented by the gleaming white pyramid dramatically dominating the grounds here, and employed to age wines. Stephen believes that the pyramid's rejuvenating energy improves good wine as well as improving the spirit and well-being of those who spend time inside. The memorable tours of the pyramid often include brief periods when visitors are invited to sit in contemplative silence. When does that happen in today's frantic world?

Stephen, an engagingly mercurial personality, was born in New York in 1944 and succeeded in real estate before moving to the Okanagan in 1986 in search of a more environmentally positive lifestyle for himself and his family. Sons Ezra and Ari share those values. Summerhill grows grapes organically in its 20-hectare (50-acre) vineyard and has been adopting biodynamic practices. Most of the winery's 14 contract growers also have been converted to organic production. Since 2007, the winery itself has been certified to make wine organically.

EZRA CIPES

Veteran winemaker Eric von Krosigk spent much of his career with Summerhill before joining Frind Estate Winery, another organic producer, in 2019. He drove the winemaking style that persists at Summerhill. "We want to let the grapes speak for themselves," Eric has said. "Our ultimate goal here is that if there was ever an ingredients list on a bottle of wine, it would say just 'Grapes.'"

MY PICKS

The winery built its reputation with sparkling wines like Cipes Gabriel and Cipes Brut. Riesling stars in a table-wine range that also includes Ehrenfelser, Gewürztraminer, Pinot Gris, Pinot Noir, and Merlot.

OPENED 1992

4870 Chute Lake Road
Kelowna, BC V1W 4M3
T 250.764.8000
1.800.667.3538 (toll-free)
W summerhill.bc.ca
Restaurant: Summerhill Organic Bistro, open daily 11–9 for lunch, tapas, and dinner

SUNNYBRAE VINEYARDS & WINERY

TAPPEN

The large framed photograph in the tasting room of Sunnybrae Vineyards & Winery—a picture of a muscular farmer with his team of Belgian draft horses—conveys heritage. The man is the late Mac Turner, the father of the late Barry Turner who, with his wife, Nancy, and their family, founded his winery beside Shuswap Lake. A stylized Mac Turner and his team appear on Sunnybrae wine labels.

The Turner family has farmed in the Sunnybrae district for five generations. The winery's 3.2-hectare (8-acre) vineyard is part of an 8-hectare (20-acre) property that once belonged to a Turner ancestor, a Major Mobley, said to have been one of the first non-native settlers. Barry's ancestor sold the land in 1907, and Barry reacquired it in 2000. "It's a beautiful field if you did something with it," Barry once told me. "Everybody told me it was an ideal spot for grapes. It has gravel soil, probably eight inches of topsoil, with a south slope of up to six percent."

Barry's career as a heavy-equipment operator and a road builder often took him away from home and family. "My plan was, later in life, to phase out of that and get into this full-time," he told me when he began planting the vineyard in 2006. "I didn't even grow grapes for a hobby before," Barry added. Sadly, cancer took Barry's life in 2017. Nancy and daughter Kristie continue to run the winery but have considered selling it.

The wines are all made with estate-grown fruit. The major variety in the vineyard is Maréchal Foch, and Sunnybrae has created much of its portfolio with that grape. The wine with the variety on the label is driest. Bastion Mountain Red has a hint of residual sweetness, while Redneck Red is off-dry. In 2017, the winery planted a small block of Pinot Noir to produce a grape for blending and giving additional differentiation among the red wines.

NANCY TURNER

MY PICKS

The winery makes excellent whites with Siegerrebe and Ortega, as well as a dry white blend called Turner Road. The easy-drinking reds help raise the profile of Maréchal Foch.

OPENED 2011

3849 Sunnybrae Canoe
Point Road
PO Box 22
Tappen, BC V0E 2X0
T   250.835.8373
W   sunnybraewinery.com

SYNCHROMESH WINES

Alan Dickinson champions three varietals at Synchromesh. Cabernet Franc and Pinot Noir anchor the red wines, while Riesling is almost an obsession with him. "I really like old Rieslings," he says. "When you start laying Riesling down past 15 years, there is magic that happens under cork." The magic, in fact, comes from Alan's singular style. Synchromesh Rieslings invariably balance high residual sugar with racy acidity, recalling fine age-worthy German Rieslings. There are many top Okanagan Riesling wines but few that compare with Synchromesh.

Born in Vancouver in 1982 and trained in marketing and entrepreneurship, Alan was a founder of Vancouver Wine Vault, which stores private wine collections. When they decided to participate in the wine industry directly, Alan and his wife, Amy, searched the Okanagan for good Riesling sites for 18 months. In early 2010, they bought a 2-hectare (5-acre) piece of land that included a four-year-old block of Clone 21B Riesling. They have since replaced all the other varieties on the property with Riesling and Pinot Noir. In 2017 they purchased an adjoining 41-hectare (102-acre) block of raw land. About a third has been planted with Riesling and Cabernet Franc, while the remainder is preserved as natural habitat. The soils are lean. "The greatest German Rieslings are basically grown in slate, with no soil whatsoever and very little nutrient," Alan says.

The block wraps around the base of 600-metre-high Peach Cliff, the most prominent geological feature at Okanagan Falls. Peach Cliff absorbs summer heat, creating updrafts that deflect rain and hail, which is why the original vineyard here is called Storm Haven. The wide diurnal temperature swing—as much as 20°C (36°F) between night and day—make this "perfect Riesling country," Alan says.

ALAN DICKINSON

He also sources Riesling, along with Cabernet Franc and Merlot, from contract vineyards on the Naramata Bench and near Oliver. Alan made his first Riesling vintage in 2010, signalling his style by labelling the wine *halbtrocken*, or off-dry. Alan has not used German on the labels since, but what's inside remains true to the style.

MY PICKS

Everything: The Rieslings are extraordinary. The flagship red is a Cabernet Franc/Merlot blend called Tertre Rouge, taken from a famous corner at the Le Mans racetrack. Alan's father, John, once competed in motor races in Britain.

OPENED 2011

4220 McLean Creek Road
Okanagan Falls, BC
V0H 1R0

T   250.535.1558
W   synchromeshwines.ca

TALL TALE WINES
VIRTUAL WINERY

Kyle Lyons's first job in the wine industry in 2004 was as what he terms a "warehouse grunt" at Sumac Ridge. He recalls the first staff party at the home of Harry McWatters, the Sumac Ridge founder. Asked if he would like Riesling, Kyle said he had never tasted one. "Your first one had better be something special," Harry told him and opened a 1978 German Riesling. "Within the first year of being at Sumac Ridge, I realized that wine was something I preferred as a career," Kyle says.

In 2010, after five years at Sumac Ridge, he joined Artus Bottling, the Okanagan-based company whose mobile bottling lines service most BC wineries. "It was a great opportunity," Kyle says. "I got to visit a different winery every day, and I made some good connections." Wanting to be more involved with winemaking, Kyle worked the 2015 harvest at Bannockburn Vineyards in Australia and then returned to the Okanagan as a cellar hand at Liquidity Wines. Subsequently, he was promoted to assistant winemaker there.

With his sister, Kristin, Kyle launched Tall Tale in 2016, making just 300 cases—Pinot Blanc, a little sparkling wine, and his signature red, a Syrah Nouveau. He had discovered that fresh, fruity style of Syrah in Australia and decided to emulate it here. "There are so many BC wineries competing to be the best at the same thing," Kyle says. "I wanted to come out with something just a little bit different but still approachable."

The style of Tall Tale wines is natural. Kyle ferments with wild yeast. "There are no additions, no nutrients, no enzymes, just a little bit of sulphur at the end to help protect the wines," he says. A recent vintage included an orange wine made with Gewürztraminer crushed by foot and fermented on the skins.

The Tall Tale label shows a farmer with an unlikely team—a

KYLE LYONS

bear and a moose—pulling the plow. "The label specifically relates to my maternal grandfather, who would tell me that, when he arrived here by boat, he did not have enough money to buy horses," Kyle says. "He had to tame a moose. I wasn't very old before I figured out that was bull. He never arrived by boat at all." Kyle carries on the tradition of exaggerating with outrageous stories on the back labels of his wines.

He is several years away from basing this virtual winery in its own physical location. If the regulations ever allow it, he would like to share quarters with a small group of like-minded vintners.

MY PICKS

The racy Riesling, the Pinot Noir Blanc, the Sémillon, and the Syrah Nouveau are delicious.

OPENED 2016

T   250.486.5953
W   talltalewines.com
    No tasting room

TANTALUS VINEYARDS

The first Reserve Pinot Noir from Tantalus Vineyards, from the 2016 vintage, was in a bottle that consumers were reluctant to recycle. The label was a gold-hued mask by the renowned Tahltan/Tlingit artist Dempsey Bob. His highly valued art is sought both by museums and by private collectors. One of those collectors is Eric Savics, the Vancouver investment dealer who, in 2004, bought this historic property and rebranded the wines with images of masks from his own collection.

This East Kelowna property is one of the Okanagan's oldest vineyards, and one of the first to grow wine grapes in quantity. It was planted by horticulturalist J. W. Hughes and then sold to his foreman, Martin Dulik. Martin's son, Denny, planted Riesling in 1978, an excellent variety for this terroir. When his granddaughter Susan opened Pinot Reach Cellars, her Old Vines Riesling drew international acclaim. Eric Savics expanded the Riesling plantings significantly here and on recently acquired adjacent vineyards. The winery farms 30 hectares (75 acres). The wines are all estate grown, and Old Vines Riesling remains the flagship at Tantalus.

David Paterson, the New Zealand–trained winemaker who joined Tantalus in 2008, credits the site for the exceptional quality of Old Vines Riesling. "It is all of the terroir," he says. "The aspect, the elevation, the soils. The root system has gone down a long, long way and draws up a lot of minerality. The root system is so deep now and so established that they buffer themselves against hot and cold vintages. We get a very consistent product. It has very little to do with winemaking. I put my stamp on it, I suppose, but at the end of the day, the grapes are really, really good."

When Eric rebranded the awkwardly named Pinot Reach, he drew on a knowledge of Greek mythology. "Do you know the background of Tantalus?" Eric asks. "Zeus was quite angry with

WINEMAKER DAVID PATERSON

Tantalus [his son], who had been behaving terribly, to the point that Zeus finally sentences Tantalus to live forever in purgatory. There is water up to his knees and hanging above him are big fat delicious grapes. When Tantalus, being thirsty, reaches for the water, the water recedes. Being hungry, he reaches for the grapes and the grapes recede. So he is being tantalized." That aptly describes the wines.

MY PICKS

Everything. Rieslings are the established stars, ably supported by Chardonnay, Pinot Noir, and sparkling wines—including the rare Old Vines Riesling Brut.

OPENED 1997
(AS PINOT REACH CELLARS)

1670 Dehart Road
Kelowna, BC V1W 4N6
T   250.764.0078
1.877.764.0078 (toll-free)
W   tantalus.ca

TENDER HOPE WINERY

Efi Perel, the founder and winemaker at Tender Hope Winery, had to be creative to start a winery without a lot of capital. In addition to taking partners, he established the winery in a leased space in a West Kelowna industrial park. With no vineyard of his own, he secured a commercial licence. He made his first wines primarily with Washington State grapes while also sourcing fruit from Okanagan vineyards. "A winery would be an investment of $4 million, $5 million," Efi says. "It is not viable for young people to start something from scratch. That is the reason we are here in a leased space."

He was born in Jerusalem in 1970, with Canadian roots. His grandfather had migrated from Poland to Ottawa early in the 20th century, and his father resettled in Israel where Efi grew up. "I have worked in agriculture since I was 12," Efi says. He developed a taste for wine in Spain, where he lived for two years after doing military service in Israel. He returned to work in Israeli vineyards. Then he enrolled in university for East Asian studies. That led to a scholarship to Taiwan, where he met his wife and settled into 14 years in corporate sales. But he continued to taste wine and to read extensively about the topic.

"At some point, I decided I don't want to get up in the morning and go to the office," Efi says. "I wanted to do what I like." In 2014 he moved his family to the Okanagan and, to get practical experience, worked as a cellar hand at Summerhill Pyramid Winery, Nagging Doubt Winery, and Grizzli Winery. He began making wines for Tender Hope in 2016 at another winery before moving to his West Kelowna facility.

Tender Hope's first wines were made with fruit from premium vineyards in Washington State. "I fall in love with vineyards," Efi says. "There are vineyards there that I visited and really liked, and

EFI PEREL

I wanted to make some wines from there." The varieties include Cabernet Sauvignon and Syrah. "These are high-quality wines." In subsequent vintages, he has sourced Okanagan fruit, making wines that are eligible for VQA.

"I work with some growers that are the best in the Okanagan," Efi says. "I feel our area is more suitable to Merlot and Cabernet Franc. Merlot is phenomenal here. It has the weight, but it is also very elegant."

MY PICKS

The winery debuted with excellent whites from Chardonnay and white Rhone varietals. The reds, including Syrah and Bordeaux varietals, are bold in structure and flavour.

PROPOSED
OPENING 2020

350 – 1405 Stevens Road
West Kelowna, BC V1Z 3Y2
T   613.983.2556
W   tenderhopewinery.com

TERRAVISTA VINEYARDS

PENTICTON

When Dallas and Eric Thor acquired Terravista Vineyards in 2019, it was the culmination of the wine journey Eric began as a bar manager in a Vancouver restaurant in 2000. He was showing off his wine knowledge to a guest. Then he discovered he was talking to Harry McWatters, the founder of Sumac Ridge, who promptly hired him to work that fall's vintage. He even got to put the Christmas lights on Harry's house before work ran out at Sumac Ridge.

Eric, who was born in 1978 and grew up in Penticton, went back to school to learn accounting. In 2003 he joined Point Grey Research, a technical start-up (digital cameras) launched by five University of British Columbia graduates. Eric had become the company's chief financial officer by 2016 when Point Grey was taken over for $250 million. Eric's share was more than enough to get him and Dallas, his wife, back into the wine business.

A teacher with a master's degree in science, she shares his passion for wine. In 2016, when they were buying an ocean-going catamaran in the South of France, they lived for seven weeks at the village of Canet-en-Roussillon, working the harvest at a small winery. They returned to Penticton to buy some land in 2017 on the Naramata Bench for a vineyard. And they asked Senka Tennant to be their consultant.

Senka and her husband, Bob, are legendary in the Okanagan. They were co-founders of Black Hills Estate Winery, where the flagship red, Nota Bene, acquired a cult following. Two years after Black Hills was sold in 2007, they established Terravista Vineyards, based on a 1.6-hectare (4-acre) vineyard with the Okanagan's first planting of Albariño and Verdejo, two Spanish white varieties. Once again, the wines attracted a cult following.

DALLAS AND ERIC THOR

Senka thought it was premature for Eric and Dallas to seek her advice before they had planted a vineyard. (A small block of Pinot Noir was planted in 2019, while Syrah was scheduled for planting in 2020 on most of their 2-hectare/5-acre vineyard.) The Thors continued to consult Senka, and they joined Terravista's wine club. The relationship blossomed. "They did not bother letting us know they were selling for a couple of meetings," Eric recalls. "When they decided we would be suitable candidates to take over their baby, they let us know they were selling."

To ensure a continuity of Terravista's style and quality, the Thors have continued their relationship with Senka. They also hired Nadine Allander, a New Zealand–trained winemaker who worked previously at TIME Winery and Poplar Grove Winery. "She eats and breathes wine," Eric says.

MY PICKS

Everything, especially Fandango, the Albariño/ Verdejo blend, and Figaro, a blend of white Rhône varieties.

OPENED 2011

1853 Sutherland Road
Penticton, BC V2A 8T8

T 778.476.6011

W terravistavineyards.com

TH WINES

SUMMERLAND

Since 2012, Tyler Harlton has become the Okanagan's most visible *garagiste* winemaker. Unlike many *garagistes*, which are side projects of winemakers or incubators for future estate wineries, Tyler pursued his passion in the 1,500-square-foot garage in the industrial park tucked behind Giants Head mountain in Summerland. His final vintage here was made in 2019. Having decided to explore other opportunities in agriculture, he will close the winery when the 2019s are sold. "You don't *need* to do more, and I'm really conscious of [that]," explains Tyler. "As you expand, it can change the nature of the business. The nature of this business currently is a lot of working by hand."

"By hand" is the mantra that has guided his winemaking since leaving behind a career in law. Born on a Pense, Saskatchewan, wheat farm in 1976, he played professional hockey at the major junior level between 1993 and 2002. He switched to law, graduating in 2008 from McGill before coming to Penticton to article. Soon entranced with the wine industry, he changed careers to work literally from the ground up as picker and then cellar hand for Osoyoos Larose. He moved around to other wineries as he gathered experience for his own winery.

With a commercial winery licence, he is not required to own his own vineyards, so he works with growers throughout the South Okanagan to source his grapes. "I'm really just trying to work with that [Old World] wine tradition and then just apply it to the grapes here. And the Okanagan has amazing grapes." The core of his portfolio currently revolves around Viognier, Riesling, Pinot Noir, and Cabernet Franc, but he is sometimes offered small lots of other varieties, which are often released only through his wine club. The wines he makes reflect his personal preferences for dry, elegant, and complex wines that reflect the vintage, even if that means large

TYLER HARLTON

variations from year to year. "That's our selling point," says Tyler. "They're interested in a brand that's not stuck in one regime or one recipe."

With a total production hovering around 1,800 cases, Tyler also does most of his selling by hand as well, establishing solid relationships with restaurants and wine stores that sell his wine. This gives him the opportunity to explain each wine's production. Knowing how a wine was produced is part of his lore. "That's a different style to have something fermenting for four months, no sulphur, at the mercy of your cellar, and so that expression is different. But again, that's the kind of wine that I drink."

In November 2019, Tyler announced that the 2019 vintage would be his last. The wine shop will remain open for the summer of 2020, presumably until all wines have been sold.

MY PICKS

All wines are complex, and the vintage variations mean that every visit to the wine shop is a new experience. The whites benefit from time to mature in bottle. The Pinot Noir and Cabernet Franc are both elegant, and the Pinot Noir rosé, if available, is excellent. Tyler leaves winemaking when he is at the top of his game.

OPENED 2012

1 – 9576 Cedar Avenue
Summerland, BC V0H 1Z2
T 250.494.8334
W thwines.com

THERAPY VINEYARDS

NARAMATA

Wine lovers and home winemakers, Mike Boyd and partner Jacqueline Johnson planned to retire to a small winery on leaving the oil and gas business. Mike, who had been in the oil industry since high school, had founded Elite Energy Products in 1999 in Nisku, Alberta. The company was selling oil-field products around the world when it was acquired in 2015 by a competitor. For Mike, who was born in 1967, this premature retirement was the opportunity to move to the Okanagan and buy a winery.

Mike and Jacqueline sought to buy Mt. Boucherie Estate Winery, then in receivership. When a higher bid won that winery, they purchased a 24-hectare (60-acre) vineyard property at the north end of Naramata Road in 2016. When they realized how long it would take to develop a winery from the ground up, they looked again at wineries for sale and found Therapy Vineyards.

The property was the original Red Rooster Winery. When Red Rooster moved to its Naramata Road location in 2004, a group of investors relaunched the property as Therapy Vineyards. The winery started strongly but was hampered by internal dissension among the investors. In 2017, Mike acquired the holdings of all of Therapy's 124 shareholders and set to work learning the wine industry. It was, he says, like "drinking from a firehose."

Crucial to Therapy's future, he hired New Zealand–born Jacqueline Kemp as Therapy's chief winemaker. "I was introduced to wine when I was seven, eight, nine, ten," she remembers. "It is part of your meal. I was getting to taste wine when I was little and really enjoying it." In 2000, after an honours degree in nutrition, she switched to wine studies at Lincoln University and worked at wineries in both Australia and New Zealand before coming to Canada in 2008. Prior to joining Therapy, she made the wines for Moraine Vineyards and designed that producer's new winery. At Therapy,

MIKE BOYD

WINEMAKER JACQUELINE KEMP

Mike immediately tasked her with improving the viticulture and designing more efficiencies into the Therapy winery.

She came to Therapy for the opportunity to make sparkling wine, which was Mike's original intention when he bought the Naramata Road vineyard. "Our real desire in getting into wine was that we really enjoy Champagne and sparkling wine," Mike says. "We knew there was land there to plant grapes for a traditional-method sparkling wine."

MY PICKS

The whites, notably the Riesling and Pinot Gris, are refreshing, as is Pink Freud, a Merlot rosé. The top reds are Pinot Noir and two Bordeaux blends, Ego and Super Ego.

OPENED 2005

940 Debeck Road
Naramata, BC V0H 1N1

T 250.496.5217

W therapyvineyards.com
Accommodation: Inn with
five suites

THORNHAVEN ESTATES WINERY

SUMMERLAND

Thornhaven's Southwest-adobe-styled winery perched on a sun-baked southern slope of Giants Head mountain is one of the most architecturally striking of Summerland's wineries. There is a vineyard on the long slope and, beyond that, views of the bucolic Summerland countryside. The wines, consistent in quality, always live up to the promise of the location.

The vineyard was planted in the 1990s by Dennis Fraser, a Dawson Creek grain farmer who purchased and converted a former orchard. He began making wine in 1999, the same year that he phoned his cousin Jack to tell him about a property down the street that was for sale. Jack and his wife, Jan, had been living overseas, working in oil fields for 24 years, and were ready to return to Canada. In 2002, they also bought property for Jan's brother, Bryan Kolodychuk, also a partner in the winery. In 2005, Jack and Jan purchased the winery from Dennis. They operate it with their son, Jason, the winemaker, and daughter, Cortney Riep, who looks after marketing. Everybody pitches in to prune the vines, a major task since the Frasers now farm three vineyards totalling 7.5 hectares (18½ acres).

Thornhaven's portfolio is focused on the grapes that they grow themselves. Dennis originally planted the vineyards with Pinot Noir, Chardonnay, and Pinot Meunier—the classic grapes of Champagne—along with Gewürztraminer. Jack believes that Dennis originally intended to produce a traditional-method sparkling wine. That is not likely to happen now because Thornhaven has developed a following for each of those varieties. It is still the only winery in BC to produce a single-variety red from Pinot Meunier. The flagship wine is Gewürztraminer, a multiple award winner made with grapes now grown on all three vineyards.

JASON FRASER, CORTNEY RIEP, JACK AND JAN FRASER

Thornhaven offers a warm welcome in its cozy and casual wine shop. The large shaded patio accommodates guests who wish to linger with their own picnics and with glasses of Thornhaven wine, enjoying the view or listening to frequent live music. The parking lot is often full, but there always seems to be room for more.

MY PICKS

Thornhaven's Gewürztraminer is one of the best in the Okanagan. The entire portfolio is sound; not to be missed are the Pinot Meunier and Brooklyn's Blend, a field blend of Chardonnay and Sauvignon Blanc.

OPENED 2001

6816 Andrew Avenue
Summerland, BC V0H 1Z7
T 250.494.7778
W thornhaven.com

THREE SISTERS WINERY

PENTICTON

In 2003, when John Lawrence ended his 40-year accounting career in Calgary as a partner with PricewaterhouseCoopers, he and his wife retired to a 3-hectare (7½-acre) vineyard on the Naramata Bench. "My family still farms in England," he explained in a 2016 interview. "I always wanted a farm, but in England, unless you inherited one, it was pretty hard to get a farm."

The retirement scheme, which he once called a "hare-brained" venture, ballooned to become Earlco Vineyards Ltd. and the associated Three Sisters Winery. Earlco manages close to 81 hectares (200 acres) of vineyards both for other owners and for the winery, which is run by John's daughter Rebecca and her winemaker husband, Matt Mikulic.

Matt, who trained at Fresno State University, came into the Lawrence orbit early in 2012 when he answered an Earlco advertisement for vineyard help. "My father and I had started a vineyard and farm in Croatia," Matt says. "Being a Canadian, I always wanted to come back and see what they were doing here." Then he met Rebecca, who had been working as a wine agent. Once Earlco had a winemaker in-house, it was a short step to licensing a winery in 2013 and making 800 cases that vintage.

The initial winery was not practical for sales from the wine shop because it was at the end of a narrow road up the mountainside. The problem was solved in 2016 by the purchase of the recently closed Stable Door Cellars, whose property fronted on busy Munson Avenue. By July, a Three Sisters tasting room had opened. The success of that location triggered an aggressive business plan. The new winery built in 2018 is producing 7,500 cases and has considerably more capacity.

MATT MIKULIC

The winery is called Three Sisters because John Lawrence has three daughters, Emily, Abigail, and Rebecca. Coincidentally, Matt also has three sisters.

MY PICKS

Matt has a good touch with reds, including Cabernet Franc and Tempranillo, and a sure hand with Chardonnay, Riesling, Gewürztraminer, and Auxerrois.

OPENED 2013

1250 Munson Avenue
Penticton, BC V2A 8S5
T   236.422.2296
     604.363.3402
W   3sisterswinery.ca

TIGHTROPE WINERY

The seed for Tightrope Winery was planted in the decade that Lyndsay and Graham O'Rourke spent working in bars and restaurants at the Whistler ski resort. The jobs supported their skiing, Graham's fly-fishing, and their shared meals in fine restaurants.

"The thing about Whistler is that you get spoiled because there are so many fine dining restaurants for such a small town," Lyndsay says. "You get a lot of chances to go out and try nice wines with good food." Graham agrees. "My wine experience all started with really good wine," he says. "I did not grow up drinking Baby Duck and the box wines."

Both were born in 1971. Lyndsay, whose geologist father, Grenville Thomas, is a diamond explorer who is in the Canadian Mining Hall of Fame, has a University of Windsor business degree. Graham, the son of an accountant, grew up near Sarnia and learned to fish during summers in a family cottage on the river. His love of the outdoors led to a University of British Columbia degree in wildlife management.

They moved to the Okanagan in 2003. Immediately drawn to the vineyard lifestyle, they both took Okanagan College courses in grape growing and winemaking. To further improve their skills, they went to Lincoln University in New Zealand for honours degrees in those disciplines. The studies paid off quickly. When they returned, Graham joined Mission Hill for six years as a vineyard manager before, with a partner, setting up his own vineyard-consulting firm. Lyndsay became the winemaker for Ruby Blues Winery for several years before devoting herself totally to Tightrope.

In 2007, the couple bought a 4-hectare (10-acre) Naramata Bench property with a million-dollar view over the lake. They

GRAHAM AND LYNDSAY O'ROURKE

planted 2.8 hectares (7 acres) of grapes—Pinot Gris, Riesling, Viognier, Pinot Noir, and Merlot, with small blocks of Cabernet Franc and Barbera. They made the first 900 cases of Tightrope wines in 2012, using the Ruby Blues winery until they built their own in 2014.

On the winery's Facebook page, they set out the rationale for the winery's name: "The journey of bringing grapes to the bottle is a tightrope walk of variables from vineyard management, to winemaking, to the weather and even balancing the cheque book. Please enjoy the final culmination of our balancing act!"

MY PICKS

Everything, especially the Pinot Noir, the Riesling, the Pinot Gris, and the Viognier.

OPENED 2013

1050 Fleet Road
Penticton, BC V2A 8T7
T   778.476.7673
W   tightropewinery.ca

TIME WINERY

In 2015, Harry McWatters had already begun construction of TIME Winery on his Black Sage Road vineyard when the Phantom Creek Estates winery bought the entire property. Harry did not miss a vintage. He purchased a recently shuttered four-screen movie theatre in downtown Penticton (as a teenager, he once took a date to a Saturday matinee here). By 2018, it had been converted into the largest of Penticton's urban wineries, with a capacity to produce 25,000 cases a year and room to expand, and with winemaker Graham Pierce running the cellar.

Harry had a history with urban wineries in Penticton. His first winery job (in sales) was in 1968 with Casabello Wines, then a major producer with a winery on the city's Main Street. After Casabello was folded into the Jackson-Triggs Winery, the Main Street property was redeveloped with retail stores. Fortunately for the approvals that TIME needed, there was a history of truckloads of grapes moving on the streets of Penticton during vintage.

TIME is Harry's second major winery: he founded Sumac Ridge winery in 1980 and sold it in 2000 to the group now called Arterra Wines Canada. Harry, who died in 2019, preserved the McWatters family legacy with TIME. Both his daughters, Christa-Lee and Darrien, are active in the winery. Christa-Lee has succeeded him, as chief executive of both TIME and Evolve Cellars, a sister winery.

After selling Sumac Ridge, Harry had to sell grapes from his Black Sage vineyard, which was renamed Sundial. That inspired the TIME name. When Harry launched his second major winery in 2013, the first wines were released under the McWatters Collection label. "I never planned to put my name on it," Harry said at the time. "It was Christa-Lee and Darrien that encouraged me to do it."

GRAHAM PIERCE   HARRY MCWATTERS   CHRISTA-LEE MCWATTERS

The first McWatters wine was a 2007 Red Meritage. It is likely there will always be red and white Meritage wines in the TIME and McWatters portfolio. The Meritage term—it rhymes with *heritage*—was created in California for wines made with Bordeaux varieties. Sumac Ridge was the first Canadian winery to release a Meritage after Harry secured the rights to use the name.

MY PICKS

Everything, especially the Meritage wines. Wines under the McWatters label are structured for longer aging, while the TIME wines are approachable when younger.

SALES BEGAN 2013

361 Martin Street
Penticton, BC V2A 5K4
T   236.422.2556
W timewinery.com
Restaurant: The Kitchen,
open daily noon–9

TINHORN CREEK VINEYARDS

OLIVER

Tinhorn Creek Vineyards draws its name from the Tinhorn Quartz Mining Company, which mined the mountainside between 1896 and 1910. The remains of the stamp mill are a brisk uphill hike behind the winery's Gewürztraminer vineyard. A map to the Golden Mile hiking trail is available in the wine shop. Famished hikers are welcome at the top-rated Miradoro Restaurant, which opened in 2011 next to the winery. The views of the valley, whether from the winery, the restaurant, or the trail, are spectacular.

One of the South Okanagan's earliest wineries, Tinhorn Creek was launched in 1994 after the founders bought 20 hectares (50 acres) of Golden Mile vineyard and planted 40 hectares (100 acres) in what they called the Diamondback Vineyard across the valley, on Black Sage Road. Sandra Oldfield, the winemaker and later winery president, came from California, where she had graduated from the University of California's legendary winemaking program. By the time she left in 2017, when Andrew Peller Ltd. acquired Tinhorn Creek, she had turned over winemaking to Andrew Windsor, a Canadian trained in Australia.

Tinhorn Creek, now producing 40,000 cases a year, has set trends. In 2004, it was one of the first Okanagan wineries to start bottling its wines under screw cap. Since 2009, the winery has embraced sustainability with a wide range of practices to reduce Tinhorn Creek's impact on the environment. These include recycling, the use of lightweight bottles, drip irrigation in the vineyards, and biodiesel in farm machinery. Tinhorn Creek also led the campaign that resulted in the 2015 designation of the Golden Mile Bench as the Okanagan's first sub-appellation.

Its wine club was one of the first in the Okanagan and is believed to be the largest. That speaks to the consistently rising quality of Tinhorn Creek wines. This resulted from significant

ANDREW WINDSOR

improvements in both viticulture and in the winemaking cellar, where wines are aged in 1,100 French, American, and Hungarian oak barrels. Reserve-tier wines, now called Oldfield Reserve, were added in 2004. A flagship Bordeaux blend called 2Bench Red was first produced in the 2007 vintage. Beginning with the 2014 vintage, this elegant and age-worthy wine was renamed The Creek.

MY PICKS

Everything, including the winery's bestselling Merlot, Cabernet Franc, Pinot Gris, and Chardonnay. The Oldfield Reserve wines are intense and sophisticated.

OPENED 1996

537 Tinhorn Creek Road
Oliver, BC V0H 1T1

T   250.498.3743
1.888.484.6467 (toll-free)

W tinhorn.com
Restaurant: Miradoro
Restaurant (250.498.3742),
open daily (except
January and February) for
lunch, afternoon tapas,
and dinner

TOWNSHIP 7 VINEYARDS &

WINERY

PENTICTON

Nearly half the wine portfolio at Township 7 is reserved for members of the wine club that was set up in 2013 by Mike Raffan, the former owner and now the general manager. "We went on a mission of direct-to-consumer sales because we control our relationship with the consumer," Mike says. Previously a restaurateur, he understood that demand from restaurants can be fickle. Wine club members, on the other hand, are among the most loyal of consumers.

With a partner, Mike owned Township 7 from 2006 to 2014, having purchased it from founders Gwen and Corey Coleman. They established the original Township 7 in South Langley in 2001, adding the Okanagan winery in 2004. Under the Raffan ownership, Township 7 doubled production to 7,000 cases. Then, in 2014, the winery was acquired by Ge Song, a Beijing businessman. He retained Mike as his manager and expanded the winery to a capacity to make 12,000 cases a year. He also recruited Mary McDermott, who had been a senior winemaker making premium and sparkling wines in Ontario for Andrew Peller Ltd. She has had a profound impact on the quality of the wines. And she has driven the expansion of Township 7's sparkling-wine portfolio, recognizing the best use for the grapes from the cool South Langley vineyard.

In 2018, Township 7 remedied a vulnerability the winery had lived with since the start: owning barely a few hectares of vineyard, it relied on growers for most of its grapes. Threatened by a looming shortage of grapes, the winery purchased the 4.9-hectare (12-acre) Blue Terrace Vineyard near Oliver. Township 7 began buying Blue Terrace grapes soon after the vineyard was planted in 2001. Along with long-term grower contracts, the winery now controls the supply of the premium grapes to make the wines that keep wine club members (and other consumers) loyal.

MARY MCDERMOTT

Everything. The red wines— Merlot, Cabernet Franc, Syrah, and Reserve 7—are bold and age-worthy. The whites, notably Pinot Gris, Sauvignon Blanc, and Viognier, are packed with flavour. The three Seven Stars sparkling wines, Equinox, Eclipse, and Polaris, are elegant.

OPENED 2001

1450 McMillan Avenue
Penticton, BC V2A 8T4

T   250.770.1743
W   township7.com

UPPER BENCH WINERY & CREAMERY

The best of both worlds is offered here by the owners. Gavin Miller produces an extensive wine portfolio, while Shana, his wife, makes at least eight cheeses. The wines and the cheese are available in the tasting room as well as in the dining patio.

The winery has undergone a profound transformation since 2011 when Gavin, backed by a silent partner, a businessman named Wayne Nystrom, acquired what was then known as Stonehill Estate Winery in a bankruptcy court auction of the winery and its 2.8-hectare (7-acre) vineyard. The partners started almost from scratch, including a new name, turning the page on the struggles of previous owners. German brewmaster Klaus Stadler originally planted the vineyard in 1998. He launched Benchland Winery three years later to such a lukewarm reception that he stopped making wine after the 2002 vintage and returned to Germany, selling the winery in 2004 to orchardist Keith Holman. Renamed Stonehill, it specialized in port-style wines before slipping into bankruptcy in 2010 with the other six Holman wineries.

Rebranding the winery, which is within Penticton's city limits, has enabled Gavin and Shana to make a new beginning with high-quality wines and cheeses. "I am really pleased we got this winery," Gavin says. "I always thought it had good bones, this place. It was never used to its potential."

Born in Britain in 1965, Gavin was a sales manager in London when he came to Penticton on vacation in 1995 and met Shana. They lived in London for a year before returning to the Okanagan in 1997. Drawn to wine after a year as a sign maker, Gavin took Okanagan University College courses. That launched him on a career that began in the vineyard at Lake Breeze, the cellars at Hawthorne Mountain Vineyards, the tasting room at Sumac Ridge, and then winemaking, first at Poplar Grove and then at Painted

Rock, where he made award-winning wines before leaving after the 2010 vintage.

Shana, a Nova Scotian, was working in Montreal when, on a whim, she decided to move to the Okanagan. "I was 25 at the time and had a pretty stressful accounting job, which I hated," she recalls. Travelling with four cats, she needed to stay on a farm. Ian and Gitta Sutherland, who were just planting the vineyard for Poplar Grove Winery, welcomed her. When Poplar Grove subsequently added a cheese plant, Shana learned the art of cheese making.

MY PICKS

Everything, including the Pinot Gris, Cabernet Sauvignon, Zweigelt, and Pinot Noir, especially when paired with King Cole, Upper Bench's semi-soft blue cheese. In 2018, the winery added a premium Bordeaux blend called Altitude.

OPENED 2001 (AS BENCHLAND WINERY)

170 Upper Bench Road South
Penticton, BC V2A 8T1
T 250.770.1733
W upperbench.ca
Food service: The Oven, 11:30–5 (closed in winter), with cheeses for sale in the wine shop

VALLEY OF THE SPRINGS WINERY

NAKUSP

Breaking new ground on a wine region is always risky, but from the perspective of owner Jody Scott, the risks are minimal compared to his notoriously dangerous former career as a tree faller. Born in Saskatchewan, Jody came to British Columbia as a six-year-old when his parents moved to a fruit-producing area near Nakusp. The construction of the Hugh Keenleyside Dam at Castlegar forced the family to relocate to higher ground as the water level of the Arrow Lakes rose 12 metres above its natural level, submerging arable land. The region ceased to be a significant fruit-producing valley.

Jody's father made wine from local fruit, and Jody also became a home winemaker, initially with wine kits. When Jody and his wife, Brenda, a fourth-generation resident of Nakusp and a Red Seal chef, built their dream house overlooking the Kuskanax River, they operated Sunset Ridge Bed and Breakfast.

While touring Salmon Arm wineries in the early 2000s, Jody discovered Siegerrebe, subsequently his favourite white variety. He cleared land to plant his vineyard with cuttings obtained from a winery in the Shuswap. While researching what to plant, Jody found like-minded people also interested in becoming grape growers. A group started the Arrow Lakes Grape Growers Society, which is completing a massive 10-year study of the grape varieties suited to the region's climate. With help from Salt Spring Island viticulturist Paul Troop and former provincial grape specialist John Vielvoye, the association is ascertaining the potential of the Arrow Lakes as a wine-growing region.

Jody began planting his vineyard in 2007 with many different grape varieties to see what would work, including Pinot Gris, Gewürztraminer, Auxerrois, Zweigelt, Ortega, Pinot Noir, Maréchal Foch, and of course Siegerrebe. The rocky

(L TO R) STEPHANIE RÖGER, OWEN, JODY, AND BRENDA SCOTT

soil made planting particularly difficult. "It's just boulders and gravel," explains Jody. "Straight glacial till." In the summer, the temperature can reach 35°C (95°F). Vineyards must be irrigated since water drains quickly through the vineyard's rocky subsoil. At 520 metres in elevation, the vineyard gets significant snowfall to protect the vines in the winter. The short growing season requires early-ripening grape varieties.

The first vintages from Valley of the Springs, a name that evokes the region's natural hot springs, was released in the spring of 2019. The initial production was only about 260 cases of wine: 130 cases of Bacchus, 40 cases of a white aromatic blend consisting of Siegerrebe, Ortega, and Madeleine Angevine, 40 cases Gewürztraminer, and 40 cases Maréchal Foch. The production was supplemented with fruit purchased from the Okanagan, although the winery intends to use only fruit from the Arrow Lakes region in future vintages. Jody has more land to plant and will be purchasing from other growers in the valley as they establish their vineyards.

MY PICKS

Vista's bright, fresh flavours are appealing, as are the aromatic whites— Gewürztraminer and Bacchus. Maréchal Foch is very fruity and well made.

OPENED 2019

890 Alexander Road
Nakusp, BC V0G 1R1
T   250.265.3075
W   valleyofthespringswinery.com
Accommodation: Bed and breakfast

VAN WESTEN VINEYARDS

NARAMATA

Every wine that Robert Van Westen releases has a name that begins with V—sometimes with a hilarious result. The winery's first Cabernet Franc was released in 2010 as Vrankenstein because the variety is usually harvested on Halloween. It is now called Vulture. The winery's first Riesling, released in 2019, was called Viscous. But even if the wine labels sometimes are a lighthearted stretch, the wines are serious.

Rob and his father and brother (both named Jake) are some of the best farmers on the Naramata Bench. The family, now with 21 hectares (52 acres) of cherries, apples, and grapes, has farmed on the Naramata Bench ever since Jake Van Westen Sr. emigrated from the Netherlands in 1951 after graduating from agriculture school. Rob, tall enough to tower over his vines, was born in 1966. He left school after Grade 10 and worked at construction in Vancouver until 1999, when he returned to help with the family's newly planted vineyard. He embraced viticulture with a passion, studying at Okanagan University College and, when he began making wine, spending nearly four months at wineries in Australia and New Zealand.

CedarCreek Estate Winery began buying Van Westen grapes. Impressed with the quality of the fruit, CedarCreek's winemaker at the time, Tom DiBello, encouraged Rob to make wine. Since the 2011 vintage, after Rob had planted Pinot Noir, he and Tom have collaborated on making a wine from that variety. The wine is called VD, for Van Westen/DiBello.

The Van Westen winery, which began marketing its wines in 2005, is established in a former apple-packing plant on one of the family properties. Four years later, Rob added the rustic tasting room where he and his staff preside at friendly and informal tastings.

ROB VAN WESTEN

The Van Westens have 4.9 hectares (12 acres) of vineyards, with another hectare or two slated for planting. They grow Merlot, Cabernet Franc, Pinot Gris, Pinot Blanc, Riesling, and Pinot Noir— but no Chardonnay. "I've never been a Chardonnay drinker," Rob admits. Conveniently, considering the winery's V theme, he does grow Viognier.

MY PICKS

Everything, including the ripe, full-flavoured Viognier. Voluptuous, always a single-vineyard blend of Merlot and Cabernet Franc, and V, a Bordeaux blend, are powerful reds built to be age-worthy, collectible wines.

OPENED 2005

2800A Aikins Loop
Naramata, BC V0H 1N1
T   250.496.0067
    250.462.8463
W vanwestenvineyards.com

VANESSA VINEYARD

CAWSTON

The tasting room here is perched just above the highway, with the Similkameen Valley spread out below. The more important view is to the rear, where the rugged, rock-strewn 30-hectare (75-acre) vineyard climbs toward a mountain. This sun-drenched slope grows red varieties almost exclusively.

"Some people said we should plant some whites," says Suki Sekhon, a partner in Vanessa with retired investment dealer John Welson. "We said we have chosen the best red site in Canada. Why would we plant whites? If we want to do that, we will just go buy another site." Richard Cleave, their viticulture consultant, had recommended reds for what is one of the hottest sites in the Similkameen. They grow 10 hectares (25 acres) of Merlot, 8 hectares (20 acres) of Cabernet Sauvignon, 6 hectares (15 acres) of Cabernet Franc, 5.3 hectares (13 acres) of Syrah, and 0.4 hectare (1 acre) of Viognier (for blending with Syrah).

Suki, born in 1961, is a Vancouver real-estate developer. In 2005 Suki and John bought this Similkameen property, intending to lease the developed vineyard to a major winery. Then the partners discovered wineries would not commit until the quality of the grapes could be established. When the vineyard began producing, Andrew Peller Ltd., owner of the nearby Rocky Ridge Vineyards, began buying Vanessa's grapes. Howard Soon, who was then the winemaker at Peller-owned Sandhill Wines, added wines from Vanessa grapes to the Sandhill portfolio. When Howard retired in 2017 after 37 years with Sandhill and its predecessor wineries, he was snapped up by Vanessa. "I was never looking for a job, [but this is] a great property, a great terroir. Our goal is that we are going to make the best wine we can, in Canada or in the world."

WINEMAKER
HOWARD SOON

JOHN WELSON
AND SUKI SEKHON

When the Vanessa partners launched their own label before building a winery at the vineyard, the wines were made for them at the Red Rooster Winery, which is also a Peller winery. "We kind of went into this basically to build a vineyard," John Welson says. "Then, as you get into it, the industry just pulls you along."

The initial production from the 2012 vintage for Vanessa totalled 600 cases. Production from the 2013 vintage was 1,200 cases; by 2014, it was 3,000 cases. The new wine shop gives Vanessa the capacity to market between 7,500 and 10,000 cases a year. The remainder of Vanessa's superb grapes are sold to Peller.

The winery is named for one of Suki's daughters. Initially, the partners had considered calling it Stagecoach Winery because a stagecoach route once ran through the site. "But when I first went to the site, there were a lot of butterflies," Suki says. Vanessa is the name of a type of butterfly.

MY PICKS

Everything, especially the Meritage and a sister Bordeaux blend called Right Bank. All the reds are bold, as is the Viognier.

OPENED 2017

1090 Highway 3
Cawston, BC V0X 1C3
T 250.499.8811
W vanessavineyard.com

THE VIBRANT VINE

KELOWNA

Since its second season, the Vibrant Vine has had rave reviews on TripAdvisor as one of Kelowna's most entertaining wineries. The fun begins when you put on the winery's 3-D glasses and the huge mural in the tasting room immerses you in psychedelic colours and images. Similar 3-D images wrap around most of the wine bottles. The fun continues with live music on the lawn every Saturday afternoon in summer and with tours of the luxuriant gardens, perhaps with a glass of wine in hand. It is not surprising that this is also one of Kelowna's favourite wedding venues.

The winery is operated by Welsh-born Wyn Lewis and his wife, Marion. They came to Canada in 1975 after graduating from Cambridge (engineering and botany, respectively). Shortly after, they went to California, where Wyn joined the Wells Fargo bank. He was its director of international operations when he retired in 2000. They were on the way to settle in Victoria in 2003 when they first saw the Okanagan Valley. Almost on impulse–they were captivated by the region's beauty–they bought an apple orchard in East Kelowna on a plateau with a dramatic view over the city and the valley. They turned the house on the crown of the plateau into a Mediterranean villa surrounded by gardens and incorporating the winery. The apple trees were replaced with vines, including Riesling, Gewürztraminer, Pinot Gris, and Chardonnay. The wine shop opened in a yellow heritage cottage (circa 1937), which was subsequently expanded to include nine tasting bars.

They enlisted their sons in the winery. Phil, an artist with work displayed in the wine shop, created the mural and the labels. Anthony, a rock musician who formerly ran a recording studio in Denver, became the winemaker under the mentorship of consultants. He compares winemaking to sound mixing. Sometimes he uses his knowledge of music to open doors when

he needs to pick the brains of wine professionals at, for example, the research station in Geneva, New York. "I always talk about music first," he laughs. "Everybody likes to talk about music. Then after talking about drums, why don't we also talk about pH?"

Phil's 3-D art is reproduced on plastic sleeves. These become wraparound labels by being slipped onto thousands of empty bottles that are immersed into boiling water by hand, one at a time. Woops, the winery's blend of seven white varieties, resulted from an error when about 4,000 sleeves were put on upside down. Wyn embraced it as an opportunity. "This by far has become our number one selling wine," he says.

MY PICKS

The white wines, especially the Pinot Grigio; the two sparkling wines cleverly branded Vibranté; and the Merlots and the Gamay Noir.

OPENED 2010

3240 Pooley Road
Kelowna, BC V1W 4G7
T 778.478.4153
W thevibrantvine.com
Picnic area and gardens

THE VIEW WINERY & VINEYARD

KELOWNA

The View Winery is housed in the oldest building occupied by any Okanagan winery: a former fruit-packing house built about 1922 by George Ward, the forebear of winery proprietor Jennifer Molgat. Municipal inspectors tried to block a tasting-room licence, but she prevailed. The building is structurally sound. Visitors enjoy both the heritage atmosphere and the thoroughly modern wines.

Jennifer, who was born in Kelowna in 1969, was on maternity leave from teaching in 2006 when she became involved in developing the winery. Chris Turton, her father, was already selling grapes from the 20 hectares (50 acres) of vineyard on the slope behind the packing house. He was also producing apple cider at another winery. When he had to move cider production to the packing house in 2006, Jennifer helped secure the cider and winery licences. Cash flow from Wards Cider has helped power The View's growth to 10,000 cases of wine a year.

Perhaps the flagship varietal at The View is Pinotage, a grape developed in South Africa. Chris, who had a special interest in the variety, sourced cuttings in California. The Pinotage block at The View has grown to 3.2 hectares (8 acres), the largest of the three or four plantings in the Okanagan. While it is a classic red wine grape, The View also uses it for rosé (likely the only Pinotage rosé in North America), for a fruity white Pinotage, and for a component in a sparkling wine.

The vineyard is primarily planted to cool-climate aromatic white varieties (Gewürztraminer, Riesling, and Ehrenfelser). Formerly, there was a block of Optima as well; it has now been replaced with Pinot Noir, a far better fine-wine varietal.

JENNIFER MOLGAT

MY PICKS

Everything, but especially the several Pinotage wines in the portfolio. And don't overlook the several Wards Ciders, all made with cider and dessert apples.

OPENED 2008

1 – 2287 Ward Road
Kelowna, BC V1W 4R5
T   250.860.0742
W   theviewwinery.com

VINAMITÉ CELLARS

OLIVER

Ray and Wendy Coulombe, the founders of vinAmité Cellars, retired in 2009 after a long career in marketing and advertising in Montreal, buying a home south of Oliver with 2 hectares (5 acres) of neglected vines. Opening this elegant winery beside the highway was a logical step after Ray had revived the vineyard. Their daughters soon joined them in the venture. Catherine, a former caterer, became the winemaker; Nathalie, an artist whose work is displayed in the winery as well as in major galleries, has worked in the vineyard.

"It is for wine, but it is mostly for the lifestyle," Ray explained when the winery opened in 2015. "I am interested in making a successful and respected little winery, which I will leave to my children. And I will have a lifestyle to go with that dream."

Ray was born in Edmonton in 1945 and grew up in Vancouver. "We always drank wine," Ray remembers. "When I was a kid, it was always homemade stuff—a white and a red." His ability as a writer and artist earned him a scholarship to an arts college in California. After graduation, he joined MacLaren Advertising in Toronto in 1968. He was soon transferred to Montreal and found that city much more to his taste. "Compared to Toronto, Montreal was full of colour. There were people on the streets at every hour. There were sidewalk cafés and people talking. Always next to them was a bottle of wine."

He spent the rest of his business career there, first as creative director at MacLaren (Wendy joined him as art director) and then with his own agency until closing it in 2001. The search for a retirement lifestyle ultimately led to a house in the country south of Oliver. "We were in that house, looking onto that vineyard below, and I thought there should be a winery at the highway," Ray says.

Catherine, their daughter, began helping in the vineyard while on vacations from her catering job at Google's Montreal office. "My background is food," Catherine says. "They had three kitchens there. I planned the meals." She began working at the winery full-time in 2013, being mentored by consulting winemaker Philip Soo. She took over the cellar in the 2018 vintage.

The vineyard grows Chardonnay, Pinot Gris, Cabernet Sauvignon, and Gamay Noir. "I couldn't wait to start this winery for the reason of the Gamay alone," Ray says, recalling glasses of Beaujolais sipped in those Montreal cafés. "I saw our wine very much to be in the Beaujolais style."

The vinAmité portfolio has grown to suit a wider range of tastes, including a port-style wine called Ouest. The first release in 2018 was aged three years in barrel. The winery skipped a few years so that the 2020 release will have five years in barrel.

MY PICKS

Every wine is elegant and polished, ranging from the easy-drinking white blend called Chanson d'Amour to the three sophisticated Bordeaux blends: Petit Claret, Compass, and Hidden Corner. The Gamay Noir recalls well-made Beaujolais Villages wines.

OPENED 2015

5381 Highway 97
Oliver, BC V0H 1T1
T   250.498.2234
W vinamitecellars.com

VOLCANIC HILLS ESTATE WINERY

WEST KELOWNA

The winery's name was inspired by its proximity to Mount Boucherie, the stubby dormant volcano on the western shore of Okanagan Lake. The proprietors, Bobby Gidda and his father, Sarwan, have named a number of the wines with volcano terms, even polling wine-shop customers for ideas. Examples include Magma White, Magma Red, and Lava Red.

The Gidda family has a long history growing tree fruit and then grapes in West Kelowna. Sarwan, who was born in India in 1953, was the oldest of three brothers who launched the first Gidda winery, Mt. Boucherie, in 2000. Eight years later, Sarwan and Bobby broke away from that partnership to found Volcanic Hills.

Bobby, now the president at Volcanic Hills, was born in 1985. He has a degree in business administration at Okanagan College and worked in the finance department there while taking the college's winery assistant and winery sales courses. As part of the coursework, Bobby, who previously worked in the Mt. Boucherie cellar, designed Volcanic Hills, a $2.3-million winery with geothermal heating and cooling. The expansive wine shop is above the processing cellars, with a view of Okanagan Lake.

The family's 32 hectares (80 acres) of vineyard, primarily around West Kelowna, support the production of an extensive portfolio by winemakers Daniel Bontorin (the consultant here since 2010) and John Zakala, a former triathlete with enology training from Washington State University. The winery also sources grapes, primarily for big reds, in the South Okanagan and the Similkameen Valley.

BOBBY GIDDA

MY PICKS

The winery is known for its bold reds and its intense Viognier. It has white and red blends back-sweetened with Icewine that appeal to the sweet tooth.

OPENED 2010

2845 Boucherie Road
West Kelowna, BC
V1Z 2G6

T 778.755.5550

W volcanichillswinery.com
Restaurant: Blu Saffron
Bistro
(blusaffronbistro.com)

WATERSIDE VINEYARD & WINERY

ENDERBY

Some visitors take a novel way to reach Waterside Vineyard & Winery: they float from the beach in Enderby down the Shuswap River to the winery. The bucolic location of the winery attracted Jennifer Marcotte and Kevin Verschoor to buy the property in 2018 and move from Alberta. "And we were tired of eight and a half months of winter," Jennifer says.

The winery had been established in 2008 by Croatian-born Branko Juric and his wife, Debbie. They had planted a 3.6-hectare (9-acre) vineyard with six cool-climate varieties: Maréchal Foch, Siegerrebe, Pinot Gris, Pinot Noir, Ortega, and Gewürztraminer. From those and with occasional purchases of other varieties, Branko created at least 16 table and dessert wines. The portfolio they inherited from Branko includes two off-dry wines, one white and one red, called Sex in a Bottle. These are among Waterside's most popular wines.

When the Jurics, who were retiring, put the winery on the market, Jennifer and Kevin discovered it during a golfing trip to the Okanagan Valley. They were ready for a change of lifestyle, especially when Branko agreed to coach them through the 2018 vintage. In his previous career, Kevin had founded and run an oil-field service company, MSI Maintenance Solutions, based in Athabasca. He is also a member of a country music band, Brandid, which has produced two albums.

Jennifer, with an arts degree from Grant MacEwan University, has had a career that includes managing a medical imaging company and a first aid company. She also found time to write four books for children. The winery, she said in 2018, is a new experience for her. "Kevin has made wine for a number of years at home, for personal use," she said. "As for myself, other than the

JENNIFER MARCOTTE AND KEVIN VERSCHOOR

occasional glass, I had not had any dealing with wine at all." Her confident demeanour in the winery's large tasting room suggests that Jennifer is a quick study.

MY PICKS

The winery bases several wines on Maréchal Foch, including a full-bodied table wine, and several with Siegerrebe, including both a table wine and a dessert wine.

OPENED 2008

70 Waterside Road
Enderby, BC V0E 1V3
T   250.838.9757
W watersidewinery.com

WAYNE GRETZKY OKANAGAN

KELOWNA

In 2008 Wayne Gretzky, the legendary Canadian hockey star, went into a celebrity winemaking venture with a Niagara winery. When the project struggled, it was taken over in 2011 by Andrew Peller Ltd. It has since become a major success there and now includes both a winery and a distillery.

As soon as the success seemed apparent, Peller launched the Wayne Gretzky Okanagan label with a 2011 vintage red and 2012 vintage white. Gretzky is one of four major brands made at the Peller-owned Calona winery in downtown Kelowna. In style and in price point, the Gretzky wines occupy a position between the premium Sandhill Wines and two value labels, Conviction and Peller.

"The whole idea with the Wayne Gretzky brand is that you could drink it at a hockey game," says Sydney Valentino, who took over in 2019 as the winemaker for Wayne Gretzky Okanagan. "I don't sit and watch hockey, but hockey is in my DNA, being Canadian. Everybody around me is into hockey. It just runs through your blood as a Canadian. It is such a cool brand to be part of."

She is the third winemaker to make the Gretzky Okanagan brand. She was born in Winnipeg and grew up in Kelowna, majoring in chemistry and mathematics at the University of British Columbia Okanagan and graduating in 2010 and intending to be a science teacher. She did teach for a year. "I was not motivated, and it did not appeal to me," she says now. She worked briefly in a wine shop. Finding that winemaking did appeal, she joined the team at Calona Vineyards. Her university degree provided a solid technical foundation, which she augmented by taking winemaking courses and being mentored by Howard Soon, the legendary winemaker then working there.

SYDNEY VALENTINO

When the Peller group launched the Conviction label in 2015 to replace the Calona label, Sydney became the lead winemaker for Conviction until she was promoted to Gretzky. While the wines are made in the same cellar, the Gretzky wines are generally made from selected premium fruit. The Gretzky reserve tier is called Signature. In style, the wines express varietal fruit and not much oak. The exception is several blended wines that include wine that has been aged in whisky barrels. This is a recent trend in winemaking designed to add complexity to the finished wines.

The wines may be meant for hockey fans. But, Sydney believes, "once they taste it, they find it is good wine and they continue to buy it."

MY PICKS

Everything, including a dry Riesling and a fruity Pinot Grigio. Keep an eye out for No. 99 The Icon, a red Bordeaux blend priced at $99. Just one barrel is made each vintage, the one the winemaker thinks is the best barrel in cellar.

OPENED 2015

1125 Richter Street
Kelowna, BC V1Y 2K6
T   250.979.4211
1.888.246.4472 (toll-free)
W gretzkyestateswines.com

WESBERT WINERY

PENTICTON

About 70% of the 2010 graduating class from the University of the Free State medical school in Bloemfontein, South Africa, now work in Alberta. One of them is Dr. Wessel Joubert (pronounced *jou*-BEAR). A wine lover as well as a physician, he is the only one who also owns an Okanagan winery.

Wessel was born in 1986 and grew up in Johannesburg. He was still in high school when he became interested in wine. "In Grade 11, I visited a winery and just fell in love with it," he says. "In my final year, I worked at a winery during the holidays." That fired his ambition. "I have always wanted to own a winery, and I never thought it would be a possibility in my life."

After getting bachelor's degrees in medicine and in surgery, Wessel practised five years in South Africa before following his classmates to Alberta. The exodus had begun with two doctors recruited for rural practices in Alberta. When they succeeded, Wessel says, others followed. He came to Canada in 2016 and joined a clinic at Three Hills, a community in central Alberta. He discovered Okanagan wineries during a vacation the following year. "I just fell in love with the place," he says. "I began looking for a winery that I could afford."

The affordable winery had been in bankruptcy twice before Wessel bought it in the spring of 2019. It has three guest suites and is located on Naramata Road; five other wineries are in walking distance, one reason why the guest suites had an average occupancy of 80% when Wessel reopened them in June 2019. The first winery at this location, which opened in 2011, was called 3 Mile Estate Winery. When it failed in 2014, the property was taken over by Marty Gunderson, an Edmonton businessman, who renamed it Quidni Estate Winery. This winery failed in 2017. When Wessel bought it from the receiver in May 2019, he took

WESSEL JOUBERT

over 1 hectare (2½ acres) of neglected vines and a building with no winery equipment.

Wessel acted decisively. The vineyard-management company that was hired to resuscitate the vines did such a good job that the 2019 yield was 60% of a full crop. The winery, using Okanagan Crush Pad Winery's services, produced 700 cases in that vintage. "We don't have much more space to plant," Wessel says of the vineyard, which grows Merlot, Gamay Noir, Gewürztraminer, and Viognier. "We will most likely get a bit more land in the area as well as buy grapes."

His target for full production is 2,000 to 2,500 cases a year. "This is manageable for me, and this is what I can afford," Wessel says. "I am making the best of it and loving every moment of it."

MY PICKS

Current range not tasted.

PROPOSED
OPENING 2020

1465 Naramata Road
Penticton, BC V2A 8X2

T   778.738.1113

W   wesbertwinery.com
Accommodation: Three
guest suites

WILD GOOSE VINEYARDS

The bell tower above the new wine shop that Wild Goose opened in 2012 telegraphs an unintentional whiff of "I told you so." When the winery first opened in 1990, a government official suggested that founder Adolf Kruger would be lucky to sell 2,000 bottles of wine a year. Adolf proved him very wrong. Now, Wild Goose is producing about 25,000 cases of award-winning wine each year. And the bell in the tower formerly was in a German merchant ship called *Simon von Utrecht*. It was presented to the Krugers by a family friend.

Adolf, an engineer born in Germany in 1931, built a family legacy on this 4-hectare (10-acre) Okanagan Falls property that he bought as raw land in 1983. With his sons Hagen and Roland, he planted Riesling and Gewürztraminer, now signature varieties for Wild Goose. Hagen, born in 1960, became the winemaker and viticulturist. In turn, one of his sons, Nikolas (born in 1985), also became a winemaker, studying at Okanagan College and gaining practical experience at Tinhorn Creek, Hester Creek, and Bremerton Wines, a family-owned Australian winery. Hagen's other son, Alexander, has taken up viticulture. Hagen's brother, Roland, looks after marketing for the winery. The Kruger family continues to be active in the winery, with Nikolas as lead winemaker, after a majority stake was acquired in 2019 by Portliving, a Vancouver developer that is raising its Okanagan profile.

The winery now farms 16.2 hectares (40 acres) of vineyard, of which 13.4 hectares (33 acres) is owned. The family's vineyards include the 2-hectare (5-acre) Mystic River Vineyard near Oliver. Purchased in 1999, it has become legendary terroir for Pinot Blanc, Pinot Gris, and, of course, Gewürztraminer. In 2009, the Krugers planted a former orchard to develop the 3.8-hectare (9½-acre) Secrest Vineyard just north of Oliver. About a third was planted with

HAGEN AND ROLAND KRUGER

Riesling vines. The site proved too hot for that variety, and in 2019 it was replaced with Cabernet Sauvignon, Malbec, and Cabernet Franc, supplementing the Merlot and Petit Verdot already there.

In 2018 they purchased the Sumac Slope Vineyard near Okanagan Falls from Bill Collings, a grower who was retiring. The vineyard already had 1.6 hectares (4 acres) of Pinot Noir and Riesling. The Krugers cleared another 1.6 hectares, planting more red varieties including a block of Syrah on a hot slope.

The winery has been highly acclaimed for white wines with, among many awards, seven Lieutenant Governor's Awards for Excellence in BC Wine. But the increased planting of red varieties supports the determination to grow the red portfolio as well. "Hagen and Nik have done a tremendous job with the red wines here," Roland says. "It is pretty hard to find red grapes in this valley. Consequently, we are planting red grapes whenever we have the opportunity."

MY PICKS

Everything. The Gewürztraminer, Riesling, Pinot Gris, and Pinot Blanc and a white blend called Autumn Gold are simply outstanding. The reds include well-made and well-priced Merlot, Pinot Noir, and a Meritage called Red Horizon. Black Brant is the winery's delicious port-style red.

OPENED 1990

2145 Sun Valley Way
Okanagan Falls, BC
V0H 1R2

T   250.497.8919

W   wildgoosewinery.com
Restaurant: Smoke &
Oak Bistro, open noon–8
Wed. through Sun. during
summer

WILLIAM TELL FAMILY ESTATE

CRESTON

David Mutch named this producer of wine, cider, and vinegar after the Swiss folk hero William Tell because the Creston business started with apples. The Swiss legend has it that Tell, an expert marksman with a crossbow, shot an apple from his son's head in 1307 during a confrontation with a tyrannical Austrian ruler that triggered a rebellion.

Born in Creston in 1978, David grew up amid the region's apple and cherry orchards. He went to Olds College in Alberta for a degree in horticultural technology. In 2001, he joined Mission Hill as a vineyard technician, returning to Creston in 2005 to work as an inspector for the Canadian Food Inspection Agency (CFIA). The following year, he established JRD Farms on a 3.2-hectare (8-acre) property that grew apples and where he planted about 1 hectare (2½ acres) of vines—mostly three clones of Pinot Noir. It is said to be one of the highest-elevation orchards and vineyards in British Columbia, with a fine southwest exposure.

William Tell was launched in 2012 after CFIA eliminated David's position. He and Amy White, his partner, began selling apple and pear juice in 4-litre containers. The business took off after David began carbonating the juices and packaging them in 750-millilitre bottles. By 2015, William Tell moved into the production of vinegars, alcoholic ciders, and, in 2018, sparkling ciders and sparkling rosé. David, busy managing a large farm for the Lower Kootenay First Nation, employs a consulting winemaker.

"This is going to sound really weird, but I don't drink," David says. "But when I do buy a drink, I like something that has bubbles and fizzes. That is why I made sparkling ciders and sparkling rosé. I like the feel of it."

William Tell's products are sold primarily in the Kootenays. David is a regular participant at the Creston Farmers' Market. His

DAVID MUTCH AND AMY WHITE

limited production volumes do not yet justify an on-site tasting room. Besides, he is lukewarm about staffing a tasting room. "I am a control freak," he admits. "I would not like other people selling my products because they would not understand the intricacies of it."

MY PICKS
Current range not tasted.

OPENED 2014

948 27th Avenue South
PO Box 204
Creston, BC V0B 1G0

T   250.428.1442

W   williamtell.ca

No tasting room

WINEMAKER'S CUT

Classical music playing is the signature of a Michal Mosny winery. "In all the wineries I have ever worked in, there is classical music in the vineyards and classical music in the cellars," he said as speakers were being installed here in 2019. "That's a must." In Slovakia, where he was born in 1982, he and Martina, his wife, had a small winery (about 500 cases a year) near the village where Beethoven is said to have written "Für Elise."

Michal and Martina emigrated in 2011, frustrated with the obstacles to assembling vineyards in Slovakia and also wanting to travel. Martina chanced to see a television documentary about Nk'Mip Cellars. That led them to the Okanagan, where Michal set up a vineyard-management company. He spent five years as the winemaker and vineyard manager at Lunessence Winery & Vineyard near Summerland while developing Winemaker's CUT, based on the Deadman Lake Vineyard.

He had met the vineyard's owner, Colin Stevens, in 2013 while buying grapes for one of Michal's winery clients. The Stevens family had originally grown tree fruit since the 1920s on this property beside the highway midway between Oliver and Osoyoos. About 3.2 hectares (8 acres) of vines—Syrah, Sauvignon Blanc, and Cabernet Franc—were planted between 2000 and 2005. The Stevens family had considered developing a winery but never did.

Michal discovered that the vineyard, rich in organic matter and minerals, produced wines of exceptional flavour. With the 2015 vintage, he began making wines for his Winemaker's CUT label. He leased the vineyard and, after leaving Lunessence in 2019, turned a small fruit-packing house into a winery. "I am a proud *garagiste* winery," Michal said after making 800 cases in 2018 and doubling production the next year.

MICHAL MOSNY

While he purchases some grapes, the vineyard is being expanded modestly with varieties such as Grüner Veltliner and Welschriesling that Michal knows from Slovakia. "I have never worked with Grüner Veltliner in the vineyard," Michal says. "I am looking forward to that. I just love those Grüner flavours that give me goosebumps because they remind me of my home country."

MY PICKS

Everything, especially the Syrah, the Sauvignon Blanc, and the Grüner Veltliner.

OPENED 2018

3848 Highway 97
Oliver, BC V0H 1T1
T   778.931.0577
W   winemakerscut.ca
No tasting room

WYNNWOOD CELLARS

When Michael Wigen became interested in wine, a friend gave him a copy of *The Heartbreak Grape*, the classic book by Marq de Villiers with the subtitle *The Search for the Perfect Pinot Noir*. Michael, who was born in 1955 into a pioneering Creston-area lumbering family, had grown up drinking varietals, with a preference for heavy California Cabernet Sauvignons. He had also begun enjoying red wines from Beaune, unaware that those are made with Pinot Noir. The book stirred his interest. When he planted his own 4.5-hectare (11-acre) vineyard on ideal limestone soil, beginning in 2007, he committed the majority to four clones of Pinot Noir. "We are hanging our hat on the traditional varieties because we are trying to mimic Burgundy where we are," Michael says.

The idea for a winery was born that spring when Dave Basaraba, an American-born school counsellor in Creston, approached Michael about growing grapes on an excellent site, an abandoned farm above Duck Lake that Michael owned. A decisive man and a lifelong risk taker (Michael spent a decade flying a souped-up Beaver in air shows), Michael soon had bulldozers clearing the limestone slope. In a few years, when there were enough grapes to make eight barrels of delicious Pinot Noir, Michael and Dave decided to go ahead with a winery on a nearby site owned by Dave and planted in 2013 an additional hectare (2½ acres) of grapes.

Dave, who grew up near Walla Walla in Washington, had worked in agriculture there and in Alberta before settling in 1987 in the Creston area, where he became interested in grapes. In 2000, he planted an experimental vineyard of about 400 vines on his farm. That gave him a feel for the terroir and led him to approach Michael to partner in a winery.

DAVE BASARABA AND MICHAEL WIGEN

Michael's great-grandfather, O. J. Wigen, came to the Creston area in 1892, opened the first hotel two years later, and manufactured railroad ties. In 1913, he organized what is still called Wynndel Box and Lumber Company. After making boxes for the area's fruit growers, the company eventually moved to quality specialty lumber products. Michael, who studied business administration at Okanagan College, has been involved in the family business since 1977.

The winery partners—Dave is the winemaker—placed the winery and tasting room strategically on the popular and scenic Highway 3A beside Kootenay Lake. It is a short drive north of Creston, on what Michael likes to call the Creston Wine Route.

MY PICKS

The winery succeeds with Pinot Noir, Pinot Gris, Chardonnay, and Sauvignon Blanc.

OPENED 2012

5566 Highway 3A
Wynndel, BC V0B 2N2
T   250.866.5155
W   wynnwoodcellars.com

YOUNG & WYSE COLLECTION

OSOYOOS

Stephen Wyse and Michelle Young, his wife, planned to call this the Black Sheep Winery until discovering that a British brewer had once registered the name for cider while a Canadian distiller wanted to use it for rum. So they came up with a bulletproof brand—their own names.

"I kind of always have been the black sheep of the family," Stephen explains. He is referring to the family that started Burrowing Owl Estate Winery, one of the Okanagan's leading producers: his parents, Jim and Midge Wyse; his older brother, Chris, who now manages Burrowing Owl; and his sister, Kerri. Stephen, who was born in 1967, set out to be an airline pilot but earned his commercial licence just as layoffs were sweeping through the Canadian airlines. He tried real-estate sales before moving to Whistler with Michelle. She managed a major restaurant, and they both worked as mountain guides.

The Okanagan caught Stephen's attention when his parents began planting the Burrowing Owl vineyard in the mid-1990s. Stephen and Michelle moved to the Okanagan. He began working with vineyard manager Richard Cleave until construction started on the Burrowing Owl winery. Stephen became a project manager and then began being mentored by consulting winemaker Bill Dyer. When Bill left in 2004, Stephen, who had also taken Brock University winemaking courses, became Burrowing Owl's winemaker. After three vintages there, Stephen helped Burrowing Owl recruit a winemaker from outside the family, having decided that "it was time for me to spread my wings and find my own identity."

In the summer of 2008, Stephen and Michelle purchased a highway-side farm south of Osoyoos, almost at the US border, and quickly converted a former cold fruit storage building into a winery. Their first vintage, totalling 110 barrels, was made with

purchased Syrah and Merlot grapes (they started the project too late in the season to get good-quality white grapes). The fruit trees on the property were replaced in the spring of 2009 with 4 hectares (10 acres) of vines (Cabernet Sauvignon, Malbec, Syrah, Viognier, and a small block of Zinfandel). Stephen also buys grapes from other growers.

Young & Wyse now produces about 2,500 cases a year. The flagship wine is a Meritage blend called Black Sheep. Cabernet Sauvignon and Malbec grapes are co-fermented because the varieties share a block in the Young & Wyse vineyard. The reds are all barrel-aged for 18 to 20 months before the Black Sheep blend is assembled. "I don't take all of the absolutely best barrels because I keep some of the barrels I really like for single varietals," Stephen says. "I try to make a nice, balanced blend. I like to layer it, so that in the end, you have something that is very harmonious."

MY PICKS

Everything, including Merlot, Cabernet Sauvignon, Syrah, Zinfandel, and Black Sheep. The winery's whites, in addition to Viognier and Pinot Gris, include a blend called Amber after the owners' daughter.

OPENED 2009

9503 12th Avenue
Osoyoos, BC V0H 1V1
T   250.485.8699
W youngandwysewine.com

ACKNOWLEDGEMENTS

I would like to acknowledge the extraordinary co-operation from the winery owners and winemakers who have spent many hours over the past 50 years telling me their stories. I have written 18 books about Canadian wines—primarily British Columbia wines—since 1984. That was only possible because of the generous support of wine producers and the patience and encouragement of Marlene, my remarkable wife. This is expected to be my final wine book. That is why I talked my friend Luke Whittall into taking on some of the burden. We trust that our profiles do justice to producers of some of the best wines in the world.

—*John Schreiner*

I would like to thank John Schreiner for inviting me to take part in this book. The very first book about BC wine that I bought was John's *Chardonnay and Friends*, and it is a privilege and an honour to work alongside him. His books inspired me to seek out wines and learn about the many amazing producers in BC's wine industry. I want to acknowledge the support and encouragement of Valerie Stride, who helped with transcribing interviews and who is the best wine taster I've ever met. I would also like to thank my two children, Miles and Vanessa, who did not roll their eyes appreciably when they said, "Another book??"

—*Luke Whittall*

PHOTO CREDITS

Photos by John Schreiner with the following exceptions:

p. ii, vi, viii, 2, 3, 4, 23, 28–29, 49, 107, 119, 129, 141, 155, 157, 159 (left), 163, 195, 201, 265, 279 (right), 299, 305, 315, 317, 323, 377, 384, 387 (right), 391 (right), 393, 401, 419, 429, 445, 461, 465, 479, 489, 499 by Luke Whittall

p. 73, 153, 471 (right) by Christopher Stenberg

p. 109 Courtesy of Cliff and Gorge Vineyards

p. 113 Courtesy of Columbia Gardens Vineyard & Winery

p. 165 Courtesy of Fort Berens Estate Winery

p. 171 Courtesy of French Door Estate Winery

p. 221 Courtesy of JoieFarm

p. 281 Courtesy of Meadow Vista Honey Wines

p. 313 Courtesy of Noble Ridge Vineyard & Winery

p. 353 Courtesy of Priest Creek Family Estate Winery

p. 389 Courtesy of Rust Wine Co.

p. 397 by Susanne Gebert

p. 403 Courtesy of Saxon Estate Winery

p. 405 Courtesy of Schell Wines

p. 427 Courtesy of Skimmerhorn Winery and Vineyard

p. 437 Courtesy of Squeezed Wines

p. 497 Courtesy of Wesbert Winery

p. 501 by Wes Johnson

p. 505 by Jennifer Schell